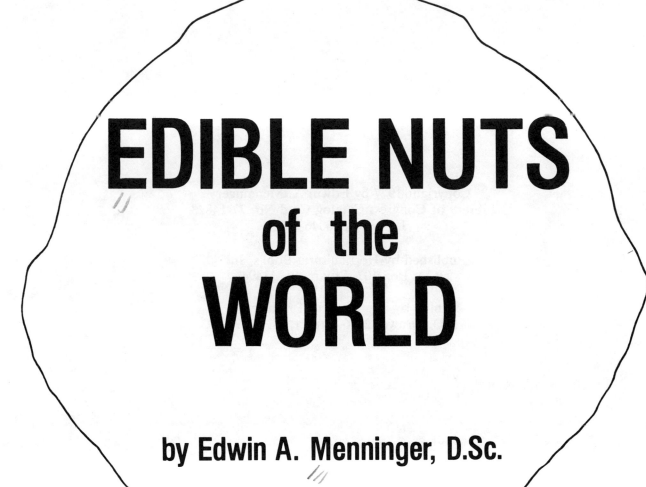

# EDIBLE NUTS
## of  the
# WORLD

### by Edwin A. Menninger, D.Sc.

Published by Horticultural Books, Inc.
P.O. Box 107, Stuart, Fl. 33494

Printed by Southeastern Printing Co.
P.O. Drawer 2476, Stuart, Fl. 33494

# EDIBLE NUTS OF THE WORLD

## Table of Contents

## Part I
## (DICOTS)

## Part II
## (MONOCOTS)

## Part III
## (GYMNOSPERMS)

## Part IV

# ACKNOWLEDGEMENTS

Compiling a book like this over a period of seven or eight years has required the inspiration and help of several hundred friends all over the world.

First of all I should name Dr. Robert L. Egolf, a physician at Land o'Lakes, Florida. Originally he was to have been joint author of this book, but circumstances prevented. He did write several chapters and these bear his name in the margin.

Chief of other helpers include:

Dr. Wilson Popenoe, fruit expert and plant explorer; he and I were boyhood playmates in Topeka, Kansas a long time ago.

Ralph Dickey of the Horticultural Staff at the University of Florida in Gainesville; we were closely associated many years in the Florida State Horticultural Society.

Dr. Harold E. Moore, Jr., of the Bailey Hortorium, Cornell University. He and I were working together at the Fairchild Tropical Garden in Miami twenty years ago.

Dr. George H. M. Lawrence, former president of the Fairchild Tropical Garden in Miami.

Dr. William J. Dress of the Bailey Hortorium at Cornell University.

Harold F. Winters, Research Horticulturist, USDA, Beltsville, Md.

Dr. Richard A. Howard, Director of the Arnold Arboretum.

Dr. Julia Morton of the Morton Collectanea at the University of Miami.

E. J. H. Corner of the faculty of Cambridge University in England; we first met as luncheon guests in David Fairchild's home. Mrs. Fairchild, who was the daughter of Alexander Graham Bell, served the meal herself.

Dr. John Popenoe, Director, Fairchild Tropical Garden, Miami.

Loyd O. Schaad, formerly of Angola, now a teacher in Botswana.

Harry Blossfeld of Sao Paulo, Brazil, a horticultural friend for twenty-five years.

D. B. Fanshawe of Kitwe, Zambia, who has helped me for years.

Rudolpho Quiogue of the Philippines.

Isaac Ho Sai-Yuen, forester of Kuala Lumpur, Malaya, with whom photography is a hobby.

K. M. Vaid another experienced plant photographer, of New Forest, Dehra Dun, India.

Dr. J. K. Maheshwari of the Botanical Survey of India.

Harold Caulfield, Botanic Garden, Brisbane, Australia.

T. R. N. Lothian, Botanic Garden, Adelaide, South Australia.

Harry Oakman, Moggill, Queensland, Australia.

My son, Edwin A. Menninger, Jr., of Stuart, Fla., who superintended production of this book.

My daughter, Barbara (Mrs. Harold J. Sack), of Tucson, Ariz., for translation of foreign languages.

Here follows a condensed list of collaborators on this book whose help in one way or another, served to expedite its publication and contributed to its completeness. If I have forgotten others, I am sorry.

## UNITED STATES

Almond Board of California, Sacramento
Geo. N. Avery, Botanist, So. Miami
California Macadamia Society, Vista, Ca.
Carl W. Campbell, Horticulturist, Univ. of Florida, Homestead
Dr. L. C. Cochran, Fruit & Nut Crops, Beltsville, Md.
Frank S. Crosswhite, Curator of Botany, U. of Ariz., Superior, Az.
Harold L. Forde, Univ. of Calif., College of Agri., Davis, Ca.
Dr. Victor Green, Horticulturist, Univ. of Florida, Gainesville
Robt. Hobdy, Forester, Dept. of Natural Res., Wailuku, Hawaii
Ron Hurov, Tropical Seeds, Honolulu
Stanley L. Krugman, Timber Management Res., Washington
H. B. Lagerstedt, Oregon State Univ., Corvallis
Elbert L. Little, Jr., USDA For. Serv., Washington
Mackenzie Nursery, Kailua-Kona, Hawaii
J. W. McKay, College Park, Md.
National Peanut Council, Washington
Steve O'Rourke, Colo. State Univ., Ft. Collins
C. A. Schroeder, Univ. of Calif., Los Angeles
Wm. F. Whitman, Rare Fruit Council Int., Inc., Miami
Allan K. Stoner, Agri. Res. Ctr., Beltsville, Md.
Edward Peterson, Theo. Payne Foundation, Sun Valley, Ca.
Dr. Louis O. Williams, Pointe Clear, Rogers, Ark.
Dr. P. van Royen, Dept. of Botany, Bishop Mus., Honolulu
Wesley Wong, District Forester, Kahalui, Maui, Hawaii
Dr. Robt. J. Knight, Jr., Research Agriculturist, USDA, Miami

## MALAYSIA AND INDIA

J. S. Womersley, Div. of Botany, Lae, New Guinea
Geoff. F. C. Dennis, Solomon Islands
Michael Galore, Asst. Dir. of Botany, Lae, New Guinea
A. L. El-Tomi, Head, Pomology, Agri. Research Ctr., Tripoli, Libyan Arab Rep.
P. F. Cockburn, Forest Botanist, Sandakan, Sabah, No. Borneo
Department of Agriculture, Sarawak, N.W. Borneo, Malaya
Benjamin C. Stone, University Malaya, Botany Dept., Alamat Kawat, Malaysia
Bureau of Plant Industry, Manila, Philippines
S. Gowers, Dept. of Agriculture, Port Vila, New Hebrides
Dr. Roberto E. Coronel, Univ. of Philippines, College, Laguna, Philippines
Matrimandir Gardens, "PEACE" Auroville P.O., 605101 South India
E. E. Henty, Forestry Service, Lae, New Guinea
Dr. Ramon Valmayor, College of Agri., Los Banos E-113, Laguna, Philippines
Concepcion A. Alba, Kawanihan NG. Paghahalaman, Maynila, Philippines

## CENTRAL AND SOUTH AMERICA

T. M. Catterson, Silviculturist, San Salvador
E. W. King, Ministry of Agri., Belmopan, Belize
Oton Jimenez, San Jose, Costa Rica
L. S. Lindo, Chief Forest Off., P.B.-148, Belize
Don Zeazer, Trop. Science Institute, San Jose, Costa Rica
Armando G. Adriasola, Servicio Agricola Y Ganadero, Santiago, Chile
Paulo Bezerra Cavalcante, Museu Paraense, Belem-Para, Brazil
John Criswick, Arcadia, East Bank Demerara, Guyana
Wm. A. Davig, Inst. de Technologia De Alimentos, Campinas, Brazil
Dr. A. Dugand, Barranquilla, Colombia
C. L. H. McKenzie, Botanical Gardens, Georgetown, Guyana
Dr. Leonam Azeredo Penna., Botanical Gardens, Rio de Janeiro
Dr. Fred M. Schlegel, Silviculture, Valdivia, Chile
Pedro Senyszyn, Ministerio de Agri. Y Pesca, Montevideo, Uruguay
R. H. Woodye, Minister of Agriculture, British Honduras

## ASIA

Hortus Botanicus, Academiae Scientiarum, Salaspils, Latvia

## AFRICA

Botanical Research Institute, Pretoria, So. Africa
S. M. Chisumpa, Forestry Dept., Kitwe, Zambia, Africa
H. L. Gerber, Dept. of Forestry, Pretoria, So. Africa
Peter Greensmith, Nairobi, Kenya, E. Africa
Dr. Alfred Heasty, medical missionary, in the Sudan
Honingklip Nurseries, Newlands Cape, So. Africa
Kruger National Park, Skukuza 1350, So. Africa
Winn J. Tijmens, University of Stellenbosch, South Africa
Dr. F. D. P. Wicker, Hazyview, Eastern Transvaal, So. Africa
Jean-Pierre Chaille de Nere, CELZA — Binga par LISALA, Zaire

## AUSTRALIA

M.S. Buttrose, CSIRO, Div. of Hort. Research, Adelaide
R. W. Johnson, Queensland Herbarium, Indooroopilly, Qld., Australia
David Noel, West Australian Nutgrowing Society, Subiaco, W. Australia
Paul Wycherly, Botanic Garden, Perth

Brazilian women preparing the nuts of the BABACU PALM *(Orbignya speciosa)* for their hungry children.

Original drawing by Percy Lau, from the book *Tipos e Aspectos do Brasil,* published by Instituto Brasileiro de Geographia e Estatistica (Rio de Janeiro). This and other drawings by Percy Lau on pages 2 and 3, are used here with permission of the publishers.

# Chapter 1
# INTRODUCTION

A thousand kinds of nuts in this world are hunted and eaten by hungry people.

They have learned by experience where grow the trees that supply their basic food needs, to protect them, to watch for ripening times, to guard the crop from animals, what to do with nuts prematurely blown off by storms. They have learned how to harvest and when, what to do with nuts when they are picked (because many kinds spoil if not protected or treated in proper manner), how to store the nuts if that is possible, how to open the shells and extract the kernels, how to protect these for future eating or packing for shipment. Many oily nuts turn rancid if not handled properly. There are lots of things to learn about nuts.

In this book the word "nut" is defined as any hard-shelled fruit or seed of which the kernel is eaten by mankind. Many fruits or seeds are thoughtlessly called "nuts" though they are never eaten and mean nothing to a hungry child. Many nuts with a pleasant flavor are chewed as you and I treat chewing gum, with no thought of swallowing. Botanists refer to these seeds as masticatories. In this book all of these so-called nuts that never reach the stomach, are dumped into a chapter entitled "Not Nuts." It is interesting but of no food value.

Many nuts contain poisons which must be eliminated by cooking, roasting, soaking in changes of water, or by other means before they can be eaten by humans, and special attention is called in this book to these dangerous foods, by a skull and crossbones in the margin. If you see this sign, beware. The CASHEW nut is loved by everybody, but it belongs to the poison-ivy family and it is dangerous until roasted. It is sparingly grown in Florida but unless you know what you are doing, let it alone.

There are hundreds of millions of people in this world who have no corner grocery store to run to, who have no refrigerator, who have no cow, but who do have a lot of hungry children. They are faced every day with the necessity of getting food into their dwelling to provide a family with nourishment, and they have learned by experience that nuts are their major source of fats and protein. As the World's population explodes, the available supply of natural foods decreases proportionately because nobody plants nut trees except for a handful of commercialized items like PECANS, FILBERTS, ENGLISH WALNUTS, MACADAMIA, COCONUTS and such. Wonderful as the BRAZIL NUT is, the nuts come only from wild trees. There are no BRAZIL NUT orchards. As Brazil becomes more and more settled, there are fewer and fewer wild trees. Millions of palms that bear edible nuts in a hundred tropical countries, are butchered every year for the cabbage or HEARTS OF PALM, which is a delicious food item but the tree dies for the benefit of a few vegetable meals. There will be no more nuts from those trees.

Commercializing reduces the edible nut supply in another way. Some nuts like those from the AFRICAN OIL PALM *(Elaeis guineensis)* are edible but they are also a major source of oil used in the manufacture of soap. As the commercial oil industry grows, the supply of edible nuts from these trees diminishes, and families that had depended on them for food have been forced to turn to other sources. Of course there are nuts now to turn to, but starvation is somewhere down the road.

Millions of people who are hungry, turn avidly to PEANUTS and other beans to catch up with their supply of fats and protein. They can grow some of these in their own gardens when the neighborhood supply of other nuts is getting low and exhaustion threatens. In southwest Africa the common PEANUT supplies 80 per cent of the fats and protein in the diets of the people there. They have no meat, except an elephant perhaps now and then. There are no cattle because no ranges to graze. And so PEANUTS are big business. Several types are cultivated, some with as many as five nuts in a shell. These are food they can stack on the closet shelf in anticipation of a few rainy days. But whatever it is, or whoever the people are, nuts are extremely important to them.

Acorns are not ordinarily included in popular lists of nuts, though they are edible morsels in hard shells, and have an important place in this book. Bush wrote:

"Acorns, the fruit of many species and varieties of OAKS have been a food from prehistoric times but never have won a place for themselves in modern nut growing. They are planted in Europe for the dual purpose of animal food and for timber. The Indians in North America, especially in the Southwest, leach out the bitterness of bitter species from the kernels. In many parts of the world hog growers have groves of OAKS where their animals are fattened. But we have not yet come to planting the trees for this purpose though there has been a little planting for game food.

"Perhaps one of the best of all the edible acorns comes from the CHESTNUT OAK found native in eastern America as far north as Hudson Bay. The largest of the acorns of this species are an inch and a half long, a starchy nut much like the CHESTNUT, not a rich, oily nut as the HICKORY or the WALNUT. They are sometimes roasted like CHESTNUTS. The commercial use of the acorn in this country is entirely out of the picture. Our city markets have lost a taste for natural things, preferring food that is sterilized, devitalized and put up in pretty packages with fancy labels."

Elizabeth Fuller Whiteman wrote for the USDA (Misc. Pub. 302) on *Nuts and Ways to Use Them* which says in part:

Nuts and nut products are steadily becoming more abundant in the markets of the United States. Four kinds of nuts, including the PEANUT, which is a legume, are produced on a commercially important scale in this country. Arranged in the order of the quantity produced, they are the PEANUT, PERSIAN (ENGLISH) WALNUT, PECAN, and ALMOND. However, the production of the FILBERT is on the increase, and many other nuts that grow wild or in small orchards are used for food.

Other kinds of nuts imported into this country in considerable quantities, are the BRAZIL NUT from South America, the CASHEW from India, and the CHESTNUT mainly from southern Europe.

Nuts are a very concentrated food and are better used as an integral part of the menu rather than as a supplement to an already adequate meal. Most nuts are extremely rich in fat. The starchy CHESTNUT is the one exception. The PECAN contains over 70 percent of fat; the BRAZIL NUT, BUTTERNUT, FILBERT, HICKORY NUT, and PERSIAN WALNUT over 60 percent. The eastern BLACK WALNUT, ALMOND, BEECHNUT and PISTACHE have over 50 percent; and the CASHEW, PINE NUT (Pignolia), and PEANUT have over 40 percent. Fresh COCONUT contains about 35 percent fat.

In protein value, the different nuts range from less than 5 percent to over 30 percent. Although nut proteins are of good quality, the high fat content of most nuts makes them unsatisfactory as a substitute for meat or other sources of animal protein. Nuts may make a useful contribution to the protein of the diet, but under most circumstances it is better to consider them as sources of fat rather than of protein, and to use them interchangeably with other fatty foods, such as butter, oils, cream, chocolate and bacon.

The total carbohydrate in nuts is less than 25 percent except in the CHESTNUT. The fresh CHESTNUT contains about

42 percent of carbohydrate, chiefly in the form of starch, whereas the proportion in the dried nut amounts to about 80 percent. Most nuts are rich sources of phosphorus and poor or fair sources of calcium. Some nuts, such as the un-blanched ALMOND and HAZELNUT, WALNUT, PECAN, and HICKORY NUT, are good sources of iron. The PECAN is also a good source of vitamin A. The PEANUT, PECAN, CHESTNUT, ALMOND, PERSIAN WALNUT, FILBERT, and BRAZIL NUT are good sources of vitamin B.

Some readers of this book will find it strange that beans are included in a discussion of nuts. This is because when we talk about beans, our first mental image is of the string beans we enjoy eating, or of the pork-and-beans combination that has been a food store staple all our lives.

However the facts are that the fruits we call beans grow on 12,000 different kinds of plants, and only a handful of them are ordinarily eaten as vegetables. We have no occasion to sample most of the other eleven thousand or so.

In this book the word "nut" is defined as any hard-shelled fruit or seed of which the kernel is eaten by mankind. People who are hungry have discovered that a great many beans come in hard shells and that when these are broken, delicious food may be found inside. Bean pods are not all alike. Some contain only one seed. Some pods are

Collecting the fallen fruits and nuts of the BRAZIL NUT tree *(Bertholetia excelsa)* in the Amazon region of Brazil. Note shields on men's heads, as the 5-pound pods fall from 150 feet in the air. Original drawing by Percy Lau. See note under frontispiece.

so hard that when they finally get ripe they explode and blow the beans all over the neighborhood.

Most Americans have no hesitancy in accepting the low-ly peanut as a nut. Yes, it is one of the most important of nuts, but it is a bean. Farmers who dig it out of the soil and glory in the nourishment provided, gladly accept it as Nut No. 1 in their experience. Commercializing it in the form of salted peanuts suddenly lifted it into the world of nuts. Commercializing the SOY BEAN has suddenly lifted it too into the world of nuts. Those two products have opened the doors of bean-land to the lover of nuts. There are many more for him to get acquainted with.

Palms are not ordinarily thought of as nut trees. Of course the coconut is excepted. But the 2500 different kinds of palms that grow in the warm parts of the earth, provide many of the necessities of life to hundreds of millions of people. Some are great producers of vegetable fats used in cooking. Many have edible fruits like the date. Many store up huge quantities of starch in their stems. Others store great quantities of a sugar-liquid in their stems that can be tapped and the sugar utilized directly or used in fermented drinks. The bud or "cabbage" of many palms is edible and millions of them are cut down for this delight. But in addition to all the above, there are perhaps a hundred palms that produce edible nuts and these are utilized by hungry people all over the world. Some of them are described in this book.

Many palm nuts are quite different from other edible nuts. The "nut" in many cases must be utilized while the fruit is still in the green stage, immature. At that point the edible part may be a liquid or pulpy. These are much eaten by hungry people; they know that if they wait till the fruit is ripe, the interior will have become inedible. The DOUBLE COCONUT *(Lodoicea)* is a good example. It takes six years to ripen. At the end of the first year, the contents is a pulpy, delicious dessert material that can be refrigerated and enjoyed over a long period. But five years later that interior material has hardened into a vegetable ivory that nobody can eat.

So there are many nut trees among the palms and folks who know which fruits to eat, and how, and when, are the winners.

Harry Blossfeld writes from Brazil: "In general, and quite different from the native Indians who consumed many sorts of palm kernels, eating them fresh, the present population of Brazil makes little use of palm nuts. This may be due to the belief that they are hard to digest, but of course palm trees are getting pretty scarce now and its use, even when it existed, is decreasing. Thousands of palm trees of many species are destroyed each year, to eat the top bud, a very appreciated dish. There is a large scale export of "palmito" in tins now, though this is mostly one species: *Euterpe edulis.*

"Most palm nuts have a stage, while unripe, when the kernel is soft and eventually liquid. But with the smaller sizes of nuts, it would be impractical to obtain this liquid, even if it were delicious. An unripe palm fruit is a fibrous matter, most of them have a bitter taste on the green shell which has to be punctured, to get at the liquid contents, and the bitter sap might spoil the pleasure.

"It may be interesting for you, that even so really good nuts as PARA NUT and CASHEW NUT have been little used in Brazil and many people have eaten the CASHEW fruit (which is not a fruit) but never tasted a CASHEW NUT. PARA NUTS are exported on a large scale for a century, but you can buy them in Rio or Sao Paulo only since World War II, when exports were reduced and part of the production had to be sold inside of Brazil. Before this, the big export firms had no interest in supplying the local market, which was not known to exist, absorbing capacity unknown, prices not established, or distribution agents not readily available."

Botanists regard the inclusion of GRAINS AND GRASSES in this nut book as "far fetched." But botanists confine their interest to plants, what they are and what they do, rather than to the utilization of the plant products.

Grains and grasses are treated as nuts in this book for one simple reason: the structure of a grain of WHEAT is no different from the structure of a PECAN, except the covering on the WHEAT grain is not as tough or as hard as the covering over the PECAN seed. Both of them are hard seeds, both eaten by mankind. Edibility is the key that locks both these fruits together in a nuts book, and botanists have no interest in edibility. A hundred years ago a man named Miers wrote a 200,000-word study of the BRAZIL NUT family *(Lecythidaceae)* and in the 150 pages of type that he consumed, describing a couple hundred different nut trees, he accidentally mentioned edibility three times.

Tubers are completely ignored in this book, though many of them are called "nuts" by millions of people, including many botanists. The TIGER NUT or CHUFA of our childhood, delicious eating though it was, is not found in this book because it is a tuber *(Cyperus esculentus sativus)*. There are many delicious tubers and they are eaten with relish and delight. But they are asexually produced, an extension of the plant's stem, and they are not nuts.

The chapter on NUTMEG and other spices was unavoidable because NUTMEG really is a nut, complete with hard shell, although when the public sees it the kernel has been grated and put in a tin can. The seeds of all the plants described briefly in this chapter are eaten with gusto by people all over the world who never stop to wonder where their special seasonings came from.

The chapter on PUMPKINS and GOURDS may seem out of place until we consider that hundreds of these fruits are prized much more for their delicious seeds than they are for the pulp. PUMPKIN pies are in great demand at Thanksgiving time but PUMPKIN seeds are prized twelve months in the year.

This book can hardly be considered complete unless someone will come forward and write a chapter on the subject of TASTE. Nuts are prized, more than for anything else, for their wonderful taste. But you sit down and try to convey to someone next to you just exactly how a MACADAMIA nut tastes. There is a frightening paucity of words in our language that enable us to describe taste. O yes, we can say something is sweet, or sour, or salty, or bitter, and, and — you are all done. There are some words in the language for the feel of the nut on your tongue — oily, lumpy, gritty, and so on, but these have nothing to do with taste. You can sometimes invoke your sense of smell by remarking on the aroma you sense in the mouth in eating certain nuts — this fragrance (or stink) may come from an oil in the nut or it may be some smell forced out of the nut by roasting.

Take *Sterculia foetida* for example. (Gee, I love that name. *Stercus* is the Latin word for manure.) The tree got this name because when it comes into bloom at night, the flowers stink to high heaven, seeking to attract night-flying insects that can smell if they can't see. When the fruit ripens some weeks later, you cut it open, extract the seed, crack it and remove the kernel and put this in your mouth. You will find it delicious — really good eating. (Gee, this is getting complicated.) Let's go back to our language difficulties.

You are still helpless when it comes to telling how the nut tastes so that another person can "visualize" what you are describing and enjoy it. Usually you just lapse into the lap of metaphor, and start insisting that this or that nut tastes "like a banana," or may be "like an onion." But usually you will just collapse and announce stentoriously that the thing you are eating, tastes "just like a chestnut." It may be you haven't tasted a chestnut in twenty years so your announcement is just an elocutionary recollection of the past.

Taste is SO important in nuts, but nobody does anything about it. In this book you can enjoy them all without having to taste any of them.

EDWIN A. MENNINGER

Collecting and preparing COCONUTS in Brazil. Original drawing by Percy Lau. See note under frontispiece.

# Chapter 2
# THE WALNUT FAMILY
## *(Juglandaceae)*
### including the Hickories, Walnuts, Pecans and some other nuts called Walnuts

Because the WALNUT and HICKORY trees are so common in the United States and many of them so well known to millions of Americans, they are grouped and described together here as one big family, starting with the HICKORIES of which there are 25 different kinds in eastern Asia and eastern North America.

Along with the story of the HICKORIES is the unfolding of the PECAN romance with its many ramifications. It is one of the HICKORIES, but it has really become a separate institution. Not only has the breeding program in search of softer shells produced many fine new nuts, but crosses with the old-time HICKORIES have produced the HICAN which deserves a story by itself.

Then come the WALNUTS of which there are 15 different kinds scattered from the Mediterranean to Eastern Asia and Indo-China, North and Central America and the Andes. Cross-breeding has brought some interesting developments in this part of the family too.

Added to this chapter as a matter of convenience is the AFRICAN WALNUT *(Coula edulis)* and some other nut trees of the Olacaceae.

Then comes the YELLOW WALNUT *(Beilschmiedia bancroftii)* of the Lauraceae, along with two allied nut trees, the BRAZILIAN NUTMEG *(Cryptocarya moschata)* and the QUEENSLAND WALNUT *(Endiandra palmerstonii).*

Last of all are some of the African CAPERS.

People who are hungry know where their favorite trees grow, when the nuts will be ripe, and what to do with them when they fall from the trees.

coastal plains of the southern states.

It is a tree to more than 100 feet but usually less, clear of branches half its height with small, open crown. The exfoliating bark detaches itself in long narrow plates, peeling back at both ends but remains fast in the middle.

The nut, about an inch long, is enclosed in an outer husk that is fleshy and green at first, becoming dry and nearly black before splitting open at maturity. The inner shell is thin but hard, light tan in color. It is ellipsoidal, somewhat flattened laterally and has four prominent longitudinal ridges corresponding to the sutures of the valves of the outer husk. The kernel is deeply divided into halves, longitudinally ridged.

Hickory nuts are not commercially important. Occasionally trees are preserved when land is cleared and may be seen in yards of farm homes. Orchard or grove planting is not practiced as suitable land is more profitable in other crops.

At present hickory nuts are simply gathered and eaten as they come from the tree. The various Indian tribes of eastern North America used the nuts in a variety of ways, dried and pounded into flour, boiled into a soup, as a source of oil both for cooking and as a hair dressing, and even pounded in water into a kind of liquor.

|  |  |
|---|---|
| *Carya laciniosa* | **KINGNUT HICKORY**<br>**SHELLBARK HICKORY** |

The KINGNUT HICKORY is found on moist bottom-land soils along the upper Mississippi and Ohio rivers. It is a large tree reaching more than 100 feet in maturity and a diameter of 2 or 3 feet. The bark is shaggy but less so than that of the SHAGBARK.

The nuts consist of an outer husk, fleshy and green at first becoming brown and dry at maturity before splitting into 4 to 6 valves to reveal the inner nut. The shell of the nut is thin and hard but brittle, marked with more or less prominent longitudinal ridges corresponding to the suture lines of the valves of the outer husk, light tan in color, and generally ellipsoidal with some lateral flattening. It is about 1 or 2 inches long without the husk. The kernel is deeply divided longitudinally into halves, each half also longitudinally corrugated or convoluted. In competition with squirrels, chipmunks, mice and birds men generally come off second best.

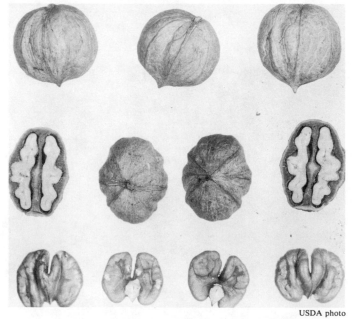

USDA photo

SHAGBARK HICKORY *(Carya ovata)*

|  |  |
|---|---|
| *Carya ovata* | **SHAGBARK HICKORY** |

The SHAGBARK HICKORY grows in the eastern United States west to the Mississippi, excepting Florida and the

4

CHINESE WALNUT or CHINESE BUTTERNUT
*(Carya carthagensis)*

Hickory nuts were an important staple for the Indian tribes of eastern North America. The nuts were pounded in water into a milky liquor called powcohicoria, hence the name Hickory. They could be eaten fresh from the tree or dried for later use, and could also be beaten into a flour.

MOCKERNUT HICKORY *(Carya tomentosa)*

### *Carya tomentosa*
### MOCKERNUT
### WHITE HICKORY
### BULLNUT

This moderately large tree to 100 feet and a trunk diameter of 3 feet, but usually much smaller, grows in the eastern United States from the Mississippi valley, the pine forests of the coastal plains along the Gulf of Mexico and the southern Atlantic coast.

The nut, about an inch or an inch and a half long, is very thick-shelled by hickory standards, the shell four ribbed corresponding to the valves of the outer husk. The kernel is small but very sweet.

In its eastern distribution this tree was probably the first Hickory noticed by the European colonists in this country. The name MOCKERNUT is thought to be a corruption of the Dutch word "mokker" a kind of heavy hammer, in reference to the force required to break the very heavy, hard shell.

PIGNUT HICKORY *(Carya glabra)*

### *Carya glabra*
### PIGNUT
### REDHEART HICKORY

The PIGNUT grows through the southern states, usually 60 to 80 feet tall, but occasionally to more than 100 feet.

The nuts are small, about an inch and a quarter long, unridged, with a small kernel that is sometimes sweet but often bitter. The outer husk is quite thin and splits at maturity about half way along its length.

The PIGNUT may be taken as representative of a variable group of other hickory species that are either of restricted occurrence or bear such small or else bitter nuts as to make them unimportant as edible nut trees. Among these would be included such species as BITTERNUT HICKORY *(C. cordiformis)*, the NUTMEG HICKORY *(C. myristicaeformis)*, the WATER HICKORY *(C. aquatica)*, the SAND HICKORY *(C. pallida)*, the BLACK HICKORY *(C. texana)* and others.

PECAN *(Carya illinoinensis)*

USDA photo

### *Carya illinoinensis*
### PECAN

The PECAN grows on the rich forested bottomlands of the Mississippi Valley as far north as Indiana and Illinois and west into Texas and Kansas. PECAN occurs locally to the north and east of this range, and at higher elevations south into central Mexico.

The PECAN is a spreading tree often more than 100 feet tall, and recorded to 140 feet. The main branches are ascending, resembling in their outward arching, when bare of leaves, the vase-shaped configuration of the AMERICAN ELM.

The ellipsoidal nuts are carried in clusters of 4 to 12, each nut 1½ to 2½ inches long by an inch through. They are individually enclosed in a thin four-valved husk which opens in the fall when the nuts mature. The rosy-tan inner shell is rounded in cross section and thin walled. The nut is deeply divided longitudinally, somewhat grooved and convoluted, but not closely adherent to the shell.

5

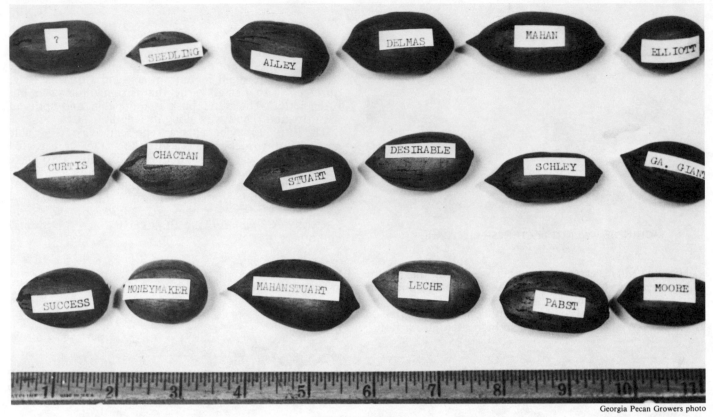

PECAN HYBRIDS

The PECAN is the most important native nut tree of North America, and the only one that has been widely planted in orchards and become an important crop. The annual PECAN crop in this country that enters commercial channels has been estimated at 52,000 tons. The most important PECAN producing states occur in a belt from Georgia in the east to Texas and Oklahoma in the west. A PECAN breeding station is maintained by the United States Department of Agriculture at Brownwood, Texas, and the Department maintains standards for grades of both shelled and unshelled nuts. On the larger plantings, some of them encompassing thousands of acres, the operations are almost entirely mechanized, with gigantic tree shakers and nut sweepers and vacuums utilized in the harvest. As with other major crops there is an industry association, the National Pecan Association, made up of growers, processors, and other industry connected people to pursue the interests of the PECAN industry at all levels.

PECAN varieties, of which there are more than three hundred named, may be divided according to their adaptation to particular growing conditions into three main groups, the southern group with a growing season of 200 days or more and 40 inches or more annual rainfall, the western group with a rainfall of 20 inches or less each year, and the northern group adapted to cold winters and a short growing season of less than 165 days. There are large, medium, and small fruited varieties in all these groups, as well as early and late bearers. The oldest PECAN variety, Centenniel, was originated by a slave gardener, Antoine, on the Oak Alley Plantation of Governor Telephore J. Roman in St. James Parish, Louisiana. The most widely planted and important commercial variety today is the Stuart but many others follow closely behind.

6 per cent of the PECAN crop is sold in shell and 94 per cent shelled. 36 per cent of the crop goes to bakeries, where the chief PECAN using products, among several hundred, are fruitcakes, custard pies, cookies, nut breads, and cake fillings. 24 per cent of the crop is sold in retail packages, 19 per cent goes to candy makers, 6 per cent to ice cream makers, and the rest to a variety of smaller users. PECAN

shells are used as paving for walks and driveways, for fuel, as mulches for ornamental plants, as soil conditioners, for stock and poultry litter, as filler in feeds, insecticides, and fertilizers, for tannin and charcoal, and are ground into a number of grades of flours, for use as soft abrasives in hand soap, non-skid paints, and metal polishes and as fillers in plastic wood, adhesives, and dynamite.

Although the PECAN is a tree of interior North America, coming down to the coast only along the Gulf of Mexico, it was discovered to Europeans as early as 1541. In that year the party of Hernando DeSoto came upon a tree, growing in abundance on the high grounds west of the Mississippi bottom swamps in what is now eastern Arkansas, they described as bearing thin shelled walnuts. This could only be the PECAN. The value of the PECAN as a nut tree was early appreciated. The famous PECAN praline appeared in Louisiana in 1762. Thomas Jefferson planted Pecans, called at that time Illinois Nuts or Mississippi Nuts, at Monticello and sent nuts from his trees on to George Washington at Mount Vernon. These were planted out by Washington in the summer of 1786 and may still be seen, the oldest trees at Mount Vernon, near the southeast corner of the mansion.

### THE HICAN

Bush in the *Nut Grower's Handbook* says:

"The HICAN is a cross between the PECAN and one of the HICKORIES. Many natural crosses have been found. More attractive HICANS have the long shape of the PECAN but in other ways show the parentage of the HICKORY. The shells of the nuts are not as thin as those of good PECANS but the kernels are rated as of better quality.

"The largest HICAN is the McAllister, at its largest is two and a half inches long and more than half as thick. It is said to be the largest American nut. Except in special instances the McAllister has not been productive. This in time may be corrected. Another variety, the Bixby, is nearly as large as the McAllister. The original tree has borne heavily."

6

## *Carya cathayensis* MOUNTAIN WALNUT

MOUNTAIN WALNUT in China, is a tall, deciduous tree with compound leaves 20 - 30 cm. long, alternate; leaflets 5 - 7, green above, rusty brown below. Fruit is globose to oblong, with a 4-angled outer layer. Inside the hard fibrous husk which is slightly wrinkled at surface there is an oily, corrugated seed, 4-celled at base, 2-celled at apex, edible. It is commonly eaten roasted with salt or goes into prepared confections. A considerable amount of this seed is used for processing of oil.

The MANCHURIAN WALNUT *(J. mandshurica)* and the CHINESE WALNUT *(J. cathayensis)* are closely allied species.

Here are five more genera in the Walnut family, scattered over more remote parts of the world:

*Alfaroa.* One species in Costa Rica.

*Engelhardtia.* Five species from the Himalayas to Formosa.

*Oreomunnea.* Three kinds in Mexico and Central America.

*Platycarya.* Two species in eastern Asia.

*Pterocarya.* Ten kinds from the Caucasus to Japan. *P. caucasica* in the Orient, produces an edible nut.

## *Juglans sp.* WALNUT

The trees collectively called WALNUT comprise 15 different trees originating from the Mediterranean, to eastern Asia, Indo-china, the United States, Canada, Central America and in the Andes. All of them produce delicious edible nuts, some hard to get at, and only one in this country of any commercial importance. They are, of course, allied to the hickories and pecans.

Bailey says: "As with nuts of the hickory species, the walnuts vary greatly in size, form, thickness of shell and, except in abnormal cases, which are very rare, the kernels are formed in two distinct halves, or cotyledons. The kernels of both are rich in valuable oils, which doubtless eventually will come into general use in the making of salads and for other purposes of cooking, but which are now used mainly in arts and paints, and as illuminants or lubricants. In color, the walnuts range from the light yellow or orange of the PERSIAN WALNUT to the dark brown or black, of the BLACK WALNUT. With the exception of the BUTTERNUT, or the "white walnut," as it is quite largely known, which is fairly cylindrical, and about one-third longer than thick, and which has a rough sharp-pointed surface, the several species of American walnuts and a number of the foreign walnuts, are spherical or spheroidal in general form.

"The usual difficulty with which the kernels are separated from the thick shell of the common BUTTERNUT and BLACK WALNUTS has prevented the nuts of either species from becoming generally popular on the market."

Downward photo

ENGLISH WALNUT *(Juglans regia)*
also called PERSIAN WALNUT and MADEIRA NUT

## *J. regia* ENGLISH WALNUT

Although usually called ENGLISH WALNUT in this country, despite the fact it has no connection with England, the nut has a lot of other prefix names: PERSIAN, ROYAL, ITALIAN, MADEIRA, EUROPEAN, FRENCH, CHILE, CAUCASIAN, CIRCASSIAN, MANCHURIAN.

It is a big tree growing both wild and cultivated from Greece and the Caucasus to Japan at elevations up to 10,000 feet.

Sturtevant says: "According to Pliny, it was introduced into Italy from Persia, but it is mentioned as existing in Italy by Varro, who was born B.C. 116. In many parts of Spain, France, Italy and Germany, the nut forms an important article of food to the people, and in some parts of France considerable quantities of oil are expressed from the kernels to be used in cooking. There are many varieties; those of the province of Khosistan in Persia are much esteemed and are sent in great quantities to India. In Georgia, they are of a fine quality. In North China, an almost huskless variety occurs. In France, there is a variety called Titmouse walnut because the shell is so thin that birds, especially the titmouse, can break it and eat the kernel."

USDA photo

CARPATHIAN WALNUT (var. of *Juglans regia*)

Watt says: "The albuminous kernel affords, by expression, about 50 per cent of a clear sweet oil, largely used in the hills for culinary purposes, but rarely seen in the plains. Stewart states that a large proportion of the hill walnut oil is prepared by simply bruising the kernel between stones. It is one of the most important vegetable fixed oils of Europe, and is said to form one-third of the total oil manufactured in France. In Spain and Italy also, outside the olive-growing regions, it is largely expressed. Spons' *Encyclopedia* says: "The oil should not be extracted from the nuts until two to three months after they have been gathered. This delay is absolutely necessary to secure an abundant yield, as the fresh kernel contains only a sort of emulsive milk, and the oil continues to form after the harvest has taken place; if too long a period elapses, the oil will be less sweet, and perhaps even rancid. The kernels are carefully freed from shell and skin, and crushed into a paste, which is put into bags and submitted to a press; the first oil which escapes is termed "virgin" and is reserved for feeding purposes. The cake is then rubbed down in boiling water, and pressed anew; the second oil called 'fire-drawn' is applied to industrial uses.

"The virgin oil, recently extracted, is fluid, almost colourless, with a feeble odour, and not disagreeable flavour. In the fresh state, it is largely used in Nassau, Switzerland, and other countries as a substitute for olive oil in salads, but is scarcely to be considered a first class alimentary oil."

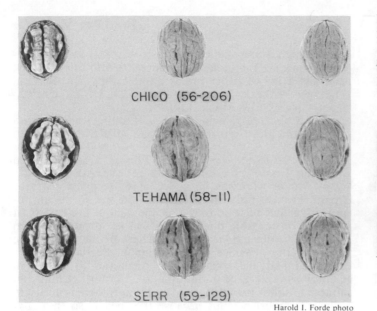

Three new cultivars of *Juglans regia* developed at
University of California, Davis.

Watt continues: "The fruit ripens in July-September, and consists of two seed-lobes (the edible part) crumpled up within a hard shell. The wild tree bears a nut with a thick shell and small kernel, which is rarely eaten. Of the cultivated varieties the best is a thin-shelled form. The WALNUT forms an important article of diet in Kashmir and the northwest Himalaya, and is exported in considerable quantities from these localities, also from Afghanistan and Persia, to the plains."

BUTTERNUT *(Juglans cinerea)*

### J. cinerea                    BUTTERNUT

Few persons nowadays know the BUTTERNUT tree when they see it, or have ever tasted the fruit, though those who know, rate it "tops" for flavor among nuts. It looks like a BLACK WALNUT tree, except that the trunk, black at the bottom, has a whitish cast in its higher reaches. Also distinguishing it is the fact that the nut hulls do not stain the fingers, as BLACK WALNUT shells do.

Sturtevant says: "The BUTTERNUT was called by the Narragansett Indians wussoquat, and the oil from the nut was used for seasoning their aliments. The nuts were used by the Indians to thicken their pottage. The immature fruit is sometimes used as a pickle and is most excellent. The kernel of the ripe nut is esteemed by those occasionally grown as a shade tree and for its nuts. In 1813, a sample of BUTTERNUT sugar was sent to the Massachusetts Society for the Promotion of Agriculture."

BLACK WALNUT *(Juglans nigra)*

### J. nigra                    BLACK WALNUT

This tree has been prized for 200 years in this country for its beautiful wood. The nuts have been incidental, although much enjoyed as tidbits by nut lovers.

Sturtevant wrote: "The kernel of the nut is sweet and less oily than the BUTTERNUT but greatly inferior to the MADEIRA NUT. It is eaten and was a prized food of the Indians."

This tree grows also in north and central China where the seeds are eaten raw or are used in making candy.

### J. ailanthifolia     JAPANESE WALNUT / HEARTNUT

This big tree to 60 feet, bearing its fruits in autumn, is endemic to Japan and very common along streams and on wettish plains. It is one of the trees most familiar to Japanese villagers because of its edible fruits and because of the usefulness of the fruit-hulls in fish-poisoning. Woodruff says:

"The HEARTNUT resembles the American BUTTERNUT in productivity, flavor and uses. The nut resembles a heart in shape, both before and after being hulled, and the kernel is heart-shaped.

"Production of HEARTNUTS in the United States is on the increase, especially from Missouri to the Atlantic. The nuts are produced in clusters of ten or more, are smaller than BLACK WALNUTS and have a rather thick shell. They are about the size of large HICKORY NUTS. Cracking is easy and the kernels come out either whole or in halves."

### Anacolosa luzoniensis     (Olacaceae)     GALO

This is a Philippine tree to 50 feet, rare and apparently never cultivated.

Brown says: "The tree is distributed in forests at low and medium altitudes from northern Luzon to Mindanao.

"The fruit is a nut produced in the axils of the leaves, with a thin shell about 2 centimeters in diameter and containing an edible kernel of good quality and taste. According to Wester the kernel of GALO contains 38.50 per cent water, 3 per cent ash, 11.1 per cent protein, 8.03 per cent fat, 39.46 per cent carbohydrates, and gives 2,733 calories per kilo. This analysis shows that GALO is a very nutritious food."

Burkill says the trees range from India to the Pacific, but are extraordinarily rare. He adds: "The Malayan *A. heptandra*, was found in Malacca in 1867 by Maingay, but has not been found there since; it was found in Singapore by Ridley in 1909, on ground since cleared."

## Coula edulis    (Olacaceae)    AFRICAN WALNUT GABOON-NUT

This medium sized tree to 60 feet grows from Sierra Leone to Gaboon and Belgian Congo, now called the Republic of Zaire.

The fruit is more or less walnut-like. Irvine describes it: "Fruit a drupe, ellipsoid-globose, 1 1/2 × 1 1/8 in., nut-shell hard, rough, 1/6 in. thick, breaking into 3 portions when ripe, difficult to break.

"The fruits are sold in Cameroon markets. The kernels are edible and of agreeable taste, resembling hazelnuts or chestnuts, and are suitable as dessert nuts. They are eaten fresh, or boiled in the shell, or roasted. Boiled and pounded, they are also made into cakes. Sometimes they are pounded with meat, or fermented before pounding. Nearly half the weight of the kernel is oil which is edible. It consists of 87 per cent oleic acid."

Dalziel says: "The kernel is of agreeable taste and quite suitable as a dessert nut either fresh or after boiling in the shell or roasted. Some tribes make a special dish from the fresh nuts pounded with meat, or the nuts are buried in mud to ferment for one month, after which they are pounded in a mortar and cooked with meat. The kernel is said to yield nearly half its weight of oil."

Schaad writes from Angola: "These trees are found in the Cabinda District of Angola, north of the Congo River. They produce edible oily nuts that mature from December till April, and during this period these nuts serve as a large part of the native diet in this forest area, and also are appreciated by the Europeans."

## Heisteria parvifolia    (Olacaceae)

Dalziel says of this plant in west tropical Africa:

"A very handsome ornamental shrub with dark glossy foliage; the persistent calyx of the female flowers enlarges and turns deep scarlet."

"The fruit is whitish with edible kernel. According to Cooper, it sometimes is used as food by the people in Liberia."

## Ongokea    (Olacaceae)

*Ongokea* is an unbuttressed tree to 125 feet in Sierra Leone, Angola and Zaire. Irvine says the fruits are "1¼ inches in diameter, depressed-globose, yellow drupes, with offensive odour, calyx persistent and enlarged, splitting into 3-4 lobes; nut spherical with crustaceous shell and large oily albuminous flesh, embryo very small. Fruits are said to be edible when ripe. The seeds are eaten in small numbers in French Equatorial Africa and Zaire."

Isaac Ho Sai-Yuen photo

WOODLAND ONION *(Scorodocarpus borneensis)*. Boiled and eaten by natives in Malaya and as a substitute for garlic sometimes.

## Scorodocarpus borneensis    (Olacaceae)    WOODLAND ONION

This tall tree is found in Sumatra, the Malay peninsula and Borneo.

Burkill says: "The garlic smell, present in the timber, is present also in the leaves, flowers and fruit. The jungle tribes eat the fruit."

Ho Sai-Yuen writes from Malaysia: "The seed is edible. There is, it appears, very little fleshy pulp for eating because the outer layer of this fruit is about 1.5 mm. thick. It is locally called Kulim."

## Strombosia pustulata    (Olacaceae)

This evergreen tropical African tree grows to 100 feet, bears round or ellipsoid fruits ½ inch diameter, containing a single seed.

Dalziel says: "The fruits have a waxy or hard cheesy kernel and thin brittle shell. According to Unwin, the nutlike fruits after falling break up into a white putty-like substance with a peculiar sulphurous or phosphoric smell. They are not used in Nigeria. The fresh kernels have been found to contain only 2-3 per cent of a golden-yellow oily matter. Kernels of *S. Scheffleri* in Angola have been found to contain 15-58 per cent of oil, and the people are said to eat them in scarcity, but only in small amount as they cause vomiting."

Irvine says: "The kernels of *S. grandifolia* are roasted and eaten in Belgian Congo."

WILD OLIVE *(Ximenia americana)*

FALSE SANDALWOOD *(Ximenia caffra)*

### *Ximenia americana* (Olacaceae) WILD OLIVE WILD PLUM FALSE SANDALWOOD SEASIDE PLUM TALLOW—WOOD

This small, spiny shrub or small tree, parasitic on the roots of other trees, and sometimes even on its own roots, is found more or less all round the world.

Burkill says: "The fruits taste like sour apples, and are yellow, or orange-coloured, thin skinned, with greenish flesh as firm as that of a cherry: they are eaten fresh, or pickled, but are very acid like citrons.

"They contain a large oily seed. The oil in it amounts to 65 per cent, and more; when the seed is crushed it is turbid and difficult to clarify. It is used in cooking in southern India.

"The nuts are eaten, but only a few can be taken at a time; many cause deleterious effects. They are rich in proteins."

Dalziel says: "The most varied opinions have been recorded as to the taste and quality of the fruit, and the kernels have been regarded by some as edible like filberts, and by others as strongly purgative or even poisonous."

BEILSCHMIEDIA ROXBURGHIANA *(Lauraceae)*

### *Beilschmiedia bancroftii* (Lauraceae) YELLOW WALNUT WANGA

Some 200 kinds of these trees grow in tropical Australia and New Zealand. Of this species Maheshwari wrote: "Kernel of large seed, after treatment, provided the most favoured source of flour amongst aboriginals of the rain forest."

Another species of *Beilschmiedia,* formerly known as *Tylostemon mannii,* and commonly called TOLA or SPICY CEDAR, is described by Dalziel thus: "A tree in Tropical Africa 40 feet or more high, with shining foliage, more or less resembling the Kola tree; found by stream banks. In Liberia it is said to attain 100 feet with over 3 feet girth and a straight bole.

"TOLA seeds are sold in West African markets, and are sometimes confused with the BITTER KOLA *(Garcinia Kola),* but are readily distinguished by being easily separable into two cotyledons. They are somewhat oily and are used in food, roasted and ground, and added to soup, rice, vegetables, etc., as a condiment and enricher of the ordinary native goods."

The North Queensland Naturalists' Club bulletin says of this species: "Kernel of large seed, after treatment provided the most favoured source of flour amongst aboriginals of the rain forest."

### *Cryptocarya moschata* (Lauraceae) BRAZILIAN NUTMEG

Sturtevant says this tree produces the spice known as BRAZILIAN NUTMEG.

Howes says of *C. peumus:* "These oily seed kernels from a Chilean tree are used as food after cooking by the poorer classes in times of scarcity, notably in the province of Alconcagua. In size they are rather larger than a Barcelona nut and quite soft."

### *Endiandra palmerstonii* (Lauraceae) QUEENSLAND WALNUT

This genus comprises 80 species in Malaysia, Australia and Polynesia. Maheshwari writes of this species: "The kernel of the large seed is prepared for flour."

The North Queensland Naturalists' Club, in its bulletin says *E. indignis* is called BOOMBAN and continues: "Kernel of nut eaten after being roasted, beaten up and steeped in running water."

So. African Forestry Service photo
*(Boscia albitrunca)*

### *Boscia angustifolia* (Capparidaceae) KURSAN (Arabic)

This shrub or small tree to 25 feet from Senegambia to East Africa, bears ½-inch bitterish berries. Irvine says these and the seeds are edible. Dalziel says the seeds are eaten cooked.

Regarding another species *B. senegalensis,* which grows from Nigeria to the Sudan, Dalziel says:

10

"Like *B. angustifolia* but with spherical, sometimes warted fruit up to ¾ in. in diameter; often found in barren and fire-scorched soil.

"The berries are sold in markets in the North for use as food, cooked and put in soup, or mixed with cereal pap or couscous, etc. In the E. Sudan the fruit has been a very valuable emergency food in times of scarcity. The roasted seeds have been used as a substitute for coffee."

Describing the same species, Irvine says: "The fruits are edible and many people are said to have subsisted on them during a drought and famine in Kordofan (Sudan) in 1900. The fruits, after soaking for 3-4 days, are cooked and eaten with *Hibiscus sabdariffa* as an emergency food in absence of *Cadaba.*"

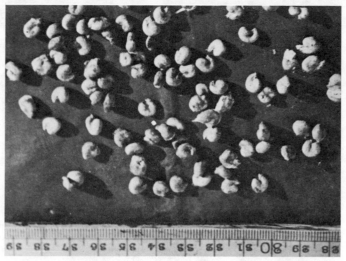

K. M. Vaid photo

*(Crateva religiosa)*

## *Buchholzia coriacea*          (Capparidaceae)
### MUSK TREE

This shade-loving tree to 50 feet in the semi-deciduous rain forests from Guinea and Ivory Coast to Cameroons, is one of four species.

Irvine says: "Fruits in November, long-stalked, yellowish green, like Avocado pears with several irregular knobs, up to 4½ × 3 in., woody, skin up to ½ in. thick, odour disagreeable; seeds generally large, blackish, 3, each up to 2 × 1 in. with flattened sides and resembling COLA nuts. They have a spicy taste and are known as KILA PIMENTE on the Ivory Coast, ELEPHANT COLA in Ghana.

The fruits are collected by the Binis of S. Nigeria and stored for a few days before being boiled and eaten.

Dalziel says: "The kernel can be used as a condiment, or as a cough medicine."

## *Crateva religiosa*          (Capparidaceae)

This small genus of trees in the tropics of both hemispheres, share some qualities of capers. The leaves and fruit of some kinds are eaten, but not commonly.

Irvine says this species, common through dryer areas of north tropical Africa, bears fruits in April that are sub-globose, up to 3 in. diameter, yellow or orange when ripe, on a long strong stalk, pericarp hard; seeds numerous dark brown, and kidney-shaped. The fruit is occasionally eaten and usually roasted. The seeds, according to Lynn, are eaten by the Nankanis.

# Chapter 3
# FILBERT — BEECH
# OAK — CHESTNUTS

These four nuts and their relatives make a splendid early chapter for this book on nuts, because they have been household words in this country for generations.

All of them grow wild in America, different kinds in different places, and memories of them and our experiences with them, well up in every American conscience.

BEAKED HAZEL NUT *(Corylus r. cornuta)*

USDA photo

COB NUT *(Corylus avellana)*

Downward photo

HAZEL NUT *(Corylus avellana)*

Downward photo

### *Corylus avellana*     (Corylaceae)    FILBERTS HAZEL NUTS COB NUTS

These three are really all the same, different names in different places for hundreds of hybrids of a delicious, favorite nut, cultivated for thousands of years.

There are fifteen species in the world, scattered across the temperate regions of North America, Europe, northern Africa, and Asia. They are mostly shrubs resulting largely from the extensive formation of suckers, according to Willis, and they form thickets in cool, deciduous woodlands. Some species aspire to being fair sized trees, and at least one, the TURKISH TREE HAZEL *(C. columa)* grows to 120 feet. All of them bear nuts that are more or less edible, and all are eaten to some extent where they grow. Of them all, however, only two or three species are of any importance in producing HAZEL NUTS, COB NUTS, or FILBERTS of commerce. There are two HAZEL NUTS native to the eastern United States: *C. americana* and *C. rostrata*. A form of the latter *C. rostrata* var. *californica,* grows on the west coast from California to the Hudson Bay region of Canada. These native nuts are not very useful for commercial nut growing, although *C. americana* has been hybridized with commercial varieties to some extent.

The HAZELS flower during the winter and produce their nuts the following fall. On the wild species in this country the nuts are rather small but very sweet, and in the wild they are a staple food for squirrels and other small animals. Each nut is set in a characteristic husk of papery bracts that varies in lengths, some being shorter than the nut, and others extending far enough beyond it to form a

12

sort of tube. *C. cornuta* is characterized by its long tubular husk and has the common name of BEAKED HAZEL.

In days gone by the nut was called a FILBERT if the husk was longer than the nut, a COB if nut and husk were much the same length, and a HAZEL if the husk was very short.

The extreme confusion in this field was unravelled for this book by H. B. Lagerstedt, research horticulturist with the U.S.D.A. at Oregon State University, Corvallis, Ore., as follows:

> HAZEL terminology is a problem. I have consulted several sources to determine what is right, but I find as many contradictory opinions and statements as I find sources.
>
> The Royal Horticultural Society Dictionary reserving "filbert" for the nuts of *C. maxima* is no longer valid. *C. maxima* and *C. avellana* cross readily and have been hybridized repeatedly during the past few hundred years. All the varieties and species of *Corylus* we have worked with appear to be self-unfruitful, thus cross-pollination is essential. It has been our observation that segregation for husk length is highly variable. Since we have *C. avellana* varieties with both long and short husks, or round and long nuts these characteristics lack validity for determining which species a variety belongs to.
>
> Some say the word FILBERT originated for the cleric Saint Philibert. *Webster's Dictionary* describes Saint Philibert as a French Abbot 1684 A.D. whose feast falls in the nutting season. The date August 22 is dedicated to him and corresponds to the ripening of the earliest nuts. In *Sturtevant's Notes* a quote from Peachans in Desraeli Curios 1858, states that Philibert was a King of France. To this we can add from *The Nut Culturist* (Fuller Judd), that the English name FILBERT comes from "full beard." This of course had reference to varieties with husks extending beyond the nut.
>
> The term COBNUT is strictly an English term. According to the *Journal of the Royal Horticultural Society,* 1918, an article by E. A. Bunyard says the origin of the word COB is unknown. It was suggested that its use for the FILBERT could be compared with its use for a stout smaller horse which was also called a cob in slang.
>
> What we commonly call the FILBERT in the Northwest and, as custom dictates, the HAZEL in the East also has a large number of other synonyms used at various times and in various places. For example, Pliny mentions it was brought to Greece from Pontus and thus was known as the PONTIC NUT. Theophrastus, the father of Botany, called them HERACLEATIC NUTS due to their origin on the Black Sea. In addition they were for a period known as BARCELONA NUTS or SPANISH NUTS. Fuller indicates that *Corylus* comes from "korys" a hood, bonnet, or helmet. Robert M. Morris in *Nut Growing* states that the common name HAZEL comes from the Anglo-Saxon "haesel" meaning a hood or bonnet.
>
> To sum up, in the Northwest where 99 per cent of the U.S. FILBERTS are commercially produced, the term FILBERT is universal. It is recognized that on the East Coast the same nut is called HAZEL. Characteristics such as husk length, nut size and nut shape no longer distinguish the FILBERT from the HAZEL, now the difference depends mainly on custom and common usage.

HAZEL NUTS may be eaten with no preparation other than removing the husk and shell, or they may be beaten to a powder and used like flour to make a FILBERT bread, which is said to be delicious.

Commercial orchards are mostly found in the northwest of the country, in Oregon and Washington. The Willamette Valley of Oregon is the center of United States FILBERT growing. In Europe commercial production is found in the countries that border the Black Sea and the Mediterranean. Orchards were planted at one time in the eastern United States, but failed due to the presence of a fungus disease among the native wild plants, of little account to them, but deadly to the commercial varieties which are of European stock. In recent years there has been some renewed interest in FILBERT growing in the east, more by hobbyists than by commercial growers.

The nuts of commerce are for the most part hybrids and selected varieties of *C. avellana* and *C. maxima.* Of these

*C. avellana* is of more widespread natural occurrence, being found in Europe, including England, northern Africa, and western Asia. The other *C. maxima* is more or less confined to southern Europe. The most important commercial varieties in the United States are Barcelona and Daniana with the latter being the pollenizer of the former. Varieties differ in productivity, sweetness, size of nut, and season.

CHINESE CHESTNUT *(Castanea mollissima)*

## *Castanea mollissima* (Fagaceae)
### CHINESE CHESTNUT

Chestnuts must be tops among the nuts of the world. This conclusion is inescapable because at least fifty authors quoted in this book, trying to describe the superior qualities of at least fifty different nuts, insist that they "taste like chestnuts". But the praise does not stop there. At least one tuber described herein, is called a nut and is reported as tasting like chestnuts.

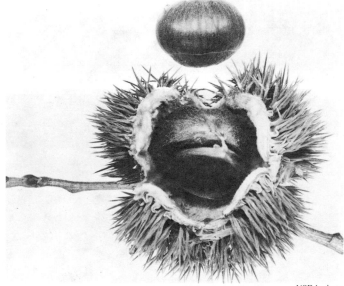

AMERICAN CHESTNUT *(Castanea dentata)*

The AMERICAN CHESTNUT *(C. dentata)* was virtually wiped out by a blight in the early years of this century, though efforts continue to develop a disease-resistant strain of this favorite monarch. But today the CHINESE CHESTNUT is stepping in to become the chief commercial form of this favorite fruit, with great promise for the future.

R. C. Moore wrote: "A national survey in 1960 by Northern Nut Growers Association to determine future prospects showed that CHINESE CHESTNUTS are orchard-type trees about the same size as apple trees and require much the same cultural care. They bear at five or six years and produce large crops that ripen in September and early October.

"The burs open and the chestnuts fall to the ground where they are picked up by hand. The largest commercial growers are in Georgia. The trees grow best where peaches are most successful.

"According to the survey, commercial orchards include 5165 trees of ages up to 25 years. Growers believe that this new industry will expand as its problems are solved. One of the chief problems is weakness of the graft union, the cause of which is not fully understood.

"The most popular method at present is to top-graft all seedlings two or three years after planting. This reduces transplanting loss of nursery-grafted trees and results in uniform orchards of good varieties. Research studies of the relationship between rootstock and scions may be expected to solve this problem.

"The standard varieties Nanking, Meiling, Kuling, and Abundance are most popular. At least two varieties should grow near each other to provide cross-pollination, without which burs will grow but the chestnuts will not have kernels.

"Another problem, especially among larger growers, is marketing the crop. Chestnuts that were harvested from the earliest plantings were sold chiefly for seed at very profitable prices. Recently, as the supply of chestnuts increased, demand and price for seed have decreased.

"In the future it is expected that much of the crop will be sold for eating purposes. Few consumers know of the superior eating quality of CHINESE CHESTNUTS and frequently confuse them with the imported cooking chestnuts that offer strong competition in eastern markets.

"Harvesting is a high-cost item. In order to reduce the hand harvesting cost, breeding is underway to develop new varieties in which burs drop to the ground before the chestnuts fall out. Mechanical harvesters may then gather up these partly-opened burs and thresh out the chestnuts.

"Those who are well informed on the subject believe that a new CHINESE CHESTNUT industry has started."

The SPANISH CHESTNUT *(C. sativa)* has long monopolized the American market, but it is not as large or as tasty as the Chinese species. Sturtevant says of it:

"The native country of the chestnut is given by Targioni-Tozzetti as the south of Europe from Spain to Caucasus. It is evident from the writings of Virgil that chestnuts were abundant in Italy in his time. There are now many varieties cultivated. Chestnuts which bear nuts of a very large size are grown in Madeira. In places, chestnuts form the usual food of the common people, as in the Apennine mountains of Italy, in Savoy and the south of France. They are used not only boiled and roasted but also in puddings, cakes and bread. Chestnuts afford a great part of the food of the peasants in the mountains of Madeira. In Sicily, chestnuts afford the poorer class of people their principal food in some parts of the isle; bread and puddings are made of the flour. In Tuscany, they are ground into flour and chiefly used in the form of porridge or pudding. In the coffee-houses of Lucca, Pescia and Pistoja, pates, muffins, tarts and other articles are made of chestnuts and are considered delicious. In Morea, chestnuts now form the principal food of the people for the whole year. Xenophon states that the children of the Persian nobility were fattened on chestnuts. In the valleys inhabited by the Waldenses, in the Cevennes and in a great part of Spain, the chestnut furnishes nutriment for the common people. Charlemagne commended the propagation of chestnuts to his people. In modern Europe, only the fruits of cultivated varieties are considered suitable for food."

Burkill says of it: "There are many varieties, and Bean suggests that the 'merit of the better forms seems to be due largely to their being able to suppress all but one of the three or four nuts, which each burr normally encloses. This enables the survivor to develop into a fine nut.' "

Bailey says: "The JAPANESE CHESTNUTS are usually of very inferior quality, except when boiled, roasted, or otherwise prepared."

Hardin photo

CHINQUAPIN *(Castanea pumila)*

Downward photo

SPANISH CHESTNUT *(Castanea sativa)*

The only others of the chestnut group are the CHIN-QUAPINS *(C. pumila)* of which Woodruff wrote: "These are widespread west of the Cascade Mountains of Oregon and Washington. They are common in the foothills where they at times are very abundant. The trees recover from forest fires ahead of most forest trees. The evergreen trees reach a height of 50 to 100 feet.

CHINQUAPINS known as bushy chestnuts are also grown as small trees in the Appalachian areas, extending south to middle Georgia. The trees are relatively resistant to chestnut blight. No efforts have been made in the United States to cultivate CHINQUAPINS.

The nuts are small, resembling chestnuts and are relatively hard to shell from the spiny burs. CHINQUAPIN nuts are sweet, more palatable than chestnuts, and were prized as food by the Indians and early Americans. They have been traded or marketed for more than two centuries. The numerous burs are an inch and a half in diameter, commonly arranged in a spikelike cluster. The plant blooms in June and the brown nuts ripen in September. The burs contain one and rarely two nuts. The nuts are round, somewhat pointed at the top and about half as large as the AMERICAN CHESTNUT. They have much the same appearance of small acorns.

CHINQUAPINS contain about 5% fat, 5% protein, 40% starch, and 1800 calories per pound. They are eaten raw, roasted in the shell and used similarly as chestnuts.

*(Castanopsis sp.)* in Malaya

GON CHESTNUT *(Castanopsis argyrophila)*

*(Castanopsis acuminatissima)*

KAT *(Castanopsis tribuloides* var. *longispinus)*

15

(Castanopsis lamontii)

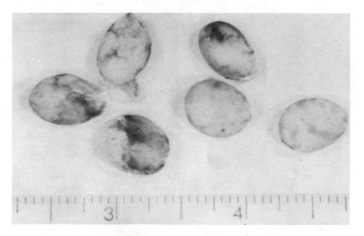

(Castanopsis sempervirens)

## Castanopsis (Fagaceae)

This genus of 120 kinds of big trees, is restricted to tropical and subtropical Asia, except for one species in northwestern United States.

Burkill summarizes the distribution of the trees in Asia:

"As the generic name indicates, they are closely similar to *Castanea,* the SPANISH CHESTNUT; and the nuts which the various species produce can be arranged in a series from an edible state, almost equalling that of the CHESTNUT, to a quite inedible condition. *C. inermis, C. wallichii,* and perhaps *C. costata* give the best nuts among the Malayan species. The inferior species are commonly regarded as pigs' chestnuts.

"CHESTNUTS derived from three species of *Castanopsis* are used in the Himalayas but none of the three extends southwards to Malaya, though one of them reaches Siam. A dozen species are said to furnish edible nuts in Indo-China, one of them being cultivated. In the Dutch Indies there are six species with edible nuts."

In addition to these, there is *C. chinensis,* sometimes called CHINESE CHINQUAPIN, cultivated in Yunnan and Kwantung, a big evergreen tree. The nut is eaten roasted, and is notable for its sweet smell; it is a popular food in many parts of Kwantung.

Also in the Philippines comes *C. philippinensis,* of which Brown says:

"*C. philippensis* is a tree usually 15 to 25 meters in height. The fruit grows on spikes, and contains an edible, oblong nut up to 3.5 centimeters in length. The flavor resembles that of a chestnut. There are several other species of this genus in the Philippines, having edible nuts, but they are of little importance as a source of food."

Burkill describes six species in Malaya that have edible nuts:

*C. costata.* A tree of moderate height found widely in western Malaysia; in the Peninsula it occurs in Perak. Wray records that the nuts are edible, in which respect this species agrees with *C. javanica* which is planted sparingly in Java for the sake of the nuts.

*C. hullettii.* A rather tall tree found here and there from Penang to Singapore. Alvin says that the prickly chestnuts are eaten boiled.

*C. inermis.* A rather tall tree found in Sumatra and the Malay Peninsula; in the Peninsula especially in the north, it is frequently cultivated. The chestnuts, which lie in a spineless case, are edible, and are considerably used, parched, roasted or boiled. In southern Sumatra they are very common in the markets, in season. In Malaya they are not quite so often seen, but they are not neglected.

*C. malaccensis.* A tree found in Malacca, Negri Sembilan, and Singapore. Alvins said that the chestnut is edible; he adds that too many cause diarrhoea.

*C. megacarpa.* A rather tall tree found from Province Wellesley to Singapore, common in the lowlands. The chestnuts are edible. Ridley records, from Malay sources, that they purge and produce flatulence, but others say they can be eaten with impunity, though distinctly bitter. It is extremely probable that more than one species is confused in these statements.

*C. wallichii.* A rather tall tree, found from Penang to Singapore. The chestnuts, which lie in a very spinous case, are edible, and Ridley records this of them: "They are small and have a hard rind, which makes them troublesome to open. They have quite the flavour of the English chestnut, and are used by the Malays to ornament cakes."

The Forest Service at Lae, New Guinea, writes of *C. accuminatissima:* "This has nuts which are eaten either raw or cooked. This is a tree, often common in fagaceous forests, mostly between altitudes of 3000′ to 7000′, often associated with disturbance (landslips, cutting, etc.). Mature trees are characterized by profuse coppice growth from the base."

For this book H. G. Hundley in Rangoon, Burma, sent three packs of *Castanopsis* fruits, illustrated here, with this note:

"Fruits of *Castanopsis argyrophylla,* commonly called GON.

"Fruits of *C. tribuloides* var. *longispinus,* called KAT.

"Fruits of *C. tribuloides* var. *ferox,* called KYSIN.

"These are Burmese chestnuts that are roasted and eaten like the Chinese chestnuts."

WEEPING EUROPEAN BEECH *(Fagus sylvatica* var. *pendula)*

EUROPEAN BEECH *(Fagus sylvatica)*

USDA photo

AMERICAN BEECH *(Fagus grandifolia)*

*Fagus grandifolia*     (Fagaceae)     **AMERICAN BEECHNUT**

Ten kinds of beech trees are found in the north Temperate Zone.

Of the fruits of this American BEECH, Bailey says: "Small triangular seeds which in form and general appearance greatly resemble overgrown seeds of BUCK-WHEAT. In character of shell and in flavor of kernel, BEECHNUTS greatly resemble the chestnut. Owing to the tediousness of separating the kernel from the shell, these nuts are not so largely harvested as undoubtedly would otherwise be the case."

The BEECHNUT trees thrive in the Allegheny mountains as far south as Florida and Texas, doing best at higher elevations. The nuts fall in autumn and soon spoil unless collected and dried.

Bailey says further: "From the seeds of the European BEECH *(F. sylvatica),* which also are edible, there is obtained a valuable oil, used as food."

Willis says the European BEECH often forms homogenous forests, and continues: "Each cupule encloses 2 nuts; an oil is expressed from the nuts. BEECH hedges in many districts; growing low it does not drop its leaves. The BEECH flowers only every few years."

Sturtevant says of the European BEECH: "In Hanover the oil of the nut is used as a salad oil and as a substitute for butter. In France, the nuts are roasted and serve as a substitute for coffee. Sawdust of BEECH wood is boiled in water, baked and then mixed with flour to form the material for bread in Norway and Sweden."

Maheshwari says the European BEECH is found in Kulu and the Nilgiris where the seeds are eaten.

*(Nothofagus glauca)*

## *Nothofagus sp.*

*Hortus Third* says this comprises "about 40 species of deciduous or evergreen beechlike trees or shrubs, native to temperate South America, New Zealand, Tasmania, southeast Australia, New Caledonia and New Guinea." This book describes several of them which have been tried in coastal areas of California. The trees are prized chiefly for timber, but a few bear edible 3-angled nuts, usually borne in threes in a scaly pod.

Bailey lists 6 species introduced into European gardens and adds: "These have proved fairly hardy in S. England and Ireland. They are all trees or sometimes shrubby, with small leaves, ½-1 in. long. One is deciduous, the others evergreen. They are perhaps oftener enumerated under *Fagus,* but besides the difference in the flowers, they are

AMERICAN BEECH *(Fagus grandifolia)*

17

different in habit, especially on account of their very small leaves, large only in *N. procera.*''

*(Lithocarpus corneus)* Hong Kong herbarium label says: "Tree 21 feet high in mixed woods. Fruit brown."

MALAYAN OAK *(Lithocarpus sp.)*

5 CM
Isaac Ho Sai-Yuen photo

## *Lithocarpus corneus* (Fagaceae)

Regarding *Lithocarpus corneus*, Bailey calls it an "edible acorn" and continues: "The seed of an evergreen tree of China, closely related to the oak. Now being tried out in this country by the Office of Foreign Seed and Plant Introduction, which says regarding it: 'The nuts are as thick-walled as hickory nuts; the kernels are white and of characteristic shape, and have a sweet very agreeable flavor. In China, they are sold on the market as are chestnuts here.

The nuts are very broad in proportion to their length, presenting a flattish appearance.' ''

Regarding *L. cuspidatus* which Bailey also calls an "edible acorn," his account continues: "Described as being a small acorn, edible and sweet, when ripe or after frost, boiled or roasted. From Formosa, Korea and milder parts of China."

Acorns of *L. corneus* are reported edible, by a Chinese author Chan Wing (1937): *The Classification of Chinese Trees.*

Some 300 species of *Lithocarpus* trees have been described from eastern and southeastern Asia and Malaysia.

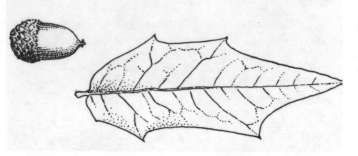

EMORY OAK *(Quercus emoryi)*

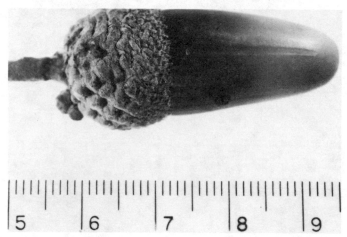

*(Quercus lobata)*

USDA photo

CHESTNUT OAK, BASKET OAK *(Quercus prinus)*

## *Quercus sp.*     (Fagaceae)     OAK

The 450 kinds of acorns that fall from that many different kinds of oaks, useful, valuable monarchs of forests all over the world, are highly popular with squirrels, and a lot of them are eaten by people.

A bulletin from U.S. Forest Service says:

"Though it is a common belief that acorns are fit only for feeding hogs, many kinds can be made edible and nourishing for people as well. The Indians gathered and stored quantities of acorns, which were ground into meal and baked into an unleavened pasty, nutritious bread. The tannin, which causes the bitter and astringent taste in raw acorns, was removed by soaking in water and filtering, or by boiling and leaching with ashes. Acorns were also eaten roasted. As a rule, acorns of the species in the WHITE OAK group are less bitter, and better for food than those in the BLACK OAK group which mature in two years instead of one. The following kinds of white oaks in eastern United States have sweetish acorns that can be eaten roasted or raw made into bread: WHITE OAK *(Q. alba)*, SWAMP WHITE OAK *(Q. bicolor* or *Q. michauxii)*, CHESTNUT OAK *(Q. prinus)*, CHINQUAPIN OAK *(Q. prinoides)*, LIVE OAK *(Q. virginiana)*, POST OAK *(Q. stellata)*, and BUR OAK *(Q. macrocarpa)* (the species with the largest acorns.)

Indians and Mexicans in the Southwest eat the sweetish acorns of EMORY OAK *(Q. emoryi)*, which are known by the Spanish name of bellotas — pronounced bay-YOH-tahs. In California the Indians hoarded acorns of CALIFORNIA WHITE OAK *( Q. lobata)*, CANYON LIVE OAK *(Q. chrysolepis)*, CALIFORNIA LIVE OAK *(Q. agrifolia)*, and CALIFORNIA BLACK OAK *(Q. kelloggii)*.

Acorn meal is prepared by grinding the shelled kernels in a food chopper. The bitter tannin is removed by spreading the meal about one-half inch thick on a porous cloth and then pouring on hot water to percolate through, repeating once or twice as needed. Or the kernels may be boiled for two hours before grinding and then soaked in hot water with occasional changes until the bitter flavor is lost. After being dried and parched in an oven, acorn meal is used like corn meal in recipes for bread or muffins, alone or mixed with equal parts of corn meal or wheat flour."

Burkill says: "The acorns of *Q. robur* (ENGLISH OAK or TRUFFLE OAK) have served man as a famine-food in Europe. Bread made from them is detestable, but is said to have been used, at times, in large quantities. Washing in water and burying in the soil are processes which lessen the bitterness. Various ills and a malady called 'trousse galante' followed acorn eating during a famine in France.

"But acorns of some species of *Quercus* are eaten regularly in countries where food is often scarce. Certain tribes of North American Indians, for instance, depended in the past very greatly upon their acorn crops, and in order to store them, built granaries.

"Perhaps the most edible of all acorns is that of *Q. ilex* (HOLLY OAK), but among edible acorns are various Malayan species."

Bailey says: "The acorns of several species are edible, in America especially those of *Q. prinus, Q. emoryi* and *Q. lobata;* in Europe those of *Q. ilex* var. *Ballota* and *Q. aegilops,* in Japan those of *Q. glauca, Q. prinus,* and *Q. emoryi.*"

Sturtevant's *Notes on Edible Plants* describes nineteen kinds of edible acorns as follows:

### *Quercus aegilops*     CAMATA
South Europe and Syria. The ripe acorns are eaten raw or boiled.

### *Q. agrifolia*     CALIFORNIA FIELD OAK
The acorns are eaten by the Indians.

### *Q. alba*     WHITE OAK
Northeast America. The dried acorns are macerated in water for food by the natives on the Roanoke. Acorns were dried and boiled for food by the Narragansetts. Oak acorns were mixed with their pottage by the Indians of Massachusetts. Baskets full of parched acorns, hid in the ground, were discovered by the Pilgrims, December 7, 1620. White oak acorns were boiled for "oyl" by the natives of New England. The fruit of some trees is quite pleasant to the taste, especially when roasted.

### *Q. cerris*     TURKISH OAK
Europe and the Orient. The trees are visited in August by immense numbers of a small, white coccus insect, from the puncture of which a saccharine fluid exudes and solidifies in little grains. The wandering tribes of Kurdistan collect this saccharine secretion by dipping the branches on which it forms into hot water and evaporating to a syrupy consistence. In this state, the syrup is used for sweetening food or is mixed with flour to form a sort of cake.

### *Q. coccifera*     KERMES OAK
Mediterranean region. The acorns were used as food by the ancients.

### *Q. cornea*
China. The acorns are used for food. Loudon says the acorns are ground into a paste in China which, mixed with the flour of corn, is made into cakes.

### *Q. cuspidata*
Japan. This species is enumerated by Thunberg among the edible plants of Japan.

### *Q. emoryi*
Western North America. This tree furnishes acorns, which are used by the Indians of the West as food.

### *Q. garryana*     WESTERN OAK
Western North America. The acorns furnish the Indians with food and are stored by them for future use.

### *Q. ilex*     BALLOTA, HOLLY OAK
Mediterranean region and the Orient. From varieties of this tree, says Mueller, are obtained the sweet and nourishing BALLOTA and chestnut acorns. Figuier says this species is common in the south of France, and that the acorns are sweet and eatable. Brandis says the acorns form an important article of food in Spain and Algeria. The acorns are eaten in Barbary, Spain and Portugal under the name of BELOTE. In Arabia, also, they are eaten cooked, and an oil is extracted from them. In Palestine they are sold in all the bazaars.

### *Q. lobata*     CALIFORNIA WHITE OAK
California. The acorns form a large proportion of the winter food of the Indians of North California. The acorns, from their abundance and edible nature, form a very important part of the subsistence of the Digger Indians and are collected and stored for winter use.

### *Q. oblongifolia*     LIVE OAK
California and New Mexico. This species furnishes the Indians of the West with acorns for food use.

### *Q. persica*     MANNA OAK
Persia. The acorns are eaten in southern Europe and, in southern Persia afford material for bread. Bartholin says that in Norway acorns are used to furnish a bread. During a famine in France in 1709, acorns were resorted to for sustenance.

### *Q. phellos*     WILLOW OAK
Eastern States of North America. The acorns are edible.

### *Q. prinus*     CHESTNUT OAK
Northeastern America. The fruit is sweet and abundant.

### *Q. robur*     BLACK OAK / TRUFFLE OAK
Europe and western Asia. Varieties are mentioned by Tenore as bearing edible acorns.

### *Q. suber*     CORK OAK
South Europe and northern Africa. Bosc alleges that its acorns may be eaten in cases of necessity, especially when roasted.

### *Q. undulata*     ROCKY MOUNTAIN SCRUB OAK
California. The acorns are sweet and edible.

*Q. virginiana*                                           LIVE OAK

Eastern North America. Eastern Indians consumed large quantities of the acorns and also obtained from them a sweet oil much used in cookery.

Russell Smith in his book *Tree Crops,* says:

"Any balanced presentation of the economics of the acorn must point out its great nutritive value and its great use as human food. It may be possible that the human race has eaten more of acorns than it has of wheat, for wheat is the food of only one of the four large masses of humans, the European-North American group. The other three groups, the Chinese-Japanese, the Indian (Asiatic), and the tropical peoples, pay small attention to wheat; hundreds of millions of their people have never heard of it. Meanwhile those humans (and possibly pre-humans) who dwelt in or near the oak forests in the middle latitudes — Japan, China, Himalaya Mountains, West Asia, Europe, North America — have probably lived in part on acorns for unknown hundreds of centuries, possibly for thousands of centuries.

"It is almost certain that wheat has been of important use only in the era of man's agriculture, while the acorn was almost surely of importance during that very, very long period when man was only a food gatherer."

During the food hysteria of the World War, C. Hart Merriam pointed out that for an unknown length of time acorn bread has been the staff of life for the Indians from Oregon to Mexico except those in the desert; that there were 300,000 of these Indians in California when it was discovered by the white man. Acorns of several species were eaten by various eastern tribes from Canada to the Gulf of Mexico.

Merriam said in the *National Geographic* that John Muir often carried the hard dry bread of the Indians during his arduous tramps in the mountains of California and deemed it the most complete strength-giving food he had ever used, as the very high percentage of fat makes it as nutritious as richly buttered bread. Dr. Merriam pointed out that one part of acorn and four parts of corn or wheat make palatable bread and muffins, adding to the cereal the value of a fat nut product.

Missouri Botanical Garden Bulletin on acorns and muffins made from them, said:

"With modern kitchen equipment acorn meal can easily be prepared at home. After husking the acorns they should be ground in a handgrist mill or food-chopper. The meal is then mixed with hot water and poured into a jelly bag. The bitter tannin, being soluble, will be taken out by the water, but sometimes a second or even third washing may be necessary. After washing, the wet meal is spread out to dry and is then parched in an oven. If it has caked badly, it should be run through the mill again before using.

"In cooking, acorn meal may be used in the same way as cornmeal. Its greatest fault is its color, muffins made from it being a dark chocolate brown. The taste suggests a mixture of cornmeal and peanut butter, and some people relish it at once, but others, it must be confessed, have to be educated to it. Because of the high oil and starch content of the acorn, it is very nutritious and is reported to be easily digested. Only acorns from WHITE OAKS should be gathered, as those from the BLACK OAKS are too bitter. Typical Missouri representatives of this group are the WHITE OAK, the SWAMP OAK, the BUR OAK, and the CHESTNUT OAK.

"In this age more and more food is being prepared in factories and delivered to the consumer in packages ready to serve. Many new materials are contributing to the success of machine production. In Michigan prepared wheat bran is put into boxes in factories, and millions of people eat it with apparent relish.

"The Californians are making human food of CAROB beans and selling it in California. Some factory may soon be giving us artistic boxes of acorn cakes under an attractive name. We need be surprised at nothing now that the food factory has come. One man is now selling each week one and one-half million sandwiches made of PEANUT butter and crackers. A few generations ago the PEANUT was unknown. Then for a few decades it served as the pocket food of the socially unsophisticated while enjoying the circus or the horse race. Finally some enterprising enthusiast took the PEANUT to the factory. Millions now eat the one-time lowly nut in its various dignified forms. PEANUT butter and the salted PEANUT have an established place at the American table.

"Will the acorn be next, blended with some other cereals? The fact that the acorn carries its own butter is an attractive feature. Its amazing keeping qualities are also greatly in its favor. The acorn bread of the California Indian keeps indefinitely. This is a wonderful quality for factory foods that are to be distributed in packages.

"Then there is that 6 percent of tannin. How easy for the chemical engineer to get it out if he had 50,000 tons of acorns a year to deal with! Tannin is worth money. We scour the ends of the world for it. It is quite possible that income from tannin might put a premium price on bitter acorns."

Dr. Merriam showed that the acorn can probably be kept for a longer time and more easily than any other food product. A common method of storage by the Indians was to bury acorns in mud kept cold by a spring of water. Dr. Merriam reports the discovery of such caches as these that had lain for a period of thirty years in which the acorn remained unsprouted and unspoiled. They were merely discolored.

### *Pasania cornea*                                    (Fagaceae)

Bailey says: "This is the seed of an evergreen tree of China, closely related to the oak. The nuts are as thick-walled as hickory nuts; the kernels are white and of characteristic shape, and have a sweet, very agreeable flavor. In China, they are sold on the markets. The nuts are very broad in proportion to their length, presenting a flattish appearance.

"*P. cuspidata.* A small acorn, edible and sweet, when ripe or after frost, boiled or roasted. From Formosa, Korea and milder parts of China."

20

# Chapter 4
# THE MACADAMIA

The MACADAMIA is a nut which in a few recent years, has risen high in public favor and has become one of the choicest of morsels, largely because of exploitation of the trees in Hawaiian orchards. There are 10 kinds of MACADAMIA trees but only two of the five Australian species have become important food producers. There are other species in New Caledonia, the Celebes and Madagascar.

The MACADAMIAS are an important number in the *Protea* family, just one of 62 kinds of trees and shrubs which almost all grow only in climates where there is annually a long dry season. Only one or two of the Proteaceae survive in Florida, and the family is largely concentrated in South Africa, California and dry parts of Australia.

There are some other nuts in the MACADAMIA family and some of them are presented here.

David Noel photo

**WILD ALMOND**
*Brabejum stellatifolium* shows the peculiar germination mode (second nut from the right) and the root grows from this.

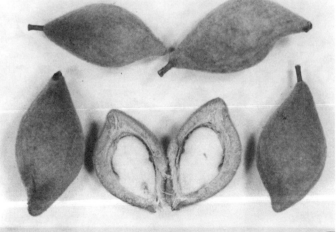

WILD ALMOND *(Brabejum stellatifolium)*

### *Brabejum stellatifolium* (Proteaceae)
### WILD ALMOND, WILD CHESTNUT

Palmer & Pittman wrote: *"Brabejum* is a genus of only 1 species, and is confined to the extreme southwest Cape, in South Africa.

"The WILD ALMOND is a densely growing tree to 25 feet or a shrub, where it grows wild along streams. Van Riebeeck planted a hedge of WILD ALMONDS as a boundary to the Colony and to prevent Hottentots stealing cattle. In his journal of 1661 he wrote that he was marking off the fence "with wild bitter almonds which will in a few years become a fine, thick, and high hedge." They did, and the remains of this historic hedge are to be found on the left from Kirstenbosch Botanical Gardens by the south gate. It is still known as Van Riebeeck's hedge.

"The fruit is about 1 to 1½ inches long, 1-seeded, enclosed in a golden velvety coat and very much resembles the fruit of the cultivated almond. It ripens in the late autumn.

"At one time the roasted kernels were used as coffee. The seed, however, is poisonous unless well soaked."

Sturtevant quotes Thunberg. "The Hottentots eat the fruit of this shrub and it is sometimes used by the country people instead of coffee, the outside rind being taken off and the fruit steeped in water to deprive it of its bitterness; it is then boiled, roasted and ground like coffee."

Forestry Service photo, New Guinea

*(Finschia chloroxantha)*

### *Finschia* (Proteaceae)

*Finschia* is a genus of seven kinds of edible nut trees that grow from New Guinea to the Solomon Islands and New Hebrides. When this author tried to get seeds from the Forest service in Lae, New Guinea, he received this note: "Seed of this tree is hard to come by as the native people value it highly as a food."

Later, E. E. Henty of the Botany Division wrote: "Of species here *F. carrii* seems to be the same as *F. rufa*. It is not much collected as yet and we have no reports that the nut is eaten. The other species are *F. ferruginiflora* (the seeds are cooked and eaten by natives) and *F. chloroxantha* which is quite often planted near villages as a food tree. It is quite variable in foliage over its extensive range.

"Fruits of this *Finschia* are collected as they mature and fall. The fruit is roasted to help crack the shell and the kernels eaten there and then as a sweetmeat. When in season there is invariably a fireplace near a *Finschia* tree. As the crop advances the heap of shells increases to quite sizeable proportions."

Marie C. Neal writes: "This tall nut tree is distributed in the western Pacific, where the nuts are a source of food for the natives. Many small, yellowish, slightly brown-hairy flowers develop in foot-long spikes below the leaves. Fruits are indehiscent, yellow, slightly flattened and round-oblique, 1.5 inches long, have a hard shell with a thin, soft coat and a thick, edible kernel. *F. ferruginiflora* from New

Guinea is similar, but the edible fruits are larger and globose.''

*(Gevuina avellana)*

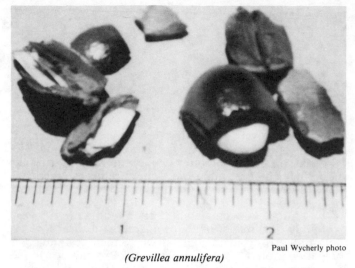

*(Grevillea annulifera)*

## AVELLANO CHILEAN NUT
### *Gevuina avellana* (Proteaceae) CHILE HAZEL

Of this nut, Bailey says: "Small seeds of an evergreen tree from Chile. Globular in form, with smooth, tough shell and a kernel much like that of a hazel in both appearance and flavor. Seeds borne within a coral-red fruit.''

These nuts have been distributed from Chile for a hundred years and there are big trees to 50 feet and more in Ireland, southwest England, California, and other suitable mild, moist climates.

Britton called it "one of the most beautiful of all trees.''

The *Botanical Magazine* says: "This very handsome and decorative tree appears to be little known outside its native country. It is a small tree or shrub, attaining 10-12 (rarely 15) meters only under the most favourable conditions, as in the rain-forest of Valdivia and Chiloe. Within this area the tree is a common constituent of the mixed rain-forest and of the scrub, growing highest in the shelter of taller trees, where it finds protection from heavy winds which it is not able to resist owing to the great weight of its foliage. It flowers from February to May, the late Chilian summer and autumn, at the same time as the fruits of the previous season ripen. It may be found in both stages in October and November. The flowers are white (snow white to ivory white). When white, the contrast with the glossy, dark green foliage is very fine indeed.''

## *Grevillea annulifera* (Proteaceae)

*Grevillea* is a genus of 190 kinds of trees and shrubs in eastern Malaysia, New Hebrides, New Caledonia and Australia. Of this species, Paul Wycherly, director of the botanic garden at Perth, writes:

"This shrub of the sandplain heaths of the Irwin district bears relatively papery fruits enclosing two hard-shelled seeds in each. The shell is fairly difficult to crack and the edible seed is relatively small, therefore there is no commercial harvest which would give an economic return, however, quite a number of people do eat them as tidbits.''

Harold Caulfield of the botanic garden at Brisbane writes: "Caution is advised in eating 'nuts' from many of the *Grevilleas*. It may be possible to eat a few seeds, however, quantities are not advised.''

Barrau says: "The seeds of *Grevillea elaeocarpifolia* are eaten on Pentecost Island, New Hebrides.''

*(Helicia diversifolia)*

## *Helicia* (Proteaceae)

There are 90 kinds of *Helicia* in southeast Asia, eastern Australia, and Indo-Malaysia, some with very beautiful fruit but whether anybody eats the kernels is not certain. Burkill reports that *H. cochinchinensis* has "seeds that are said to be edible.'' Manson Bailey's *Queensland Flora* seems to indicate *H. youngiana* fruits are poisonous.

Dr. George H. Hewitt whose photograph of the fruit appears here, writes: "I have never tasted *Helicia* fruits and do not expect to try.''

The *Helicia* nuts are borne by plants so obscure amidst the general luxuriance of the tropical vegetation as to be scarcely known beyond the localities where they actually occur, and with nuts, according to those who have tasted them, unlikely to appeal to the civilized palate.

## *Kermadecia* (Proteaceae)

This genus, closely allied to the CHILEAN HAZEL *(Gevuina)* includes 12 kinds of trees in Polynesia, Fiji, and Northeastern Australia. Barrau says the "nuts of *K. leptophylla* require lengthy washing and cooking before they are ready to eat."

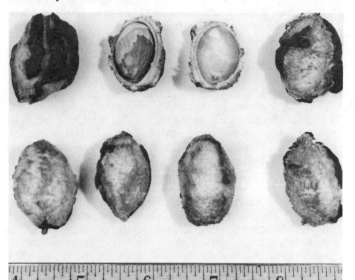

*(Hicksbeachia pinnatifolia)*

## *Hicksbeachia pinnarufuda* (Proteaceae)
### MONKEY NUT
### REDNUT

Lord says the MONKEY NUT is an 80-foot tree in New South Wales and Queensland, on rich, warm East Coast soils. He says the tree has striking, 24-inch leaves, light green, deeply lobed, and 12-inch spikes of small yellowish flowers, and adds: "Hard, red, oval nuts, 1½ inches, edible."

Neal writes: "The REDNUT from Australia, like the *Macadamia* in some ways and much different in others, with fruit globose, orange, about 1 inch in diameter, with a thick, woody shell and an edible nut."

Dr. Wm. J. Dress of Bailey Hortorium writes: "The nut of *Macadamia integrifolia* is globose, whereas those of *M. ternifolia* tend to be pointed at both ends."

Harry Oakman photo

QUEENSLAND NUT *(Macadamia integrifolia)*

## *Macadamia integrifolia* (Proteaceae)
### *M. tetraphylla* MACADAMIA
### *M. ternifolia* QUEENSLAND NUT

The MACADAMIA originated in the coastal rain forest and scrubs of Queensland in northeastern Australia. Today the nuts are a prized delicacy throughout the world.

The nuts are borne on the trees in hanging clusters of a dozen or more. Each nut is brown, spherical, ½ to ¾ in. across, with a smooth or slightly roughened exterior husk. The shell is very hard. The trees bear continuously when mature, and as the ripe nuts are difficult to distinguish from the immature ones on the tree they are commonly harvested from the ground after they have fallen. Hybrids and selected clones of Hawaiian origin are Kakea, Ikaiki, Wailua, and Nuuanu.

It is remarkable that the QUEENSLAND NUT is the only commercially important food plant ever to come from the Australian continent. *Macadamia* nuts were grown in Australia fairly soon after the plant itself was discovered and the nuts found good, and at the turn of the last century, about 1892, orchards were started in Hawaii, where the nuts have become an important crop. Over the years there has been much improvement in the Hawaiian plants and nuts through selective propagation and the replacing of seedling orchards by those of grafted origin.

For many years the edible-fruited MACADAMIA was called *Macadamia ternifolia,* but this application of the name has been found to be incorrect; the name *M. ternifolia* actually belongs to a species with bitter, inedible nuts. Botanists now generally agree that the commonly cultivated kinds with sweet, edible nuts belong to two other, closely related species: *Macadamia tetraphylla,* with prickle-edged leaves arranged usually in whorls of four around the stems, and *M. integrifolia,* with smooth-edged leaves mostly in whorls of three. These plants interbreed easily, and all degrees of intergradation may be found, often on the same tree, but most of the best varieties of nut producing trees are of predominantly *integrifolia* stock. The tree itself, in its native coastal scrubs, is a small evergreen, seldom reaching more than 30 or 40 feet in height, with flowers in pendant racemes, followed by the nuts hanging in clusters of 10 or 20, each nut about an inch, or slightly less across.

Neal says: "The first MACADAMIA trees were planted in Hawaii by E. W. Jordan about 1890. They grew and bore so well that an orchard of 2,000 trees was later planted on Round Top, Honolulu, and 6,000 trees were planted in Kona. Other orchards on Maui and Kauai bring the total area to about 4,000 acres."

Burkill says of the MACADAMIA: "The flavour of the nut is excellent and the tree is cultivated on account of it, at the present time, in several countries. The kernels contain upwards of 76 per cent of a colourless oil, suitable for human food, and the residual press-cake, after crushing for oil, contains 35 to 36 per cent of protein. They hold no starch, but nearly 6 per cent of a sugar."

MACADAMIA NUTS are most commonly used in fancy pastries, candies, and ice cream. The nuts have the unique advantage of retaining their texture and flavor without becoming stale when used in these ways.

CSIRO photo

QUEENSLAND NUT *(Macadamia whelanii)*

There is another kind of MACADAMIA in Australia with very large nuts 2 or more inches across, *M. whelanii,* but these nuts contain dangerous quantities of cyanide and are eaten by the aborigines only after special preparation to remove the poison.

F. M. Bailey, in his *Queensland Flora* says about this: "The nuts seem to be largely used by the natives of the locality along Tringilburra Creek for food, as we found large quantities of the broken shells as well as the whole nuts at all their camps."

––––

## (AN AUSTRALIAN CONTRIBUTION)

Lying close behind the eastern coast of the Australian continent, extending through the states of Victoria, New South Wales, and Queensland, from Wilson's Promontory in the south, to Cape York in the north, opposite Papua, is a more or less continuous series of uplands and low mountain ranges, known in aggregate as the Great Dividing Range. West of this divide much of Australia is an arid land. Over a continental territory of thousands of square miles there is not to be found a single permanently flowing river or stream. In this country life depends, uncomfortably, on a small number of isolated water holes. Such a desolate land held no interest for the earliest European discoverers of Australia, coming upon the forbidding western coast by accident in their voyages to the Spice Islands, and eastern Australia was not seen, by Captain James Cook, until late in the 18th century.

East of the Dividing Range the aspect of the country changes. Here, along a narrow coastal corridor more than 2,000 miles long, rain falls in abundance, brought by the southeasterly trades of the southern hemisphere. Under these rains the eastern mountain slopes, the valleys and gorges, and the narrow coastal plains are blanketed in luxuriant vegetation. Through this verdant, often rugged, country numberless crooked streams and rivers find the

ocean, in the south through steep sided gullies lined with gum trees and tree ferns, but in the north, above the Tropic, more often through a tropical rain forest, related by proximity to the forests that clothe the tropical islands of the South Pacific. In these tropical forests and scrubs of the north, in Queensland, and extending south into the northern part of New South Wales, is found the MACADAMIA or QUEENSLAND NUT.

Originally this tropical coast of northeastern Australia belonged to the Aborigines. These native Australians have felt the hot sun of civilization, but they were, and are yet in some places, a stone age people, naked, making fire by friction, but without metals or even pottery. Without herds or agriculture they have subsisted, as other hunting peoples, on what they could find or kill. In this primitive economy the men hunt and the women gather. It seems likely that Aborigine women, dark skinned lubras, must have gathered MACADAMIA nuts, but of this there is at least a shadow of doubt. They cannot themselves be asked, because in this part of Australia they are vanished, or else detribalized and partly assimilated. At least one account says the Aborigines did not eat the MACADAMIA nuts, and that their edibility was discovered by a small boy, employed by the curator of the Botanical Garden at Brisbane to crack the nuts for planting in the Garden, who was found eating them, as small boys will, with no ill effect; this happening, obviously, at no very early date.

There is another MACADAMIA, closely related to the one bearing edible nuts, with temptingly large nuts filled, unfortunately, with toxic quantities of prussic acid or cyanide. The Aborigines, who distinguish the plants they lived among with scarcely less nicety than a trained botanist, would hardly be confused by such similarities. Even so, the poisonous nuts were eaten by grinding them to a coarse meal, which was treated by soaking for two days in running water before being used, the water serving to remove the soluble poison. We may wonder how necessity could find a way to use the poisonous nuts and yet allow the edible ones to remain unnoticed.

––––

J. W. Endt wrote in the Orchardist of New Zealand as follows:

"The MACADAMIA of eastern Australia is represented by two species *M. integrefolia,* or smooth-shelled and *M. tetraphylla,* rough shelled. These two hybridise, although there are differences.

"*Tetraphylla:* Spiny leafed, no leaf stalk, sometimes a short leaf stalk. Young growth, usually red or brown tree, very upright in growth. Nuts often spindle-shaped and pebbled.

"*Integrefolia:* Leaf margins smooth or with few spines. Young leaves light green, tree more spreading and willowy. Long leaf stalks. Nuts round and smooth.

"Encouraged by the economic success of the Hawaiian industry, many other subtropical regions have started planting MACADAMIA in the last five years or so. Big acreages are being planted in South Africa, Rhodesia and Malawi, and in parts of South and Central America. Southern California and Australia are entering commercial production. The varieties used have mainly been the Hawaiian clones. However, it has been found that the tetraphylla varieties have been developed in Australia and California. In New Zealand the tetraphylla species is most common.

"What are the varieties to plant? It seems likely that the MACADAMIA will be sold as a fresh nut product. A variety should be chosen which has a thin shell, easy to crack. In the tetraphylla range I would recommend Elimbah, Sewell and Probert 2.

"The integrefolia type usually has a thicker shell. Varieties suitable for processing are Keauhou and Ikaika.

"A hybrid variety which produces a good crop of thin-shelled nuts is Beaumont. Because of the long period of nut shedding, this variety is recommended for home gardeners.

"Nuts fall off the tree when ripe. They should never be picked. All harvesting is done by gathering nuts from the ground. So far no mechanical harvesting device has proved practicable. After collection the nuts are husked, then air-dried to reduce the moisture content to low levels. This prevents the nuts from going mouldy and rancid. Once dried, the nuts will keep for 12 months or more."

---

Chapter 5

# THE PILI NUT AND THE KENARI NUT

## (Burseraceae)

*Canarium* is a genus of big shade trees in the Old World tropics, chiefly Malaysia to the Philippines. They are prized not only for their resins, but because they produce lots of edible fruits and nuts.

They are of two kinds: Some like *C. album* in Indo-China whose fruits are eaten like an olive, i.e. the flesh is the part sought, not the kernel. In Malaya the kernels of these fruits are pickled for later use. The kernels contain an edible oil, but the hard stone renders crushing impractical.

In other species, headed by *C. ovatum,* the PILI NUT, of the Philippines, the kernels are large enough to be worth extracting and enjoying as nuts.

*C. ovatum* and *C. luzonicum* are among the most important nut-bearing trees of the 75 kinds in this family, and they are No. 1 producers of fat and protein in the diet of residents of the far Pacific. *C. luzonicum* also produces the resin called Manila elemi, and *C. strictum* of south India, and some other species produce the black dammar of commerce. It is a highly important tree family.

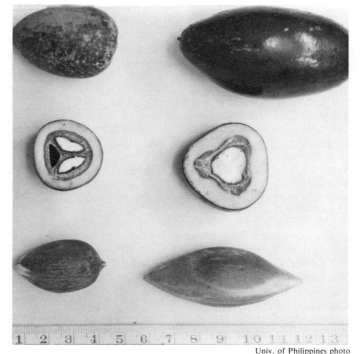

Univ. of Philippines photo

PILI NUT *(Canarium ovatum)*

J. K. Maheshwari photo

INDIAN OLIBANUM *(Boswellia serrata)*

### *Boswellia serrata* (Burseraceae)
### INDIAN OLIBANUM

This common tree of central India and eastward into Burma, is cultivated chiefly for its fragrant gum-resin, and for its useful timber; the wood also is used to make paper.

Watt says: "The flowers and seed-nut are eaten by the Bhils."

Maheshwari reports: "The flowers and seeds are edible."

JAVA ALMOND *(Canarium luzonicum)*

## PILI NUT
## *Canarium ovatum* (Burseraceae) PHILIPPINE NUT

The most important of all the nuts in the world to the millions of people who depend on it for food, is the PILI NUT of the Philippines and its relatives. Seventy-five kinds of these nuts grow in enormous quantities from Africa through India to northern Australia, Malaya and on the Pacific Islands.

Burkill says: "The PILI NUT is found in great abundance throughout a very large part of the islands. The fruits are produced in considerable quantities — upwards of 70 lb. per annum for a tree; they are collected and enter trade. The shell is hard, but the kernel, when extracted and roasted, has a delicious flavour, and is claimed to be superior to almonds. Before marketing, the pericarp outside the shell is removed by dipping the fruits in hot water."

Bailey says: "These nuts are slender, sometimes attaining a length of 2½ inches and a middle diameter of about ¾ to 7/8 of an inch, though sometimes they are short and blunt-pointed with about the same diameter. Typical specimens taper gracefully from near the middle into long, sharp-pointed ends. Inside the shells, which are exceedingly difficult to crack, are single kernels."

Brown says: "The nuts of this species are very rich in oil, and when roasted have a delicious flavor. They are served in the same manner as almonds, and by many are considered superior to the latter. The nuts are also used considerably in the making of confections. In Camarines, the roasted kernels are used to adulterate chocolate. The uncooked nuts have a purgative effect. In 1913, 1,186,173 kilograms of PILI NUTS were exported from Manila. The oil obtained from the nuts is sweet, and suitable for culinary purposes. The fruits are 6 to 7 centimeters in length and consist of hard, thick-shelled, triangular nuts surrounded by a small amount of pulp. This pulp, which is edible when cooked, also contains an oil which is occasionally extracted locally and used for lighting and in cooking.

"E. Tabat who kept a record of the yield of a number of trees, found that an average tree produced 33 kilos of nuts in one year.

"*Canarium ovatum* is a tree reaching a height of about 20 meters and a diameter of about 40 centimeters. It is very abundant in southern Luzon.

"Another Philippine species, often called PILI NUT, is *Canarium luzonicum,* a tree reaching 35 meters and a diameter of 1 meter or more. The fruits are somewhat oval, about 3 centimeters long and contain a thick-shelled, triangular, edible nut. This species is very abundant in the primary forests of Luzon at low and medium altitudes and is also found in Marinduque, Ticao, Mindoro, and Masbate."

*(Canarium vulgare)*

*(Canarium kepalla)*

*(Canarium oleosum)*

*(Canarium commune)*

26

J. K. Maheshwari photo

*(Canarium indicum)*

J. S. Womersley photo, Lae, New Guinea

*(Canarium indicum)*

Worthington photo

*(Canarium zeylanicum)*

These two Philippine species of *Canarium,* and the Chinese *C. album* and *C. pimela,* commonly known as CHINESE OLIVES, are the only *Canarium* fruits that reach the world markets. The others are consumed locally.

Some *Canarium* are planted as shade trees along highways, and in nutmeg plantations, preferably *C. vulgare* and the Ceylonese *C. zeylanicum.*

*C. vulgare* and *C. indicum* are closely related and are called JAVA ALMONDS.

The Malaysian species of *Canarium* are described thus by Burkill:

"The JAVA ALMOND or KENARI NUT *(C. indicum)* is a tree of considerable size, native of eastern Malaysia and New Guinea; Rumpf says it is endemic in Amboina. In eastern Malaysia it has several races, the most important of which is perhaps *C. amboinense,* with round fruits, hard to shell.

"The tree can be used for shade, and the magnificent avenue in the Botanic Garden, Buitenzorg, now more than one hundred years old, is made of it. It grows fairly fast, but the soil of Singapore and some other parts of the Peninsula suits it little.

"The nuts are its most important produce. They have one kernel in a rather hard shell. This kernel is oily and has a very delicate taste, that of some races being better than others. In Malaysia it takes the place of almonds for sprinkling over cakes, and the local demand absorbs the supply. The production of one large kernel, as a rule, by this species is an important feature; wild species of *Canarium,* as a rule, have three small ones.

"The fresh oil from the nuts is used for cooking in eastern Malaysia where the coconut is scarce. For the purpose of oil-extraction, the nuts are allowed to get absolutely ripe, but for eating they are pleasantest at an earlier stage. When eaten, the seedcoat must be removed, as it carries some substance producing diarrhoea. The nuts do not keep well, going rancid soon, and would not seem to be an article for export; but Boorsma has found the oil capable of use in an emulsion as an artificial milk for feeding infants in the tropics.

"Nuts purchased in Singapore and examined at the Imperial Institute contained 72 per cent of fat, 13.5 per cent of proteins, and 7 per cent of starch.

"*C. rufum.* A tree of moderate size, found from Larut to Singapore. The kernels can be eaten, but are worth little, owing to their hard shell and rather small size; but people with nothing to do pick them up and amuse themselves by cracking the shell and eating the kernel. The amount of oil in the seeds was found at the Imperial Institute to be 70 per cent and the proteins 16 per cent giving a high food-ratio."

Barrau says: "The nuts of various species of *Canarium (C. mehenbethene), C. salomonense, C. commune,* and *C. nungi,* are relished and extensively eaten, particularly in New Guinea, the Solomons, and the New Hebrides. In the Solomons they are gathered by a system of intensive foraging and are sometimes preserved in special huts, particularly on Malaita."

Geoff. F. C. Dennis on Santa Ana Island, Solomon Islands, sent seeds of *Canarium indicum* with this comment:

"70-80 feet tall, straight-trunked tree, slightly buttressed, plum-size fruits ripening a prune color; 3-angled seed coating is extremely hard and kernels are extracted after hammering with special round stone atop another suitable larger stone, some of which — in the vicinity of large trees — are 'peck-marked' from use by generations of fruit-gatherers. Called 'Galap-nut' in Papua, New Guinea pidgin, and 'Ngali' in the Solomons. Kernels are eaten raw on the spot, or collected for baking in stone ovens, or as a tasty additive to puddings made from cassava, yam, or sweet potato. Trees usually uncultivated, but there are some cultivars in the Reef Islands (Eastern

27

Solomons) as a reselective planting by many generations of Polynesians, some of which bear fruits with seeds twice the usual size."

In Africa the chief food-providing species of this genus is *C. schweinfurthii,* commonly called INCENSE TREE or BUSH CANDLE TREE.

Irvine says: "Distribution: Senegal to Angola, Sudan and E. Africa. A large tree to 120 ft. high and 12 ft. in girth; bole straight and up to 90 ft., without or with very slight and blunt buttresses; fruits (June) nearly 1½ in. long, bluish black, glabrous and narrowly oblong-ellipsoid, with a hard, fluted stone.

"The fruits are eaten in many parts of Africa, and are sometimes sold in African markets, the greenish oily pericarp being edible uncooked, though it is somewhat of an acquired taste. They are best softened in warm water before eating. The very hard nuts are sometimes made into necklaces, or carved. The seed contains an oil which is a possible substitute for shea butter. The seeds are sometimes cooked with food and are only eaten cooked."

Dalziel says of this tree: "Abundant in hill forests with a good rainfall; sometimes planted. On the Bauchi Plateau it is believed to have been introduced by the local pagans. The leaves differ from those of *Pachylobus edulis,* with which it is confused. The fruit is like an olive or date, 1½ in. long, blue-black, with a triangular calyx persisting at the base. It is sold in markets in areas where the tree occurs; the slight greenish outer pulp is of oily consistency and edible. The nut is very hard; the seed is cooked with food, and yields an oil, sometimes used as a substitute for shea butter."

Fanshawe writes: "Seeds are cooked and eaten in Uganda. The kernels yield an oil occasionally used in Africa as a substitute for shea butter."

Even Central America is much involved with the PILI NUT. Wilson Popenoe wrote this author in 1973:

"On whatever basis you go ahead with the nut business, don't forget to give the PILI NUT plenty of space. We have been growing it in Panama and Honduras for more than 40 years, and still we have not been able to commercialize it though it is a fine tree for the wet tropical regions and at one time, years ago, they used to export PILIS from the wild in the Philippines. I don't know why they stopped.

"I am much interested in the PILI, on which I have done a bit of work ever since United Fruit Company introduced it into Panama, and I brought it from there to Lancetilla. It has done remarkably well there, and I have been feebly attempting to encourage its cultivation in the wet tropical regions of Central America. You know that we do not have many fruits or nuts for the wet tropics. Robert P. Armour published a good paper on the PILI in *Proceedings of the American Society for Horticultural Science.*"

The North Australian Naturalists Club reports on *Canarium muelleri:* "The nuts (very small) are eaten here."

## *Santiria trimera*                    (Burseraceae)

There are 6 kinds of *Santiria* in west Africa and 17 more in Malaysia. Irvine says of this species:

"A tree up to 50 ft. high with stilt-roots. Fruits (Sept.-Dec.) black, ellipsoid, flattened, up to 1 x ½ in., smelling of turpentine. The fruits are edible and appear in S. Leone markets. The oily seeds are eaten in Liberia."

# Chapter 6
# THE ILLIPE NUT
# MIX-UP

For no special reason, there has been a mix-up in the nuts grown in the far Pacific which are called ILLIPE NUTS. They grow on two different, quite unrelated trees that have nothing in common except the common name. The first one, of the genus *Madhuca,* belongs to the Sapotaceae along with the MAMEY SAPOTE and a lot of other delicious fruits. The other belongs to the Dipterocarpaceae, which includes a lot of big timber trees but no fruit worth mentioning. Here these two ILLIPE NUT trees are described side by side for the reader's convenience.

### *Madhuca latifolia* (Sapotaceae) ILLIPE NUT ILLIPE NUT

This genus comprises 85 kinds of trees in Indo China, Indo-Malaysia, and Australia.

*M. latifolia* is a tree of northern India and is described by Bailey (under the old name of *Bassia latifolia*) thus: "The long-oval, smooth-surfaced, coffee-colored seed of a tree native to the East Indies. Typical seeds measure approximately 1½ inches in length by ½ inch in diameter. According to the Daily Consular Reports, ILLIPE NUTS are used to manufacture an edible oil similar to lard. There are two crops a year, one large and one small."

Burkill says that *Madhuca* "has fleshy fruits, but as a food, is of scarcely any value."

K. M. Vaid photo

INDIAN BUTTER TREE *(Madhuca butyracea)*

K. M. Vaid photo

*(Madhuca latifolia)*

Regarding this species Burkill says: "The seeds yield oil, which is used in food, as a substitute for ghi, or sometimes for adulterating ghi. The oil under the name ILLIPE BUTTER is an export for the manufacture of margarine.

"There is a saponin, or sapo-glucoside, in the seeds which has a destructive action on the blood."

Sturtevant says: "*M. butyracea.* East Indies. An oil is extracted from the seeds, and the oil cake is eaten, as also is the pure vegetable butter which is sold at a cheap rate."

Regarding this INDIAN BUTTER TREE, Watt says: "The seeds on expression yield a concrete oil. This is extracted by beating the seeds to a consistence of cream, and placing the mass thus obtained in a cloth bag, upon which a weight is laid until all the oil or fat is expressed. This becomes of the consistence of hog's lard, is inodorous, and of a delicate white colour; it contains 34 parts of fluid oil and 6 parts of vegetable matter. It dissolves readily in warm alcohol, leaving the vegetable impurities undissolved. At 95° it retains its consistency, but melts completely at 120°. This vegetable butter, being cheaper than ghi, is sometimes used as an adulterant. The oil is both eaten and used as an adulterant for ghi."

Of *M. utilis* K. Heyne says: "The seed yields oil of culinary use in Siak."

Of *M. longifolia,* in the East Indies Sturtevant says: "The oil pressed from the fruits is to the common people of India a substitute for ghee and coconut oil in their curries."

### *Shorea macrophylla* (Dipterocarpaceae) FALSE ILLIPE NUT ENGKEBANG NUTS

This genus composes 180 kinds of trees from Ceylon to Malaya and south China, many of them valued for timber. This species from Malaya and three others from Borneo, supply ENGKEBANG NUTS, often mistakenly called ILLIPE NUTS. It is not desirable to use this common name here because the true ILLIPE NUTS come from the Sapotaceae *(Madhuca, Palaquium,* etc.) From *Shorea* nuts is derived a substitute for cocoa butter in chocolate manufacture.

Sarawak Dept. of Agric. photo

False ILLIPE NUTS *(Shorea gysbertsiana)* Sarawak name is Engkabang jantong.

Burkill says: "Engkawang fat is a tallow-like substance extracted from the seeds of several trees. Borneo produces the greatest amount. When fruiting occurs, the fruits must be gathered at once. This is done by picking them from the ground and scooping them out of the streams by which the trees grow. Men, women, and children go into the forest at the right time, and having erected shelters for themselves, await the falling of the fruit: bad weather hurries it, and so the greater their discomfort the sooner their work is done. The seeds are incapable of resting; they germinate at once, and the more readily after gathering as they are heaped together wet, or put into baskets which are deliberately submerged in water.

"The seedlings in growing burst the fruit-wall, and the collectors, after shelling them, dry the germs in order to keep them until it is convenient to extract the oil, or to sell them for that purpose. Naturally there is some loss in quality due to the germination, but no alternative process promises any more economical return; and there is another reason for submerging the seed, almost as important as the securing of the bursting of the seed-wall, namely, the killing by drowning the grubs, which devour an enormous proportion of seeds of Diptercarps. This fat consists largely of the glyceride of stearic with that of palmitic and oleic acids. During the voyage to Europe, the respective fatty acids are liable to be freed so that the value of the produce deteriorates. The fat is greenish in colour.

5 CM

Isaac Ho Sai-Yuen photo

*(Shorea sumatrana)*

"In the East, the fat is used as food, and the tribes which use it take some care to ensure that the fat is not rancid; in fact, they take more care than when their object is to sell the dried cotyledons. In Borneo its place in the diet is important — a little being mixed with their rice, like butter, to adjust some of the dietetic deficiencies of the rice.

"Allan describes the native way of winning the fat, as follows: the 'padi tengkawang' is pounded in a rice-pounder, and the pounded mass is boiled in water: the fat rises and is skimmed off; after straining it is left to set in joints of bamboos. When fat prepared in Malaysia comes to Europe, it is shaped like thick candles, due to the moulding effect of the bamboos.

"In Singapore and other parts of the East the fat has a local industrial use, being employed for greasing the pans in which sago and tapioca are torrefied. Otherwise it is used for cooking. For cooking, the collectors prefer it to coconut oil."

K. M Vaid photo

*(Shorea robusta)*

Hewitt wrote that he found the seed of *S. gysbertsiana* to fetch the highest price in the Sarawak market and adds that the tree is actually planted, and invariably occurs, in the vicinity of rivers."

A report by B. E. Smythies of the Dept. of Agriculture, Sarawak, describes the two chief Borneo species:

5 CM

Isaac Ho Sai-Yuen photo

*(Shorea gysbertsiana)*

"*S. gysbertsiana.* This species produces the largest nut of all, and also has the advantage of being riverine, so that the nuts are easy to collect and load into a boat. Many nuts can be collected by putting a net or temporary fence across a river and trapping the nuts as they float down. Probably some 80 per cent of the nuts exported come from this one species.

"*S. seminis.* This is a small nut but produces an oil of good flavour and excellent quality. It is often collected by

---

30

natives for their own use, which includes eating with rice as a sort of vegetable butter."

## *Vateria indica* (Dipterocarpeae) DAMMAR

Sturtevant says: "East Indies. This species is a tree of Ceylon from whose seeds the natives make a kind of bread."

## *Argania sideroxylon* (Sapotaceae) ARGAN TREE

Sturtevant says: "From the seeds, the natives of Morocco extract an oil that is used for cooking, and lighting. When ripe, the fruit, which is an egg-shaped drupe, falls from the trees and the goats then enter into competition with their masters for a share in the harvest. The goats, however, swallow the fruit only for the sake of the subacid rind and, being unable to digest the hard seeds, eject them during the process of rumination, when they are gathered and added to the general store for oil making."

## *Butyrospermum parkii* (Sapotaceae) SHEA BUTTER TREE

This small, spreading tree to 40 feet with bole to 6 feet in diameter, grows from Senegal to Uganda. In April it bears fruits 2 inches long containing usually one seed, sometimes 2 or even 3. The shiny brown seeds have a thick rind and contain a large, white kernel.

Bailey explains: "The outside fleshy pulp, whose weight is approximately equal to that of the nut, rots away in time and splits, leaving the nut exposed. The natives hasten its removal by burying the freshly gathered fruit in a pit for some days. The nuts, divested of their outer covering (pulp), are dried, either by being placed in the sun for about twelve days or by heating in an earth oven. In this process the nut loses 30 to 40 per cent of its weight. The skin is removed and the kernel remains. The SHEA-BUTTER content of the decorticated kernel is 40 to 60 per cent of this weight of the kernel.

"Purified SHEA-BUTTER is edible and suitable for use in the preparation of artificial butter by chocolate manufacturers, etc., and the principal European demand is for this purpose."

Irvine says: "The fruit-pulp, though sometimes eaten, is usually eaten by animals, e.g. elephants.

"The kernels are rich in oil (45-55 per cent by weight) which is extracted entirely by women. They pound the usually roasted kernels, and grind them to an oily, chocolate-coloured paste, which contains tannin and is not edible until it has been boiled and the oil skimmed off, as many impurities as possible being removed in the scum.

"In commerce SHEA BUTTER is used in soap, and candle-making, also in the manufacture of butter substitutes. When extracted in Europe it is known as 'shea oil'. Its main local use is in cooking. If carefully prepared and clarified it is a good substitute for lard."

Dalziel explains the after-harvest procedure in some detail:

"In some districts the fruits are spread out in the sun until the pulp separates, in others they are fermented by being kept moist for weeks or months in large earthenware jars, and the nuts are thereafter roasted. In general, as collection takes place during the rains, a period which also favours early germination, the nuts (in the shell) are often stored in huts until the dry season in districts where they are not immediately supplying a demand by European firms.

"SHEA BUTTER appears in markets in the form of loaves, commonly about 5-6 lbs. in weight, but sometimes up to 20 lbs. or in smaller balls, etc., in shapes which differ from one village to another. In Lagos it is sold in large ovoid masses in palm-leaf casings. In retail it is often sold in sections more or less resembling cut cheese or soap. It is usually oily to touch. Hausa butter prepared from unroasted kernels is light yellow. It is sometimes tinted by yellow dye. The mass generally has a strong odour, which is more pronounced when the unpurified butter is warmed. Properly prepared butter keeps perfectly but loss of keeping quality may result from adulteration with water and yam-flour, etc. The deeper the colour the stronger the odour and taste, and these qualities are said to be the result of decomposed proteins which occur in proportion to the degree of fermentation of the nuts and to over-roasting. Butter prepared from nuts which have been subjected to little fermentation, as when clean nuts are lightly sun-dried without previous masceration of the pulp, is almost tasteless and odourless. Such nuts are the best for export, and they also contain more sugars and tannin and less protein. Thus it is quite possible to obtain a deodorised and neutral product which does not turn rancid.

"The variability of commercial shea nuts in free fatty acid in the fat is due to faulty handling after it leaves the producer. The native sells chiefly for local use, and sells only the kernel which is generally dealt with without delay by the makers of SHEA BUTTER. When the native stores the fruit to await purchase by middlemen for Europeans it is stored in the shell, in which state it is not readily damaged and suffers little deterioration. The storage of kernels in a damp state, or of kernels purchased fresh and not immediately dried before storing in bulk, accounts for the high proportion of free fatty acid, and at present there is no means of distinguishing by external appearance sound kernels from those damaged in storage.

"Export of the butter itself is undesirable and requires metal containers. If clarified, native-prepared SHEA BUTTER can be used quite acceptably for European cooking. Treatment of the melted butter by steam removes volatile acids and part at least of the odorous matter. Washing the heated butter with alcohol to dissolve out nitrogenous matter with other impurities yields an almost tasteless and odourless product.

"Thoroughly dried kernels represent about one-third of the original weight of the fresh nuts. From the native point of view a kerosene tinful of kernels, representing about 27 lbs., will yield 7 lbs. of SHEA BUTTER."

## *Ganua motleyana* (Sapotaceae)

Burkill says: "A large tree found in Sumatra, the Malay Peninsula and Borneo; it likes swampy soil.

"The tree has a little importance as a source of oil, or rather fat, obtained from the seeds, which comes to market. This fat suggests, in odour and colour, the oil of bitter almonds. It is extracted, considerably, in Borneo. The seeds and native-made fat were reported yellow, like paste, free from hydrocyanic acid (which is expected in almond oil), composed chiefly of glycerides of oleic and stearic acid. The amount of fat in the kernels is 51 per cent."

## *Magonia pubescens* (Sapotaceae) TINGUI

Mors & Rizzini say of this Brazilian tree: "MAGONIA is quite abundant in the dry forests and high cerrados of the state of Minas Gerais. Its seeds are large and disc-shaped, existing in great quantity within the large fruits. The copious seed oil is used locally in soap manufacture and for cooking. It is light-colored and of fine consistency."

31

*(Mimusops caffra)*

*(Mimusops obovata)*

### *Mimusops djave* (Sapotaceae) DJAVE NUT, FALSE SHEA BUTTERNUT, AFRICAN PEARWOOD

This is a giant tree of the evergreen forest in West Africa.

Dalziel says: "The fruit is the size of a fist, smooth, the pulp with a sticky latex when unripe, but mealy, slightly acid and edible when ripe.

"DJAVE NUT kernels yield by solvents 60% or more of an oil or fat resembling SHEA BUTTER and of similar composition, but having a lower melting and solidifying point. The fresh seeds contain some gutta-like substance and starch as well as fat. The residue after extraction of the fat (by expression) is poisonous to fowls and animals in general. The bitter principle can be removed without much difficulty, rendering the fat suitable for alimentary purposes. The native use of the fat is as a food in cooking, especially in Cameroons; in Nigeria its use is mainly restricted to some Cross River tribes in Oban district, etc. The method of preparation is more or less as follows: after thoroughly drying the nuts the shells are removed for use as fuel for the operation; the kernels are ground finely on a stone, then spread out and moistened frequently with boiling water; the mass is then manipulated with added water into lumps or balls until the fat appears dark in colour. Sometimes the residue after a first extraction is dried again for a day or two and treated a second time. The extraction may be made by mechanical means, the smoothly-ground mass being put in a press; the oil so expressed soon thickens, and is said to have a pleasant taste free from the bitterness of the residue."

*Mimusops heckelii* is a similar tree in Sierra Leone, Ivory Coast, southern Nigeria and the Gold Coast.

Dalziel says of it: "The fruit is 4-5 in. long by 3-4 in. broad, greenish-yellow. Under the thin shell is a yellow pulp about 1 in. or more thick, juicy, but with an unpleasant smell and bitter taste. The kernels of the seeds are composed of two large fleshy cotyledons rich in fat, which is used by the forest tribes to make soap, as a food in cooking and as a medicine or pomade. The fruit-pulp rapidly decomposes on the forest floor and the seeds are collected, broken between stones and the kernels broken into fragments, which are put to dry for some weeks on mats in the open by day, but placed under cover by night; the fat oozes from the kernel fragments, which are then pounded to a paste, boiled with a little water and the fat skimmed off. The fat so prepared is yellowish, semi-fluid capable of being poured into bottles; it is edible and, when freshly prepared, free from bitterness or unpleasant flavour. 'Baco' kernels have been found to yield 60-65%, or 21% by weight of the nut in the shell, of a solid, creamy-white fat resembling that of djave, and regarded as suitable for soap manufacture. It has been called 'Dumori butter.' The kernels themselves are intensely bitter, so that the residue after extraction is unsuited for use as a feeding-stuff. The people are said to prefer it to palm oil for cooking, but as collection and the method of preparation is slow, much of the produce is left ungathered."

### *Nephelium mutabile* (Sapotaceae) PULASAN

This tree of medium size grows wild in the Philippines.

Burkill says: "The fruits are delicate and the tree is much grown for them. The stone is large as a rule: but seedless races exist.

"Boiled or roasted seeds may be used for the preparation of a drink like cocoa.

"These seeds contain 29 per cent of fat, formerly used as a lamp oil. Georgi found it to make 64 per cent on the dry weight of the seed. He found it a firm, white fat, melting at about 40 to 42 °C, to a yellow oil, with a faintly sweet smell, and suitable for use in food. The amount of oil in the moisture-free kernel was 74.9 per cent."

According to Ridley, the flavor of this fruit is decidedly superior to that of the RAMBUTAN *(N. lappaceum).*

Burkill says of the RAMBUTAN: "There is present in the seeds a fat like cacao-butter, to the extent of 37 per cent of dry weight. It is hard and white at ordinary temperatures, and turns on heating to a yellow, pleasant-smelling oil. Georgi says it would be suitable for edible purposes."

### *Palaquium gutta* (Sapotaceae) GUTTA PERCHA

This tree among 150 species in Formosa, southeast Australia and Indo-Malaysia was long the sole source of GUTTA PERCHA, but because the wild trees were slaughtered to get the latex, it is now extinct in the wild and is found only in cultivation. GUTTA PERCHA is obtained from other species.

Burkill says: "As far as we know, the seeds of all the *Palaquim* contain fats. Long before any thought was directed towards the exploitation of the trunk for gutta, the concrete oil was slightly commercial. The best kinds of fats from these Sapotaceae are confused with the fats of the Dipterocarps — *Shorea* and *Isoptera.*

"It has been necessary to mention the difficulty in getting seed for stocking plantations; how much greater the difficulty of getting seed for an oil industry. This difficulty is, of course, less in well-settled country such as are parts of Java, where the fat of *P. javense* is exploited somewhat.

"Georgi has given the constants of one oil, but its source was not ascertained. It was a hard white fat, with a pleasant smell, which would be used for edible purposes, as well as for soaps and other products, such as are made by the use of Borneo tallow and Illipe fat.

"The oil of *P. philippense* is used for food and illumination in the Philippine Islands. It is called limpid.

"Saponin is present in the foliage and seeds — at least at times. The saponin of *P. gutta* stands high in the table of toxicity of the saponins."

Burkill continues: "*P. gutta*. The seed is rich in fats.

"*P. hexandrum,* Sumatra. The sour fruit is said to be eaten, and the seed to yield a fat which contributes to the supplies of 'vegetable fat of Siak'.

"*P. rostratum*. A gigantic tree. The fruit is green, sweet and edible. The seed contains oil, and is very bitter in taste."

## MAMEY SAPOTE
## *Pouteria sapota*  (Sapotaceae)  SAPOTE

*Pouteria* (formerly called *Calocarpum,* or *Lucuma)* is a genus of 100 kinds of fruit trees that grow in Malaysia, Australia, islands of the Pacific, and South America. Many of them are prized for their edible fruit, and a number of them have been introduced into Florida.

Dr. Wilson Popenoe, writing in *Bailey's Cyclopedia,* says of this species: "The most important member of the genus is without doubt the MAMEY SAPOTE, a common fruit in Cuba, and not infrequently seen on the Central American mainland. It can be grown in extreme south Florida."

*(Pouteria hypoglauca)*

This dean of fruit experts of tropical America could be wrong, for he failed to consider the many species in other parts of the world.

Popenoe's description continues: "The fruit is commonly elliptical, and about 6 inches in length. Within the thick woody skin, somewhat rough and rusty brown on the sur-face, is the soft melting flesh, of a beautiful reddish salmon color, and of about the same consistency as a ripe canteloupe. The large elliptical seed can be lifted out of the fruit as easily as that of an avocado; it is hard, brown and shining, except on the ventral surface, which is whitish, and somewhat rough. The seed contains a large oily kernel, which has a strong smell and a bitter taste. According to Pittier, it is used in Costa Rica, after being finely ground, to prepare an exquisite confection; the same authority states that it is sometimes used by the Indians, after being boiled, roasted and ground, to mix with cacao, imparting a bitter taste to the beverage."

Popenoe in his own book *Manual of Tropical and Sub-Tropical Fruits,* continues: "The seed is an article of commerce in Central America, where the large kernel is roasted and used to mix with cacao in making chocolate."

William Francis Whitman of Miami Beach, distinguished leader of the Rare Fruit Council the past few years in South Florida and elsewhere, writes this author:

"Your definition of a nut opens up a whole new world and just how far it goes is anyone's guess. If you regard the seed of the MAMEY SAPOTE as a nut I assume the GREEN SAPOTE *(P. viride),* the CANISTEL *(Pouteria campechiana),* the ABIU *(P. caimito),* the LUCUMA *(P. abovata)* and many others would also fit into this category."

Dr. Carl Campbell at the University of Florida Institute of Food Sciences at Homestead, wrote this author:

"It is my opinion that seeds from plants of the genus *Pouteria* can be called edible nuts (at least those of some species). I must admit that I have never actually witnessed anyone eating them; however, I know several reliable people who say that poor people in Central America do eat them. I suspect that they do this only in times of need, when corn and beans are scarce."

Mr. Whitman wrote further: "Elling O. Eide has grown and fruited the MAMEY SAPOTE in Sarasota. During the winter he gives the tree some cold protection. In the mid-1950's I visited Havana, Cuba and brought back six hundred MAMEY SAPOTE seeds, hoping to get this worthwhile fruit tree better established in Florida. I was able to purchase the seeds for ten cents each, most of these being retrieved from garbage cans. Because of this it would appear that the Cubans did not place much value on this as a nut for eating. A common belief among Cubans in Florida is that it is illegal to bring MAMEY SAPOTE seeds into the United States because they can be used to cause abortions. When told they can be grown and fruit here they frequently stare in disbelief."

Dr. Campbell wrote of two newer fruit trees of this family for the Florida State Horticultural Society in 1964, thus:

"Two species which have been found to be promising enough for trial in gardens of South Florida are *P. hypoglauca* and *P. caimito*. Both are in the Sapotaceae, a family which includes such well known fruits as the CANISTEL, MAMEY SAPOTE, SAPODILLA and STAR APPLE.

"*Pouteria hypoglauca* is native to El Salvador, where it is esteemed as a source of food.

"*Pouteria caimito* is relatively well known to tropical fruit enthusiasts. It is native to the warm regions of Peru east of the Andes, and is grown extensively in the Amazon region and other parts of Brazil, where the fruit is called ABIU."

# Chapter 7
# THE BRAZIL NUT FAMILY
## (Lecythidaceae)
### *with Barringtonia and the Myrtles*

This comprises 325 kinds of nut-bearing trees in the American tropics, divided among 15 genera. They are all wild trees, a majority of them growing in wet or waterfront locations along the Amazon and contributing rivers all the way from the Atlantic to the mountains of Peru, a distance of 2400 miles.

Many of the nuts are eaten by mankind. The genus *Bertholetia* in which our beloved BRAZIL NUT is dominant, comprises 75 species. The genus *Lecythis* in which the MONKEY POT trees are numbered, includes 50 species of trees. And there are delightful nuts in many of the other genera in this huge family, mostly consumed locally.

Also in this chapter are the *Barringtonia,* edible nuts from all over Malaysia and Polynesia; and the MYRTLES that bear edible seeds, growing all over the world.

Pan American Union photo

The BRAZIL NUT tree *(Bertholetia excelsa).* Often 150 feet high and 6 to 8 feet in diameter.

Isaac Ho Sai-Yuen photo

BRAZIL NUTS *(Bertholetis excelsa)*

Tourist souvenir. A BRAZIL NUT pod, with window to show how BRAZIL NUTS fit inside. *(Bertholetia excelsa)*

### *Bertholettia excelsa*  (Lecythidaceae)
**BRAZIL NUT**
**NIGGERTOE**

Outstanding among the great nut trees of the world, *Bertholettia* is unique in many ways. It is enormous in size, often 150 feet or more with a straight, bare trunk to 75 feet or more, the massive top standing high above the surrounding forest in low, river bottom land. Although the nuts are loved and enjoyed all over the world, they are not eaten in Brazil, and the seeds are not planted there. There are no BRAZIL NUT farms, no society of growers, no effort to gather nuts from any except wild trees.

The extremely large and heavy pods develop in groups of 3 or 4 on a 12-inch stout stalk 100 feet or more in the air. These pods are 4 to 6 inches in diameter with a rough, brown, very hard shell which is ½ inch thick and lined with hard fibres. Inside are two concentric rings of 3-sided nuts, each 2½ inches long, packed around a core. The pods weigh up to 5 pounds each. Often there are 300 pods on a tree.

Dahlgren wrote: ''The fruits can be collected only when they fall to the ground on ripening. Although the related CANNON-BALL fruit, in spite of the name, never functions as a projectile, the BRAZIL NUT fruits, are dreaded as bombs. Their weight is not inconsiderable and the momentum acquired by them as they drop is so great that the fruit becomes imbedded in the ground.

''The collecting of BRAZIL NUTS is performed mostly by Indians, who at the proper seasons make their way in

34

canoes up the rivers on the banks of which these trees grow.

"Harvesting BRAZIL NUTS is a hazardous occupation. Wild animals and jungle fevers are taken for granted, but there is more. A BRAZIL NUT pod is heavy and it comes to the ground from 100 feet up with frightening force and velocity. It is, in fact, an exceedingly dangerous missile. Every year there are reports of Castanheiros (the name given to the Indians or migrant laborers who gather the nuts) killed or badly injured by falling fruits. Mostly the gatherers stay clear of the trees when it is raining or windy, but occasionally they work carrying a round wooden shield over their heads to ward off the falling pods. The entire BRAZIL NUT industry, set in the suffocating tropical forest of the Amazon, with itinerant gatherers bartering their nuts to jungle traders operating from wheezy boats or tiny trading factories, is in startling and delightful contrast to the mechanized, scientific agriculture we know."

Dahlgren continues: "The extremely hard shell of the fruit yields to a few blows of an ax and the nuts are gathered into baskets with which the canoes are filled.

"The large rodents of the region are able to open the fallen fruits by means of their powerful incisor teeth, especially after decay has partly softened the shell. The larger monkeys, who are also fond of the seeds, are said sometimes to seize the favorable moment to drive the rodents away and to snatch the coveted contents for themselves."

The top end of a BRAZIL NUT pod has a small aperture which is closed by a lid, which can be removed only with difficulty, and it is still tightly closed when the fruit hits the ground. Contrariwise, the lids of the related SAPUCAIA NUT trees *(Lecythis sp.)* fall out while the pods are still on the trees, releasing the nuts which scatter over the ground and are wildly chased by monkeys that can run faster than men can. Result: SAPUCAIA NUTS are rare on the market.

Miers wrote: "The seeds, well known as the BRAZIL NUTS of the shops, are easily distinguished from SAPUCAIA NUTS by their acutely trigonoid form. The hard fruits which fall to the ground are broken in the forests by Indians, where a man and a boy will break about 300 of them daily, yielding them about 2 alquieres of the nuts. The kernels of these nuts, broken in a similar manner, are subjected to pressure, when they yield an oil greatly esteemed for domestic purposes and for export, each pound of the kernels furnishing 9 ounces of oil. This oil, according to Martius, consists, per cent, of 74 parts of elaeine, and 26 of stearine.

"The question here naturally arises, how do the seeds germinate and strike root, confined as they are in an inextricable prison? For it is manifest they cannot find an exit through the opercular opening, and they cannot escape by any other means than by the rotting of the thick pericarp on moist ground; and it would probably require three years' exposure to the sun and moisture before so thick a shell could decay sufficiently to allow liberation of the seeds, and then perhaps another year's exposure before the thick testa of the seeds could rot sufficiently to allow the embryo to germinate. This shows an extraordinary power of vitality in the embryo, which would seem to remain four or five years in a dormant state. Oily seeds are generally supposed to ferment and decay soon; but that perhaps is where the oil-cells are contained in albumen; here, however, we find a reverse condition. I have been told that when the embryo of *Bertholetia* has been extricated, and planted under the most favourable circumstances, it takes a whole year before it begins to germinate. Is this inertness due to the large amount of stearine in the oil-cells, which preserves it from decay?"

## Allantoma cylindrica (Lecythidaceae)
### SKITTLE NUT

*Allantoma* is a genus of 15 kinds of nut trees in Guyana and Brazil. Of this one Miers wrote:

"The pyxidium (seedpod) is 5 in. long, cylindrical, and 1¾ in. diameter. The seeds are 1½ in. long. Mr. Farries states 'that its flat seeds are good eating, yielding a crop once a year; the fruit is called SKITTLE NUT because it is like a skittle.' "

## Eschweilera subglandulosa (Lecythidaceae)
### GUATECARE
### WATERCARE

Williams describes it: "A large tree in Trinidad reaching over 100 feet, and 2 to 3 feet in diameter. Two varieties are recognized, black and white; black is the better wood. Fruit, a hard capsule opening, as it were, by the lid coming off, containing one to three conspicuously veined seeds, much eaten by agouti."

The genus comprises 120 kinds of nut trees in tropical America.

## Holopyxidium jaraua (Lecythidaceae)

This is a genus of 3 trees in Brazil, in the Amazon region, bearing edible nuts.

Georgetown Botanic Garden photo

SAPUCAIA NUTS from Guyana. *(Lecythis zabucajo)*

## Lecythis zabucajo (Lecythidaceae)
### SAPUCAIA NUT
### PARADISE NUT

Of the fifty kinds of these MONKEY POT trees in Brazil and Guyana, this is perhaps the biggest tree and most important nut producer. Macmillan says: "Closely allied, but superior, to the BRAZIL NUT. The oblong, wrinkled nuts (seeds), about 2 in. long, enclosed in a very large, brown, woody shell, are of a delicate flavour and considered by some to be the finest nut known. As distinct from the BRAZIL NUT, the shell is furnished with a large lid, which when ripe becomes detached and allows the seeds to drop out. Owing, therefore, to the difficulty of collecting these, they are more rare and command a higher price than the

BRAZIL NUTS. The nuts are used in chocolates and other forms of confectionery.''

Kennard & Winters wrote: "The irregular oblong ridged nuts, about 2 inches long, are enclosed in a heavy grayish-brown, woody fruit 8 inches long and 10 inches wide.

"Although the brown shell bears several parallel ridges, it is less sharply angled than in the BRAZIL NUT. The shell is also softer.''

The various species of *Lecythis* have common names all their own, but these are used carelessly in referring to different species, and confusion results.

Regarding the MONKEY CHESTNUT *(L. grandifolia),* Dahlgren wrote: "The name MONKEY POT has reference to the characteristic shape of the fruit, which is like a vase or small urn with the opening neatly closed by a lid. The seeds are packed within these containers, more or less after the manner of BRAZIL NUTS. There are many species of MONKEY POT trees and bushes, differing from each other in the particular size and configuration of their fruits as well as in various other respects.

"The best known of all is the GREAT MONKEY POT which in size is second only to the BRAZIL NUT trees. Its fruits measure six to seven inches in diameter. The lid closing this seed pot becomes detached at maturity while the fruits still hang on the trees, affording a feast for parrots and monkeys who fight over the seeds. 'The battle-cry of both of these animals then resounds far and wide in the forest,' says the botanist-traveler Ave-Lallemant. The seeds are called MONKEY CHESTNUTS.''

Ward photo

Another MONKEY POT. *(Lecythis elliptica)*

Regarding one SAPUCAIA NUT *(L. elliptica),* Kennard & Winters wrote: "Although not a well-known tree, *L. elliptica* deserves to be more widely planted. It is a highly ornamental, small tree, which often begins to fruit when only about 6 feet tall.

"The grayish-brown, globose, woody capsules measure about 3 inches in diameter and contain about 8 nuts each. The capsule remains attached to the tree for some time after dehiscence of the lid, while the nuts gradually dry and fall to the ground. The nuts are about 1.25 inches in length, chestnut brown marked with yellowish anastomosing lines. They have a delicious flavor and a high oil content.''

Regarding a MONKEY POT in Guyana, *L. davisii,* Fanshawe wrote: "The large, obovoid pots contain about 50-70 grey-brown, fusiform seeds of an oily nature which are very palatable. They could be used as a substitute for SAPUCAIA NUTS in chocolate manufacture. Unfortunately the nuts are highly prized by wild animals and it is difficult to obtain any great quantity.''

SAPUCAIA NUTS from southern Brazil *(Lecythis pisonis)*

*(Lecythis pisonis)*

Harry Blossfeld writes from Sao Paolo: "The species we have here in southern Brazil is *L. pisonis.* It is deciduous for a few weeks only. In some years it blooms while the old leaves are dropping and the new foliage sprouts, which is a beautiful pinkish copper red when coming out. The tree then is a lovely sight, with the old empty pods still dangling from the branches. The nuts of this species are highly perishable. They get rancid in a week or two, though delicious when fresh, but quite soft, not crisp as the CASHEW NUT.

SAPUCAIA NUTS are not commonly eaten in Brazil, except here and there. The nuts are never sold in the markets. Maybe in rural villages, where the tree still occurs, sometimes nuts or entire pods may be offered for local sale, but the pods do not drop as a whole, as the BRAZIL NUT pod does. It stays on the tree, and the lid falls off, and then monkeys and bats and birds draw out the nuts one by one, which is not an easy matter, because they are closely packed. Some time or other, a nut or two may drop to the soil, but unless the tree is climbed and the pods hewn off, they are not available for humans.

"The nuts are very similar to the BRAZIL NUT in size and shape, but on the tip they have a big, irregular and crested arillus protruding from the brown nut proper. This arillus is butter-colour or may be white, when the nut is fresh; when fresh and good, this nut is delicious.

"The tree is present in many settlements in the interior and well known but scarcely anyone tries to eat the nut, fearing it might be poisonous or too oily to be good. The nut, once dropped from the fruit that remains on the tree, must be eaten within a few days.

"But there is a common use for the SAPUCAIA fruit pod in Brazil. Peasants bore a hole through it and put a wire or a string through it and bind it to a fence post. Then they put a handful of maize into the pod and leave it on the ground near their corn field. When there are monkeys about to plunder the corn fields before the ears are ripe, they will be attracted by the maize and put a hand through the round opening each pod has. When grasping the maize, the full hand won't go through the hole any more and the monkey is so terrified by the idea that he won't open the hand but struggles instead to pull off the entire pod. Then the peasant can approach and catch the monkey.

"There is a much quoted saying in Brazil: 'An old monkey will not put his hand into a SAPUCAIA hull;' Indeed, it is the young monkeys that are caught, and they are tamed and kept as pets in many houses.

"By the way, the tree has excellent timber — almost all species — and so it has become a rare tree. As things are going here, some species may become extinct in the near future."

Under certain soil conditions, *Lecythis* nuts may be poisonous. For details see *Economic Botany* 20 (2): 187-195 (1966); 23 (2) 33-4 (1969).

David Noel photo

F. C. Hoehne wrote: "Of *Lecythis,* which are the SAPUCAIAS, we have many species, whose enumeration and classification would be boring. All of them produce good nuts, though structurally quite different from the first ones. Because they are not well known, their commercial development is still very small. Nevertheless, it would be worth it to plant some 'Sapucaieiras' if you are trying to combine three excellent benefits in one bag: have beautiful trees with excellent wood, have them as an ornament because of their beautiful flowers, and have them so as to have the nuts."

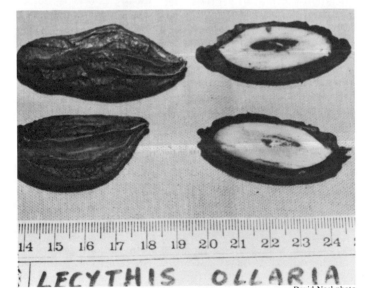

*(Barringtonia asiatica)*

David Noel photo

Kernels of *Barringtonia reticulata*

*(Barringtonia sumatrana)*

## *Barringtonia*         (Barringtoniaceae)

*Barringtonia* comprises some 39 species of trees and shrubs. Dahlgren says these "are scattered over a wide area extending from East Africa and India, over the islands of the East Indian Archipelago and of Oceanica, even to Australia. Floating *Barringtonia* fruits are familiar objects of the tidal drift in the oriental tropics. The are pyramidal in shape, with four bulging faces and rounded edges, of a tan-colored leathery exterior, and light as cork. The single large seed within begins to germinate early and is usually in an advanced stage of development when the fruit floats out to sea."

Burkill says: "Most of the species carry saponins and on that account are fish-poisons. The greatest quantity of this substance seems to be in the seeds."

However, he goes on to explain the way of making a starchy food from the seeds of one Malayan species, *B. racemosa*. He ways: "The Sakai pound the fruits and let the starch settle, then decant the liquor and make the starch into cakes which they eat. They know that the juice would make them vomit."

Burkill adds: "Seeds are said to be used as food, also in Borneo." He quotes Wray as saying: "The seed of *B. scortechinii* might be used as a flavoring with food."

*(Barringtonia edulis)*

*(Barringtonia racemosa)*

Geoff. F. C. Dennis on Santa Ana Island, Solomon Islands, sent seeds of *Barrington edulis* with this comment: "25-30 feet tall, sparsely branched tree with handsome large leaves, bronze-colored when young, and 2-3 feet long pendent racemes of yellow to red flowers — very showy — fruits ripening green to reddish-brown. Seeds eaten raw with flavor of raw peanuts. Two very similar species bear edible fruits: *B. niedenzuana* and *B. novae-hyberniae*. All three species are called 'cut-nut' in Solomons pidgin. Cultivated or semi-cultivated."

Sturtevant describes four other species with edible nuts:

*B. butonica.* Islands of the Pacific. This plant has oleaginous seeds and fruits which are eaten green as vegetables.

*B. careya.* Australia. The fruit is large and is edible.

*B. excelsa.* India, Cochin China and the Moluccas. The fruit is edible.

*B. edulis.* Fiji Islands. The rather insipid fruit is eaten either raw or cooked by the natives.

Parham who lived for years in Fiji, says of the latter species:

"A tall tree with large glossy leaves and pendulous racemes of white or pink flowers. The fruit is an ovoid nut with a large edible kernel."

Barrau says the seed of several species are eaten, "*B. edulis* and *B. magnifica* for instance, particularly in the Solomons, the New Hebrides and Fiji."

S. Gowers of the Department of Agriculture, New Hebrides, says the kernels of *B. edulis* are eaten and are "very popular." The kernels of a green unidentified *Barringtonia sp.* are also eaten.

## *Careya arboeea* (Barringtoniaceae) PATANA OAK

This Indian tree is one of four species in Indo-Malaysia. Both Watt and Burkill assert that "the seed is said to be more or less poisonous" (whatever that means), but Maheshwari says: "The seeds are edible."

## *Chydenanthus excelsus* (Barringtoniaceae)

Six species of these trees are found in New Guinea, Borneo and Burma. The fresh nuts of the various species are much eaten by the Melanesians.

5 CM

Isaac Ho Sai-Yuen photo

GUAVA *(Psidium guajava)*

## *Psidium guajava* (Myrtaceae) GUAVA JAMBU

*Psidium* is a genus of 150 kinds of trees and shrubs in the West Indies and Tropical America, of which this one is best known for its jelly.

This is grown also in Malaya and Ho Sai-Yuen writes of it: "The JAMBU seeds are eaten apart from the fleshy pulp. Personally, I take this fruit quite often and it is rich in iron."

Burkill says: "There is a little oil in the seeds to the extent of 14 per cent of dry weight, along with 15 per cent of proteins, and 13 per cent of starch."

In the Quito region, says Herrera, "There are *guayabos* that produce fruit like apples, with many kernels, some white and some red, well tasted and wholesome. The fruit is globular, varying from the size of a plum to that of an apple."

## *Umbellularia californica* (Myrtaceae) CALIFORNIA LAUREL

Kirk: *Edible Wild Plants* says: "The thin-shelled nuts may be parched and eaten, or ground into flour and baked as bread."

# Chapter 8
# COLA, JAVA OLIVES, and CHOCOLATE

Big business is involved in three kinds of tropical trees in the *Sterculia* family — 125 African trees called COLA which are not cultivated but which are important to millions of people all over the world for the stimulating effect of the seeds; 300 kinds of *Sterculia* trees and shrubs that supply edible nuts often called JAVA OLIVES, and last but not least the 30 kinds of tropical American trees that produce COCOA and CHOCOLATE.

Seeds of all three come buried in pulp inside big pods, some of which are heavy enough that they must hang on the trunk of the tree.

Dr. Francis Halle photo

KOLA NUT *(Cola digitata)*

*(Cola acuminata)*

*(Cola gigantea* var. *glabresens).* This enormous leaf was from a 30-foot tree at the U.S. Plant Introduction Garden at South Miami, Fla., formerly known as *Sterculia* sp. P.I. 73070. The seed of it was collected by Dr. David Fairchild in 1927 near the village of Dable, between Akkra and Winnaba, Gold Coast. His note on it said: "A large handsome tropical tree with deep green leaves and pods the size of an apple."

## *Cola nitida*　　　(Sterculiaceae)　　　COLA NUT

The most important nut crop in Africa, next to the oil palm *(Elaeis guineensis)* is the COLA NUT but there is much confusion over whether this name refers to *C. nitida, C. acuminata,* or *C. vera.* Apparently it makes little difference; there is a world-wide demand for them to chew, like so much chewing-gum, or to eat — in both cases to obtain the stimulus of the caffeine they contain.

Burkill says: "*C. nitida* yields the best commercial nuts," and continues:

"In Africa fruits of *C. nitida* are collected from both wild and cultivated trees, and marketed fresh. They are packed in bundles with green leaves rolled round them, and, by changing the leaves every few days, are carried fresh for great distances to the markets of the interior. It is said that with care they can be kept saleable for 8-10 months. When the nuts cease to be fresh they are a different product.

"The fresh nut is used as a masticatory. It tastes bitter, then after eating it a sense of well-being spreads through the body and a sweet taste is in the mouth, which makes any food or drink, taken afterwards, also seem sweet. This effect is physiological and depends on the substances absorbed in the eating. Two are important: caffeine, which is present to the extent of 2-2.25 per cent, by which the nut stimulates the body as coffee does; and a glucoside kolanin which stimulates the heart. As the nut dries, the kolanin is acted on by an enzyme, and gives rise to a red colour with the formation of kola-red — a compound very similar to

40

phlobaphene. In this way the old nut loses the stimulant value of the kolanin, and in the eyes of any habitual chewer is no longer the same thing as the fresh fruit. Along with the caffeine is a trace of theobromine.''

Bailey says that from the seeds of *C. acuminata* is obtained ''the stimulating drink, long used in the tropics and now very common as a summer drink in this country. The seeds are borne in long pods, containing from five to twelve seeds each. The cola-nut is described in the *United States Dispensatory* as being irregular in form, reddish gray in color, from ¾ of an inch to 1¼ inches in length, flattened and rounded upon one surface.''

*U.S.D.A. Misc. Pub. 801* says: ''The fruit is a follicle, which is corky or rough on the surface and may be 8 inches in length. The ovoid or angular seeds are covered with a white skin that is thin but rather fleshy. Within the seed-coat the seeds are commonly red, but may be pink or white. The cotyledons are tender and succulent but bitter in taste. The COLA NUT is widely grown in West Africa and has particular uses in the social life and religious customs of the people. In Nigeria and the British Cameroons, four species of *Cola* with edible seed have been distinguished.''

Of the other 120 different kinds of *Cola* trees in west Africa, all of them with hard-shelled fruit, a few are important in this book. Irvine says: ''The MONKEY COLA *(C. caricaefolia)* has edible seed kernels; the seeds of *C. heterophylla* (probably another MONKEY COLA) are eaten in French equatorial Africa; of *C. millenii* ''the viscid kernels are eaten like KOLA; of SLIPPERY COLA *(C. verticillata)* the seeds are edible and are indistinguishable from true *Cola* in appearance, and are sometimes chewed where found, though considered to be inferior to the genuine species, being very bitter and considered unfit to eat.''

Dalziel describes the KOLA nut in some detail:

''The natural range of *C. acuminata* is from S. Nigeria to Gabon and the Belgian Congo. The fruit is smooth, lacking the dorsal keel. The seeds are usually 5-8. The nuts of some varieties are more viscid than those of *C. nitida*. Elephants eat the fruits of KOLA and damage the tree in procuring it.

''*C. nitida* has a more westerly range than *C. acuminata*, and is a typical species of the Ashanti forests of Gold Coast, Ivory Coast and Liberia. The fruits are commonly longitudinally rugose and wrinkled and nodular in varying degree and dorsally keeled; the seeds are separable into only two cotyledons. KOLA nuts of this species are the more appreciated and usually contain more caffeine. It is the species almost solely cultivated by Europeans in West Africa, and thus furnishes most of the nuts in European commerce.

''FALSE KOLAS are commonly seen in markets, and are often chewed but are probably now a rare adulterant of true KOLAS. They are derived from other species of *Cola* and from other trees. The loose term MONKEY KOLA may mean any FALSE KOLA.

''KOLA nuts are classed according to colour, red, white or pink. White are preferred and command a much higher price. The same tree may bear nuts of different colours, but trees grown from white seeds produce, if self-pollinated, only white ones; the production of coloured nuts may therefore be due to cross-pollination.

''The KOLA nut of commerce is the seed freed from its thin white covering, usually after soaking or by fermentation in broad leaves; occasionally the nuts are buried to keep them sound for a favourable market; in the equatorial region this is said to be done in ant hills. The main trade is in good-sized nuts, small nuts being almost unmarketable. Packing is done in baskets along with broad leaves; with occasional moistening the nuts can be transported thus for a month free from mould. For longer journeys repacking, with washing of the nuts, and repacking in fresh moist leaves is necessary. KOLA hampers contain about 3 cwt. of nuts.

''To the European importer it is the caffeine that matters. The amount of caffeine in dried KOLA is usually between 1.1% and over 2%. Caffeine alone acts rapidly, the effect passing off comparatively quickly. The effects of the nut itself are more slowly produced and more lasting, and it has also 50% of nutritive matter. In the Belgian Congo the daily use of the nut has been advised, especially for workers, both European and African, and the recommendation is made that every company or mission, etc., should have at their disposal enough KOLA trees to supply a reasonable amount of fresh nuts to their personnel.

''Early accounts (Sixteenth Century) mention that the people of the Cape Verde region chewed KOLA nuts to enable them to go without food, to quench thirst, and (like the olive in Europe) to improve the quality of drinking water. Present day uses are similar, and, apart from social ceremonial, the nut is chewed mainly as a stimulant and conserver of strength, acting without inducing a drug habit.''

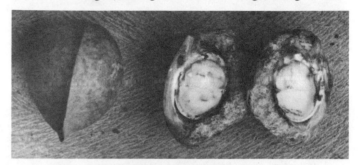

*(Heritiera littoralis)*

## *Heritiera littoralis* (Sterculiaceae)

Burkill says: ''A low-growing, much-branched tree found on the warmer coasts of the Indian and Pacific Oceans.

''The seeds are eaten with fish when the seeds of *Parinari glaberimum,* which are preferred, cannot be obtained.''

Dalziel says: ''The seed of *H. minor* is starchy and it is reported that it may be used as a famine food, provided the tannin is first removed by means of treatment with cold water.''

K. M. Vaid photo

*(Pterygota alata)*

## *Pterygota alata* (Sterculiaceae)

An avenue tree in India. Burkill says: ''The seeds are eaten in Burma and have been used as a substitute for opium, but this needs confirmation.''

PANAMA TREE *(Sterculia apetala)*. A leaf from a lower branch. To get the leaf to lie flat for a photograph, the two bottom lobes were over-lapped about 6 inches. In nature the leaf hangs like an umbrella on a long stem that supports it in the center.

*(Sterculia quadrifida)*

Leaves and fruit of *Sterculia foetida*

## *Sterculia foetida* (Sterculiaceae) JAVA OLIVES

*Sterculia* is a genus of 300 kinds of tropical trees scattered all over the world. Most of them bear edible nuts. Burkill says of this species:

"A tall tree found from Africa to Australia. It would make an excellent avenue tree, were it not for the stench of its flowers; they smell of skatol. (*Stercus* is the Latin word for manure.)

"The seeds have a pleasant taste, and are eaten as nuts by the Malays, and in other countries. Hunter stated that the Chinese in 1800, in Penang, ate the seeds of *'Sterculia balanghas'* by which name he may have meant this species.

"There are several of these seeds in each of the large red pods, but their production high up on the trees and the tough parchment-like skin which covers them are disadvantages which prevent them from being convenient to obtain and use: and, moreover, they have a purgative action. They may cause headaches: and very large quantities of the seeds are said to bring about abortion.

"In India they serve as a famine food. They taste like cacao, and are sometimes used to adulterate it. They may be eaten roasted as well as raw. In frying the skins burst. Soaking for a time also enables the skin to be removed.

"The seeds of many species contain oil and are edible. The most important of these is *S. foetida*. In the Philippine Islands the similar seeds of *S. oblongata,* are eaten as nuts; and those of *S. urceolata,* and *S. treubii* in the Lesser Sunda Islands. In some parts of the East, the oil is extracted from the seeds of these and other species. Crevost says that seeds of several are crushed for oil in Indo-China, chiefly at Quang-ngai, apparently in a domestic way."

Winters & Kennard say of *S. foetida*: "Because of the extremely unpleasant odor of the flowers it is recommended that this tree be planted at some distance from dwellings.

"The fruit has 1 to 5 smooth, rounded, reddish carpels, each 3 to 5 inches in length. At maturity these split open to reveal 10 to 15 gunmetal-colored seeds, each about 1 inch long, arranged along the edges of the opening. The seeds are eaten raw, roasted, or fried. They are oily with a pleasant flavor. Like many nuts, they have a purgative effect if too many are eaten.

"The PANAMA TREE, *S. apetala* from Panama yields seeds that may be eaten in the same way. It differs from the JAVA OLIVE in that the large leaves are lobed but not divided to the base. The fruits are lined with irritating hairs and are less colorful than those of the JAVA OLIVE."

Blossfeld writes from Brazil about *S. chicha,* called MARANHAO NUT. The pod is a huge flat and woody fruit that splits open on one side and opens like a book, showing a red inside. On the rim are fastened the black seeds, each an inch in diameter, with a papery or half-woody hull and an almond-like taste. They are mostly roasted for human consumption. Some species have a chocolate taste, others have a taste like GROUND-NUTS. The trees are not planted, but they are frequent in some States in Brazil and the raw nuts are eaten by porks, that fatten on the diet in harvest season."

Caulfield warns from the Brisbane Botanic Garden: "According to Everist in his book *Poisonous Plants of Australia,* sheep and cattle have died after eating seed and pods of some *Brachychiton (Sterculia)* species. Therefore, it may be inadvisable to include these as edible."

Sturtevant suggests some other edible species:

*Sterculia alata.* BUDDHA'S COCONUT. East Indies. The winged seeds of its large fruit are eaten.

*S. balanghas.* Tropical eastern Asia. The seeds, when roasted, are nearly as palatable as chestnuts. Rumphius says the seeds are considered esculent by the inhabitants of Amboina, who roast them. Unger says the nuts are eaten by the natives of the South Sea Islands generally.

*S. carthaginensis.* Tropical America. The seeds are called chica by the Brazilians and panama by the Panamanians and are commonly eaten as nuts.

*S. diversifolia.* BOTTLE TREE. Australia. The seeds are eaten.

*S. guttata.* Tropical India. The seeds are eaten by the natives of Bombay.

*S. tomentosa.* Equatorial Africa. The seeds are eaten in famines.

*S. urens.* East Indies. The seeds are roasted and eaten by Gonds and Kurkurs in Central India, according to Brandis. The seeds, according to Drury, are roasted and eaten and also made into a kind of coffee. Maheshwari lists these additional Indian species:

*S. quadrifida.* GORARBAR. Seeds roasted for eating.

*S. ramiflora.* AN-JI-UR. Seeds roasted for eating.

*S. trichosiphon.* BROAD LEAVED BOTTLE TREE. Seeds roasted for eating.

*S. rupestris.* NARROW LEAVED BOTTLE TREE. Seeds roasted for eating.

F. C. Hoehne wrote: "In early times, botanists included the genus *Cola* in *Sterculia,* of which Brazil has half a dozen indigenous representatives worthy of attention. They are beautiful trees. *S. chicha* has capsules in a whorl at the ends of the flowing branches which, after maturity, open and for a time let the nuts hang from the open shells. *S. striata* has the same kind of leaves and fruit.

"The flavor of the almonds of *Sterculia* is very pleasing. Doubtless, once these have been thoroughly studied, they will reveal themselves to be bearers of stimulating substances and could become sources of new industries. Would that we always were careful to use the genuine material in the different industries not only to guarantee the products, but even more to safeguard public health."

Howes says: "The seeds of *(Sterculia)* are pleasant in taste and of good eating quality either raw or roasted. They are used as nuts by the inhabitants in many areas. The tough parchment-like skin in which the kernels are enclosed may militate against their more general use as edible nuts."

Buttresses often change direction as they grow, as evidenced by this Indo-Malaysian tree *(Sterculia alata),* on the grounds of the Thomas A. Edison estate at Fort Myers, Fla. Manager of the estate, Robert E. Halgrim, is almost hidden by one of the buttresses.

*(Sterculia lanceolata)*

Forestry Service photo, Lae, New Guinea

*(Sterculia schumanniana)*

43

*S. schumanniana* is a very common and widespread tree in Papua New Guinea, at low altitudes. Usually it is not very large (70-90 ft.) and the timber is white and soft. The fruit is bright orange-red at maturity, opening to expose the black seeds. Dept. of Forests — Papua and New Guinea.

American Cocoa Research Inst., photo by E. P. Imle

Native boy by a slender *Theobroma* tree, ready to harvest the crop.

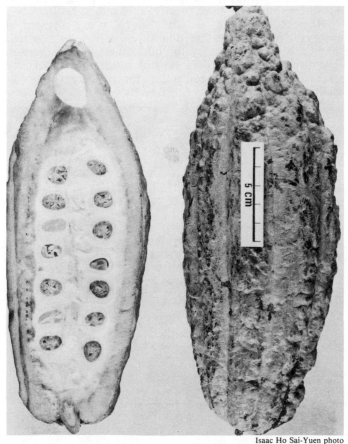

Isaac Ho Sai-Yuen photo

Detail of the pod of *(Theobroma cacao).*

Wolfe Worldwide Films

Dried COCOA beans being sacked at Guayaquil, Ecuador.

## *Theobroma cacao*     (Sterculiaceae)     COCOA CACAO

The oldest and one of the largest commercial food enterprises in the United States, centers around nuts — the seeds clustered in the big pods that hang on the trunk of a tropical American tree known to all the world as the source of chocolate. In the United States the Baker chocolate business was established in 1765 on the banks of the Neponset River, just 7 miles from Faneuil Hall. Chocolate continued to be made on that site until ten years ago when the General Foods Company moved the operation to a more central location.

Williams: *Useful and Ornamental Plants of Trinidad* pictures the nut which built a world:

"The name *Cacao* has come to embrace all the commercial varieties of *Theobroma* although originally it was usually restricted to the CRIOLLO types, native of Central America. Some authorities consider the purple types to belong to *T. leiocarpa* and the bulk of West Indian FORASTERO cocoa to be a series of hybrids between these two.

"The trees range in size from delicate CRIOLLOS rarely exceeding 15 feet in height to impressive FORASTEROS attaining a height of 50 to 60 feet or more.

"The young seedling has large, oval leaves spirally arranged on the stem. At about 3 to 5 feet the terminal bud dissipates into three to five lateral branches which bear leaves in two ranks. The portion of the plant which bears spiral leaves, i.e. below the fork, is termed chupon-growth as opposed to fan-growth above the jorquette.

"Flowers and fruit are borne on spur shoots or cushions on the trunk and branches. The fruit is a pod with 20 to 50 oval seeds embedded in a white pulp. The beans are extracted, fermented and dried before being converted into chocolate or cocoa. The pods vary in length from 4 to 18 inches, are generally oval, sometimes with a pronounced wartiness and pointed apex. The colour of the pods ranges from unpigmented green to heavily pigmented, almost purple hues.

"The CRIOLLO varieties have either unpigmented or heavily pigmented pods, but always white. *Leiocarpa* varieties have unpigmented pods but pigmented seeds. In FORASTERO, the commercial mixture, all gradations of pod colour and bean colour occur. CRIOLLOS tend to be delicate, *leoicarpa* varieties robust.

"Plantations in Trinidad range from one acre to over 1,000 acres. Trees are spaced 12 feet or 14 feet apart in the field. When young the space between each is used to grow vegetables which serve also as shade for the young cocoa. Plants may be either seedlings, budded, grafted or rooted cuttings. Trees come into bearing in the third to fifth year and continue to bear heavily for 30, 50 or more years on good soil. Pods are reaped during the greater part of the year. The beans are fermented for five to seven days, spread on large trays to dry and then polished before being bagged for sale. The dried beans are the CACAO of commerce."

American Cocoa Research Inst. photo

CHOCOLATE pods *(Theobroma cacao)* hanging on the tree's trunk. The flowers, just above the upper pod, are quite inconspicuous.

Burkill summarizes the nut's history:

"In the sixteenth century, Cortez and the Spaniards with him found CACAO in use among the Indians of Mexico, and ascertained that the tree yielding it was cultivated. The seeds, indeed, were so valued that they passed as a means of exchange. Those who could made a drink from them: the common people, if they were not able to afford that, used them sparingly as one would a spice, to flavour food. The drink was made by pounding the seed with maize and boiling it with cayenne pepper. This beverage the Spaniards did not like: however, before a century had passed they had discovered a way, by mixing it with sugar, of brewing a different drink that they appreciated and introduced to Spain. An import began, first of cakes prepared by pounded beans, and then of the beans themselves. The cakes were spiced.

"The popularity of such cakes, from the CACAO beans spread in Europe. At first Mexico alone produced the beans, and the price was kept high: but in 1634 Venezuela joined in the export of them, and the produce began to go to Amsterdam, though the Spaniards tried hard to keep the trade in their own hands. From Venezuela, CACAO exporting spread to the southern of the West Indian Islands, the tree having indeed been in Trinidad from 1525. In the seventeenth century planting extended almost throughout the islands, their produce gaining ground in the markets. Considerable changes have followed this spreading, and now in most of the old CACAO countries production is either declining or stationary; while among the new CACAO countries — most of them in Africa, a few in South and Central America and some in Asia — here and there it is expanding. Of Asiatic countries Ceylon and Java, which are among the oldest of the new CACAO countries, have a declining production."

45

# Chapter 9

# THE MANGOSTEEN FAMILY

## (Guttiferae)

This most delicious of fruits, along with a tree that ranks very high among the beautiful flowering trees of the world *(Mesua ferrea),* gets into the nuts book because a few of the trees in the family do have seeds that are rich in edible oil.

Among these nut trees is the BITTER KOLA.

### *Allanblackia floribunda*  (Guttiferae) TALLOW TREE

This tree to 100 feet in Sierra Leone, Cameroons, Congo and Uganda, bears large and showy, fragrant white flowers, followed by sausage-shaped 18-inch seed pods, 5 inches in diameter that contain up to 100 red-brown seeds. These are irregular in shape, with flattened surfaces, about 1½ x ½ inch in size.

Irvine says: "Antelopes are said to eat the fruits. The kernels, composing about 62 per cent of the seeds, contain when dry about 73 per cent of solid white fat, which is suitable for soap-making (also probably for edible purposes) and from which pure stearic acid can be obtained. The residual meal is too bitter for cattle food. The yield of seeds per tree is large, and the nuts travel well without deterioration. Okisidwe (Ashanti, 'rat's nut') is so called because rats are sometimes specially trapped with it. Dalziel states that the similarity between the appearance of these seeds and those of *Carapa procera* and *Pentadesma butyracea* has led to confusion."

### *Garcinia kola*  (Guttiferae)  BITTER KOLA FALSE KOLA

The 400 kinds of *Garcinia* in Asia and South Africa include one of the most delicious of fruits, the MANGOSTEEN *(G. mangostana),* but it also includes many species like this one, having nuts that are somewhere between chewing gum and food. Dalziel describes this in west tropical Africa:

"The seeds are the important product, and are seen in markets from Senegal (obtained from Sierra Leone) to S. Nigeria and to parts of the interior. They do not separate into two cotyledons. They have in chewing a bitter, astringent and resinous taste, somewhat resembling that of the raw coffee bean, followed by a slight sweetness, and are appreciated rather as an adjuvant than a substitute for true KOLA, increasing the user's enjoyment of the latter and allowing of the consumption of larger quantities without indisposition. Similarly they enhance the flavour of native liquor. The residue after chewing is white. They are eaten raw and not in prepared food."

Watt describes *G. indica* which produces in India what is called KOKAM BUTTER: "A slender tree with drooping branches, found on the Ghats most commonly in the Southern Konkan, and considerably cultivated in gardens. It bears a conspicuous spherical purple fruit, the size of a small orange, which ripens about April.

"A valuable oil, KOKAM BUTTER, is obtained from the seeds of the fruit to the extent of about 30 per cent. The kernel is pounded and the pulp with some water is kept in a large vessel and allowed to settle for the night. During the night the oil rises to the surface and forms a white layer which is removed in the morning. The mixture is then churned, and the oil which, like butter, rises to the surface in a solid form, is removed by the hand.

"KOKAM BUTTER, as found in the bazaars of India, consists of egg-shaped or concavo-convex cakes of a dirty white or yellowish colour, friable, crystalline, and with a greasy feel like spermaceti. When fresh it has a faint, not unpleasant smell."

This butter is used mostly for making soap, but Sturtevant says: "The oil from the seeds has been used to adulterate butter. About Bombay the oil obtained from the seeds is used for adulterating ghee or butter."

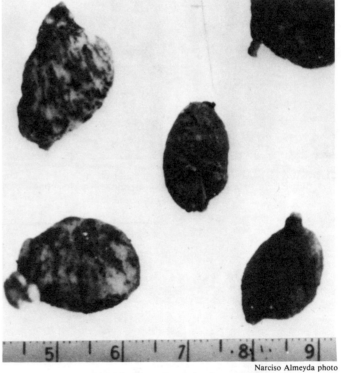

Narciso Almeyda photo

MANGOSTEEN *(Garcinia mangostana)*

*G. mangostana,* the MANGOSTEEN, is prized for the delicious fruits. The seeds are eaten raw or in various preparations, according to Uphof.

Uphof says the seeds of the following species also are edible: *G. barrettiana* of the Philippines, *G. conrauana* of the Cameroons; *G. cowa* of India; *G. lateriflora* of the Philippines; *G. planchoni* of Indochina and others.

*(Garcinia picrorhiza)*

***Mesua ferrea***      **(Guttiferac)**      **IRONWOOD**

Sturtevant says: "Java and East Indies. The fruit is red-dish and wrinkled when ripe, with a rind like that of the CHESTNUT. It resembles a CHESTNUT in size, shape, substance and taste."

***Pentadesma butyracea*** **(Guttiferae) TALLOW TREE**
**BUTTER TREE**
**CANDLE TREE**
**BLACK MANGO**

This large, buttressed evergreen tree to 100 feet grows throughout tropical Africa from Guinea to the Cameroons.

Irvine says: "The fruits (Feb.-June, July-Oct.) 6 in. by over 4 in., pointed, broadly ellipsoid, brown, with large persistent sepals at base, with yellow-red latex when cut; seeds 3-10 or more, in a yellowish pulp; brown, with flattened sides, resembling those of *Carapa procera,* vinous red in section and very bitter, formerly used to adulterate true cola, but easily distinguished.

"The seeds are said to be edible when young, but sour when old. They are sometimes offered as a KOLA substitute. A pale greyish-yellow and granular fat is extracted from them much in the same way as SHEA-BUTTER, which it resembles in many respects, and is used for cooking. It is soft at European temperatures, but fluid in the tropics. Air-dried seeds yield 32-42 per cent of solid fat, pale to dark brown, almost tasteless, and with a pleasant smell. Only fully ripe fruits should be used for extraction, and the seeds should be thoroughly dried before shipment, when they should yield about 40 per cent of readily saleable fat."

Dalziel says: "The fat is extracted from the seeds in the same way as from those of the SHEA BUTTER tree. Its native use is as a cooking fat. The crude fat is pale greyish-yellow, granular, with an odour like that of SHEA BUTTER, which it resembles in general characters, but it is free from the bitter latex which necessitates special refinement of the latter; it clarifies to a greenish-yellow and does not readily become rancid. In Dahomey the two kinds of butter may be mixed. Air-dried seeds yield from 32-42% of a solid fat, pale yellow to dark brown in colour, with a pleasant smell. Fat extracted from fresh seeds is but slightly coloured, and the colouring is probably proportional to amount of desiccation. The yield of fat varies in different samples; only those from fully ripe fruits should be collected for export, and the seeds should be thoroughly dried for shipment. They then should yield about 40% of fat and would be readily saleable."

Burkill says: "The seeds are sometimes offered as a substitute for KOLA NUTS. When young they are edible. The absolutely dry kernels hold 42 per cent of oil. It is a pale yellow fat with a slightly agreeable odour, and of a rather soft consistency at temperatures usual in Europe, but fluid in the tropics."

# Chapter 10
# THE CASHEW FAMILY

The delightful CASHEW NUT that everybody loves, is characteristic of the POISON IVY family. It is dangerous until roasted. Here is the CASHEW in all its glory, along with the MANGO and other close relatives, and when the seeds are sought for food, it is important that precautions be taken. Each subject is fully explained.

Julia Morton photo

The CASHEW tidbit is contained in a hardshelled nut that protrudes beyond the apex of the soft fruit.

*Anacardium occidentale*
**(Anacardiaceae)**

**CASHEW**
**GAJUS** *(Malaya)*
**MONKEY NUT**

The highly popular CASHEW nut that originated in the West Indies, has spread its blessings all over the world so that the nut and its products have become commercially important all over Africa, in India, and in many parts of Malaya. It is a 40-foot tree that grows easily from seed and starts producing nuts when it is 3 or 4 years old. It is adapted to moderately dry areas near the sea.

The kidney-shaped, hard shelled nut is borne on a much-enlarged, fleshy receptacle, the CASHEW "apple," which is about 2 inches in diameter and 4 inches long. At maturity the apple has turned bright red or yellow. The shell contains an oil that is highly irritating to the skin, and the nuts should be heated to render the oil less caustic before the kernels are extracted. Since the caustic oil is expelled from the shell during roasting, the smoke must not come in contact with the eyes or skin. This tree belongs in the same plant family with poison ivy and sumac, which may explain its dangers. The CASHEW is one of the most delicious of nuts after being roasted and is rich in protein and fat. The oil, contained in a spongy layer of the shell, has become of great commercial value.

Allen, who reports the tree highly successful in Malaya where Portuguese explorers brought it four hundred years ago, describes it:

"GAJUS fruits more or less all the year round in Malaya, but bears heavier crops after a dry period. In wild trees the apple seldom ripens, for children, birds, and squirrels eat them, and so do the large flying foxes. Although the apple has an attractive smell the flesh is watery and often causes a tickling in the throat. Nuts must be heated, either boiled or roasted, before eating to destroy the irritant poison, and care must be taken to avoid the steam or smoke, and when picking, not to damage the shell. Once heated they are harmless."

Blossfeld writes from Sao Paulo: "The CASHEW is native of the coast of northern Brazil. But again, the nut is very rarely consumed in Brazil, and only since a few years, it started to become an export commodity here, while from India, it has been an export article for a hundred years. There is some difficulty in getting the nut out of its shell. This is done by roasting and during the process, the hot resinous sap of the shell squirts out. This sap is highly caustic and being hot, leaves dangerous burnings on the skin. It is a most disagreeable job, always done by hand, also in India. So it can be done only where labor is very cheap."

A. J. Melville Williams, writes in the *Christian Science Monitor:*

A tree that is not native to Africa is a big moneymaker for Mozambique, Portugal's east African territory.

Centuries ago Portuguese seamen brought seeds of the CASHEW nut trees from Brazil to be planted by the early settlers along the coasts of east Africa.

The tree took root and thrived. It was not long before it was growing wild along the entire coast of Mozambique.

Uncared for and uncultivated the ripe nuts were primitively harvested by the African natives and later sold to Portuguese traders who in turn disposed of them to merchants who shipped the nuts to India. The cashew-nut tree prevented soil erosion and at the same time provided sustenance for the African natives.

The days of the easy exploitation of resources long have passed. The CASHEW nut is big business and on the way to becoming Mozambique's most important industry and earner of foreign exchange.

Secondary industry has followed in its wake, and emphasis is being laid on the need for increasing national development and the necessity of making use of go-ahead methods.

Mozambique's CASHEW exports, both processed and unprocessed, totaled 612 million escudos (nearly $22 million U.S.) in 1967 and are increasing. This export figure is expected to reach 1.5 billion escudos within the next few years.

A $3 million CASHEW nut plant, able to process 35,000 tons a year, has been erected at the little port of Nacala, situated on the finest natural deep-water harbor on the east African coast nearly 1,000 miles north of the capital city, Lourenco Marques. The factory is staffed by Portuguese technicians from metropolitan Portugal and some 1,500 semi-skilled and unskilled workers, mostly African women.

There are eight licensed mechanical plants in Mozambique capable of processing 85,000 tons of raw nut annually. If the CASHEW nut trade progresses at the present rate, it well could exceed the total figure for Mozambique's chief exports within a few years.

Processed CASHEW nuts bring about $500 a ton, more than twice that paid for unprocessed nuts.

CASHEW nut shell liquid, generally known as CNSL, an oil extracted from the raw nut during processing, has high polymerizing and friction-reducing properties and is used largely in the paint and varnish industry in the United States.

It also has a strategic value in that it is used as a component of space-rocket lubricants.

There are more than 300 patented uses for CASHEW by-products including cattle feed. The kernel with its high vitamin content is regarded as a dainty.

The biggest kernel buyer is the United States with a consumer market accounting for some 40,000 tons annually and still growing.

The New York price for whole kernels has been remarkably buoyant, with prices tending to remain firm even with greater increases in production.

Thousands of Africans experience a better living standard and generally benefit with the development of the CASHEW industry.

Ralph Dickey photo

CANDLE NUT *(Aleurites moluccana)*

## *Aleurites moluccana*      (Euphorbiaceae) CANDLE NUT

This Malayan tree is somewhat larger than its relatives, the MU-OIL or the TUNG, reaching 60 feet, but greatly resembling them in other respects. It is the only common evergreen *Aleurites.*

The nuts are round, 1½ to 2 inches across, and flattened laterally. They contain 1 or 2 seeds. The outer hull of the nut is thin and papery but the rough inner seed coats thick and hard.

Where the TUNG and the MU-OIL will not grow, in tropical regions, and where land and labor are cheap, CANDLE NUT oil may be produced. It is said to be of lower quality, slower drying, and more nearly resembling linseed oil than the others. It grows chiefly in the Philippines, Malaya and Ceylon, and throughout the South Pacific.

Bailey says: "Irregularly rounded to spheroidal nuts, from 1 to 2 inches in diameter, ranging in color from mottled gray to nearly black, and having a hard but brittle shell, about 1/8 inch in thickness. Borne in fruits, 2 or 3 inches in diameter, containing about five nuts each. From the kernels of these nuts which are considered edible only from certain species, and when half-ripe and roasted, there is obtained a valuable oil, known as country walnut oil, artists' oil, kekune (Ceylon), or kukuii (Sandwich Islands) oil."

There is some uncertainty about the edibility of CANDLE NUTS. They are reliably reported as being eaten in some places after being roasted. For some people, however, they act as a powerful purgative.

These five species of *Aleurites,* starting from the ruler, are:
1. *A. trisperma.* SOFT LUMBANG
2. *A. moluccana.* CANDLE NUT
3. *A. fordi.* TUNG OIL
4. *A. montana.* MU OIL
5. *A. cordata.* JAPAN WOOD OIL

Maheshwari says: "Nuts eaten after roasting."

Watt says: "The nuts contain 50 per cent of oil, which is extracted and used as food and for burning. It is cultivated for the sake of its fruit, which is generally 2 inches in diameter."

Roxburgh says: "The kernels taste very much like fresh walnuts, and are reckoned wholesome."

Burkill says: "The seeds are used a little in food, chiefly among the Javanese: they enter into a sauce which is an almost invariable associate of the green vegetables eaten with rice. Thus used in sauce, no great amount is demanded, for only a very little is eaten at a time: but the use is so wide that the local produce does not suffice, and there is an import of nuts into Java from the east of Malaysia. In the preparation the kernels are crushed and oil is extracted which is used as an illuminant.

"The kernels are also eaten, but sparingly, roasted. The nuts are put in the fire until half the shell has been burned; then they are cracked open and the kernel removed. This roasted kernel — it would be dangerous to eat it raw — is pounded with such other flavorings as salt, chillies, and shrimp-paste and eaten as a relish."

49

Ochse says: "CANDLE NUT oil is used in some places to fry food, but is likely to be poisonous unless the oil has been obtained from well-ripened seeds. Pulverized seeds steeped in running water for 48 hours and then steamed are sometimes eaten in Indonesia."

### *Antrocaryon micraster* (Anacardiaceae)

This is one of six species of trees in West Tropical Africa, extending from Sierra Leone to Uganda.

Irvine says: "A large tree to 150 ft. and 9 ft. in girth; crown spreading, bole twisted near top, buttresses slight, or none, bark thick, fragrant and gummy, slash pink, white-streaked, resinous, branchlets stout and somewhat angled; fruit (Apr.-June) strong-smelling with hard several seeded stone.

"The plum-like fruit is eaten in various parts of Tropical Africa, and a fermented beverage could be made from it. The seeds are edible and rich in oil, but difficult to extract from the fruit, though the hard endocarp bursts in hot cinders."

Dalziel writes: "The people eat the plum-like fruit. The kernels are oily and edible, but difficult to remove from the sea-urchin-shaped nut."

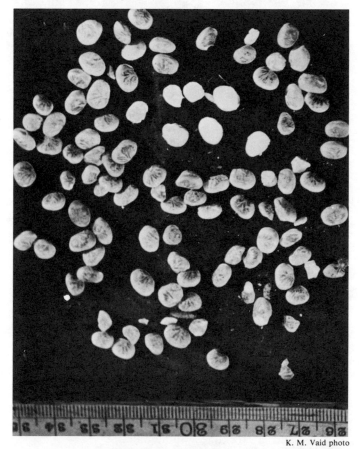

K. M. Vaid photo

*(Buchanania lanzan)*

### *Buchanania lanzan* (Anacardiaceae)

This 50-foot Indian tree, one of 20 species scattered throughout east Asia, Malaysia and northern Australia, bears edible nuts considered superior to cashews, according to Macmillan. The pear-shaped kernels are rich in oil.

Brandis says: "The fruit has a pleasant, sweetish, sub-acid flavor and is an important article of food of the hill tribes of central India. The kernel of the seed tastes somewhat like the PISTACHIO nut and is used largely in native sweet-meats."

Drury says: "These kernels are a general substitute for almonds among the natives and are much esteemed in confectionery or are roasted and eaten with milk."

Burkill says: "Kalompang or Calumpang seeds are now sold in England as 'almondettes'. They are rich in oil; the oil is rarely extracted, as the seeds are in great demand as a sweetmeat.

"Analyses of calumpang-nuts, from the Philippine Islands, gave 51-78 per cent of oil, 21-61 per cent of starch, 12-10 per cent of protein, 5 per cent of sugar on dry weight. The oil expressed is sweet, of a light yellow colour, and physically closely resembles olive-oil. It is without any irritant action and could be used for culinary purposes in the place of olive oil."

Howes says: "Roasted or slightly charred it constitutes an excellent after-dinner dish, and is relished by Europeans in India. In some parts of India the dried fruits and the kernels are baked together into a sort of bread."

### *Caryodendron orinocense* (Euphorbiaceae)
### TACCY NUT

Howes says: "In Colombia the seeds of this tree are valued for eating and are consumed after roasting. They are very prevalent in some parts of the country, especially the Llanos of San Martin. The thin brown shell surrounding the kernel, which is about an inch in length, is easily broken with the fingers."

### *Cnidoscolus oligandrus* (Euphorbiaceae)

This genus comprises 75 kinds of trees and shrubs in South America.

Mors and Rizinni report on this species in Brazil: "The large fruits contain seeds with 40 to 50 percent oil and serve as food for the local inhabitants during times of severe drought, which frequently scourge parts of the waterless northeast."

### *Dracontomelum mangiferum* (Anacardiaceae)
### BELGIAN WALNUT

This is a genus of mostly small trees extending through southeast Asia.

Hundley writes: "The BELGIAN WALNUT is a large, evergreen tree with young growth tawny-pubescent; has a range from the Andamans and Nicobars through the Malay peninsula to coastal Burma. The fruit is a drupe 1 inch in diameter, depressed, with a flat stone containing 2 to 5 cells each holding a small almond. These are edible."

Isaac Ho Sai-Yuen photo

TAPOS *(Elateriospermum tapos)*

## Elateriospermum tapos (Euphorbiaceae) TAPOS

This handsome tree, often more than 100 feet high and more than 3 feet in diameter, is found throughout western Malaysia.

Burkill says: "The seeds, which are nearly 2 inches long, contain an abundance of oil. There seem to be some races in which the seeds are not poisonous in a fresh state. These races are rare. Usually the seeds are slightly poisonous from the presence of hydrocyanic acid, and cannot be eaten raw.

"The seeds are an important article of food among the jungle tribes. The commonest way of using them is to rasp or pound them with a little water, pack them into a bag, or a bamboo, which is buried in wet earth for a month or more, sometimes for several months. This preparation is fermented, and has a strong flavour, which is greatly appreciated by those who eat it. Sometimes the seeds are boiled or roasted whole. In Sumatra a paste made from them, is wrapped in a bamboo leaf, and commonly sold in the markets, for use as a flavouring. Malays sometimes make a salt pickle from them. Javanese eat them roasted or boiled as a tidbit."

## Gluta elegans (Anacardiaceae) RENGAS

*Gluta* is a small genus of trees in Malaysia. The common name RENGAS indicates it is poisonous. Burkill describes them:

"All the species are called RENGAS by the Malays. This indicates a plant growing to a tree, containing a sap which produces sores on the skin.

"*G. elegans* is a small tree very common in Penang. Its new foliage is of an intense violet colour, and makes the tree very conspicuous for a few days at the time of new leaf.

"*G. renghas,* is a tree of fair size found in western Malaysia. It gives a beautiful red timber, which is not much used, as workmen are afraid of splashing the latex on to their skin in felling the tree. Should any fresh latex fall on the skin it blisters it, and sores follow, which are very obstinate.

"The seed, which is like a small billiard-ball, can be eaten after it has been roasted.

"*G. velutina.* Botanically very close to *G. renghas,* but usually of smaller size. It occurs on the coasts of the Gulf of Siam, western Sumatra, the moister parts of Java and Borneo. It grows on the water's edge. The seed is edible. Ridley once met a European who had tasted a fruit and had suffered from violent diarrhoea afterwards."

*(Lannea sp.)*

## Lannea stuhlmannii (Anacardiaceae)

Fanshawe writes: "In Zambia the seeds are crushed and boiled with salt to produce a local relish."

Bill Lane Photo

MANGO *(Mangifera indica).* Zill hybrid.

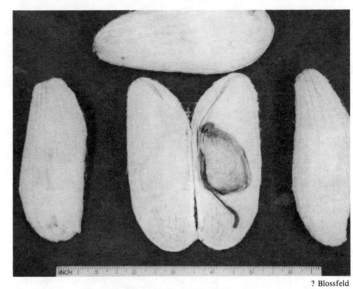

? Blossfeld

MANGO *(Mangifera indica).*

## Mangifera indica (Anacardiaceae) MANGO

This Indian tree, cultivated in the tropics everywhere for its fruit, is being improved in taste and size by many fruit experts like John G. DuPuis, Jr., of Miami and David Sturrock of West Palm Beach, so that the finest fruits nowadays are very delicious and often weigh 2 pounds or more.

The seeds and their kernels are worthless to Americans, but millions of people value them for hundreds of medicinal uses, and even for food.

Dalziel says: "The kernel is starchy and can be eaten roasted, or dried and pickled, etc. In some places the half-ripe fruit is sliced and partially cooked, and then dried in the sun to preserve."

Watt says: "The kernels are eaten in times of famine, and by the poorest classes in many parts of India they are boiled and eaten with greens. They are also ground into meal and mixed with various other ingredients to form the relish known as am-khatai. When stuffed with coriander, turmeric, and other spices, and boiled in mustard oil, they are esteemed a great delicacy."

## *Manniophyton fulvum*      (Euphorbiaceae)

This straggly bush or lofty, hairy, woody climber grows in tropical Africa from Sierra Leone to Zaire and Nyassaland. It is the only species. Irvine says: "Fruits 3-lobed, nearly spherical, with raised ribs 1 in. long, rusty-tomentose.

"The large round white kernels, when boiled, become mealy, and are sold in Nigerian markets for food. They contain about 50 per cent of a yellow, tasteless oil."

Dalziel says: "The fruit is 3-lobed or nearly spherical with raised ribs and contains an oil-seed. The cooked nuts are sold in markets in S. Nigeria, the large round white kernel, about 1 in. in diameter, being edible and mealy when well boiled."

## *Omphalea*      (Euphorbiaceae)

*Omphalea* comprises 20 species of vines that grow in tropical America, Africa, Madagascar, Indochina, West Malaysia, Celebes, New Guinea, Queensland and the Solomon Islands. It stretches around the world and produces its edible seeds everywhere.

Sturtevant describes two species: "*Omphalea diandra* COBNUT. West Indies. This tree is cultivated in Santo Domingo and Jamaica under the same of noisettier, or COBNUT, from the resemblance of the flavor of the seeds to that of the European nuts. The embryo is deleterious and requires to be extracted.

"*O. triandra,* COBNUT. Tropical America. The seeds are edible after the deleterious embryo is extracted. The tree is called COBNUT in Jamaica. The kernels of the nuts in the raw state are delicately sweet and wholesome. When roasted they are equal, if not superior, to any CHESTNUT. By compression, they yield a sweet and fine-flavored oil."

Bro. Alain Liogier writes of the latter species: "This seems to be popular in some parts of Hispaniola. It is called AVELLANA in Santo Domingo. Said to be tasty."

Fanshawe wrote from Guyana regarding *O. diandra:* "The fruits of this vine contain edible nuts of an oily nature."

A friend writes from Australia: "*O. queenslandiae* might look the most promising of nuts (produced by a large vine of the lowland rain forest), but the nut sometimes has purgative effects, and a peculiar 'short' texture and poor flavour make it unattractive to me."

Irvine writes of *O. megacarpa* in Africa, called HUNTER-MAN'S NUT: "A woody native vine with fruit 3 to 4 inches diameter, round, containing 2 to 3 seeds, roundish, about 1¾ inches long. These yield a pale-yellow, faintly bitter oil, resembling castor oil, although it is less viscous and without unpleasant taste. It is regarded as a valuable non-irritant purgative, a teaspoonful being considered sufficient for a dose."

Maheshwari says of this same plant in India which he calls RUSSELL RIVER NUT: "Large nut eaten raw."

Julia Morton photo

EMBLIC MYROBALAN *(Phyllanthus emblica)*

## *Phyllanthus emblica*      (Euphorbiaceae)

This genus comprises some 600 species in the tropics and subtropics.

A correspondent in Taiwan writes that the seeds of this species "are edible if eaten before ripening, and they are very good for soothing a dry throat."

Watt says: "The acid fruit, which is of the size of a small gooseberry, with a fleshy outer covering, and a hard three-celled nut containing six seeds, is used, among other purposes, for food and preserves by the Natives. It is made into a sweetmeat with sugar, or eaten raw as a condiment and is also prepared as a pickle."

## *Pimeleodendron amboinicum*      (Euphorbiaceae)

Burkill calls this a small genus of trees found in Malaysia and New Guinea. He says this species "furnishes edible seeds which taste like HAZELNUTS."

Ben Stone, Professor of Botany, University of Malaya, Singapore writes: "This supplies edible seeds."

USDA photo

PISTACHIO NUTS on the tree. These grape-like clusters are about ready to harvest.

PISTACHIO NUTS *(Pistacia vera)*

## *Pistacia vera*    (Pistaciaceae)    PISTACHIO NUT

The PISTACHIO NUT, enjoyed as a tidbit throughout the world, came originally from Asia Minor, but its cultivation now extends into India, the Far East, southern United States to California, Mexico into Europe and north Africa.

Watt says: "A small tree, forming forests at altitudes of 3,000 feet and upwards, in Syria, Damascus, Mesopotamia, extensively cultivated in Syria, Palestine and Persia.

"The value of the forests of indigenous PISTACHIO lies in their yield of nuts, but the harvest is a precarious one, generally due to the tree being dioecious, and to fertilisation being frequently unaccomplished.

"The nuts on some of the trees are partially dehiscent, whereas in others they are quite indehiscent. So well is this known to the people of the country that in collecting nuts for eating, should they chance to come on a tree of which the nuts are indehiscent, they just move on until they come to a tree bearing dehiscing nuts. In the latter case a slight crushing of the nut with the fingers gives exit to the kernels, whereas in the former each nut has to be broken up, as we would a hazel, before the kernel can be got at. On many trees the female flowers are found not to have been fertilised; these develop into a nut-like form, and when these unfertilised ovaries are examined they are found to be quite hollow, the walls being apparently analogous to the covering of the fertilised nut.

"From the great trade-value of the nuts and of the galls, there is much jealousy as to the forest rights, as to whom they belong, and in what proportion to each tribe. Half the blood-feuds of the nomads originate in their quarrels over the rights of produce in their forests.

"All persons connected in the rights to the forest and produce unitedly collect the nuts, and the general harvest is subsequently divided in the allotted proportions to those to whom they may belong. In the meanwhile the Amir's tax collectors are at hand ready to carry off the usual tax imposed on produce before it is permitted to leave the ground.

"The PISTACHIO NUT is oval-shaped and varies in size with the amount of cultivation which the tree has received. It has a brittle shell, enclosing a kernel, generally about half an inch in length, of a greenish colour and agreeable flavour. The wild fruit is smaller and more terebinthinate in flavour than the cultivated, but is preferred by many. In India the nut is much appreciated by all classes. By Natives, the nuts are generally roasted in their shells in hot sand, and then thrown into a hot paste of salt-water, and stirred so as to make the salt adhere to the shell, much as sugar does to a burnt almond. They are hawked about the street of large towns."

The Agress Nut & Seed Co., New York leading importers, report: "Most of the farm processing is done by hand. The clusters of nuts are knocked from the limbs with bamboo poles onto cloths spread below. The soft husk that surrounds the shell is removed by hand squeezing. Empty shells are removed by floating off in a tank of water, while the full nuts sink. The full nuts are then carefully dried in the sun.

"Roasted PISTACHIO NUTS are hygroscopic — they will draw moisture from the air and become soggy. To preserve the roast, packing must be in a moisture resistant medium. When properly packaged, they have a shelf life in excess of 24 months, and maintain their full flavor.

"For many years, vending machines accounted for a substantial part of PISTACHIO NUT sales. With the advent of prepackaging, methods of distribution changed and this field now leads in sales."

---

*\* Pistacia was long kept in the CASHEW family, but now is established in a family of its own Pistaciaceae. For convenience it is kept here in this book.*

\*There are ten species of PISTACIO\*. Sturtevant describes three others with edible nuts:

"*P. lentiscus.* MASTIC TREE. Southern Europe, northern Africa and western Asia. Mastic is the resin obtained from incisions in the bark of this tree and is produced principally in the Island of Scio and in Asiatic Turkey. MASTIC is consumed in large quantities by the Turks for chewing to sweeten the breath and to strengthen the gums. The tree is cultivated in Italy and Portugal. From the kernel of the fruit, an oil may be obtained, which is fine for table use.

"*P. mexicana.* Mexico. A small tree with edible nuts found near the mouth of the Pecos.

"*P. terebinthus.* CYPRUS TURPENTINE TEREBINTH. Southern Europe. A large tree of the Mediterranean flora. The nuts are shaped like the filbert, long and pointed, the kernel pale, greenish, sweet and more oily than the almond."

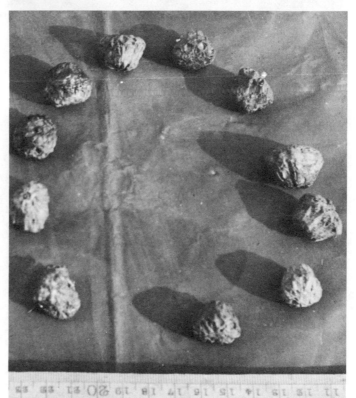

K. M. Vaid photo

BURDEKIN PLUM *(Pleiogynium cerasiferum)*

## *Pleiogynium cerasiferum*    (Anacardiaceae)    BURDEKIN PLUM

This is a genus of two kinds of trees that grow in the Philippines, Australia and New Guinea, and are cultivated in Florida, California and Hawaii where the delicious fruit is used for jellies.

Uphof says the large seeds have a pleasant flavor and are eaten in Australia.

## *Plukenetia conophora*    (Euphorbiaceae)    OWUSA NUT

This cultivated woody vine to 20 feet in tropical Africa has seeds producing oil that is used by natives in food, according to Uphof.

Howes says: "The thin-shelled seeds are about an inch in length and contain a yellow oily kernel. They have a pleasant odour and taste and are eaten raw as nuts by the natives. Sometimes they are consumed along with other foodstuffs."

MANKETTI NUT. MUGONGO NUT. *(Ricinodendron rautanenii)*

### Ricinodendron heudelotii (Euphorbiaceae) and  *R. rautanenii*

MANKETTI NUT
ZAMBEZI ALMOND
MUGONGO NUT

There are only two species of these medium-sized, soft-wooded quick-growing trees in central Africa, both prized for their nuts which are about the size of pecans. The nuts are devoured by many animals but the extremely hard-shelled nut within is difficult to crack. Fanshawe says the kernel within is about the size of a HAZELNUT, palatable, nutritious, containing 57-63% of edible oil. In Malawi the nuts are roasted under a layer of sand, cracked, and the kernel extracted; it is used in stews or eaten as a relish.

A forester in Rhodesia sent this author some MANKETTI nuts and on the package under the scientific name *Ricinodendron,* he had written "Recovered from elephant dung". This startled me. The nuts are like oversized pecans which have had smallpox and were covered with pock marks. I wrote the forester to ask why the special inscription, and he replied that there are 3 reasons: (1) The elephants eat the fruits greedily and it is much easier to let the elephants do the job of picking; (2) The seed will not germinate until it has spent a week inside the elephant, and (3) The elephant enjoys the fruit but his digestive mechanism does not affect the extremely hard shell and the nut inside. The natives of Rhodesia, therefore, follow the elephant, recover the hardshelled nuts where they have been dropped, clean and dry them, then crack the extremely hard shell, and find the contents perfectly delicious. This story is a bit grizzly, but it is part of the nut story and it is only one of a thousand local color stories that make this book on nuts entirely different.

### *Sclerocarya caffra*   (Anacardiaceae)   MAROELA

Of the five species of *Sclerocarya* in tropical East and South Africa, Sturtevant says that on the Zambezi, the seeds of this tree are eaten by the natives.

Williamson: *Useful Plants of Nyassaland* says: "This is a fair sized handsome tree to 45 ft. The trees are conspicuous in May with their yellow edible fruit the size of a plum with a strong odor when ripe. The male tree is a beautiful sight in October with its red catkins coming out before the leaves. The fruit is edible with a turpentine-mango flavor. Elephants are very fond of the fermented fruit which they pick up from the ground."

*Sclerocarya* nuts are contained within an edible fruit and good eating although the kernels are hard to extract. The local tribesmen manufacture a special nut-picker for the express purpose of digging out the kernel.

Lloyd Schaad writes from Angola: "*Sclerocarya* is a large tree up to 18 meters in the southern part of Angola. The seeds are edible, with the fruit used at maturity by the natives to make a much-appreciated alcoholic beverage."

Th. Mueller, director of the Botanic Garden at Salisbury writes: "*Sclerocarya* fruit in Rhodesia is relished by the indigenous people and some Europeans, including myself, enjoy it also."

Sturtevant wrote of *Sclerocarya birrea* in eastern equatorial Africa: "This is a forest tree on the upper Nile. The kernels of the fruit, whose unripe sarcocarp is apple-scented, are milky and are eaten like GROUND NUTS. This species affords the natives of Abyssinia an edible kernel, while its fruits are employed in Senegal in the preparation of an alcoholic drink.

The Lady Rockley wrote: "The tree has a large crown of leaves for its height of 15 to 30 feet, and the fruit comes on one tree, the male catkins on another. These are a striking red and make a beautiful show in October before the leaves appear. The fruit is the size of a golf-ball, and is yellow with a hard bitter skin, but the soft part inside is fit to eat."

H. A. Lueckhoff, Secretary for Forestry in Rhodesia, wrote: "The fruits are much sought after by the Bantu population. The pulp is eaten fresh but is mainly used for the manufacture of an intoxicating beverage. They are also relished by many wild animals and make a good table jelly. The kernels of the fruits are rich in edible oils and proteins and are used for food purposes by the Bantu. The MAROELA nut is not, however, a commercial nut in South Africa. The kernel is small, and the shell very hard, and it is unlikely that the nut will ever become a commercial proposition."

Dalziel wrote: "The fruit is yellow, with leathery rind like a mango and similar fibrous soft pulp covering the stone. The taste is acid, but of pleasant flavour when fully ripe. From the expressed juice a fermented beverage like cider is prepared. According to Ozanne, the juice is boiled down to a thick, black consistence and used by the people for sweetening their Guinea-corn gruel. The kernel is oily and edible."

MAROELA *(Sclerocarya caffra)*

ORIENTAL CASHEW *(Semecarpus anacardium)*

K. M. Vaid photo

*(Semecarpus anacardium)*

### *Semecarpus anacardium* (Anacardiaceae)

**MARKING NUT**
**MARANY NUT**
**MARSH NUT**
**ORIENTAL CASHEW**

This genus comprises 40 species in Malaysia, Micronesia and the Solomon Islands.

Bailey explains: "The black, lobe-like, somewhat contorted seed of about 1 inch in length, by ¾ inch wide, and 3/8 inch thick, of an evergreen tree native to the warmer parts of Asia. A very useful ink is made by mixing lime with the green juice of these seeds. It is said that to a considerable extent the natives roast and eat these seeds.

"Unless roasted, these nuts should be handled with great precaution, as in the raw condition they possess extremely poisonous properties similar to those of the American poisons, ivy and sumac, and the cashew, to which it is closely related.

"The tree is abundant in northern and central India. The nut is produced on the apex of the edible enlarged fruit-stalk. The outer shell of the nut yields a black resinous juice which when mixed with lime, makes the ink."

Burkill says: "*Semecarpus* is a genus of 5 kinds of trees in tropical Asia, Malaysia to Australia and Polynesia. Some species have in them an abundance of the poisonous resin which characterizes *Gluta* and *Melanorrhoea*.

"Among others, with less of this resin is *S. anacardium* — MARKING NUT which has, as is well known, an edible fruit. It is the pedicel which swells under the fruit, and can be eaten; when roasted it tastes like an apple. The kernel may be eaten, with caution, and is sometimes on sale in Singapore. The very young fruit, as a pickle in salt and vinegar, is eaten in India. The kernels contain a sweet oil.

"Some species have seeds which serve as food, but they seem to be used with caution. Man *(The Andaman Islanders)* says the Andamanese keep the seeds of the species which they eat for some time before they use them. The preparation is by removing the fruit-wall and licking the seeds clean; then par-boiling, wrapping in bundles in leaves, burying in the soil for several weeks during which fermentation takes place, unearthing and drying; and finally baking.

"In the Moluccas *S. cassuvium,* is one of the species with edible pedicels. Its fruits are even sold in the markets of Amboina. They, too, taste like apples. The fruit itself is oily, and the oil may carry the irritant substance. The kernel is edible, but only if caution is exercised in shelling it, for if juice from the fruit-wall gets on the tongue it is painful."

Sturtevant says: "The nuts of various species of *Semecarpus* are sometimes eaten, particularly those of *S. atra* in New Caledonia, although the fruit contains a latex which can cause extensive blistering.

### *Sorindeia longifolia* (Anacardiaceae)

Dalziel says of this plant in French Guinea:
"The fruits are in grape-like clusters, about 1 in. long, splitting in two leathery halves, with fleshy oily kernel (cotyledons) edible."

HOG PLUM *(Spondias dulcis)*

*Spondias sp.* (Australia)

### *Spondias monbin* (Anacardiaceae) MONBIN HOG PLUM YELLOW SPANISH PLUM

A dozen species of this tree are scattered from Indo-Malaysia to tropical America, with 1-to-5 seeded fruits, several of them edible. The trees are often cultivated. Dalziel says of this one in tropical Africa:

"The fruit is plum-like, with thin, smooth, yellow skin and acid pulp agreeable to the taste; it is supposed to cause dysentery when eaten to excess. The seed also is edible."

## *Tetracarpidium conophorum*    (Euphorbiaceae)

This woody liane up to 100 feet high grows from Sierra Leone to Zaire. Irvine says of it:

"Sometimes cultivated in parts of Africa, for its edible nuts, especially on recently cleared land, and fruiting in its second year. The seeds, which are sold in Freetown market and elsewhere in Fr. Equat. Africa and are palatable, are cooked (e.g. roasted) and often eaten with maize on the cob. They are edible even when raw, and have a bitter taste and a tonic effect like COLA. The leaves and young shoots and fruits are eaten with rice in S. Leone.

"The seeds are eaten like walnuts and can be roasted in the embers."

Dalziel says: "The fruit is a 4-winged and ribbed capsule 2½-3 in. across, containing subglobose seeds about 1 in. long with thin brown shell and yellowish kernel. The kernels of fruits obtained from Cameroons yield up to 59 per cent of a rapidly drying oil, whitish-yellow, with agreeable taste and odour, having a high iodine index, and with physical and chemical characters similar to linseed oil. It is suggested as possibly suitable for edible purposes and for soap-making, and as certainly suitable as a substitute for linseed oil in the varnish and lacquer industry. In Sierra Leone the plant, though growing wild, is often cultivated."

Douglas Elliott photo

KARAKA *(Corynocarpus laevigatus)*

## *Corynocarpus laevigatus*    (Corynocarpaceae)*
### KARAKA

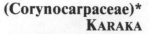

This highly ornamental New Zealand tree with its rich, dark green glossy foliage, was prized by the Maoris as a prime source of food in season.

Laing and Blackwell wrote: "The kernel of the orange-colored, damson-shaped fruit was one of the staple articles of their diet.

"The fruit was first baked for some hours in an earth oven, and then placed in baskets and soaked for a day or two in the waters of a stream or lagoon. The kernels were thereafter washed and knocked about to rid them of adhering flesh and skin, stored away in new baskets, and reserved for use at feasts, or as gifts for neighbouring friendly chiefs."

The *Botanical Magazine* says: "KARAKA of the natives, upon which the eye of the traveller rests with pleasure, furnishes a plum-like fruit, of which the drupaceous coat, when fully ripe of a sweetish taste, is eaten by the natives. The nut or kernel also, upon being deprived by steaming and maceration in salt water of the poisonous property it is said to possess, is held in considerable estimation by the New Zealanders, who collect and use it for food, in seasons of dearth. If eaten without this necessary preparation, the person becomes seized with severe spasmodic pains and convulsions; from which the sufferer, in some cases, does not recover but has been observed to die in great agony in a few hours."

Other species of this tree grow in New Hebrides, New Guinea, New Caledonia and Queensland.

V. C. Davies wrote: "The Maoris had two varieties of this tree they called KARAKA. This is poisonous to eat in its raw state, but was steeped in brackish water for about a month and then used by grinding into meal and is then considered fit to eat. These trees are found growing mostly in coastal areas inhabited by the Maoris."

*Included here because plant families are closely related.

# Chapter 11
# THE ALMOND
## *Queen of the Rose Family*

The ALMOND is unquestionably the Queen of the Rose Family which includes such things as apples, pears, prunes, raspberries and a lot of other delicious eatables. There are a few other edible nuts in the family but they are of little importance either as tidbits or as commercial crops.

The 1974 crop was 230,000,000 pounds (shelled basis) with a farm value of $171,000,000. It accounted for one-half the world's supply. The balance was produced mostly by Spain and Italy, with lesser amounts from Portugal, Morocco, Iran, and other countries of the Mediterranean

ALMONDS in the hull just prior to harvest. The outer hull is removed, revealing a shell, which in turn is removed to obtain the almond.

### *Prunus dulcis*     (Rosaceae)     ALMOND

The ALMOND is a round-headed, bushy tree 20 to 30 feet. At one time orchard trees were pruned to branch low to the ground to facilitate hand harvesting, but now they are trimmed higher to accommodate mechanical equipment.

The ALMOND has been cultivated around the Mediterranean from the most ancient times. Because so extensively planted there, the exact original range is obscure. It is found wild in Algeria and from there into the countries of western Asia bordering the eastern end of the Mediterranean and the Black Sea.

ALMONDS are among the most exacting of all nut crops in their climatic requirements. California is the only state where ALMONDS are grown in commercial quantities. Ideal conditions are found in the great Central Valley (the Sacramento and San Joaquin River basins). In the 400 mile area from below Bakersfield in the south to Red Bluff in the north, 304,000 acres are under cultivation. More than 230,000 of these are in production and another 74,000 are non-bearing, less than four years ago — so bigger crops are in prospect.

In terms of California acreage, ALMONDS are now second only to grapes (646,000 acres) and outrank oranges, walnuts, peaches, and other fruit and nut crops.

region. Today. U.S. imports are negligible. Exports of California ALMONDS, often more than half the total crop, have been rising steadily and reached 104 million pounds (shelled) in 1975. West Germany was our biggest customer.

Each major ALMOND variety is self-sterile (will not pollinate itself), so an orchard must have trees of more than one variety. Nonpareil variety, which is the most consistent and heavy producer, accounts for 55 per cent of all plantings. For pollination, other varieties such as Mission (16 per cent of plantings) and NePlus (7.5 per cent of plantings) are planted in rows with Nonpareil, for a total of 50 to 90 trees per acre. In a good year, many well-managed orchards will produce 2,000 pounds or more of nut meats per acre.

Nonpareil ALMONDS are sold in whole kernel form for a wide range of uses. They are also the basic raw material for manufacturing sliced, blanched, chopped, and slivered almonds, the forms housewives often find in cello bags in the supermarket. Several other varieties of similar characteristics, lumped under the name "California" may also be used.

Other varieties have characteristics that make them useful in specialty products. Mission, for instance, is a shorter, plumper nut, and is quite flavorful when roasted. Thus, it is in demand for chocolate candy bars and in roasted-salted form for snacks. NePlus is a long, thin nut,

The ALMONDS shown in the photograph are: (1) At the top, in the shell; then to the right, (2) Whole natural; (3) Sliced blanched; (4) Diced (or chopped); (5) Blanched slivered; (6) Whole blanched; (7) Sliced natural. The term "natural" in the industry is used to designate almonds that have been shelled but still have their skins on. The process of removing the skin thus results in "blanched" almonds. Both natural and blanched almonds may be further processed into chopped or sliced or slivered forms.

especially useful for candy-coated "Jordan" ALMONDS. Another variety, Peerless, has a hard but light-colored shell, making it most attractive for sale in-the-shell and in nut mixes.

At one time, ALMONDS were sold almost exclusively in-the-shell; now the industry offers barely five per cent that way, and instead sells shelled products in a wide range of convenient, ready-to-use forms.

The ALMOND is a plant of biblical lands and is mentioned often in the Bible. In the 17th chapter of the Book of Numbers the Rod of Aaron is placed in the Tabernacle by Moses and brings forth flowers and ripe ALMONDS, signifying God's special commission to the house of Levi.

It is the opinion of some botanists that the ALMOND of agriculture is not a true species, but rather a very ancient natural hybrid among at least three of the many species of wild ALMONDS found in the arid mountains of the near East and central Asia. The species most frequently thought to have contributed to the cultivated ALMOND are *Prunus bucharia,* a small tree of Russian Turkestan, *P. fenzliana,* a shrubby tree of the dry mountain slopes of Armenia and eastwards, and *P. ulmifolia,* another large shrub or shrubby tree found on the rocky slopes of the Tian Chan and Pamirs in central Asia.

Of the nearly 50 species of wild ALMONDS only a few have sweet kernels. The rest contain a bitter substance, amygdalin, that makes them unfit for most uses although the liquid ALMOND extract used in cooking is generally made from BITTER ALMOND kernels. The occurrence of sweet kernels, and the degree of sweetness, in the ALMONDS, and in the other stone fruits as well, is very sporadic, differing even in different strains of the same species. With the exception of the CHINESE ALMOND, which is the kernel of a variety of plum, none of the other stone fruit kernels, including those of the wild species of ALMONDS, are of any importance as nuts.

## APRICOT
### *Prunus armeniaca* (Rosaceae) CHINESE ALMOND

The apricot is an important fruit in many countries, but only in northern China is it cultivated primarily for the edible kernels. These are an important market crop there.

The kernel is mostly indistinguishable from a small ALMOND. The shell is quite different, however, being darker than the almond, without the pits, and having a thickened rim along the suture line joining the halves.

The CHINESE ALMONDS appear in many traditional Chinese recipes, and may be used as well in the same ways as the ALMOND.

E. H. "Chinese" Wilson, famed plant explorer and later Director of the Arnold Arboretum of Harvard University, reported the use of apricot kernels in China in his *Agricultural Explorations in the Orchards of China.* He wrote:

> Foreigners in China are often served in various homes and hotels with so-called almond cake. One of the main ingredients of this cake is sweet kernels, so closely resembling ALMONDS that even intelligent foreigners believe that they are eating genuine ALMONDS. This supposition has given rise to the statement that ALMONDS grow in China. These so-called CHINESE ALMONDS are the kernels of a particular kind of apricot *(Prunus armeniaca)* grown exclusively for its seeds.
>
> There are several varieties of APRICOTS that produce these seeds. The best one has small red fruit with large, medium-soft stones and sweet kernels. The tree of this particular variety is of very erect growth, quite distinct from all other varieties of apricots. It is propagated by grafting upon seedling stock.
>
> Another variety bears somewhat larger fruit, also of a red color, but the tree is of an open habit. Then there is a yellow-fleshed variety that resembles the preceding one very much in habit of growth. The stones of the last two varieties are not so easily cracked, however, as those of the first-mentioned kind.
>
> Another variety that came under the writer's notice has a bitter kernel, used only in small quantities to give flavor to confectionery.

Sturtevant wrote: "In the oases of Upper Egypt, the fruit of a variety called musch-musch is dried in large quantities for the purpose of commerce. The fruit in general is roundish, orange or brownish-orange, with a more or less deep orange-colored flesh. The kernel in some sorts is bitter, in others as sweet as a nut. Erdman describes the 'wild peach' of Nerchinsk, Siberia, as a true APRICOT, containing a very agreeable kernel in a fleshless envelope."

### *Prinsepia utilis*                                   (Rosaceae)

This is a deciduous, thorny shrub found on the dry rocky hills of the eastern Himalayas. Watt says: "The seed yields an oil by expression which is much used in the North-West Himalaya, for food."

Sturtevant says: "In India an oil is expressed from the seeds, which is used as food and for burning."

COCOPLUM *(Chrysobalanus icaco)*

northern South America, and to tropical Africa. In form, the COCOPLUM varies from a low spreading shrub to a small tree. The fruits are 1 to 2 inches in length and ovoid or globular. The thin skin of the fruit varies from pinkish white, to red, to purplish black. The white, cottony pulp adheres to the single large seed and is somewhat insipid in taste. The COCOPLUM is generally stewed with sugar after the skins have been removed and the seeds can be roasted as nuts.''

Botanists have now moved the COCOPLUM into a family of its own, *Chrysobalanaceae.*

*(Parinari curaetellifolia)*

## COCOPLUM
*Chrysobalanus icaco*  (Rosaceae)  ICACO

Sturtevant says: ''African and American tropics. This tree-like shrub, with its fruit similar to the damson, grows wild as well as cultivated in the forests along the shores of South America, and in Florida. Browne says in Jamaica the fruit is perfectly insipid but contains a large nut inclosing a kernel of very delicious flavor.''

The fruit is ovoid, up to 2 inches long.

Kendal and Julia Morton wrote: ''In the Bahamas, where it may be seen as a low, spreading plant, or as a fair-sized tree, it is so common that the natives go out to gather the fruit in season as one goes out to gather wild strawberries in the North. The fruits are smooth and attractive while on the plant, but the skin is so thin and the white, cottony pulp is so soft that picking and handling leaves the fruits dented and misshapen. This does not impair their usefulness, however, and preserved cocoplums are a popular native product.

''The fruits are generally peeled and cooked down with a good deal of sugar and this causes them to turn a deep purplish-red. In preserving the fruits, each is generally punctured with an ice pick or sail needle, which is driven through the thin shell and kernel of the single large seed. This permits the sirup to penetrate, and the nut-like kernel, after separation from the shell, is eaten with the fruits. Jam and jelly may also be made from the cocoplum and the seeds may be roasted as nuts.''

Kennard & Winters wrote: ''The COCOPLUM is indigenous to the coastal regions from southern Florida to

## *Parinari curatellifolia*  (Chrysobalanaceae)

Willis says that of the 60 kinds of *Parinari* trees scattered through tropical Africa from Senegal, Gold Coast, Nigeria and eastward, some have edible seeds.

Regarding this species which is a small tree to 25 feet bearing hard, brown fruits 1½ inches long, in June, Irvine says:

''The fruits and kernels are eaten in various parts of Tropical Africa. The fruit-pulp is of pleasant flavour and sometimes thought to be one of the best of African wild fruits. The shell is thick.''

Dalziel reports: ''The fruits are also eaten by various animals and have a characteristic sickly smell when decaying. Their pulp has a peculiar flavour like that of an avocado pear, and has been used at times as an important emergency food. A fermented beverage is also made from it. The rather oily kernel, from which a fat can be extracted, is also eaten, and is then mixed with other foods.''

Dale & Greenway say: ''Both pulp and kernels are used for food in West Nile and Madi.''

Sturtevant describes other edible species as follows:

''*Parinari campestre* — French Guiana. The drupe is small, oval, yellow. The single seed is edible.

''*P. montanum* — French Guiana. The drupe is large, ovate, smooth and fibrous, has a thick, acrid rind, and the nut or kernel, is sweet and edible.''

Williamson says the seeds of *P. mobola* or *C. curatellaefolia* make an excellent substitute for almonds.

# Chapter 12
# The
# TROPICAL ALMOND
# and the
# BOMBAX Family
## along with CARYOCAR
## and the SOUARI NUT

In this chapter are several hundred big trees of the tropics in whose fruits are buried seeds that hungry people like to eat.

A lot of them are very big trees, to 100 feet or more. All of them grow only in tropical countries. Perhaps the most famous of them all is the DURIAN which bases its fame on its awful smell. But why should smell interfere with something to eat? Here they are in all their glory.

TROPICAL ALMOND *(Terminalia catappa)*

### *Terminalia catappa*          (Combretaceae)
###                               TROPICAL ALMOND

*Terminalia* comprises 250 kinds of tropical trees mostly in India and Malaysia, prized chiefly for timber, some for dyestuffs, but the fruits of many are edible, a few very fine flavored.

Macmillan says of this species: "A handsome spreading tree, 40-50 ft. high, with large leathery leaves, native of Malaya, commonly grown in most tropical countries. The fruit is of the size of a plum, slightly compressed on two sides, and contains a 1-seeded kernel (drupe), which is edible and not unlike an almond. Firminger considered this to be 'beyond comparison the most delicious nut of any kind India affords'. The tree is deciduous twice a year and bears two crops annually. Thrives from sea-level to about 2000 ft."

Kendall and Julia Morton wrote: "Unrelated to the true ALMOND the TROPICAL or so-called INDIA ALMOND has its origin in southern Asia and has been widely planted throughout the tropical world for ornament and shade.

"The fruits, unlike typical nuts have a tender skin and a thin layer of edible, subacid, juicy flesh. Beneath the flesh, there is a thick, corky shell, and within this is a small, slender kernel with a very thin light brown skin, and crisp, white meat of mild but pleasant flavor. Because of the small size of the kernel and the difficulty of cracking the spongy shell, the nut is little used in the Western Hemisphere."

Kennard & Winters wrote: "The fine-flavored kernels are edible raw or roasted, but very few of the fruits produced in the Western Hemisphere are utilized for food because of difficulty in cracking the shell. Cracking is easier after the nuts dry out, and it might be possible to devise some mechanical means of cracking and cleaning them. In the West Indies they are often cracked between stones by children.

"The kernels yield an edible oil of excellent flavor. Asenjo and Goyco obtained a yield of nearly 55 percent by extraction and 35 percent by expression."

Burkill wrote: "The edible part of the fruit is the green rolled-up embryo. It is exceedingly delicate in flavour, but the trouble of breaking the tenacious husk, in order to get it out, is great. Half the weight of this embryo is in a pale yellow, or pale green odourless oil, which is very like almond oil; but as less than 10 percent of the fruit is embryo, the oil amounts to only 5 percent, which is not enough to pay for extraction."

BELERIC MYRABALAN *(Terminalia belerica)*

Burkill describes another species *T. bellerica* of which he says: "The kernels of the fruit can be eaten, but are dangerous, as they produce what Graham and Roxburgh call intoxication, but Dutt says is a narcotic effect."

60

*Terminalia kaernbachii*. These are the weathered nuts, very different in appearance from the fruits with flesh adhering.

FRUITS bigger than golf balls *(Terminalia kaernbachii)*

head. The flavour is mild and pleasant; nutty, of course. The meat is less oily than *Canarium*."

Macmillan says: "*T. okari*. OKARI-NUT. A large handsome tree bearing ovoid or obovoid fruit, about 7 in. long by 3 in. diameter, deep reddish-purple when ripe. The large kernel, surrounded by a fibrous shell, is about 3 in. long by ¾ in. diameter, and has a dark-brown testa. In its native home the nut is much relished by all classes, being eaten raw or cooked, and prepared in different ways. Probably one of the finest of tropical nuts."

A leaflet from New Guinea botany division says of this nut: "Trees to 140 ft., with spreading crown, diameter to 9 ft., flange-buttressed up to 10 ft. Fruits ellipsoid, more or less laterally compressed, 2.5 - 7 by 1.75 - 3.25 by 1.3 - 2.5 inch, slightly beaked at apex, at first tomentose, nearly glabrous when ripe, the endocarp on cross section with a broad band of very hard sclerenchymatous tissue including in it some irregularly shaped and spaced air-chambers and a rather large cell containing the kernel. Fruits plum red when ripe, slightly succulent.

"Due to its value of a foodstuff for local people this tree is usually excluded from timber lease agreements. An analysis of the fat from the kernel made some years ago by C.S.I.R.O. Division of Organic Chemistry revealed that oil was remarkably similar to butter in constitution and could be described as a vegetable butter."

*Terminalia langanda*

Watt describes these two Indian species with edible nuts: "*T. glabra*. The fruit when ripe is occasionally eaten. The oily kernel, like those of other species of the genus, tastes like a filbert, and is used as an article of food.

Perhaps most astonishing of *Terminalia* seeds, at least on first acquaintance, are those of the OKARI NUT *(T. kaernbachii)* of Papua and New Guinea. They are almost as big as tennis balls and heavy. A dozen of them by airmail from New Guinea cost $38 postage.

Leonard J. Brass of the Archbold Expedition, wrote this author years ago about the OKARI NUT:

"The big, well-flavored OKARI NUT should have a place in your book. P. van Royen' *Manual of the Forest Trees of Papua and New Guinea,* says of it: 'A relatively common, frequently cultivated tree in the lowlands (up to 3,000 feet) from New Georgia to the Aru Islands, including the whole of New Guinea.' In many places the species is without doubt exclusively cultivated. David Fairchild knew of this nut and tried to arrange for its introduction into Hawaii, but I seem to recall that attempts to do this failed, due to the extreme perishability of the seeds. Devilled in the frypan by the camp cook, these nuts go very well with the sundowner, when one is camped in the rain forests of Papua."

E. E. Henty of the Botany service in Lae, New Guinea, wrote: "The kernel varies in size, from 3 cm x 1 cm (spindle-shaped) to the size of a small hen egg. There are 3-4 cotyledons, which are wrapped around each other and in the larger kernels look something like a small cabbage-

*(Terminalia citrina)*

K. M Vaid photo

*(Terminalia chebula)*

"*T. chebula.* Breaking of the nuts is a tedious and costly operation. The kernel resembles an almond or fresh filbert in flavour, and is largely eaten by Natives. It is very palatable, fairly wholesome and nutritious, and is a pleasant dessert fruit."

Sturtevant describes other species bearing edible nuts:

*T. glabrata.* Friendly and Society Islands. The kernels of the fruit are eaten and have the flavor of almonds.

*T. latifolia.* Jamaica. The kernels are eaten and have the flavor of almonds.

*T. litoralis.* Fiji Islands. The seeds are sometimes eaten by children in Viti.

*T. mauritiana.* FALSE BENZOIN. Mauritius and Bourbon. The kernels of the fruit are eaten.

*T. pamea.* Guiana. The tree is cultivated on the Isle of France and elsewhere. The almond-like kernels are good to eat and are served on the better tables of the country.

Seeds of two unidentified species of *Terminalia* from the Solomon Islands.

Regarding Polynesia, Barrau says: "Various species of *Terminalia* produce edible nuts which are commonly used by the Melanesians. *T. catappa* is probably the most important. The nuts of certain other species of *Terminalia* require washing and cooking before being eaten."

Geoff. F. C. Dennis on Santa Ana Island, Solomon Islands, found two unidentified *Terminalia* trees and sent the seeds (pictured here) with this comment: "Beachside trees of medium height and leaning habit. Its many small red fruits are valued for both their sweet flesh and the seed kernels, eaten raw, especially by children. This collection is from two separate trees, growing in contact with each other, one bearing much pulpier fruit than the other. Uncultivated."

Julia Morton photo

RANGOON CREEPER *(Quisqualis indica)*

## *Quisqualis indica*        (Combretaceae)
### RANGOON CREEPER

Sturtevant says: "An erect shrub, for a few feet, grows into a large woody vine from 6 to 25 feet long. It is from southeast Asia and Malaysia, including the Philippines, and is grown ornamentally in many other regions. Ripe seeds taste like coconut and are used for food, though even a few seeds cause some people to become ill.

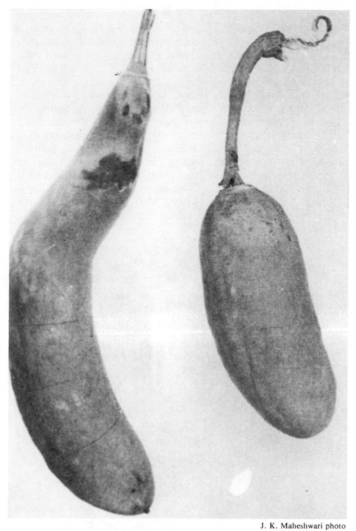

BAOBAB *(Adansonia digitata)*

## *Adansonia digitata* (Bombacaceae) BAOBAB, SOUR GOURD MONKEY BREAD

One of the largest and also one of the most useful of trees is the BAOBAB with its 30-foot-diameter trunk. In full leaf, in flower and fruit, it is also one of the most beautiful of trees. Loyd Schaad, writing from Angola says: "These very useful plants with large groupings of trees found in present and especially past village locations, are resistant to the annual winter dry season grass fires. Gossweiler states that 300 years ago the tree was especially useful to the local natives for their fibers, even to the making of a coarse cloth. These days they continue to use the hand-made strings and ropes from the trunk of these trees for sewing the umbrella fern or papyrus mats, making ropes for their bird and animal snares, hunting nets, and every-day ropes. The leaves of these trees are useful cooked as a vegetable. The dry pulp is said to contain cream-of-tartar and is eaten raw or made into drinks by the villagers. Throughout the large seed pod there are small black seeds imbedded and used in the native diet, especially in drought years or at the end of the winter dry season when food is scarce. Our family has eaten the oil-rich seed that takes a lot of time and patience to prepare, because it is small and has to first be soaked overnight in water and then shelled before cooking — takes a lot of seeds about the size of an apple seed to fill a small pan. The seedcoat is black but the inside is white."

Fanshawe writes from Zambia: "Roasted seeds are used in Malawi as a relish in place of groundnuts. Roasted seeds are also used as a coffee substitute. Seeds have an oil content of up to 11%."

Irvine says: "The seeds, widely used as food, are prepared sometimes by roasting, sometimes by soaking and fermenting in much the same way as those of *Parkia,* and are said to taste like almonds. Ground and mixed with millet meal, they are made up into thin gruel and drunk. Washed, pounded and steeped in water for 10 days, they are used in NW. Ashanti to flavor soup. Nankanis boil the seeds, together with those of BAMBARRA *(Voandzeia)* and GEOCARPA *(Kerstingiella)* groundnuts for food.

"The thick seed-coat is hard to separate from the kernel, and forms more than half the weight of the seed. Decorticated, the kernels have yielded nearly 15 per cent of fat by ether extraction. In parts of Senegal the oil is extracted by boiling, and used in a certain festive dish, while in Fr. W. Africa groundnut oil is diluted with it; but on the whole it is rarely used in W. Africa."

Sturtevant says: "The BAOBAB is cultivated in many of the warm parts of the world.

"The earliest description of the *Baobab* is by Cadamosto, 1454, who found at the mouth of the Senegal, trunks whose circumference he estimated at 112 feet. Perrottet says he has seen those trees 32 feet in diameter and only 70 to 85 feet high."

Burkill says: "A genus of six to eight trees most of them African or Madagascan, two or three in Australia. Seeds are often cooked and used as food, tasting like almonds."

Audas: "*Native Trees of Australia* wrote of *A. gregorii:* "The large seed cones which are hairy when young and hard-shelled when mature, about 8 inches in length, contain a mass of bread-y matter used by the aborigines, with numerous seeds about the size of a large pea, which are held to be nutritious."

SILK COTTON TREE *(Ceiba pentandra)* in Thailand

## *Ceiba pentandra* (Bombacaceae) SILK COTTON

Originally South American, the SILK FLOSS tree is now planted around villages throughout the tropics, for it produces great quantities of many useful products. The trees are chiefly in secondary forests, and special precautions are taken to protect them from fire.

Irvine writes: "One of the largest trees in W. Africa, up to 160 ft. or more high, diameter 6 ft. or more, girth up to 25 ft. above buttresses, latter prickly, plank-like, and extending 12 ft. or more up the trunk; crown pyramidal and spreading, main branches horizontal and bracketed to stem, young trees with whorled branches. It is irregularly deciduous, even from branch to branch. Flowers (Nov.-Feb.) at ends of branches, creamy white, when leafless, sometimes flowering progressively from branch to branch. Fruits (Jan.-Mar.), capsules up to 6-10 in. long x 2-3 in. turning brown and usually splitting into 5 valves. An adult tree produces 1,000 - 4,000 fruits.

"The seeds contain 22-25 per cent of oil, 17-18 per cent, of which can usually be expressed. Cold-drawn oil can be classed with GROUND NUT oil and used for culinary purposes. It has an agreeable taste and smell rather resembling cotton-seed oil, but is slightly more drying. Though not used in Ghana, it is suitable for lubrication and soap-making as well as for cooking; and it has been tried in Senegal on the railway as a lamp oil and in paint-making.

"Pounded and ground to a meal (the oil not being expressed), the seeds are often used in W. Africa in soup, or eaten, after being roasted, by the Hausas. Coull states that in the N. T. they are prepared as a food or seasoner like those of *Parkia*."

Burkill says: "In various places the seeds are eaten. This is recorded as done by Malays, Javanese, and in Celebes. Sometimes they are germinated before use. Only small quantities are consumed, as they upset the digestion."

DURIAN FRUIT *(Durio zibethinus)*

Isaac Ho Sai-Yuen photo

## *Durio zibethinus* (Bombacaceae) DURIAN NUT, CIVET FRUIT

These prized edible seeds are from a big, famous Malayan tree to 80 feet or more, the fruit of which is distinguished for its fine flavor and disgusting smell.

Lindley says: "The fruit varies in shape, being either globular or oval, and measures as much as 10 inches in length; it has a thick hard rind, entirely covered with very strong sharp prickles, and is divided into five cells, each of which contains from one to four seeds rather larger than pigeon's eggs and completely enveloped in a firm luscious-looking, cream-colored pulp."

Bailey says: "The seeds are roasted and eaten as are chestnuts."

Macmillan says: "This celebrated fruit produced on strong, mature branches, varies in shape from round to ovoid, is yellow when ripe and usually weighs from 6 to 8 lbs., sometimes as much as 10 lb. or more. It is armed with thickly set, sharp-pointed spikes about ½ in. long, and possesses when mature a very offensive odour, more especially so on first acquaintance. The white custard-like pulp surrounding the seed is highly relished and regarded as an aphrodisiac by Malays and others; it is also esteemed by some Europeans who acquire a taste for it once the smell is overcome. It has been described as resembling blanc-mange, delicious as the finest cream, whilst according to Russel Wallace the sensation of eating durians is worth a voyage to the East. Others have compared it to French custard passed through a sewer pipe. Malays preserve the fruit in salt for use all the year round. The large seeds may be roasted and eaten like nuts."

Botanic Garden, Penang photo

DURIAN

Ochse says: "The seeds from ripe fruits are often roasted in hot ashes, cut into slices and fried in spiced coconut oil to be eaten with rice, or covered with sugar and consumed as a sweetmeat."

Anton Smith photo

GUYANA CHESTNUT *(Pachira aquatica)*

## Pachira aquatica      (Bombacaceae)
### GUYANA CHESTNUT

This 15 foot tree from the American tropics is cultivated all over the world for its delicious, edible seeds. Of trees in Hawaii, Neal writes:

"The woody, ovoid, five-valved fruit is 4 to 12 inches long and contains rounded seeds, without floss, 0.5 inch or more in diameter, edible raw or roasted. This tree is sometimes called MALABAR CHESTNUT in Hawaii. Among Central American names are SABA NUT and PROVISION TREE."

Schaad writes from Angola: "*P. aquatica,* called the CASTANHA DE GUIANA by the local Portuguese, is growing in limited amounts on their plantations. It is grown commercially in the Congo. It is a low-growing evergreen tree very resistant to drought and adverse conditions, reaching about 10 feet or so in height. When the large fruits are ripe they split open like a walnut and discharge their many nuts to the ground. If there are showers they will sprout on the surface of the soil. Without rains they will sun-dry, or must be protected from moisture until dried in the sun. They are a tasty nut when roasted or fried with oil. Enclosed is a picture of the fruit before opening, being held by one of our school girls. We have about a dozen of the trees growing here on the mission station."

Barrau wrote: "The GUIANA CHESTNUT *(P. aquatica)* has been introduced into Ponape and into Tahiti."

Standley, writing of *P. aquatica* in Mexico. says: "Seeds cooked and eaten, taste like chestnuts."

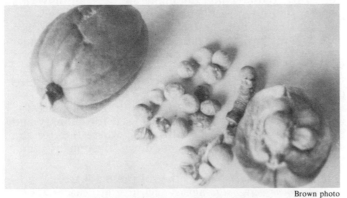

GUYANA CHESTNUT *(Pachira aquatica)*    Brown photo

SABA NUT *(Pachira aquatica)*    Loyd Schaad photo

Sturtevant says: "When roasted, taste like chestnuts. The young leaves and flowers are used as a vegetable. There is nothing better than this chestnut cooked with a little salt." He continues:

"*P. grandiflora,* West Indies. The seeds are eaten as chestnuts are.

"*P. insignis,* Mexico and Guiana. The seeds, young leaves and flowers serve as food."

Burkill says: "The seeds contain oil, as do those of *Bombax, Ceiba, Gossypium,* and other allied genera. This oil makes about 50 per cent of the weight of the seeds of *P. aquatica* and *P. insignis.* The oil has a smell suggesting liquorice and fenugreek."

F. C. Hoehne wrote: "The seeds of many species of the *Bombax* family are rich in oil which is edible. The *Pachina insignis* is an indigenous species which could and should be considered a fruit, because it produces seeds contained in capsules which are commonly called MARANHAO NUT and should not be confused with the PARA NUT nor its far-reaching benefits as edible material. Other species of the genus have edible seeds, but of little nutritive value."

Photo from *Fifty Tropical Fruits of Nassau* by Kendal and Julia Morton
ROSELLE *(Hibiscus sabdariffa)*

### RED SORREL
## Hibiscus sabdariffa    (Malvaceae)    ROSELLE

This seems to be the world champion all-around food plant, native of west tropical Africa. Dalziel writes:

"Cultivated for leaf, fleshy calyx, seed or fibre. Wild or naturalised forms are often spiny.

"The succulent calyx, after the flower fades, is used either fresh or dried, as a common pot-herb for soup or in the form of a sauce or relish. Soup made from the dried article is sold in markets. In cakes or balls it is called chafalfalo in Hausa markets. A beverage is also made by boiling, sweetening with sugar-cane and flavouring with ginger, Guinea grains, etc. Europeans use the calyx for jelly, chutney, etc.; also as a refreshing drink or made into a wine or syrup. The leaves are used as a pot-herb.

"The seeds pounded into meal, are used as food, chiefly as an oily soup or sauce made after roasting. The oil is extracted by parching the seeds and then placing them for three or four days in water made alkaline with ashes, after which they are pounded and the oil floats off; or the seeds are crushed and boiled and the oil skimmed off, the residue being used for food, either in soup or made up with beans and other articles into cakes, etc."

65

SOUARI NUT *(Caryocar nuciferum)*

## *Urena lobata* (Malvaceae)

Fanshawe writes: "The seeds are used in W. Africa in soups and cereals for their mucilaginous qualities."

## *Caryocar nuciferum* (Caryocaraceae)
## SOUARI NUT
## BUTTER NUT

Of the 20 kinds of *Caryocar* trees in northern South America, this is perhaps best known. Macmillan says: "This is a handsome lofty tree, attaining 80-100 feet. It bears a large, roundish, woody fruit, about the size of a child's head, containing 3-5 large, kidney-shaped seeds, which have a very hard, woody, warty and reddish shell. The kernels have a pleasant nutty taste, and are esteemed for confectionery and fruitarian dishes; they contain 60 per cent of fatty oil."

Blossfeld writes from Brazil: "The fruit is a globular berry with a rather hard outer shell, though not woody. The shell is covered by corky ridges and contains a sweet pulp, that may be drawn off by making two holes on opposite sides and sucking on one of them. Thereafter, the shell is crushed and the seeds withdrawn. In some species, these have terribly hard spines on the seed coat, and offer a real danger to the unprepared consumer. But with a pair of pliers, the spiny shell can be removed and the kernel, after roasting, is delicious. It can be roasted or cooked in salt water and contains much oil, though this hardens at ordinary temperature like butter, but is excellent for preparing meat, fish, or bakery. The SOUARI NUT, along with PUPUNHA *(Bactris)* and ACAI *(Euterpe oleracea)* are the most popular articles of food in the Amazon region.

Bailey says: "In fineness of texture and in richness of flavor, this nut is said to excel any other nut of the tropics."

John Chiswick wrote from Guyana: "The SOUARI NUT trees (pronounced SOW-A-REE, the sow to rhyme with HOW) that I have seen were growing on white sand and leafmould about 25 miles south of Georgetown, where the vast equatorial forest of South America begins. They were large, lofty, spreading-trees with several sturdy, 15 foot buttresses. The nuts were scattered among the rotting leaves on the forest floor, and care had to be taken in searching for them as the deadly fer-de-lance lies coiled among the fallen nuts, waiting for the rodents which will come to eat them. A large percentage of the kernels are spoilt through insect damage. It is a less oily nut than the BRAZIL NUT *(Bertholettia excelsa)* and has a flavor similar to filberts or Kentish COB NUTS. Unfortunately it is difficult to open the shell without fragmenting the delicate kernel.

"It was grown experimentally at the Government Experimental Farm at Ondemeeming early in the century, but as far as I am aware, it is nowhere cultivated in Guyana today. I have found seedlings difficult to grow, even here."

Regarding another species, *C. brasiliensis* which grows near the sea farther south in Brazil, Blossfeld writes: "In early fall it produces a great quantity of oval fruits, covered by a pulp which may be eaten, but is laxative. The seeds are generally in number four or six and have a rough surface and an oily kernel. This kernel is much appreciated by the poor people as a substitute for fat, for making all kinds of food. When the kernels are shelled and pressed cold, the fat is of excellent taste and solid like butter; when boiled, it becomes almost liquid, but has not so good a taste.

"There is another species in northeastern Brazil, *C. coriaceum*. The fruit is spherical, at first green, yellowish when ripe, with a whitish pulp. The pulp is oily and may be eaten raw, but is mostly cooked with rice, to prepare a nourishing food. This species has generally but one seed, but sometimes two or up to four. The seed has a shell full of sharp, hard and dangerous spines. Removing the spiny shell, one obtains the clean, oily nut, highly esteemed as a nourishing food, mostly added crushed to other food and cooked with beans or rice. But in some areas, where the tree is frequent, the nuts are gathered and their oil extracted by cold pressing, obtaining an excellent oil with a peculiar, not disagreeable odour, highly nourishing.

"This tree has been protected against destruction by law in several regions, where the people at harvest time wander for long distances to stay in the natural groves for several weeks, extracting nuts, pressing oil and selling the pulp from the fresh fruits. This happens annually in the Cariri district of northeastern Brazil.

"There are several other species in Brazil, all called PEQUIA and of several, the seeds are used for culinary and other purposes, in the rural districts, where the tree can still be found. But is has been cut down for so many years, that it is scarce now."

Sturtevant describes five other of these nut trees:

*Caryocar amygdaliferum.* A high tree in Ecuador. The kernel of the nut is edible and has the taste of almonds.

*C. amygdaliforme.* Peru. The tree bears nuts that taste like almonds.

*C. butyrosum.* Guyana. This plant is cultivated for its nuts in Cayenne. These are esculent and taste somewhat like a BRAZIL NUT.

*C. glabrum* Guyana. It furnishes edible nuts. It is sometimes cultivated. Natives make much use of the nuts.

*C. tomentosum.* Guyana. The plant bears a sweet edible nut.

A. Dugand writes from Colombia: "*C. amydaliferum* is found in humid evergreen forests in the Central Magdalena Valley. A related species grows at the eastern base of the Eastern Cordillera, in the drainage system of the Orinoco and Amazon Rivers, and at least three others are found along the Rio Guaninia on the Colombia-Venezuela border.

"The Central Magalena species, locally known as ALMENDRON (meaning "big almond"), is a large tree about 30 meters tall. The drupe-like fruit is somewhat globose, with a yellow pulp containing three to four bean-shaped seeds which are woody and covered with thorn-like tubercles; the oily kernels are edible; the thick oil is sometimes used by natives for cooking, and the nuts are roasted and eaten."

# Chapter 13
# SANDALWOOD —
# Australia's Delight

The genus *Santalum,* always referred to by its common name of SANDALWOOD, comprises some 25 kinds of trees in Malaysia, India, and Australia to eastern Polynesia, but only a few of its relatives are commercially important. Most of the 400 plants involved are semi-parasitic herbs, shrubs or trees, rather after the style of MISTLETOE *(Loranthus).*

However two or three kinds in Australia are cultivated for their edible nuts. The famed fragrant SANDALWOOD of commerce, is supplied by a tree in India, but it is not a nut-bearer.

Harry Oakman photo

NATIVE PEACH *(Eucarya acuminata)*

## *Eucarya acuminata* (Santalaceae) NATIVE PEACH

This northern Australian tree, according to Burkill, bears fruit "which is much eaten. The kernels are edible and very rich in oil."

It is possible this author confuses this tree with *Santalum acuminatum.* (q.v.)

QUANDONG *(Santalum acuminatum)*

## *Santalum acuminatum* (Santalaceae) QUANDONG NATIVE PEACH

P. R. Wycherley, director of the Botanic Garden at Perth, West Australia, writes:

"*Santalum acuminatum.* The outer flesh of the fruit is red and pulpy. It is cooked in pies, made into jam and chutney. The nut, enclosed in the flesh, although quite hard to crack, has a kernel eaten by many people, both aborigines and others.

"*Santalum spicatum.* This is the sandalwood (timber) of commerce in Australia. The trees have been very heavily exploited in the past. The outer flesh of the fruit is too thin to be eaten or cooked. The hard shell (probably endocarp) is thinner than is *S. acuminatum* and the edible seed is somewhat larger. The hard shell of *S. spicatum* can be crushed by hand, whereas you must take nutcrackers or a hammer to *S. acuminatum. S. spicatum* kernels are edible and eaten. I classify them as the best of the local nuts, both for flavour and relative ease of extraction.

Paul Wycherly photo

QUANDONG *(Santalum acuminatum)*

"*S. acuminatum* occurs disjointedly throughout the southwest and into the desert areas of central Australia. *S. spicatum* is somewhat more restricted in distribution; it occurs on slightly heavier soils and in areas of lower rainfall than *S. acuminatum.*"

Dr. M. S. Buttrose, CSIRO, Box 350, Adelaide, South Australia 5001, has been studying the QUANDONG with a view to its improvement as a soft fruit and/or nut. He writes:

"Both the flesh and the nut are edible. The nut is really good eating if slightly roasted. It has a high oil content (60%), and about 25% protein. The plant grows in low rainfall country, but responds well to better conditions. It is a partial root parasite.

"Our aim is to understand how the plant works so that we can get it established easily and possibly overcome the need for a host plant. Our second aim is to improve fruit and nut quality by selection and, later, breeding."

67

SANDALWOOD *(Santalum spicatum)*

Paul Wycherly photo

*Santalum* is described in various reference books under the generic names *Fusanus* and *Eucarya,* although Willis keeps Eucarya distinct as comprising four species in southern and eastern Australia.

J. M. Black in the *Flora of South Australia* indicates that not only is the succulent covering of the stone eaten by natives, but the seed is cracked and the kernel is also used for native food.

A. B. & J. W. Cribb: *Wild Food in Australia* says: "*Santalum acuminatum (Fusanus acuminatus).* This small inland tree is best known for its edible fruits, but within the pitted stone is an oily, edible seed."

J. H. Maiden: *Useful Native Plants of Australia* says:

"The kernels of the nuts (QUANDONGS) of this small tree are not only palatable and nutritious, but they are so full of oil that if speared on a stick or reed they will burn entirely away with a clear light, much in the same way as CANDLE NUTS *(Aleurites triloba)* do. QUANDONGS are so abundant in parts of the country that they may possibly be used as oil-seeds in the future."

# Chapter 14

# GUARANA

## *The Most Exciting Nut in the World*
## With the AKEE and the GENIP

The reader will find the Sapindaceae one of the most interesting families in this book. Even the television announcers have not yet dreamed up a vision like this.

### *Paullinia cupana* (Sapindaceae) GUARANA

The following is an abridged translation from Vol. 3 of M. Pio Correa's *Useful Plants of Brazil* by Harry Blossfeld of Sao Paulo:

"One of the species in warm America, this is a climbing shrub, up to 10 m. high, with very dark bark and clustered branches of 4 - 8 mm. diameter, deeply furrowed by 4 to 5 angles, dark pubescence on young parts; basic trunk single and woody (hence it may be called a tree); leaves pinnate, with 5 leaflets on a common petiole 7 to 15 cm. long, glabrous same as rachis, which however is channelled above and concave below, and somewhat striated.

"Flowers small, aromatic, with 3 to 5 sepals of 3 mm. length and oblong petals of 3-5 mm. length, very hairy, having on the inside crested scales. Inflorescence in pendulous circinnate cymes — 10 cm. long; fruit a pear-shaped capsule, divided into 3 splitting locules, 1 cm. in diameter — of red or yellow color — containing one or two globular or ovoid seeds 12 mm. length, black with an arillus that changes color from white to yellow and red. This plant has never been found in a wild state and has been cultivated for centuries by a few Indian tribes, specially by the Maues who lived at the middle and superior Amazonas region and were known as living in fixed settlements as keen agriculturists. At present about 60.000 kilograms of prepared GUARANA is sold per year through the markets of Manaus and principally Cuiaba, since the latter capital of the State of Mato Grosso is the center of popular demand of the product.

"The seeds are plucked one by one by measure of their successive ripeness, the pulp and arillus are removed by rubbing in water, the clean seeds are then dried in the sun and then roasted on a pan or earthenware pot with frequent, frequent stirring, until the shells become brittle. Then the hot seeds are put into a strong bag of tucum fibers and beaten with a kudgel, to remove the shells, which is afterwards completed by hand. The clean kernels thus obtained are then crushed in a mortar, eventually after again being baked a short time, to expel their humidity. Thus is obtained a fine, dry powder, which is exposed during one night to the humid air and dew, absorbing so much humidity that it can be formed into cakes, bars or figures of a lizard, a snake etc., these cakes are then slowly dried in an oven, with little heat, during two or three weeks, the fires kept uninterruptedly by day and by night and after this period the prepared cakes become as hard as a brickstone, reddish black or purple black and when polished may look like a piece of hard asphalt. This is the GUARANA of commerce. It contains about 5% of caffeine, much more than coffee, tea or cacao, and a number of other alkaloids with stimulating and digestive properties. The commercial modern GUARANA is not prepared by crushing in a mortar, but the whole roasted seeds are ground without previously removing the hulls, so that the final product contains only 4.2% of caffeine.

"The stick of GUARANA is present in each and every house in Mato Grosso for daily use. It is rubbed against a grate or against the palatine bone of the piracuru-fish which is like a file with sharp and hard teeth, so that a powder is obtained, of which a teaspoonful is spread on the surface of a cup with cold water. The GUARANA powder dissolves readily and a reddish brown solution is then drunk which has a very agreeable taste when mixed with sugar but is quite bitter when consumed alone. In spite of the high caffeine content, it acts extremely slowly, and during four to six hours it stimulates circulation and entirely frees the human body from the drowsy condition overcoming a person that took a heavy meal with plenty of meat or fish into a stomach that did not receive any food since the previous evening. The Brazilians do not eat anything in the morning and work hard from sunrise to midday. The GUARANA drink eliminates the siesta which is the rule in other parts of Latin America and imposes to the Brazilians another regime of living without the two-hour interruption at noon. The custom of taking a GUARANA refreshment is little known outside of Brazil and is peculiar to the two neighboring states of Mato Grosso and Amazonas, where the plant is supposed to be native. People who are accustomed to it, swear that it improves health, helps digestion, prevents sleepiness, increases mental activity and many whisper, that it improves also sexual activity, though doctors believe that this may be, but also it might act as a limiting factor to fertility.''

Sturtevant says: ''Brazil. The seeds are mingled with cassava and water and allowed to ferment, forming the favorite drink of the Orinoco Indians. The pounded seeds form GUARANA bread. This bread is made by the Indians and is highly esteemed in Brazil. The bread is grated into sugar and water and forms a diet drink. Its active principle is a substance called guaranine, which is identical in composition with the thein of tea.''

Henfrey says of *P. subrotunda:* ''The seeds of this plant are eaten.''

MAHOE *(Alectryon macrococcus)*

## *Alectryon macrococcus* (Sapindaceae) MAHOE

This Hawaiian tree is very rare, and is to be found only in isolated forest areas. Rock says other species grow in New Zealand and Malaya.

Rock continues: ''The MAHOE is medium-sized to 25 feet, an ungainly tree.

''The fruits, which are of very large size, have the color of a potato and are perfectly smooth. They hang in clusters from the branches and become ruptured when mature, the fissure being irregular, exposing a bright scarlet aril and the glossy surface of the chestnut-brown orbicular seed, giving an altogether unpleasing contrast.

''The MAHOE is endemic to the Hawaiian Islands, and is remarkable for its fruits, which are the largest in the genus.

''The name MAHOE meaning 'twins', undoubtedly refers to the double fruits, which are not uncommon in our *Alectryon.*''

Degener says: ''Mature fruit 3-7 cm. in diameter, subglobose and simply of one coccus or more or less double with second coccus normal or commonly more or less aborted, pendent, glabrous. Aril firm, fleshy but hardly juicy, scarlet throughout, edible, shiny, slightly softer than

apple in consistency and resembling peach in flavor and odor. The Hawaiians ate both the aril and the kernel.''

Julia Morton photo

AKEE *(Blighia sapida)*

## *Blighia sapida* (Sapindaceae) AKEE

Sturtevant quotes Under as saying: ''The seeds have a fine flavor when cooked and roasted with the fleshy aril.''

Neal says: ''A native tree of Guinea, named for Captain Bligh of the Bounty, is an ornamental tree 30 to 40 feet high. The fruit is attractive — a yellow to red, thick-walled, three-valved, somewhat pear-shaped capsule about 3 inches long, containing firm, white, nut-flavored pulp and three globose, shiny, black seeds. The raw pulp is said to be poisonous when green or overripe, but if ripe is wholesome food. It is also fried or boiled. The seed coat is poisonous.''

Isaac Ho Sai-Yuen photo

NOSSI BE *(Crossonephelis penangensis)*

## *Crossonephelis penangensis* (Sapindaceae)

Willis says there is only one species, on the island of Nossi Be, Madagascar.

In *Pflanzenreigh,* Baillon describes *C. pervillei* as an 18-foot tree with sparse small foliage, small flowers in spikes, but there is no mention of fruit.

Isaac Ho Sai-Yuen, a forester in Kuala Lumpur, Malaya, supplied the accompanying photograph of the fruit of *C. penangensis,* with this note: "Kernel boiled and eagerly eaten."

### *Cubilia blancoi*    (Sapindaceae)    KUBILI

This Philippine tree, found also in the Moluccas and Celebes, reaches 50 feet. Brown says of it:

"The fruit is oval, about 5 centimeters long, and covered with very numerous, pointed projections. It contains a large, starchy nut which is about the size and color of a chestnut, and in Baguio, where it is sold in the market, is called CASTANAS. The nut is of good quality but is rather lacking in flavor. According to Wester the edible portion contains 48.24 per cent water; 1.47 per cent ash; 1.21 per cent crude fiber; 5.20 per cent protein; 1.92 per cent fat; 23.13 per cent starch; 18.83 per cent other carbohydrates; and gives 2,057 calories per kilo. These figures show that the nut is really very nutritious."

But there are differences of opinion. Otto Weber wrote: "It is one of the good-flavored nuts, boiled or roasted."

Fuller says: "The nut is said to be of excellent quality when boiled or roasted and consists mainly of starch or carbohydrates with about 2 per cent fat and 5 per cent protein."

### *Cupania americana*    (Sapindaceae)

*Cupania* is a genus of 55 kinds of trees in warmer parts of America. This species grows in Mexico. Sturtevant says:

"The sweet, chestnut-like seeds are used in the West Indies as a food. The seeds have the flavor of chestnuts or sweet acorns and are used on the banks of the Orinoco to make a fermented liquor."

The Australian tree *Cupaniopsis anacardioides* which is occasionally planted in Florida as a salt-resistant street tree, is not related to *Cupania.* Australians called their tree TUCKEROO, CARROTWOOD, and unfortunately, sometimes CUPANIA. Its seeds are inedible.

*(Deinbollia oblongifolia)*

### *Deinbollia grandifolia*    (Sapindaceae)

*Deinbollia* is a genus of 40 species of trees in tropical Africa and Madagascar.

Dalziel says of this species: "The fruit contains a single seed in a pulp which is said to be edible. Also the seeds are slightly oily and edible."

Julia Morton photo

GENIP *(Melicoccus bijugatus)*

### *Melicoccus bijugatus*    (Sapindaceae)    GENIP MAMONCILLO SPANISH LIME

This West Indian fruit was described by Kendal and Julia Morton thus:

"The MAMONCILLO is grown both as an ornamental and as a dooryard fruit tree and, with its limbs laden with their big clusters of fruits, it is exceedingly handsome.

"The fruits are much like small green limes in outward appearance and have a leathery but somewhat brittle skin and a thin layer of pulp that clings tenaciously to a large seed. They are popular with children who are adept at popping open the shell and letting the slippery, juicy ball of pulp and seed slide into the mouth. Fruits of normal size have a single oval seed, while the occasional larger fruits have two, and the starchy white kernels of these seeds are sometimes eaten as nuts, preferably after roasting."

Neal says: "A slow growing tropical American tree is cultivated in Hawaii for its fruit, both the pulp and the roasted seeds of which are edible. The fruit is a smooth-skinned, green ovoid drupe about 1 inch long and has yellow, juicy, grape-flavored, scanty pulp surrounding one large seed."

### *Otophora fruticosa*    (Sapindaceae)    LANAU

This small genus of trees is found in southeastern Asia and Malaysia.

The fruits of some species are eaten. The dark red fruits of *O. fruticosa,* are used in the Philippine Islands, where the roasted seeds taste like chestnuts.

## Pappea capensis    (Sapindaceae)  WILD PLUM

Sturtevant says: "South Africa. The fruit is edible, and an edible, though slightly purgative, oil is expressed from its seed."

Willis says: "3 species (or 1 variable) in tropical and South Africa. This is the 'wild preume' of South Africa with edible fruit; oil is obtained from the seeds."

## Pometia pinnata    (Sapindaceae)  FIJIAN LONGAN  LANGSIR

This medium sized tree grows throughout Malaysia. Burkill says the oily seeds are eaten after roasting.

Neal says: "A medium to large tree is found from Malaysia east into Polynesia. Fruits are subglobose, 0.5 to 2 inches in diameter, with smooth, thin, brownish rind and pulpy seeds, which are edible when roasted."

William F. Whitman of Rare Fruit Council International wrote: "The newly set fruit is a vivid Chinese red which, upon reaching pea size, gradually disappears and fades into green. The smooth, nearly round to oblong-round, green fruit reaches a diameter of 1¾ inches or more at maturity. Borne in clusters like the lychee, they weigh about eleven to the pound. The semi-transparent, juicy, white flesh contains a single marble-size seed, which may be eaten boiled or roasted. The tree flowers in September in Florida and bears in December."

SOAPBERRY *(Sapindus saponaria)*

## Sapindus indicum    (Sapindaceae)

This comprises 13 species of shrubs and trees in the south Pacific, often called SOAPBERRY because the fruits of some may be used as soap.

Of *S. indicum,* Burkill writes: "The seeds contain 50 per cent of a thick, greenish, drying oil. They can be eaten when quite ripe, but care should be taken to put nothing more than the seed into the mouth as the latex, which is in the fruit wall, is caustic."

## Schleichera trijuga   (Sapindaceae) CEYLON OAK  LAC TREE

This large, deciduous tree is found from the sub-Himalayas eastward to Java. Watt says: "The seeds yield an oil which is used in Malabar for culinary and lighting purposes. It is reputed to be the original Macassar oil, and has recently reappeared in German commerce under that name."

AMERICAN BLADDER NUT *(Staphylea pinnata)*

## Staphylea pinnata  (Sapindaceae)  BLADDER NUT

There are 10 species of BLADDER NUT in the north Temperate Zone. Sturtevant says this European plant is cultivated in shrubberies. Haller says the kernels of the fruit taste like PISTACHIOS and are eaten in Germany by children.

Sturtevant adds: "*S. trifolia,* the AMERICAN BLADDER NUT, has seeds containing a sweet oil and these are sometimes eaten like PISTACHIOS."

Bailey says: "The fruit of a shrub common in eastern and northern United States. Triangular in form, measuring from 1¼ to 1¾ inches in length by about ¾ inch in width, covered with a thin papery shell of a reddish brown or buckwheat color, and having a rather long, sharp point at the apex. Fruit three-celled, each cell containing several (usually three) small, smooth and very hard shining seeds. Fruits remain on shrubs during winter. Of use only as ornamentals."

71

# Chapter 15
# The JAK FRUIT and BREAD FRUIT
## of the Mulberry Family (Moraceae)

Of the 50 kinds of trees and shrubs in this group, most are tropical and include many useful plants. Besides fruits like the FIG *(Ficus),* and those described in this chapter, it includes many useful trees like *Broussonetia* (paper), *Castilloa* (rubber), *Brosimum* (milk), *Ficus* (Caoutchouc, lak, timber, etc.) It starts off BIG with the JAK FRUIT.

Paul Root photo

JAK FRUIT *(Artocarpus heterophyllus).* This is first cousin to the BREADFRUIT *(A. communis)* but it grows much larger, sometimes to 20 pounds, so that it is forced to hang from the tree's trunk, rather than from the branches.

## *Artocarpus heterophyllus* (Moraceae) JAK FRUIT

The enormous fruits of this evergreen member of the mulberry family feed millions of people in India, Malaysia and Indo-China, growing readily from seed in wet, tropical areas. F. H. Popham writes:

"These enormous fruit hang on short stout stalks from the branches and from the trunk also in older trees, making an unusual sight. A Sinhalese fable maintains that the older the tree the lower down the trunk grow the fruit. They are usually oblong in shape, with a rough knobby surface, and they are one of the largest fruit in the world, being rivalled only by marrows and pumpkins. A well-

grown fruit weighs as much as 75 pounds and a tree in its prime can produce fifty fruits in a season.

"JAK FRUIT is eaten mostly as a vegetable in curries, being cooked within a day or two of picking. It is a bland food when cooked in simple style, being used as a substitute for rice, potatoes, manioc, and as a cheap source of bulk.

"The seeds when roasted are delicious to eat, recalling roasted chestnuts at Christmas in Western countries; they are also fried and salted to serve as a companion to drinks after the manner of olives in the Mediterranean countries and potato-chips in England. Because of its importance as a source of food, the JAK is a protected tree."

72

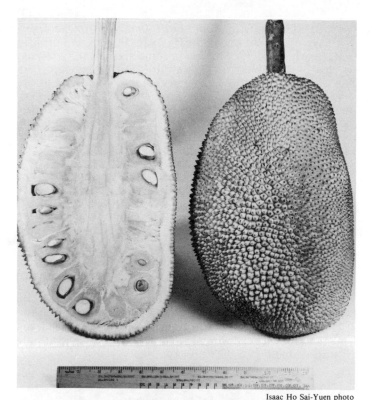

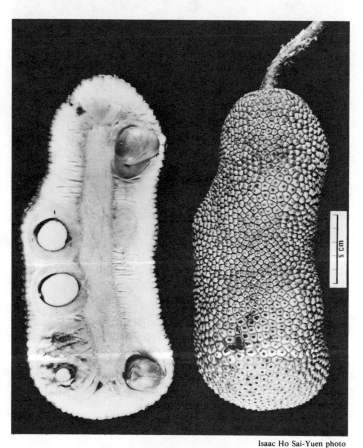

JAK FRUIT *(A. heterophyllus)*

NANGKA *(A. integra)*

Isaac Ho Sai-Yuen photo

either raw or fried, is delicious. The round seeds, about half an inch in diameter, eaten roasted, have a very mealy and agreeable taste. The tree has a very strong and disagreeable smell.''

Burkill describes some other species:

*A. odoratissima.* A tree of Borneo, and cultivated in the southern Philippine Islands. The fruit is in size like a DURIAN, with white, sweet, and aromatic flesh. The seeds are eaten roasted.

*A. elastica.* The ripe seeds can be eaten roasted. A solid oil is present in them, in very small quantities.

*A. champeden.* A tree of moderate size, much grown for its fruits. It is cultivated from Cochin-China throughout Malaysia. The wild tree is generally taller than the cultivated, and its fruits contain more seeds. The fruit of the cultivated tree may weigh as much as 60 lb. The flesh is eaten, and so are the seeds after cooking.

In a Sakai song ''pluck it, split it, and boil it'' refers to the seeds, which are of more value to the Sakai than the flesh. Elsewhere, Rumpf says that the seeds are more valued than the flesh, as they contribute more to the filling of the stomach.

BREADNUT *(A. communis)*

Christian Daniel photo

The closely allied BREADFRUIT *(A. communis)* is similar to JAK in size and pulpy contents, except there are no seeds to eat. However exceptions do arise: sometimes these BREADFRUIT by mistake do have seeds and of them Mortensen & Bullard write: ''The common forms which produce seeds are sometimes called BREADNUTS. These seeds are commonly sold in the markets in Haiti and are roasted and eaten like chestnuts.''

Sturtevant says of this fruit: ''It is considered delicious by those who can manage to eat it, but it possesses the rich, spicy scent and flavor of the melon to such a powerful degree as to be quite unbearable to persons of a weak stomach, or to those not accustomed to it. Lunan says the thick, gelatinous covering which envelops the seeds, eaten

BREADFRUIT *(A. incisa)*

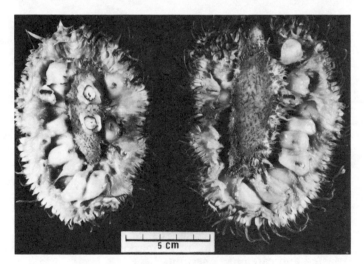

Worthington photo

*A. gomeziana.* A 50-foot tree from Andamans to Borneo.

TERAP *(A. elastica)*

5 CM

MONKEY JAK *(A. rigida)* Singapore

The USDA Bulletin: *Some Fruits and Nuts for the Tropics,* says: "The BREADNUT or PANA DE PEPITA, is a prolific seed-bearing variety common in some areas of the Tropics. It closely resembles the seedless BREADFRUIT except that the tree is a little more coarse in character. The rind of the fruit is covered with fleshy spines. Little edible pulp remains in most varieties, as it has been replaced by brownish seeds 1 inch or more in length and up to 1 inch in diameter. The seeds are edible after boiling or roasting and are said to resemble chestnuts. The seeds are a good source of calcium, phosphorus, and niacin."

When BREADFRUIT trees do bear fruits that have seeds in them, they are much appreciated by the Melanesians, according to Barrau. He adds: "They eat them roasted. In New Guinea they are eaten more often than the fruit itself."

## *Bosqueia angolensis* (Moraceae)

*Bosqueia* comprises four species of deciduous trees in tropical Africa from Guinea and Angola to Zaire.

Irvine says the drupes in January are about ¾ inch long, and adds: "The seeds are roasted and eaten. The fruit pulp is also edible."

BREADNUT *(Brosmium alicastrum)*

## BREAD NUT
## *Brosimum alicastrum* (Moraceae) SNAKEWOOD

Not to be confused with the true BREADNUT *(Artocarpus altilis),* this tropical American tree bears small, roundish, yellow or brownish seeds, an inch or less in diameter. Bailey says: "They come singly or sometimes two in a thin paper-like, but stout shell, with smooth and somewhat granular surface. They are edible only after cooking or roasting."

Standley says: "The seeds when boiled are palatable and nutritious, being consumed in substantial amounts in some regions."

*Cont. to U.S. Natl. Herb.* records: "The seeds are said to be fattening for cattle, which are fond of them, and they are used also as human food. For the latter purpose they are boiled or roasted, and eaten alone or mixed with sugar, honey or corn meal. They have a flavor resembling that of chestnuts and are very nutritious. The seeds are sometimes roasted and used as a substitute for coffee."

Sturtevant says: "The fruit, boiled with salt-fish, pork, beef or pickle, has frequently been the support of the negro and poorer sorts of white people in times of scarcity and has proved a wholesome and not unpleasant food.''

*Underexploited Tropical Plants* extols the virtues of this tree: ''The fruit's sweet pericarp and its chestnut-like seeds are eaten by humans. The seeds taste somewhat like potatoes and are eaten raw, boiled and roasted. They are also reduced to a meal that is mixed with maize meal to make tortillas, or are baked with green plantain. The seeds are gathered by the Mayans for making their native bread when stocks of maize run low.''

Bailey says: ''The small roundish, yellow or brownish seeds, an inch or less in diameter, of a large tropical American tree. These seeds are borne singly or sometimes two in a thin paper-like, but stout shell, with smooth and somewhat granular surface. They are edible only after cooking or roasting.''

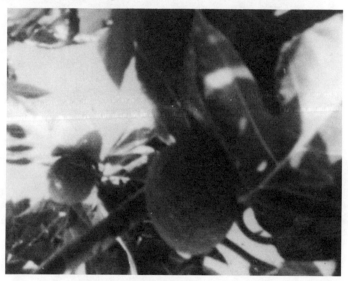

MALANANGKA *(Gymnartocarpus woodii)*

## *Gymnartocarpus woodii*          (Moraceae)
### MALANANGKA

This genus comprises three species of trees in the Philippines, Java, and Sumatra. Brown wrote of this one:

''The fruit of this species is somewhat rounded, 6 to 9 centimeters in diameter, and contains 6 to 12 chestnut-like seeds, 2 or 3 centimeters long. The seeds are eaten either roasted or boiled.

''*Gymnartocarpus woodii* is a tree reaching 20 meters and a diameter of about 40 centimeters. This species occurs in central and southern Luzon, Mindoro, Samar, and Leyte.''

## *Trophis sp.*     (Moraceae)     WHITE BREADNUT

Standley reports two of these trees in Mexico, remarking only that the fruits have scant flesh and a large seed. Willis reports 11 species scattered to Madagascar, Malaysia, and the West Indies.

R. H. Woodye of the Ministry of Agriculture in British Honduras writes: ''You might be interested to know of the YELLOW or WHITE BREADNUT *(Trophis racemosa)* that while the foliage is used for horses, the nuts are boiled for human food.''

# Chapter 16
# THE
# OLD MAN'S STICK
## *Panopsis* and *Calatola*

Common names can be dangerous. Two kinds of nut trees that grow in Costa Rica, are both commonly known as PALO DE PAPA or "OLD MAN'S STICK." Unfortunately for the common man, the trees are not related. The nuts of one are delicious and the nuts from the other are inedible. They may be poisonous.

The situation is complicated because the nuts of the second tree *(Calatola)* were described by distinguished botanists as edible; they seem to have been misled by the confusion of the common names. Here are the nuts:

PALO DE PAPA *(Panopsis suaveolens)*

## *Panopsis suaveolens* (Proteaceae) PALO DE PAPA
## PALO DE LA MONTANAS

*Panopsis* is a genus of 20 kinds of trees in tropical America, and this species in Costa Rica bears nuts the size of golf balls that enclose edible kernels. The newspaper *Tico Times* in San Jose, says:

> Don Zeazer has a novel suggestion for anyone who is a bit bored with snacks made of customary meat, fish or vegetables.
> How about a plate of "pickled panopsis" instead?
> The name may sound like some dreaded tropical disease, but Don thinks that given a more appetizing name, his unique cocktail snack could one day catch on in a big way in Costa Rican bars and restaurants.
> *Panopsis* is the Latin name for a tree commonly known as PAPA DE LA MONTANAS which grows prolifically in hilly forests around the country. The tree's big, round nuts have never generally been considered edible by Costa Ricans because they are very hard. A solution to that problem may have been found by Don, who is from Pennsylvania. (He used a hammer).
> "They're very good cut up and pickled in a sweet sauce made of *tapa dulce* (local brown sugar)" he says, brandishing a jar of the nuts, which look like artichoke hearts. "I've also mixed them quite successfully with spices and treated like a snack, they could be a valuable food source here."
> Don's "nutty" kitchen experiments are a diverting sideline to his serious research here for the Tropical Science Center into more effective use of native forests."

PALO DE PAPA *(Calatola laevigata)*

PALO DE PAPA *(Calatola laevigata)*

## *Calatola laevigata* (Icacinaceae) PALO DE PAPA

This 50-foot tree on the Honduras-British Honduras border, is one of seven species ranging as far south as Ecuador. Regarding the seeds, Standley wrote: "Fruit broadly ellipsoid, about 5 cm. long, rounded or very obtuse at each end, covered with low obtuse ridges. The curious stones of the fruit sometimes are found on Atlantic beaches of Central America, indicating that trees of the genus are not rare along the Atlantic slope; few specimens have been collected. The kernels of the seeds are white and firm, with a pleasant flavor that suggests coconut. They sometimes are roasted and eaten, and also are ground and made into tortillas, which are said to have the agreeable flavor of those prepared with grated cheese. The raw seeds are believed to be dangerous to eat, at least if consumed in some quantity.''

Standley wrote of *C. costaricensis:* "Fruit oval, 5-7 cm. long; nut globose, 4.5-6.5 cm. long, cristate. An interesting tree, easy to recognize by its fruits, especially the nuts, which have somewhat the appearance of ENGLISH WALNUTS. The seeds are white, with a consistency and flavor suggestive of coconut. The people of the volcanoes of Poa's and Barba roast and eat the seeds, and also grind them into a coarse meal with which they prepare a kind of tortilla.''

Standley's report that the nuts are edible is untrue. This mistake probably occurred because in Costa Rica, this and another completely unrelated genus, *Panopsis* (q.v.) are both commonly called PALO DE PAPA (Old Man's Stick).

*Panopsis* fruits contain an edible nut; *Calatola* fruits are not eaten.

Obviously Standley was confused, because he put *Calatola* in the Proteaceae where it does NOT belong.

Dr. L. R. Holdridge of the Tropical Science Center in San Jose, Costa Rica, wrote this author:

"As for *Panopsis* and *Calatola,* they are very distinct trees from different families. The literature does make it seem like Stanley or Pittier are talking about the same tree. I have a vague suspicion that the reporters may have actually had them confused. For one thing *Calatola* is from real wet forest areas which have only been opened up in relatively recent years. At least you will have to be careful about recommending *Calatola* as a nut. *Panopsis* is the PALO DE PAPA and the nut is used. I do not know personally that the other is.''

---

Chapter 17

# The CALABASH and its relatives

## (Bignoniaceae)

The Bignonia Family is distinguished for its beautiful flowers with thousands of magnificent trees from *Tabebuia* in the south to *Catalpa* in the north, but it is not much in the nuts area. In this chapter are a few trees of which the seeds are eaten, sometimes despite bad odor in the fruit.

Julia Morton photo

Fruit of the CALABASH *(Crescentia cujete).*

Julia Morton photo

CALABASH TREE *(Crescentia cujete).*

MARANKAS with various kinds of pebbles within, are commonly made from CALABASH fruits.

Fruits of the SAUSAGE TREE *(Kigelia pinnata)*.

## *Crescentia cujete* (Bignoniaceae) CALABASH

The CALABASH is a very hard-shelled pod that hangs from a small West Indian tree. Julia Morton wrote:

"Weirdly ornamental, and a favorite perch of orchids, the tree may reach 40 ft. It is characterized by outspread, arching branches garnished with nocturnal, bell-shaped flowers, 2 to 2½ inches long, on the trunk or along the branches throughout most of the year. The short-stemmed fruit, round, oval or oblong (sometimes artificially shaped by binding during development), varies exceedingly in size. The wild form is seldom more than 3 or 4 inches in length. Under cultivation, the fruits attain a width of 12 inches and a length of 18 inches or more. Always green and smooth on the exterior until it has dried, the shell is thin but hard and durable. The fruit is filled with a solid mass of spongy, juicy, white pulp containing a great number of dark-brown, flat seeds up to ¼ inch long.

"The seeds have been much used in Curacao to make a popular confection called 'carabobo'. Smith and Dollear found the seed oil to contain linolenic acid but otherwise to resemble peanut and olive oils. In Curacao, and in certain villages, sirup is made from the seeds.

"The mass-production method of obtaining is to dig a pit, build a fire in it and let it burn down to coals, crack a number of CALABASH fruits and roast them on the coals, take out the paste-like cooked pulp, stir it vigorously in water until the seeds sink. If the seeds only are to be used (for carabobo or for sirup), the flesh is skimmed off and fed to chickens. For sirup, the seeds are pounded fine, mixed with sugar and a little water and boiled."

The MEXICAN CALABASH *(C. alata)* grows chiefly on the west coast and uses are found for the seeds. A popular "refresco" on special occasions such as birthdays, is made of ripe seeds ground with raw rice and roasted pumpkin seeds, lemon peel, strained and mixed with sugar, water and ice.

## *Kigelia pinnata* (Bignoniaceae) SAUSAGE TREE

A spreading African tree to 50 feet, often grown in Florida and other warm areas for its curious sausage-like fruits, 3 to 4 inches in diameter and up to 18 inches long. These hang singly or in bunches from the trunk or old wood and do not open. The orange-yellow flowers with red spots often have an unpleasant fragrance.

Fanshawe writes: "The roasted seeds are eaten as a famine food in Malawi."

Other African authorities fail to mention the edibility of the seeds.

Fruits of the MIDNIGHT HORROR *(Oroxylum indicum)*. The pods are 2 to 4 feet long and 3 inches wide.

## *Oroxylum indicum* (Bignoniaceae) MIDNIGHT HORROR

A small tree found from India through southern China into Malaysia. Its very large seed pods make it a conspicuous object wherever it grows.

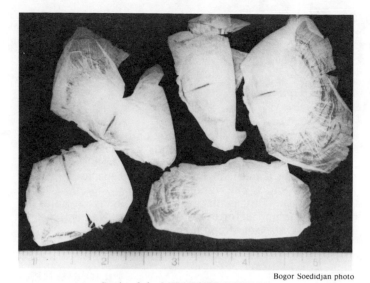

Bogor Soedidjan photo

Seeds of the MIDNIGHT HORROR.

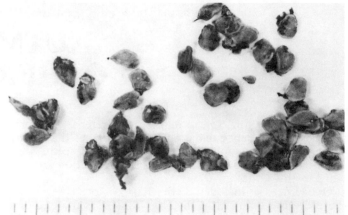

Seeds of the CANDLE TREE.

Maheshwari says: "The bark and fruits are used for tanning and dyeing. The seeds are edible."

## *Parmentiera cereifera*     (Bignoniaceae)
### CANDLE TREE

This 20-foot Panama tree bears its 2-inch white or yellowish funnel-shaped flowers directly on the trunk or larger branches. These are followed by dangling yellow fruits 18 to 36 inches long that much resemble yellow wax candles.

Sturtevant says: "The fruits are eaten in Mexico. The seeds are inside."

Paul Root photo

Fruits of the CANDLE TREE *(Parmentiera cereifera).*

# Chapter 18

# NUTMEG and OTHER SPICES

This chapter on Spices makes no pretense of completeness. It merely calls attention to the fact that many spices are seeds, and because we eat these seeds, they automatically become nuts under the definition of that word in this book.

One spice is included here that is not a seed and therefore not a nut. It is the CLOVE. This is the bud of a flower rather than the seed which follows, so it comes close.

This chapter only points the way in which small plants along with big trees contribute to human welfare, appetites and desires.

AMOMUM *(Aframomum elliottii)*

### Aframomum latifolium  (Zinziberaceae)
### GRAPE-SEEDED AMOMUM

This genus comprises 50 species of spice plants in West Africa. Of this one Dalziel says: "The seeds are like grape-stones, smooth, shining, and slightly aromatic, of weak flavour. The fruit is acid and refreshing to relieve thirst and fatigue on a journey.

"*A. longiscapum.* The seeds are angulate, brown, not shining, only slightly aromatic."

"*A. melegueta.* GRAINS OF PARADISE, GUINEA GRAINS, MANIGUETTE. Of this important spice Dalziel says:

"The name *Melegueta* is of doubtful origin. The term GRAINS OF PARADISE is loosely used but is properly referred only to *A. melegueta*. The seeds are golden-brown, angular and granular, strongly aromatic and pungent, with a CARDAMOMS flavour. The taste is due to a volatile oil, and the pungency to a resinous body, paradol, both contained in the seed-coats. The article was at one time important in trade with Europe. It was in demand as a spice and stimulating carminative, but now chiefly used in liqueurs and alcoholic beverages.

"In West Africa the fruit-pulp around the seeds is eaten, especially before maturity and is chewed as a stimulant. The seeds are a familiar spice, used in food."

*A. elliotii* (ALLIGATOR CARDAMON) is an important ginger-like spice plant from West Africa. It belongs to the GINGER family, has dark green one-foot leaves and 10-inch flower shoots which arise from basal rhizomes. Very decorative. Spice used to flavor wine, beer, foods and gingerbeer.

### Amomum  (Scitamineae)  CARDAMOM

Some 150 kinds of this plant are scattered through the tropics.

Sturtevant says: "The aromatic and stimulant seeds of many of the plants of this genus are known as CARDAMOMS, as are those of *Elettaria*. The botanical history of the species is in much confusion. One species at least is named as under cultivation, *A. angustifolium,* GREAT CARDAMOM. This plant grows on marshy grounds in Madagascar and affords in its seeds the Madagascar, or great CARDAMOMS of commerce.

### Aniba firmulum  (Lauraceae)  PICHURIM BEAN  TODA SPECIE

Sturtevant says: "Brazil. The Portuguese of the Rio Negro, a branch of the Amazon, gather the aromatic seeds which are grated like nutmeg."

Willis says there are 40 species of *Aniba* in tropical South America.

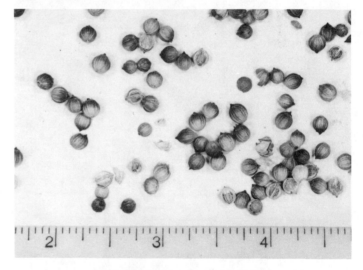

CORIANDER *(Coriandrum sativum)*

### Coriandrum sativum  (Umbelliferae)
### CORIANDER

Sturtevant says:"Southern Europe and the Orient. The seeds of this plant were used as a spice by the Jews and the Romans. The plant was well-known in Britain prior to the Norman conquest and was employed in ancient English medicine and cookery. CORIANDER was cultivated in American gardens prior to 1670. The seeds are carminative and aromatic and are used for flavoring, in confectionery and also by distillers. In the environs of Bombay, the seeds are much used by the Musselmans in their curries. They are largely used by the natives of India as a condiment. The ripe fruits of CORIANDER have served as a spice and a seasoning from very remote times, its seeds having been found in Egyptian tombs of the twenty-first dynasty, a thousand or so years later. Pliny says the best CORIANDER came to Italy from Egypt. Cato, in the third century before Christ, recommends CORIANDER as a seasoning; Columella, in the first century of our era and Palladius, in the third, direct its planting. The plant was carried to Massachusetts before 1670.

BRAZILIAN NUTMEG *(Crytocarya alba)*

## Cryptocarya moschata (Lauraceae) BRAZILIAN NUTMEG

Harry Blossfeld writes from Sao Paulo: "People who live where this big tree grows, in Minas Gerais, Mato Grosso, and the southern Amazon, have believed for 200 years that this is the true NUTMEG. (See *Myristica*). However, the kernel is much smaller and the aroma is distinct, an interesting spice.

"The stem of *Cryptocarya* is brown when young and gets almost white in age. It grows frequently as a shrub and is highly esteemed for the yellowish hard timber, but more so, because of the white fruits, surrounded by a soft pulp, containing one big seed with a ribbed and netted surface that resembles the NUTMEG. The seed has like many other Lauraceae, a pungent smell and taste and is used as a condiment."

## Cuminum cyminum (Umbelliferae) CUMIN

Sturtevant says: "Mediterranean region. This is a small, annual plant indigenous to the upper regions of the Nile but was carried at an early period by cultivation to Arabia, India and China, as well as to the countries bordering on the Mediterranean. It is referred to by the prophet Isaiah and is mentioned in Matthew. Pliny calls it the best appetizer of all the condiments and says the Ethiopian and the African are of superior quality but that some prefer the Egyptian. During the Middle Ages, CUMIN was one of the species in most common use and is mentioned in Normandy in 716, in England between 1264 and 1400 and is enumerated in 1419 among the merchandise taxed in the city of London. It is mentioned in many of the herbals of the sixteenth and seventeenth centuries and is recorded as under cultivation in England in 1594. In India, the seeds form an ingredient of curry powders and pickles and in France find use in cookery. In Holland, cheeses are sometimes flavored with CUMIN."

## Elettaria cardamomum (Scitamineae) CEYLON CARDAMOM

Sturtevant says: "East Indies. From time immemorial, great numbers of the natives have derived a livelihood from the cultivation of this plant. The fruit is used as an aromatic in medicine throughout the East Indies and is largely consumed as a condiment."

Burkill says: "A monotypic genus, wild in southwestern India, and extended by cultivation through the tropics. It is a tall herb, with erect leafy stem 9 feet high and very much shorter flowering stems, horizontal along the ground. Its dried fruits are in modern language true CARDAMOMS, but it is only one of a number of spices to which that name is applied: for CARDAMOMS, using the word in its widest sense, are the fruits of various species of no fewer than six genera- *Elettaria, Amomum, Aframomum, Languas, Riedelia,* and *Vanoverberghia*."

Burkill devotes several pages to detailed description of the various CARDAMOMS.

## Eugenia aromatica (Myrtaceae) CLOVE

Williams: *Zanzibar* says: "An upright, somewhat columnar tree 30 to 70 feet high, with shining green leaves and small myrtle-like flowers; the unexpanded buds when dried are the CLOVES of commerce.

"CLOVES and clove-oil comprise 70 per cent of the total domestic exports of Zanzibar and Pemba, and some 82 per cent of the CLOVES supplied to the world's markets. It is estimated that there are some 4,000,000 trees here on 50,000 acres.

"A rough estimate of the average yield of an individual tree is 6 lbs. of CLOVES. The harvest is a scene of intense activity, men, women and children assist in the picking; unfortunately, they do considerable damage to the trees."

## Euphorbia lathyris (Euphorbiaceae) CAPER SPURGE

Sturtevant says: "Southern Europe. The seeds are used as a substitute for capers but, says Johnson, they are extremely acrid and require long steeping in salt and water and afterwards in vinegar."

## Lunaria annua (Cruciferae) BOLBONAC

Sturtevant says: "Europe. The seed of the BOLBONAC is a temperature hot and dry and sharpe of taste, and is like in taste and force to the seed of treacle mustard."

CALABASH NUTMEG *(Monodora myristica)*

*Monodora myristica*           **(Annonaceae)**
                          CALABASH NUTMEG
                          JAMAICA NUTMEG

*Monodora* is a small genus of big trees and climbers in tropical Africa and Madagascar and it was carried to the West Indies during the slave-trade.

Burkill says: "The aromatic oil of the seeds contains limonene, myristicol, aromatic pinene, etc., which give them a close resemblance to the nutmeg oil, and cause them to be used as a flavouring."

Irvine says: "This is a tree to 80 feet, bearing fruits in April to September that are up to 8 x 6 in. suspended on long stalk, green, with numerous seeds embedded in whitish, sweet-smelling pulp, each oblong, about ¾ in. long, pale brown when fresh, seed-coat thin, kernel hard and oily (up to 36 per cent of a fixed oil).

"The seeds are aromatic. The dry seeds are sold all over W. Africa as a spice, e.g., as a condiment in soup or as seasoning by the Hausas. They are eaten in Uganda. They also form an ingredient in African snuffs and pomade."

Regarding another species *M. tenuifolia*, Irvine writes: "A tree up to 50 ft. high and 1 ft. diameter. Fruit spherical or ovoid, not ribbed, smooth and hard up to 1 in. by over 3 in., green mottled with white spots, and containing many aromatic seeds; fruit-stalk up to 4 x ¼ in. The fruits are eaten by children and the seeds used like those of other spices."

NUTMEG FRUIT *(Myristica fragrans)* just opening to release the seed which is covered by the red MACE.

*Myristica fragrans*    **(Myristicaceae)**    NUTMEG

NUTMEG is probably the only nut over which nations went to war, and innocent people were slaughtered. Harry Blossfeld writes:

"If NUTMEG is a nut, then there is a dramatic story in it. The tree is native of the Molucca Islands. The Arabs started buying the nuts from the Polynesian and Malayan native races. They settled on the islands and had a sultan residing there, who ruled over the natives that were converted to Mohamedan religion. Then arrived the Portuguese, who took over the trade, then fought the sultans and finally settled in the islands. A century later came the Dutch, ransacked the Portuguese warehouses and ships,

took over the islands and a monopoly. NUTMEGS had a price fixed and were to be delivered exclusively to the Dutch warehouses. The natives had obtained much higher prices from the Portuguese and started trading NUTMEG in their fast sailboats to Amboina (which was English) and Sumatra (which was Portuguese). There were secret plantations of NUTMEG, trees on almost all small islands of the South Seas and NUTMEG trade flowed on secret roads to Europe. So the Dutch started an eradicating program. They landed systematically on all islands outside the Molucca Sea and cut down all nutmeg trees, wild or planted, and cut the throats of any native who was growing or trading NUTMEG beyond the Molucca Sea. Still this did not work. The fast flyboats of the natives escaped with their cargo by night through the cliffs of the Molucca Sea.

"The Dutch called this contraband, and when they realized that almost all the natives of the Molucca Islands were secretly trading large parts of their harvests, they resolved to take measures. Island after island, they blocked the Moluccas with their ships, landed troops and killed every living soul, men, women, children and animals and threw all into the sea. Thus, the whole indigenous population of the Moluccas was eradicated. Later, the Dutch brought in Malayans from the superpopulated Java, and taught them to care for the NUTMEG plantations on the islands. The whole thing was so completely and entirely done, that only decades later, some Dutch officials admitted the facts, and the historical facts became known.

"I obtained the information from a resident in Maneassar, whose family came from Molucca Islands. He is descendant of a Javanese NUTMEG grower's family, that was brought over by the Dutch after the slaughter. His family tradition is that the beaches were sown with skeletons of killed 'pirates' when they arrived at the island. Some books on history of the Molucca Islands — including some printed in Holland — admit the facts. Most NUTMEG plantations are shaded by a large tree, *Canarium commune*, which is also producing an edible nut much esteemed by the Indonesians.

"Details of this history appear in O. Warburg: *Die Muskatnuss* (1897). One year later the Dutch published in Batavia *De Nootmuskaat-Cultuur* by J. M. Janse, omitting the most shocking details of slavery and slaughtering of the natives of the Banda Islands.

"The tree has been introduced twice to Brazil by the Portuguese. A few plants were growing in 1798 at Para (today Belem) on the mouth of the Amazon. In 1810 four plants were carried from Cayenne to Rio de Janeiro, when the Portuguese troops invaded French Guyana, shortly after Napoleon had invaded Portugal, and the royal family and the whole nobility had fled to Brazil. All these plants fruited during many years, but the fruits were gathered and used as condiment, nobody thinking of planting them to reproduce the tree. Thus, at the beginning of the 20th century, all trees had died of old age and none survived. Only recently, a small number of trees was obtained from East Timor, which remained a Portuguese colony. Also, from a Dutch possession in the South Sea, a few plants were obtained, a hybrid variety, and all are now being cared for in suitable climate, with the idea to use them as propagating stock for future plantations."

Kennard & Winters wrote: "Although the NUTMEG is cultivated primarily as a source of spices, NUTMEG and MACE, it is valued in some tropical areas for the fruit. Native to the Moluccas, the NUTMEG is a medium-sized to large tree, sometimes reaching more than 60 feet in height. At maturity the pale-amber fruits, which resemble large apricots, split open and release the glossy dark-brown nuts, which are partly covered by lacy red arils. When dried, the nut is the NUTMEG of commerce and the aril is MACE.

"The principal sources of NUTMEGS are the Moluccas and Celebes Islands. A considerable quantity comes from the W. Indies, especially Grenada, where the trees are often interplanted with CACAO.''

A. S. Fuller: *The Nut Culturist* says: "NUTMEG — A name applied to the fruits of a large number of trees, and of different orders of plants. The true NUTMEGS of commerce are the fruits of trees belonging to the genus *Myristica*, and of the family Myristicaceae. The oldest and best known of these is the *M. fragrans*, a small widely branching tree, growing 20 to 25 feet high, and supposed to be indigenous to the Indian Archipelago. The fruit is about the size of an ordinary walnut, with a thick rind, which, upon opening at maturity, discloses a reddish aril covering the nut within. This aril or husk is the mace of commerce, while the true NUTMEG is the center or hard seed (nut). The BRAZIL NUTMEG is longer than the true species, and is sold under the name of long nutmeg, and is the fruit of *M. fatua*. Another species the *M. oloba*, is cultivated in Madagascar, but is scarcely known in commerce.

"Another species, the *M. sebifera*, is a common tree in the forests of Guyana, North Brazil, and up into Panama. It is utilized principally for the oil extracted from the nuts, obtained by maccrating them in water, the oil rising to the surface, and as it cools skimmed off.

"The seeds of several species of conifers and laurels are known, either locally or in commerce, as NUTMEGS, or are used as a substitute for the true NUTMEG. There are three different kinds of trees, native of Guyana, in addition to the one already named, the seeds of which are employed as a spice or medicine.''

### *Nigella sativa* (Ranunculaceae) BLACK CUMIN ROMAN CORIANDER

Sturtevant says: "East Mediterranean and Taurus-Caspian countries and cultivated in various parts of the world. The seeds are employed in some parts of Germany, France and Asia as a condiment. In eastern countries they are commonly used for seasoning curries and other dishes, and the Egyptians spread them on bread and put them on cakes like comfits. The seeds, on account of their aromatic nature, are employed as a spice in cooking, particularly in Italy and southern France.''

BASIL *(Ocimum pilosum)*

### *Ocimum basilicum* (Labiatae) SWEET BASIL

Sturtevant says: "A fragrant and aromatic plant of tropical Asia, which, as a culinary plant, has been celebrated from a very early period. It was condemned by Chrysippus more than 200 years before Christ as an enemy to the sight and a robber of the wits. Diodorus and Hollerus entertained equally superstitious notions regarding it. Philistis, Plistonicus and others extolled its virtues and recommended it as strongly as it had been formerly condemned. Pliny says the Romans sowed the seeds of this plant with maledictions and ill words, believing the more it

was cursed the better it would prosper; and when they wished for a crop, they trod it down with their feet and prayed to the gods that it might not vegetate. It seems to have been first cultivated in Britain in 1548 and is now valued for seasoning. It reached America before 1806. SWEET BASIL seeds are eaten in Japan.''

*Ocimum* is a genus of 50 kinds of herbs, mostly African. Uphof says that *O. graveolens* of Abyssinia "has been recommended as a condiment for flavoring foods.''

ALLSPICE *(Pimenta dioica)*

### *Pimenta dioica* (Myrtaceae) ALLSPICE

Williams: *Zanzibar* says: "This plant is a native of Jamaica. The dried, unripe berries are known as ALLSPICE on account of a combined flavour said to resemble CLOVE, CINNAMON and NUTMEG. These should be picked when mature, but still green, and dried in the sun for a week or ten days.''

USDA Photo

BLACK PEPPER *(Piper nigrum)*

### *Piper betle* (Piperaceae)    BETEL PEPPER

Williams: *Zanzibar* says: "A climbing plant, native of the East Indies, commonly cultivated for its spicy-flavoured leaves, within which the BETEL NUT chew is folded and fastened with a clove; their cultivation constitutes quite a minor industry.

### *P. nigrum*        BLACK PEPPER

This is a climbing plant, native of the East Indies and Malaya. The fruit when ripe, somewhat resemble red currants. Dried with the outer pulp on they are the black peppercorns of commerce. Ordinary white pepper is obtained by grinding the hard round seeds after removal of the pulp."

### *Ravensara aromatica* (Laurineae) MADAGASCAR CLOVE NUTMEG

Sturtevant says: "A tree of Madagascar. The fruit, leaves and young bark, having the taste of cloves, afford one of the best spices of the island. The kernel of the fruit affords the MADAGASCAR CLOVE NUTMEGS."

USDA Photo

SESAME *(Sesame indicum)*

### *Sesamum indicum* (Pedalineae)    SESAME SIM-SIM BENNISEED

Sturtevant says: "SESAME has been cultivated from time immemorial in various parts of Asia and Africa. The seeds are largely consumed as food in India and tropical Africa, but their use in European countries is mainly for the expression of oil. In Sicily the seeds are eaten scattered on bread, an ancient custom mentioned by Dioscorides. In central Africa, SESAME is cultivated as an article of food, also for its oil. This oil which is largely exported from British India and Formosa, is an excellent salad oil; it is used in Japan for cooking fish. In China the species is extensively cultivated for the seeds to be used in confectionery. During a famine in Rajputana, the press-refuse was sold at a high price for food. This seems to be the species, which is used by the negroes of South Carolina, who parch the seeds over the fire, boil them in broths, and use them in puddings.

"SESAME was cultivated for its oil in Babylonia in the days of Herodotus and Strabo, also in Egypt in the time of Theophrastus, Dioscorides and Pliny. Its culture in Italy is mentioned by Columella, Pliny and Palladius. The seeds are used as a food by the Hindus, after being parched and ground into a meal which is called, in Arabic, rehshee. The expressed oil has a pleasant taste and is also used in cookery. In Japan SESAME is highly esteemed. In China also, the oil is used. In Greece, the seeds are made into cakes."

Dalziel says: "The seeds are smooth on the surface, without a radiate margin. In most parts it is cultivated only to a small extent amongst other culinary plants, and for local use chiefly in cooking. In Togo it is grown not for the oil, but as a food, the seeds put in soup. Barth observed that its 'cultivation imparts quite a different aspect' to many pagan districts 'as numerous tribes seem to subsist chiefly upon this article.' Amongst these BENNISEED is prominent in all religious rites. In the Benue region it is both a dry season crop and an early crop harvested in August. It is mostly grown by the Munchis (a semi-Bantu people) on farms owned by women, in rotation with yams and sorghum. The seeds, ground and roasted are used in soup, a habit which the Munshis are said to have acquired from the Hausas; also made into cakes fried with salt, pepper, etc., an article suited for journeys.

Commercialized SESAME and CORN roasted as tidbits in plastic bags.

"BLACK BENISEED amongst those of pale coulour is probably commonly an adulteration with seeds of *Ceratotheca*, at least in the Benue Basin. In the Gongola Valley, where BENISEED is purchased in three grades, grade 1 is true *S. indicum*; grades 2 and 3 are mixtures, the seeds of *Ceratotheca* being predominant, but also containing some suspected hybrid, the colour being light brown to blackish. For certain European markets only the yellow seeds are accepted, mostly destined for Turkey. In trade the permissible amount of dark seed must be less than 25% to be classed as white.

"The seeds contain 50-57% of oil, and yield by expression from 42-48%. It is a semi-drying oil, that of the first pressing being clear yellow and odourless, that of the second and third pressing being darker and of stronger flavour, but refinable. The best grade is official in the B. P. for use in India and the British colonies as a substitute for olive oil. Nigerian oil is clear yellow, odourless, and can be preserved long without becoming rancid; as a cooking oil for Europeans it is probably more wholesome than groundnut oil. Sesame oil extracted in Europe is an important edible oil, particularly on the Continent, because of the compulsory addition (about 10% in Germany, Austria, Belgium and Denmark) to margarine, etc. The object is to prevent fraud, and is based on the property of easy recognition by colour tests revealing the nature of the butter or margarine in which it is used. The ordinary uses are those of olive oil (as a salad oil or an adulterant) for cooking."

*S. orientale* — AFRICAN SIMSIM. This is a very important spice and seed oil plant in Africa. Seed oil is used in perfumery and for frying vegetables and meat. Seeds are eaten raw or fried, and are used in various types of confectionery. The plant is a 3 to 6 foot annual with white, pink or purple flowers.

### *Siler trilobum* (Umbelliferae)

Sturtevant says: "Orient, middle and south Europe. The stems and fruit are edible. The seed is like FENNEL but larger, pungent, but pleasant to taste and when in season, if broken as far as the soft part, can be eaten without salt."

### *Sison amomum* (Umbelliferae) HONEWORT STONE PARSLEY

Europe and Asia Minor. Lindley says the seeds are pungent and aromatic but have a nauseous smell when fresh. Mueller says they can be used for a condiment.

### *Vanilla planifolia* (Orchidaceae) VANILLA

Williams says: "A climbing plant with twisted furrows on the stem. The pod or bean is thin, round and several inches long. This is the most important of the VANILLAS. After reaping, the beans have to be cured. When cured, the beans should be pliable and of a dark chocolate-brown colour."

### *Xylopia aetheopica* (Annonaceae) GUINEA PEPPER

*Xylopia* comprises some 150 species of plants, mostly in tropical Africa, the fruits of many used as peppers. This species is a tree 30 feet high. It is described by Ron Hurov thus:

"An important African spice. The fruits are sold in African markets as a substitute for pepper. The powdered seeds are added to snuff, coffee, foods and palm wines. Seeds are sometimes used to purify water. The seeds contain avoceine."

### *Zygophyllum coccineum* (Zygophyllaceae)

Sturtevant says: "North Africa and Arabia. The aromatic seeds are employed by the Arabs in the place of pepper."

---

## Chapter 19

# PEANUTS AND OTHER BEANS

### (Leguminosae)

Next to the grasses, the beans are the most important family of plants on which mankind depends for food. There are 12,000 kinds of leguminous plants from tiny groundlings to great trees, and the seeds they produce are extremely important food items. In many cases the pods themselves are consumed as vegetables, but the seeds inside are of major importance in every part of the world. Most of them are edible, but a few like *Mora*, with a single big seed in a big hard pod, are not eaten by anybody. Many bean pods must be opened forcibly, just as a hickory nut is broken, and one is just as much a nut as the other, so long as it is eaten by mankind.

Beans and peas are important sources of fats and proteins. When hungry people fail in the woods nearby, to find the walnuts or filberts they love, they can always turn to legumes. They can plant peanuts in their own garden. The commercialization of the peanut does not rob the farmer with his hungry children; he can still produce his own nuts, all he needs. His family cannot be deprived of the fat and protein they need. That is why legumes are so important in a world desperate for more food.

PEANUTS in Angola. Type I. 2-3 kernels per pod, light colored seeds.
Maquela variety.

PEANUTS in Angola. Type III. Spreading, long season variety.
Kimbundu name KAMBACA.

PEANUTS in Angola. Type II. 3-5 kernels per shell, dark colored
kernels.

Virginia runner PEANUTS.

86

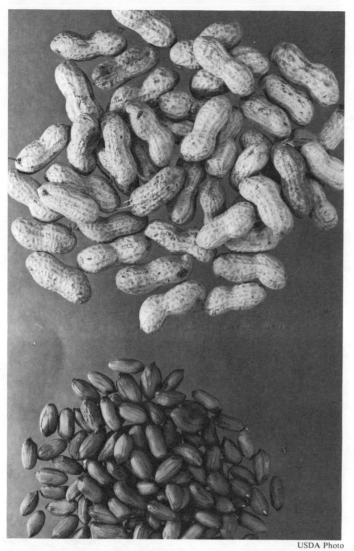

USDA Photo

Holland Jumbo PEANUTS.

### PEANUT
### GROUNDNUT
### MONKEY NUT
### GOOBER

## *Arachis hypogaea*

This Brazilian bean, now grown throughout the tropics with largest production in China and India, is often thought of as a tuber because it pushes its fruit underground where it ripens. The plants with pretty yellow flowers are 1 to 5 feet high, depending on varieties and soil, and the straw-colored pods are usually 2 to 4-seeded, more or less 2 inches long and as fat as a big pencil.

Mors & Rizzini say: "The manifold uses of the PEANUT are comparable to those of the SOYBEAN, but its oil content is twice as high, reaching 40 to 50 percent of the weight of the seed.

"The properties of peanut oil are similar to those of soybean oil, but the former is decidedly preferred in Brazilian cooking.

"From the New World the peanut was introduced into Africa, where it soon adapted well and has displaced the native 'ground peas' of the same family, which have the same underground habits (*Voandzeia* and *Kerstingiella*, *q.v.*). Today the cultivation of the PEANUT extends to all tropical and subtropical parts of the world."

Oxford Book of Food Plants says: "GROUNDNUTS have to be dug out of the soil at harvest, like a root crop. In the erect varieties, the pods are well grouped round the central stem, but in the runner varieties they are much more scattered and laborious to harvest. Most of the world's GROUNDNUTS are dug by hand, but in the United States machines are used. The nuts can be shelled out of the pod by hand or in machines. They are extremely nutritious because of their high content of both protein (about 30 per cent) and oil (40-50 per cent); they are also rich in vitamins B and E. In tropical households the whole nuts are used in cookery; and whole nuts of selected large dessert types, with the reddish skin removed, are also eaten raw or roasted in temperate countries. Peanut butter is made by removing the skin and germ and grinding the roasted nuts. There is a large export trade in groundnuts for the commercial extraction of oil. Besides being used as a cooking and salad oil, GROUNDNUT oil is one of the most important fats used for making margarine. It is also used for packing sardines. The residue left after oil extraction is one of the most used oilcakes for animal feeding. The country producing most groundnuts is India, which has little to spare for export, and is followed by China. Nigeria is the largest exporter of groundnuts, which are grown in the drier northern part of the country. GROUNDNUT exports are very important in the economy of certain smaller countries, such as Senegal and Gambia."

The enormous commercial peanut industry that has built up in the United States is an enduring memorial to the ability of one man, George Washington Carver.

## *Kerstingiella geocarpa*     HAUSA GROUNDNUT

This plant, like the PEANUT (*Arachis*) and Bambarra GROUNDNUT (*Voandzeia*), is grown in the drier parts of West Tropical Africa, where it buries its fruit in the soil.

Dalziel says: "The plant is known only in cultivation, and has a restricted range from the Upper Senegal-Niger Basin to Gold Coast, Togo, Dahomey and N. Nigeria.

"The seeds are sold in markets, and are of various colours, whitish, brown or black, and spotted or speckled. The flowers of the variety with white, sometimes black-spotted seeds are said to be usually white, those of the other varieties being tinted with bluish-purple. Chevalier mentions that in Dahomey it is a food forbidden to women; the restriction is not known in Nigeria. In N. Terr., Gold Coast, a food is prepared by adding shea butter and salt to the pounded kernels. They have an agreeable taste equal to that of good varieties of *Phaseolus*, appreciable by Europeans, and chemical analysis shows them to be of high food value, with a nitrogen content equal to that of the richest varieties of *Voundzeia*. The plant, however, gives a poor yield and the beans are comparatively small."

BAMBARRA GROUNDNUT (*Voandzeia subterranea*)

## Voandzeia subterranea BAMBARRA GROUNDNUT

Like the peanut (*Arachis*) and *Kerstingiella*, this bean buries its fruit in the soil.

Willis says: "One species. The seed is edible and the plant is largely cultivated."

Hutchinson and Dalziel say: "Herb with prostrate rooting branches. Fruits to 2 cm. long, 1-3 seeded. Seeds somewhat kidney-shaped to 1 cm. long, rich brown."

Dalziel says: "The seeds vary in colour from whitish, with or without a black areola around the hilum, to pure black or red with all types of mottling, blotching or spotting.

"Various analyses agree in placing both the albuminoid and oil content low, from 16-21% and from 4.5-6.5% respectively, and the starch content from 49-59%. It is thus not to be classed as an oil seed. Being hard, the seeds require soaking before cooking, but they are often used in the young fresh state when the taste is more agreeable. As a native food it may be classed as a pulse with rather more fat and less nitrogen than beans, etc., and it is sometimes preferred to *Arachis* in flavour and being less oily. The native methods of use are: (1) Cooked in the fresh state; (2) roasted and pounded to a meal and used in soup or as a puree; (3) the meal mixed with oil and condiments, salt, red pepper, etc., and fried; this is prepared in cakes or balls known in N. Nigeria as bakuru, an article which is believed to keep better when made from *Voandzeia* than from ordinary beans; (4) "popped" like Indian corn by roasting the seeds with sand on a pan and cracking with a stone — something to eat as a "snack."

As a human food Balland, considering the proportions of the ingredients, regards *Voandzeia* seeds as "an example of a natural article possessing the composition of a complete food."

*Acacia albida*

*Acacia nilotica*

## Acacia albida WATTLE

Of the nearly 800 kinds of *Acacia* trees scattered throughout the tropics and subtropics, most are trees and many are prized for the gum arabic that oozes from their branches and is a highly valued food product. However, only a few of the *Acacia* produce seeds that are eaten.

*A. albida* is the largest thorn tree in the savannahs of Africa, often 60 feet high and 8 feet around. The seed pods are gathered several times a year, are up to 6 x 1½ inches, slightly curved, the ends rounded.

Irvine says: "The seeds are eaten in times of famine in S. Rhodesia, being boiled first to loosen the skin. The kernels are then reboiled and eaten, the water being thrown away."

Fanshawe writes from Zambia: "*A. nilotica* seeds are roasted and eaten by the Housas as a relish."

Sturtevant suggests others with seeds that are eaten:

*A. concinna* SOAP-POD. Tropical Asia. The natives of India eat the beans after roasting.

*A. flexicaulis* Texas. The thick, woody pods contain round seeds the size of peas which, when boiled, are palatable and nutritious.

*A. leucophloea.* KUTEERA-GUM. Southern India. The pods are used as a vegetable, and the seeds are ground and mixed with flour.

*A. longifolia.* SYDNEY GOLDEN WATTLE. Australia. The Tasmanians roast the pods and eat the starchy seeds.

Uphof cites five species of which the seeds are eaten as follows:

*A. aneura* MULGA. Ground seeds are consumed as food by the aborigines of South Australia.

*A. cibaria* West Australia. Seeds are eaten by the natives.

*A. dictyophleba.* Seeds when pounded are used as food by the natives of Central Australia.

*A. oswaldii* UMBRELLA ACACIA. Seeds are consumed as food by the aborigines of Australia.

*A. rivalis* Australia. The seeds are eaten as food after being ground.

RED SANDERSWOOD (*Adenanthera pavonina*)

*(Amblygonocarpus andongensis)*

## Adenanthera pavonina

This medium-sized Indian tree, grown in gardens in Florida and throughout the tropics, is valued for its shade and useful form. The inconspicuous flowers are followed by 8 inch seed pods which hang long on the tree, finally curling up to expose the 10-12 bright red seeds within which hang on and do not drop off.

Irvine says: "The tree is propagated by seeds and transplants fairly well, but germination is slow because of the hard seed-coats. The husked kernels contain ¼ of their weight of oil with a protein content of 39 per cent, hence their agreeable soya-bean taste."

Burkill says: "Haskarl records the seeds as, in Java, roasted and shelled, and eaten with rice, tasting like Soy beans. The eating of them is also recorded in the Malay Peninsula."

Doreen Langley records the food use of the seeds by the Tongans in Guam.

Sturtevant says: "The seeds are eaten by the common people in tropical eastern Asia. The seeds of a related species *A. abrosperma* in Australia, are roasted in the coals and the kernels are eaten."

## Amblygonocarpus andongensis

This graceful tree to 60 feet, the only species, grows in moist savannahs from Ghana to tropical South Africa. Its feathery foliage, drooping at the tips is crowned with dense, yellow flower spikes in April, followed by 6-inch, tetragonal, woody, 6-inch seed pods.

Irvine says: "The seeds, after boiling and fermenting, have a meat-like taste and are used in local drinks."

Fanshawe wrote: "Seeds are boiled and allowed to ferment for three days, then eaten as a relish with meat in West Africa."

*(Afzelia quanzensis)*

## Afzelia africana

Dalziel says: "African tropics. A portion of the seed is edible.

"The fruits are very hard and woody, nearly black, bursting violently to discharge the seeds. Although the aril is edible, with a tolerably agreeable taste, and is eaten by monkeys, the seed is often stated to be poisonous. Pobeguin says the pulverised seed is regarded as a violent poison. It is possible that cyanogenetic properties develop as the seed ripens, but the writer has known of native boys chewing the young seed when immature and soft without apparent ill-effects. The seeds of an allied tree in Malaya, Intsia are used as a famine food, but require roasting and soaking for several days to render them non-poisonous."

## Amphicarpaea monoica      HOG PEANUT

Howes says: "This climbing wild bean of North America bears pods near the roots, each of which contains a brown seed about the size and shape of a peanut. These seeds are often very abundant among the dead leaves and just under the surface of the ground. They are eagerly sought by pigs running in the woods, hence the name HOG PEANUT. The seeds were much used as food by North American Indians who sometimes obtained supplies of them by robbing rodents' nests where they had been stored, leaving corn or other food in return."

ST. THOMAS TREE *(Bauhinia tomentosa)*

## Bauhinia tomentosa      ST. THOMAS TREE

This yellow-flowered ORCHID TREE from Asia is sparingly cultivated in Florida. Sturtevant says of it: "The seeds are eaten in the Punjab."

89

*(Brachystegia boehmii)*

*(Brachystegia wangermeeana)*

*(Brachystegia utilis)*

## Brachystegia spiciformis

Fanshawe writes of this tree in Malawi: "The seeds are cooked and eaten locally as a famine food."

Sturtevant says the seeds of *B. appendiculata* in tropical Africa are eaten.

## Bussea Sp.

These big trees of west tropical Africa and Madagascar, yielding extremely hard timber like LIGNUM VITAE, number four species.

Fanshawe says in east Africa: "The roasted seeds are eaten locally as a famine food."

Dalziel says: "The seeds are thick and somewhat oily; they are eaten after roasting."

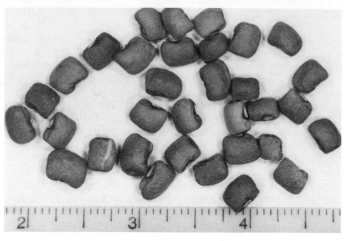

PIGEON PEA *(Cajanus cajan)*

## Cajanus cajan                    PIGEON PEA

The PIGEON PEA is native of Indonesia but has been cultivated throughout the tropics for centuries. Dalziel says: "Isert recorded the plant from Dahomey in 1783-86, and it was probably known long before from Lower Guinea. Easily cultivated, drought-resistant, and capable of yielding most of the year, it is cultivated on a considerable scale in Dahomey and Lower Congo. Some pagan tribes regard it with superstition, planting it near fetish houses, but refusing it as food except as votive offerings.

"The ripe seeds are a pulse, used in the form of meal variously cooked, but usually boiled and mixed with palm oil, salt and condiments. Europeans use the young seeds like green peas and the green pods as a vegetable.

Sturtevant says: "The PIGEON PEA is a perennial shrub, though treated generally as an annual when in cultivation. It is now naturalized in the West Indies, in tropical America and in Africa. The variety *bicolor* grows 3 to 6 feet high; the variety *flavus* grows from 5 to 10 feet high. Lunan says the pea when young and properly cooked is very little inferior as a green vegetable to English peas and when old is an excellent ingredient in soups. In Egypt, on the richest soil, says Mueller, 4,000 pounds of peas have been produced to the acre, and the plant lasts for three years, growing 15 feet tall. Elliott says the pulse when split is in great and general esteem and forms the most generally used article of diet among all classes in India. At Zanzibar the seeds are a principal article of diet."

## Calpocalyx brevibracteatus

This is one of eleven species of these trees in evergreen forests of tropical Africa, often 100 feet high and 4 feet in diameter. The 6-inch pods, sometimes 2 inches wide, curl and open when ripe, ejecting the 6 or 7 shiny brown seeds, ½ inch long.

Dalziel says that in Liberia where the trees are abundant, the seeds are eaten after cooking.

## Canavalia ensiformis

HORSE BEAN
SWORD BEAN
CUT-EYE
ONE-EYE BEAN

This small genus of climbing herbs, found in the tropics all over the world, is useful to many people.

Dalziel writes: "The beans are large, white, but sometimes wine-red; as food the white beans are considered more wholesome. Suspicion of any poisonous quality seems to be unfounded and they can be recommended as a human food of fairly good value.

"By the Yorubas the beans are regarded as a plebeian or inferior food, but they are sometimes eaten after cooking with salt or natron. The Hausas do not use it much as food, but plant it probably with some superstitious idea. The red-seeded variety is known in Hausa as 'dan sago'. Some of the pagan tribes of N. Nigeria use it as food."

Williamson says: "Two forms of this bean are recorded, a bush in the foothills up the Dwambazi River. Its fruits are said to be poisonous and it was planted as a deterrent to snakes; it has large white seeds. A climbing form bearing 9 in. pods containing large red thick-skinned beans, grows luxuriantly in villages of the Mzimba District where the garden huts are each surrounded by a lion-proof stockade on which the people have planted it for ornament and to keep away lions but do not eat the bean.

"The beans may be eaten as a pulse, but care must be taken with some varieties as they may be slightly poisonous."

## Cassia tora

STINKING CASSIA

Cassia is a genus of 600 kinds of trees, shrubs and herbs in the tropics and warm temperate zones. Senna is derived from the leaves of some. Rarely are the seeds of any species eaten. Dalziel says of *C. tora* in west Africa: "The seeds, roasted and ground, have been used as a coffee substitute. The seeds are used by the Moors as food in time of scarcity."

MORETON BAY CHESTNUT (*Castanospermum australe*)

## Castanospermum australe

MORETON BAY CHESTNUT
BLACK BEAN
AUSTRALIAN CHESTNUT

This big Australian tree to 60 feet bears pretty yellow to orange or red butterfly flowers in 6-inch clusters, chiefly on the big branches and on the trunk. For reasons unknown, the tree fails to fruit in many countries where it has been planted ornamentally.

The fruits are produced in leathery pods an inch thick and up to 9 inches long, 2 inches wide, rather spongy inside. The seeds as large as a chestnut, are rounded, spheroidal or flattened in form.

Bailey says: "The nuts to some extent are roasted and eaten by the natives but are not altogether pleasant."

Maiden: *Useful Native Plants of Australia* says: "The beans are used as food by the aborigines, who prepare them by first steeping them in water from eight to ten days; they are then taken out, dried in the sun, roasted upon hot stones, pounded into a coarse meal, in which state they may be kept for an indefinite period. When required for use, the meal is simply mixed with water, made into a thin cake, and baked in the usual manner. In taste, cakes prepared in this way resemble a coarse ship biscuit."

Caulfield writes from Brisbane: "*Castanospermum australe* is another nut which has caused many a person to become hospitalised. Recently 14 airforce personnel were admitted to the hospital after being on a survival mission and eating the seed."

## Cathormium altissimum

SPIRIT'S MARBLES

This 50-foot spreading tree with thorny branches and 20 seeds in a loose spiral pod grows from Sierra Leone to Uganda. Dalziel reports the "seeds are said to be edible", but also "the seeds are used in Sierra Leone as a fish poison." So take your pick.

## Cicer arietinum

CHICK-PEA
EGYPTIAN PEA

Sturtevant wrote: "The CHICK PEA is extensively cultivated in the south of Europe, in the Levant, in Egypt as far as Abyssinia and in India. The seeds vary in size and color. In Paris, they are much used for soups. In India, they are ground into a meal and either eaten in puddings or made into cakes. They are also toasted or parched and made into a sort of comfit.

"The shape of the unripe seed, which singularly resembles a ram's head, may account for its being regarded as unclean by the Egyptians of the time of Herodotus."

MOPANE (*Colophospermum mopane*)

## Colophospermum mopane

MOPANE

This is the only species in this genus, formerly included in *Copaifera*. Loyd Schaad writes from Botswana: "I am sending pictures of MOPANE, our most common forest tree, sometimes called BUTTERFLY TREE because of the

91

shape of the leaves. Recently I saw mention that the prolific production of MOPANE seeds should be investigated as a possible source of protein.''

### Copaifera baumiana

This genus comprises 25 species in South America and 5 species in tropical Africa.

Fanshawe writes: ''Africa. The seeds are pounded and eaten in Barotseland as a porridge.''

Sturtevant tells of another in Africa: ''*C. hymenaeifolia*. A tree which yields a red-skinned, fattening bean-like seed.

Harry Blossfeld writes from Brazil: ''*Copaifera* has a yellow, waxy aril on the seeds of some species, and the seeds are oily, but the seeds are not eaten.''

### Cordeauxia edulis                     YEHEB NUT

Howes says: ''In Somaliland this nut or bean is much relished by the Somalis and it is said that at times destitute natives have subsisted more or less entirely on it. The tree producing it occurs in the hinterland of British Somaliland and sacks of the nuts are brought down yearly to the coast and sold. The nut is rather larger than a filbert and has a fragile shell. The kernel may be eaten raw when it tastes not unlike a chestnut, or it may be boiled and served as a vegetable. The tree yielding the nut occurs in dry regions and is very deep-rooted.''

### Cordyla africana                      BUSH MANGO

*Cordyla* is a tree of French Sudan, Gambia and French Guinea. Dalziel says of it:

''The fruit is yellow when ripe, with two or three kidney-shaped black seeds in a soft pulp. By some it is regarded as one of the best of the wild fruits, by others it is said to be astringent and even to be rather unwholesome, sometimes causing vertigo.

''As this tree is capable of furnishing an agreeable edible fruit as well as shade, etc., it is to be recommended for propagation, and in Senegal it has been suggested for re-afforestation.''

Fanshawe writes: ''The seeds are occasionally eaten, raw or cooked by the Valley Tonga. Ripe seeds are ground into meal and eaten in famine times in Zanzibar.''

### Coumarouna odorata                    TONKA BEAN

The TONKA BEANS from Venezuela and parts of the Amazon Valley are not eaten directly but a lot of them end up in the mouth. Originally they were borne only on three kinds of *Coumarouna*, giants of the forest, although related, edible beans called *Dipteryx* are now included by botanists in the genus *Coumarouna*.

The three original *Coumarouna* trees furnish the big seeds called TONKA BEANS, in world-wide demand commercially. These yield coumarin, a crystalline substance with a fragrance suggesting vanilla, which is used to flavor snuff, cigarettes, cigars, cocoa, and confectionery. Coumarin is used also as an ingredient of perfumes, sachet powders and cosmetics.

Chief of these TONKA BEAN trees is *C. odorata* which in the wilds reaches 100 feet or more, but is scarcely medium sized in cultivation.

*Coumarouna* is one of the few genera among the legumes that bear ''beans'' containing a single seed and not opening at maturity. The fruit somewhat resembles that of the almond tree, and inside the fleshy oily covering is a single, black, elongated oily seed or bean shaped like an almond, but much longer, and highly fragrant. These beans mature in June-July, about nine months after flowering.

Harry Blossfeld wrote this author from Brazil: ''*Coumarouna* is no nut to eat. It is rather poisonous, containing alkaloids acting on the heart. Indeed, coumarin is the best poison for rats.''

Williams explains how the beans are cured: ''The ripe fallen fruits are gathered and spread out to dry on smooth open places; in Venezuela they are spread out on concrete pavements and turned daily like cacao. After drying the pods are carefully cracked and the chestnut coloured bean or seed removed. These are then dried in the open and are ready for curing.

''The dried beans are placed in casks or puncheons filled to about 12 inches from the top, strong spirit (minimum strength 45 per cent absolute alcohol or about 20⁰ under proof) is poured in until the cask is nearly full when it is covered over with a thick cloth. After two days the unabsorbed spirit is run off and the beans removed, spread in the open (usually on the wooden floor of a building) and allowed to dry in the shade for five or six days.

''The spirit can be used over again for curing further batches of beans as long as the minimum strength of alcohol, 45 per cent, is kept up by the addition of further cask or strong rum.''

A relative of the TONKA BEAN, *Torresea cearensis* which grows in the dry region of Bahia, Amburana, has a high oil content, and is largely exported in competition with the TONKA BEAN.

Recently a species of *Dipteryx* that grows in the botanic garden at Tingo Maria, Peru, was introduced into the U.S.D.A. experimental station at Miami. The nuts are called ''Sacha inti'' which might be translated as ''wild peanut.'' They are not eaten raw.

Another tree now considered a species of the Dipteryx-Coumarouna muddle, is described from Guam by Safford thus: ''*Bocoa edulis* or POLYNESIAN CHESTNUT.

''Local Names — If (N. Guinea); Ivi (Fiji); Ifi (Samoa); Cayam, Kayam (Cebu); Mape (Tahiti); Marrap (Ponape); Marefa (Mortlocks).

''A tree bearing an edible kidney-shaped fruit, recently introduced into Guam from the Caroline Islands, but not yet bearing. In Polynesia and in some of the Malayan Islands its fruit is an important food staple. The tree grows to a great size, often towering above the general level of the forest. When young the trunk is nearly cylindrical. It later becomes fluted, as though surrounded by adherent columns, which when older develop into radiating buttresses, like great planks. In Samoa it is one of the most striking features of the forest. Flowers inconspicuous, white or yellowish, very fragrant; pod shortstemmed, obovate, curved, hard, drupe-like, one seeded.

''In Polynesia the seed is eaten cooked when not quite ripe, and tastes much like a chestnut. In some islands it is preserved, like the breadfruit, in pits, where it is left to ferment. In Samoa it is a staple food for several months of the year.''

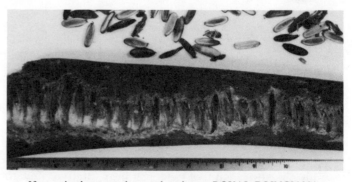

If a squirrel can reach a seed pod on a ROYAL POINCIANA *(Delonix regia)*, he chews out one whole side of the pod to get the delicious seeds within.

## Delonix regia    ROYAL POINCIANA

Nobody talks about eating the seeds of the ROYAL POIN-CIANA — it's too pretty. But the squirrels in my yard think the seeds are wonderful.

## Detarium senegalense    TALLOW TREE

Dalziel says there are two forms of this tree — one of 15-20 feet in open savannah woodlands and the other a forest tree to 120 feet and 5-foot diameter. Of the savannah tree he writes:

"The fruit is rounded or oval, flattened, 1½ in. in diameter, 1-seeded, with edible sweet greenish mesocarp which is penetrated by a fibrous network attached to the hard bony shell of the seed. The dry brown fruits are sold in markets. According to Pobeguin, vertigo is caused by eating too much of the fruit. In N. Nigeria it is used, along with that of *Diospyros mespiliformis* and of *Vitex Cienkowskii*, boiled, strained and concentrated to make a sort of sweetmeat or molasses. The tree often has small abortive fruits of quite a different shape, probably galls, which are said to be poisonous to persons who may inadvertently eat them when hungry.

"The kernel of the seed is deep purple-brown, and is more or less oily and edible.

"The fruit of the forest tree is comparatively large, 2-3 in. in diameter, with a strongly developed fibrous network through the succulent outer pulp, which has a strong sickly smell when decaying on the forest floor. The outer skin is smooth and thinly crustaceous, and the mature fruits are exceedingly like those of larger specimens of *Irvingia gabonensis*, from which they are at once distinguished by the reticulate nature of the fibre in the pulp as compared with the bristly material in that of *Irvingia*. It is very bitter, and even suspected to be poisonous."

## Dialium engleranum

*Dialium* is a small genus of trees found throughout the tropics. They produce plum-like fruits with a solitary seed and a little edible pulp. Fanshawe wrote of this species in west tropical Africa: "The seeds are eaten raw by the Bushmen after soaking in water for an hour."

## Dimorphandra mora

Sturtevant wrote: "A gigantic timber-tree of British Guiana. The seeds are used by the natives as food, being boiled, grated, and then mixed with cassava meal, giving it a brown color but a pleasant and sweetish taste. The seeds of another species are likewise used."

HYACINTH BEAN *(Dolichos lablab)*

## Dolichos lablab    HYACINTH BEAN

*Dolichos* comprises 70 kinds of beans in warm countries. This species is a vine. In Malawi it is described by Williamson:

"The beans are eaten as a side-dish. They are very hard and are said to take up to eight hours to cook but they may be ground before cooking (Karonga). They are also cooked with the skins removed as cipere. The skins are very firmly attached, hence the beans are first roasted, then ground between stones, then pounded, after which the skins are winnowed off. In spite of this drastic treatment, the cotyledons of the bean remain unbroken. Red and white kinds are boiled in their pods and the beans eaten one by one as makata (Palombe); black kinds are too bitter for this. The beans are boiled twice and the third time are mixed with maize and again boiled to form ngata (Karonga).

"The wild HYACINTH BEAN is grown in hilly areas, the beans are small and are not eaten."

## Elephantorrhiza goetzei

Fanshawe writes. "Young beans are cooked for two days in changes of water and eaten in Zambia in famine times."

K. M. Vaid Photo

*(Entada pursaetha)*

## MATCHBOX BEAN
## GILLA NUT
## Entada scandens    QUEENSLAND BEAN

This lofty vine of India and Burma, now cosmopolitan in the tropics, is described by Watt: "The pods contain large, flat, hard, polished, chestnut-coloured seeds, or rather nuts, which, on being steeped in water and afterwards roasted, are sometimes eaten by the natives."

Irvine says: "Fruits — probably the largest pods in W. Africa and almost in the world — 3-4 feet in length, woody, slightly constricted between segments, breaking between each seed; seeds large, almost circular, flattened 3-4 in. diameter, shiny, rich reddish brown.

"The seeds are roasted and eaten both in N. Australia and India. The roasted seeds are a coffee substitute. The seeds, often found on river banks or the seashore, retain their germinating ability for a long time. They are used in a game, also, having first been hollowed out, they go to make a small musical instrument.''

Burkill says: "The seed can be eaten, but without careful preparation is unwholesome. Greshoff says it requires boiling the whole day. The Anamanese eat it. As heat destroys the saponin, either roasting or boiling suffices. Heyne says, in Bali, Java and Sumatra, the poor roast the fresh seeds until the skin bursts, and then eat the rather bitter interior; or by a better method, soak the already roasted seeds for twenty-four hours in water, and boil before eating.''

Sturtevant says: "This vine is found on tropical shores from India to the Polynesian Islands. The seeds are flat and brown and are eaten cooked like chestnuts in Sumatra and Java, and the pods furnish food in the West Indies. In Jamaica, Lunan says the beans, after being long soaked in water, are boiled and eaten by some negroes.''

*CORAL TREE (Erythrina indica)*

## *Erythrina variegata*          CORAL TREE

This moderately big tree, native of India, is much planted through India to Burma and southern China, cultivated for shade and support.

Burkill says: "The seeds may be eaten after boiling or roasting but they are poisonous when raw.''

## *Geoffraea superba*          ALMENDORA

Sturtevant says: "South America. Gardner says this plant produces a fleshy drupe about the size of a walnut which is called 'umari' by the Indians. In almost every house, whether Indian or Brazilian, he observed a large pot of this fruit being prepared. The taste of the kernel is not unlike that of boiled beans. It is the ALMANDORA of the Amazon.''

USDA Photo
SOYBEANS *(Glycine max)*. Newly harvested Harosoy SOYBEANS in Ohio.

## *Glycine max*          SOY BEAN / SOJA BEAN

The SOY BEAN, a cherished food and fodder for 2,000 years in Japan, China and elsewhere in the east, is now coming into its own as a source of oil used in food preparation, and even trying to become a nut. The parched beans are sold in plastic bags nowadays in chain stores, like so many salted peanuts.

Commercialized SOYBEANS as roasted tidbits in plastic bag.

Manchuria is still the center of SOY BEAN production, though American farmers are fast getting into the picture.

Burkill devotes pages to describing various food products made from the oil, including artificial milk. In the United States it has become not only a nut, but an important ingredient in soap manufacture.

*(Guibourtia conjugata)*

94

*(Guibourtia coleosperma)*

## Guibourtia coleosperma

*Guibourtia* is a genus of trees with 4 species in tropical America, and 11 species in Africa.

Fanshawe writes from Zambia of this: "Locally the seeds are soaked in water for 1-2 days, cooked with cassava and eaten as relish."

## Indigofera

This large genus of herbs grows throughout the world, and is prized chiefly for the famous dye, indigo.

Burkill records that the seeds of several species are said to be poisonous, but Watt says that the seeds of four species are eaten as famine foods in India.

OTAHITE CHESTNUT *(Inocarpus edulis)*

## Inocarpus edulis
(Syn. *I. fagiferus*)

### OTAHITE CHESTNUT
### POLYNESIAN CHESTNUT
### TAHITIAN CHESTNUT

Burkill calls this a "smallish tree" of eastern Malaysia, extending across the tropical Pacific. Although it grows in the forests it is much planted in the villages. It bears large kidney-shaped pods each with a single seed or bean.

Safford says: "The tree grows to a great size, often towering above the general level of the forest. When young the trunk is nearly cylindrical. It later becomes fluted, as though surrounded by adherent columns, which when older develop into radiating buttresses, like great planks. In Samoa it is one of the most striking features of the forest."

Bailey says the fruits are "borne singly in flat, fibrous pods, having a smooth outer surface. They are thin and somewhat wedge-shaped. Typical specimens measure approximately 2 x 1¾ by ¾ inches."

Burkill says: "The seeds taste like chestnuts, and from this comes the English name. They may be eaten after boiling or roasting in ashes. They are indigestible, but much consumed in Celebes and to the eastward. It is best to eat them before they are quite ripe. An analysis of the seeds gives 7 per cent of fat, 10 per cent of albumens, 2.5 per cent of ash, and 80 per cent of non-nitrogenous substances on dry weight, the last apparently largely starch.

"In some of the islands of the Pacific the seeds are used in exactly the same way as BREADFRUIT seeds, i.e., they are allowed to undergo a partial fermentation in pits in the ground, by which means they can be kept into seasons when food becomes scarce."

Barrau says: "The nuts are boiled or roasted. The cooked nuts or raw ones, strung on twigs as are beads, are sold in the native markets in the Society Islands. Some Polynesians prepare flat cakes from the grated seeds mixed with coconut meat and cream and bake them in the oven in a covering of green leaves, and the Marquesas make purees from the cooked seeds, flavored with coconut cream.

"In Polynesia and in some Micronesian islands surplus pods are buried in the ground for future use."

Sturtevant says: "The nuts are eaten in the Fiji Islands, roasted or in a green state, and are soft and pleasant to the taste. They are much prized by the natives of the Indian Archipelago and in Machian the inhabitants almost live on them. Labillardiere says the fruit is eaten boiled by the natives of the Friendly Islands. Wilkes says it is the principal food of the mountaineers of Fiji. Voigt says the nuts are edible but are by no means pleasant."

*(Intsia bijuga)*

## Intsia bijuga

*Intsia* comprises 6 species of trees and shrubs from tropical Africa to Malaysia. Benjamin Stone of the botanic garden at Singapore wrote: "The seeds are poisonous but after washing and soaking 3 or 4 days, they can be eaten."

## Lathyrus                                     SWEET PEA

The SWEET PEA genus supplies not only pretty flowers but a good many edible nuts among its 150 species and *L. macrorrhizus* and other species produce tubers that are eaten like potatoes.

Sturtevant says: "*L. aphaca*. Europe and the Orient. The seeds are served sometimes at table while young and tender but if eaten abundantly in the ripe state are narcotic, producing severe headache.

"*L. maritimus*. SEASIDE-PEA. The seeds are very bitter. In 1555, the people of a portion of Suffolk County, England, suffering from famine, supported themselves to a great extent by the seeds of this plant.

"*L. montanus*. BITTER VETCH. In Holland and Flanders, the peas are roasted and served as chestnuts. According to Sprengel, the peas are eaten in Sweden and form an article of commerce.

"*L. sativus*. CHICKLING VETCH. The flour from the peas makes a pleasant bread but is unwholesome; its use in the seventeenth century was forbidden in Wurtemburg by law. The peasants, however, eat it boiled or mixed with wheat flour in the quantity of one-fourth without any harm. In many parts of France the seed is used in soups.

## Lens esculenta                               LENTIL

Ten species of this herb in the Mediterranean region and Western Asia, produce food for millions. The small round seeds split on removing the skin into orange cotyledons. They are commonly used for soup. Eaten by both Europeans and natives.

## Leucaena glauca                        HORSE TAMARIND

This South American shrub or tree grows to 25 feet, now naturalized throughout the tropics, is usually a hedge, bearing 1-inch white ball flower heads, and 6 inch pods that hang on long after the seeds are shed. The 1-inch ripe seeds are eaten raw in West Africa and Malaysia.

Burkill calls them "something tasty." Dry seeds are eaten parched.

LANCEPOD *(Lonchocarpus capassa)*

## Lonchocarpus capassa                     LANCEPOD

Fanshawe wrote: "The seeds are crushed, boiled and eaten in Zambia in times of famine."

## Lupinus hirsutus                           LUPINE

Sturtevant says: "Mediterranean regions. This plant was cultivated by the Greeks and serves now as food for the poorer classes of people, as it did the Cynics. The Mainots, at the present day, bake bread from the seeds. It now grows wild throughout the whole of the Mediterranean region from Portugal and Algiers to the Greek islands and Constantinople.

"*L. luteus*, YELLOW LUPINE. Mediterranean region. The seeds constitute a nutritious article of food for man. It is cultivated in Italy.

"*L. perennis*, WILD LUPINE. Eastern North America. Unger says its bitter seeds are eaten from Canada to Florida.

"*L. termis*. This plant is cultivated in Italy and in Egypt for its seeds, which are cooked in salt water and shelled. The peduncles, after being pickled, are eaten without cooking."

## Medicago                               BLACK MEDICK
                                             NONESUCH

Sturtevant says: "This bean of the Old World is naturalized in southern California where its seeds are much relished by the Indians."

## Monopteryx uacu

This Brazilian tree, one of three species in tropical America, bears seeds that are used to produce an edible cooking oil. This species grows in Rio Negro and Solimoes, Amazonas, where the nut kernels are eaten after being boiled or roasted.

## Mucuna sloanei                        HORSE-EYE BEAN

This genus of 100 species of vines scattered through the tropics and subtropics is famed for the stinging hairs on the fruits.

Irvine says: "A climber or climbing shrub. Fruits oblong, 6 in., with oblique furrows, almost black when ripe, with yellowish sting hairs; seeds almost spherical, slightly flattened sideways, diameter about 1 in., almost black. In E. Nigeria the plant is cultivated, being grown on tall poles as climbing beans; and the seeds are pounded, cooked and eaten, especially in soup.

Burkill says: "*Mucuna* is a genus of rather vigorous climbers, somewhat woody. Many of them possess spicular hairs on the stems and pods, which, when they penetrate the human skin, give rise to considerable irritation.

"In Florida it attracted attention and got the name FLORIDA VELVET BEAN (*M. deeringiana*).

"The demand for cattle-fodder in the United States caused more work to be done on the genus, as it was found to meet a need. No desire for fodder stimulated man in Asia to cultivate the Asiatic plants; but they were evidently his food crop. This being so, it is interesting to ask in which measure they served him. Their seeds were eaten, as they still are: but considerable care had to be taken in their preparation, for a toxic substance is found in the seed-coat and it would seem in the substance of the seeds also, though eliminated from the best by selection. Probably soaking and a double boiling were always given. Another preparation of them is fermented: the seeds are boiled; the seed-coat removed; the seed itself soaked in running water, chopped up, steamed and then left to ferment in some favourable spot, probably where such a preparation has previously been made so that fungus spores are present.

"The hairs of the wild species of *Mucuna* sting when the plants themselves have been long dead; the irritation which they produce, however severe, is mechanical.

"BLACK VELVET BEAN. Rumpf says that the seeds, when the pods are turning yellow, can be eaten and have a pleasant taste if soaked for two or three days in changes of water, finally in rain-water or sea-water, or at any rate in water with the addition of salt, until the skin is removable and then thoroughly cooked. But if these precautions are not taken, head-aches and dizziness follow eating them.''

IRONWOOD *(Olneya tesota)*

## *Olneya tesota*      IRONWOOD

Sturtevant says. ''Mexico. This tree grows in the most desolate and rocky parts of Arizona and Sonora. The seeds are eaten raw or roasted by the Indians. When care is taken to parch them they equal peanuts with no perceptible difference in taste. The Mohave Indians of Arizona store them for winter use.''

## *Pachyrhizus tuberosus*      POTATO BEAN

Sturtevant says this grows in the West Indies. He continues: ''The plant has large, tuberous roots, which, as well as the seeds, serve as food.''

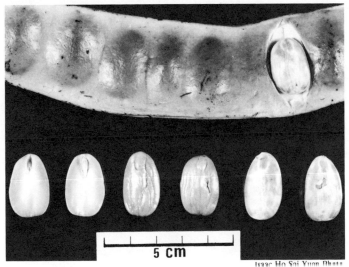

Isaac Ho Sai-Yuen Photo

*(Parkia speciosa)* in Malaya. Eaten with curry dishes either cooked or raw.

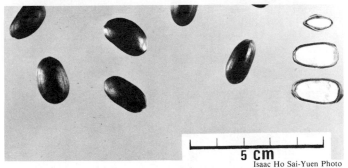

Isaac Ho Sai-Yuen Photo

*(Parkia javanica)* in Malaya. Seeds eaten by aborigines.

K. M. Vaid Photo

*(Parkia roxburghii)*

## *Parkia filicoidea*      AFRICAN LOCUST BEAN

*Parkia* is a small genus of trees found all around the world in the moister tropics.

Dalziel says: ''This species is very common in N. Nigeria and extends north to beyond Kano, to about 14° N. Lat., the most typical tree of the park savannah, and in many populous regions it may be the only tree in the landscape; often leafless when in flower, and often defoliated by caterpillars. Every locust tree in inhabited districts has an owner. The abundant leaf-fall is a valuable soil improver, rich in nitrogen and ash, and in some districts the people themselves collect the leaves for use as manure.

''The fruits are from 6-10 in. long and hang in clusters.

''The yellow pulp is a comparatively dry, soft substance in which the black seeds are embedded, and can be separated by sifting after drying. It is sold as a yellow meal like powdered biscuit and is a valuable food.

''The seeds are boiled for twenty-four hours to soften the seed-coats, pounded, washed several times to remove the broken shells; the kernels are boiled to form a paste and then set aside for two or three days to ferment. After fermentation they are made into cakes or balls. This rather strongly smelling blackish article is used as food and seasoning, commonly as a basis for soup, and, as it keeps well, it is an important article in Hausa itinerant trade, both for personal use and for barter. The odour is destroyed by frying or roasting, and its place in culinary economy is much the same as that of cheese amongst Europeans, as a concentrated food used also as a seasoner. Some N. Togo tribes grind the seeds to a fine meal and macerate in water to make a sort of gruel to be taken as a refreshing drink. The seeds contain about 17% of a semi-solid fat and a high percentage of protein, and are thus also a good foodstuff. No poisonous properties are present in seeds or pulp.''

Of the related tree, *Parkia biglobosa*, Dalziel writes: ''The fruit is known in Gambia as 'monkey cutlass,' and in Sierra Leone sometimes as 'St. John's Bread,' which is properly the locust bean of the Levant (*Ceratonia*). The farinaceous pulp, and the seeds are both used as food in the same manner as those of *P. filicoidea*. In Sierra Leone the word 'kinda' seems to have been widely used for the fermented product of the seeds.

"The seeds have been used as a substitute for coffee. From the seeds is prepared the greasy extract, of unpleasant odour and appearance called "netetou," which is preserved and used as required as a food and seasoner."

Bailey's Cyclopedia says of the NITTA-NUT or NUTTA-NUT (*P. africana*): "Edible seeds, borne within the long clustered pods of the AFRICAN LOCUST TREE. The pods, containing a sweetish farinaceous pulp within which the seeds are imbedded, are eaten entire, as is the carob or St. John's Bread."

Describing the same tree, Sturtevant says: "The natives of Sudan roast the seeds and then bruise and allow them to ferment in water until they become putrid, when they are carefully washed, pounded into powder and made into cakes, which are excellent sauce for all kinds of food but have an unpleasant smell."

Of another species *P. biglandulosa* which grows in Malaya, Sturtevant writes: "The seeds are eaten by the Malays, who relish them as well as the mealy matter which surrounds them. The former taste like garlic.

"The seeds contain about 16 per cent of a clear yellow oil. It is not employed as an oil-seed, however, but the seeds are as a seasoning and adjunct to food. They are roasted and then shelled. At this stage they can be made into a sort of coffee, but that, again, is only a minor use. Their major use is to furnish a food after being subjected to fermentation, which is sometimes short, and is arrested by the addition of salt; or sometimes is prolonged. Prolonged fermentation results in a cheesey substance with an unpleasant smell. There is a big trade not only in seeds, but particularly in these different preparations, which serve the travelling Negro as dates do the travelling Arab, adding to his diet of cooked grain a flavouring and substances which go far towards balancing it.

"The seeds are often used as a substitute for those of *P. speciosa*; but being slightly bitter are in less favour. They are roasted for eating.''

### *Pentaclethra macrophylla*

OIL BEAN TREE
ATTA BEAN

*Pentaclethra* is a huge tree to 120 feet or more and 6 feet in diameter, in the forests of Senegal, Angola and the Belgian Congo. It is often cultivated, and usually left standing when forest growth is cleared for farming.

Dalziel says: "The pods are very large, hard and strongly elastic, over 18 in. long and 4 in. wide, bursting violently, the valves curling up when dry. The beans are known as oil-seeds under the names 'fai' (Sierra Leone and French Guinea), 'obachala' (Nigeria), 'atta' (Gold Coast) and 'owala' or 'ovala' (Cameroons and Gabon). They yield about 30-36% of oil from beans in the shell, or 44-45% from kernels after removal of the seed-coats; they are rich in protein (exceeded only by the soja bean and *Vicia Faba*), but poor in starch. The oil is non-drying, with a high melting point, and has an unpleasant pungent odour.

"The beans are commonly eaten after roasting, but more as a condiment than as a staple food. In Nigeria if eaten boiled, they are cooked for twelve hours first. Cooper refers to the tree as 'Liberian wild locust,' the seeds being used to season 'palaver sauce.' In Gabor, they are sometimes an added ingredient to 'odika.' Walker describes the method of use as follows: 'The seeds are cooked, split open with a knife to separate the two cotyledons, which are cut small and put in a stream; after two to three hours they are removed, dried and ground to extract the fat, which is then kneaded in small loaves of odika.' "

Irvine says: "The seeds are red, flattened, up to 3 x 8 inches. They are edible after roasting or boiling for 12 hours, though more as a condiment than a food, e.g. in Liberia they season 'palaver sauce' because of their sweet smell, while in parts of Trop. W. Africa they are eaten wrapped in leaves after roasting, sometimes with plantains. The Ibos of Nigeria boil the seeds, remove husks, and shell the cotyledons, add salt, and allow them to ferment in a warm place for 3 days before eating. The oil, limpid or with an unpleasant aromatic and burning taste is used for cooking purposes."

Sturtevant says: "A tree, the seeds are eaten by the natives, who also extract a limpid oil from them."

### *Piliostigma thonningii*

*Piliostigma* is a genus of three kinds of trees in the drier parts of tropical Africa, Indo-Malaysia and Queensland.

Fanshawe writes of this species: "Ripe seeds ground into meal and eaten in famine times in Zanzibar."

Irvine says: "This low scrambling shrub or small and often crooked tree with a low spreading crown, grows in grass savannah forests, from the Congo to Rhodesia and the Transvaal. The pods are 6 inches by over 2 inches, seeds small, scattered throughout pods. The seeds are eaten by man in the Sudan."

Palmer & Pittman: *Trees of South Africa* says *Bauhinia thonningii* is now known as *Piliostigma thonningii*. Regarding the seeds of this tree, the book says:

"The pods are large — up to 23 cm. long and 8 cm. wide — woody, heavy, green becoming bright chestnut brown, and are covered with tiny raised lines. When in full fruit in winter and spring, the branches are weighed down by the weight of the massed pods. In times of famine Africans eat the pods and seeds."

*(Pithecellobium lucyi)* New Guinea.

5 cm

Isaac Ho Sai-Yuen Photo

JIRINGA *(Pithecellobium jiringa)*

## *Pithecellobium jiringa*      JIRINGA

This 80-foot tree through most of Malaysia, abundant in villages, is one of the 200 species that produce edible seeds.

Burkill says: "The seeds may be eaten after two or three boilings on successive days. They are mostly used as a flavouring for food, and are liked by the Malays, but to Europeans their smell is objectionable. The pods, for the purpose, come to market, and the Sakai find it profitable to barter them to their neighbours for rice. Immature seeds are used as well as ripe ones. Kerr states that in Lower Siam seeds from wild trees are preferred to those from a cultivated tree.

"The seeds contain nearly 70 per cent of starch, together with small quantities of fat. In them is a volatile oil consisting of a sulphur compound of allyl, and also an alkaloid.

"Ingested, the seeds act as a diuretic, the allyl compound being excreted by the body through the kidneys. If more than a small amount has been eaten inflammation is set up in the kidneys, blood may be passed, and stricture may follow. Death even results. An overdose is best countered by a harmless diuretic.

"There are various ways in which attempts are made to minimize the effect. One is to bury the seeds until they germinate, and only use them then. Another, is to pound the seeds and make them into wafer-like cakes which are sun-dried. This results in the removal of some of the oil."

Benjamin Stone in Malaysia says: "This has a garlicy flavor and is supposed to be helpful to diabetics."

*P. unguis-cati* is a small, spiny bush coming into cultivation in the West Indies and elsewhere. Burkill suggests: "The seeds are said to be eaten by the negroes in the West Indies."

Burkill says the seeds of *P. bubalinum* have the flavor of JIRINGA but are rarely used for it because "their action on the kidneys is dangerously powerful."

Howes says that the NGAPI NUT (*P. lobatum*) "is the seed obtained from the large twisted pod of a jungle tree in Burma. It is collected and sold in the bazaars and eaten in a variety of ways by Burmans — either raw, salted, boiled,

or cooked with coconut milk or oil. Its powerful odour renders it objectionable to many."

## *Prioria copaifera*

This vine, the only species, grows in Jamaica and Panama. Sturtevant says: "The enormous seeds have edible embryos. They are sold in Panama under the name 'cativa.'"

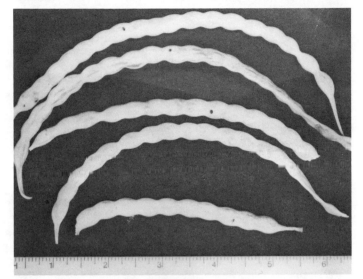

MESQUITE *(Prosopis glandulosa)*

South African Forestry Dept. Photo

*(Prosopis juliflora).*

## *Prosopis juliflora*      MESQUITE

In the arid southwestern part of the United States, MESQUITE has edible, bean-like pods with sweet pulp, and FREMONT SCREWBEAN (*P. pubescens*) has sugary, spirally-coiled pods. The Indians dried and ground these pods into meal for bread.

*P. africana* is a 60-foot spreading tree from Senegambia to the Congo and Uganda, usually in savannah forest. The 6-inch seed pods contain up to 10 seeds, loose and rattling. Dalziel says the seeds are used for food in Nigeria in much the same way as those of *Parkia*.

Sturtevant says in Argentina: "*P. algarobilla* has seeds that are sweet and nutritious. He adds that *P. dulcis*, commonly called ALGAROBA-CASHAU, produces seeds that ground to powder, constitute the principal food of many of the inhabitants of Brazil."

99

## Psophocarpus tetragonolobus     GOA BEAN

Sturtevant writes: "This plant is grown in India for the sake of its edible seeds. In the Mauritius, the plant is cultivated for the seeds. Pickering says it is a native of equatorial Africa and the kidney beans of the finest quality, observed by Cada Mosto in Senegal in 1455, belong here."

Burkill says: "A climber. It furnishes edible roots as well as pods, but in many places where it is grown the cultivators never use the roots. In Burma considerable use is made of them. They may be eaten raw, and are slightly sweet with the firmness of an apple.

"The seeds are eaten in Java after parching. Hooper's analysis of them shows 37 per cent of albuminoids, 28 per cent of carbohydrates, and 15 per cent of oil. Crevost and Lemarie say that they are indigestible."

J. K. Maheshwari Photo, National Botanic Garden, Lucknow

BIJASAL *(Pterocarpus marsupium)*

## Pterocarpus santalinoides

*Pterocarpus* is a genus of 100 timber trees of India and Malaysia, with winged seeds. Several species furnish kino, and astringent resin.

Dalziel says of this species: "The seeds are roasted and eaten in scarcity, but various informants state that, unless cooked properly or if eaten in more than small quantities, they are unwholesome, giving rise to symptoms of vertigo and vomiting. Chevalier, on the other hand, says that the tree is sometimes planted in villages of S. Dahomey for the sake of its edible fruits. The Hausas refer to the fruit a-fere (to peel or scrape off the surface), suggesting that any harmful property may be confined to the outer coverings."

Irvine says: "The seeds, after necessary cooking, are eaten in Guinea and Sierra Leone, and in Ghana, after necessary roasting, in times of scarcity."

Maheshwari says of the Indian kino tree (*P. marsupium*): "The flowers and seeds are edible."

## Sesbania aculeata

Of this low prickly shrub which is common in India and Malaya, Burkill writes: "The seeds are edible. According to an analysis they have a high food-value, associated, as far as can be told, with no deleterious substances."

Of *S. aegyptiaca* Watt writes: "The seeds were eaten at Poona during the famine of 1877-78."

## Sphenostylis stenocarpa

### GROUND SQUIRREL'S BEAN

Dalziel says: "In West Tropical Africa this is cultivated both for the seed and for the tuber.

"The seeds are rounded-oval, not flat, and vary in colour from whitish unmarked to various shades of brown with speckling and marbling. They have to be soaked for several hours before cooking."

Dalziel adds that *S. Schweinfurthii* in Nigeria "is not cultivated but the seeds can be used for food in an emergency."

Fanshawe writes from Zambia: "*S. marginata* beans have been eaten locally in famine times."

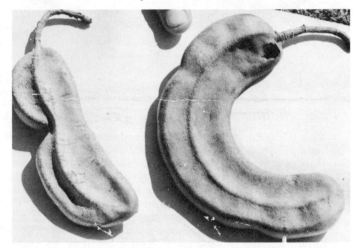

TAMARIND seed pods. *(Tamarindus indica)*

## Tamarindus indica     TAMARIND

This big, beautiful evergreen Indian shade tree bears quantities of seeds — very hard nuts in very hard pods. Hooker wrote: "The seeds are eaten in India in times of scarcity by the poorer classes, the very astringent integument being first removed, and, then roasted or fried, are said to resemble the common field-bean in taste.

Burkill says: "In India sometimes the beans are made into flour, or starch is extracted from them."

## Trigonella foenum-graecum     FENUGREEK

A strongly and pleasantly scented plant. Its cultivation extends from the Mediterranean to western India and to China. Its seeds, after roasting, are eaten in Egypt.

GEMSBOK BEAN *(Tylosema esculentum)*

## *Tylosema esculentum*      GEMSBOK BEAN
(Syn. *Bauhinia esculenta*)

This South African plant, long identified as a *Bauhinia* among the 500 different kinds of so-called ORCHID TREES, has been sparingly grown in Florida. This author wrote in his book *Color in the Sky*: "The GEMSBOK BEAN is a native of southwestern Africa. It is said to be a tree to 40 feet, but usually seen as a prostrate, trailing plant which can even be used as a ground cover. Seedlings grown at the Sub-Tropical Experiment station at Miami behave as vines and produce tendrils. The flowers are fragrant, a bright yellow in October and November. The seeds are ½ inch in diameter and are an important source of food for the African Bushmen. The seeds are rich in protein and oils, the latter 42 per cent and of a pleasant taste. The oil is similar to cottonseed oil and commercially is called GEMSBOK oil."

Loyd Schaad, a correspondent in Botswana, in southwest Africa, writes that this plant is now known there as *Tylosema esculentum*, and he sent the seeds pictured here. Seeking to verify the switch in nomenclature, this author received the following letter from Dr. Wm. J. Dress of the Bailey Hortorium at Cornell University:

"Apparently the South African botanists are recognizing *Tylosema* now as a separate genus; it was previously just a section of *Bauhinia*. It is not really a matter of right or wrong, but rather a matter of taxonomic opinion. Since the South Africans are recognizing *Tylosema* as a distinct genus, however, I think one may as well follow them in this.

"*Tylosema* is neuter in gender, so the name is *Tylosema esculentum*, not *esculenta*, even though many authors have written it the latter way."

In his book *Some Plants Used by the Bushmen in Obtaining Food and Water* Dr. R. Story wrote:

"This plant (*Tylosema*) is a runner in open grassveld, to 18 feet, but is not a climber. The vines die back during the winter and new runners are produced from the perennial underground stem. The plant bears showy yellow flowers in December, and the pods ripen from April onwards. At first they are soft and reddish brown, then light green and, when ripe, brown and woody. They contain up to six flattened seeds about the size of one's thumb nail, consisting of a hard shell and a soft nutty edible inner part. The plant is easily seen because of the craters it forms where the soil is stony, — craters a yard or more across, edged with a ring of stones which appear to have been forced to the surface by the stem beneath.

"Although the seeds are not pleasant to eat when raw, they are excellent after roasting, and analysis figures show that they are rich in protein and oil. The roasting should be carried out slowly, otherwise they may shatter with a rather disconcerting report, and to avoid this they are often roasted in sand, which probably gives a slower and more even heat. They may also be boiled to make a porridge or a drink. They will last through the winter in the field without spoiling.

"With breeding this might become a useful plant of cultivation."

## *Vigna catjang*      COWPEA

Sturtevant says: "This plant is cultivated in Portugal, Italy and India. In Martinique the seeds are highly esteemed as an article of food. In the southern states, this species has many permanent varieties, as Red Cowpea, Black-eyed pea and so on. So conspicuous is this species that in some localities it is made to carry the name of all others, all being referred to as the COWPEA. This plant is extensively cultivated in India for its pods, which are often two feet in length, contain a number of pea-like seeds, called by the Hindus chowlee, and form a considerable article of food."

## *Xanthocercis zambeziaca*

This is a genus of two species of trees in East Africa and Madagascar.

Fanshawe writes from Zambia: "The seeds are pounded and mixed with millet meal to make a sweet porridge."

*(Xeroderris stuhlmannii)*

## *Xeroderris stuhlmannii*

Fanshawe writes from Zambia: "The Valley Tonga eat the seeds after prolonged boiling in famine times."

101

# Chapter 20
# THE SUNFLOWER FAMILY
## (COMPOSITAE)

*No, the heart that has truly lov'd never forgets*
*But as truly loves on to the close,*
*As the sunflower turns on her god, when he sets,*
*The same look that she turn'd, when he rose.*

There are 110 kinds of SUNFLOWER, all of them American, so that it is a home-grown institution. There are a few other genera in the family that produce edible seeds but they are of only minor importance.

### *Balsamorhiza sagittata*  (Compositae) OREGON SUNFLOWER

Sturtevant says: "Northwestern America. The roots are eaten by the Nez Perce Indians in Oregon, after being cooked on hot stones. They have a sweet and rather agreeable taste. Wilkes mentions the Oregon SUNFLOWER of which the seeds, pounded into a meal, are eaten by the Indians of Puget Sound."

5 CM

HELIANTHUS ANNUUS
(Sunflower seeds)

### *Helianthus annuus* (Compositae) SUNFLOWER

The common SUNFLOWER that originated in North America, has become a valued food producer in countries all over the world. The seeds were first used as food four hundred years ago.

Sturtevant says: "Brewer and Watson say in all probability the wild SUNFLOWER of the California plains is the original of the cultivated SUNFLOWER and that the seeds are now used by the Indians as food. Kalm, 1749, saw the common SUNFLOWER cultivated by the Indians at Loretto, Canada, in their maize fields; the seeds were mixed with thin maize soup. In 1615, the SUNFLOWER was seen by Champlain among the Hurons. The seeds are said to be boiled and eaten in Tartary. In Russia, they are ground into a meal, the finer kinds being made into tea-cakes, and in some parts the whole seed is roasted and used as a substitute for coffee.

"In Russia, this plant yields about 50 bushels of seed per acre, from which about 50 gallons of oil are expressed. This oil is used for culinary purposes in many places in Russia."

Burkill says: "The SUNFLOWER was brought from America to Spain in the middle of the sixteenth century. Its early history in Europe is obscure, but Matthioli, who died in 1577, mentions it as frequent in gardens, and Bauhin was able to record that by 1623 it had become quite familiar and flourished particularly in Spain, attaining there a height of 24 feet.

"It was first grown as an oil crop in Bavaria in 1725, and then in France in 1787. At the present time countries in central and eastern Europe grow it as an oil crop; but the seed has no well-established place in the markets. The Russians habitually eat the seeds; and races in which these are large have been selected for the purpose. The oil is a good edible oil."

Commercialized SUNFLOWER seed as tidbits in plastic bag.

M. G. Kains, discussing in Bailey's cyclopedia the commercial uses and the cultivation of the common SUNFLOWER, wrote:

"SUNFLOWERS are cultivated extensively in Russia, India and Egypt; less widely in Turkey, Germany, Italy and France. The seeds from the large-seeded variety are sold upon the streets in Russia as we do peanuts, except that they are eaten raw. The small-seeded variety is preferred for the manufacture of oil. When cold-pressed, a citron-yellow sweet-tasting oil, considered equal to olive or almond oil for table use, is produced. The resulting oil-cake, when warm-pressed, yields a less edible fluid, which is used for lighting, and in such arts as woollen dressing, candle and soap-making. The oils dry slowly, become turbid at ordinary temperatures and solid at 4°F.

"On some farms the heads are harvested as they ripen and placed upon floors or movable pole-racks to dry. Upon larger areas they are cut to the ground when most of the heads have ripened and piled, heads up, to cure. The former method insures a much higher grade of oil, and is therefore preferred. Every effort is made to prevent fermentation, either in the heads or in the pile of seeds, since this injures the quality of oil. When thoroughly dry the heads are either placed on racks or piled, face downward, on a floor and beaten with flails. The seeds are then spread thinly, shoved over occasionally, and allowed to become perfectly dry before being sent to the mill. The average yield is about fifty bushels to the acre. The percentage of husks ranges from 40 to 60; and the oil from 15 to 28. As a general rule, 100 bushels of seed will yield 33 bushels of kernels, 100 bushels of kernels from 280 to 320 gallons of oil of both qualities. Russian SUNFLOWER, a large-seeded variety, producing a single head, grows 8 feet tall, but is less esteemed for oil-production than the small-seeded varieties."

SUNFLOWER research is now being promoted by the National Cottonseed Products Association of Memphis, Tenn., with test acreage in a dozen states. In Florida, Dr. Victor Green, Professor of Agronomy at the University of Florida, Gainesville on one acre has 14 varieties under test.

Thornton Hartley writes in the *Florida Times-Union*:

"With cotton acreage reduced in recent years, 'there is not enough cottonseed to squeeze for oil anymore' and the cotton seed mills are underused, said Dr. Green. So the cottonseed products business since 1967 has been encouraging research to see if SUNFLOWERS can be grown as a competitive oilseed crop in the cotton production area.

"Dalton E. Gandy, agronomist with the National Cottonseed Products Association and consultant to SUNFLOWER research projects in various parts of the country, says, "I feel confident we've got a winner" with SUNFLOWERS.

"He said it produces 'a premium oil.' Two companies, Proctor and Gamble and Lever Brothers, are test marketing sun oil products, a cooking oil and a margarine, Gandy said.

"Gandy, who also is president of the International Sunflower Association said, 'Florida offers greater advantages than many other areas,' because flowers can be grown almost year round here.

"At the University of Florida SUNFLOWERS also are being looked at in studies on multiple cropping. 'What we're trying to do is keep the ground covered with crops 12 months of the year,' said Dr. Green and SUNFLOWERS may fit into this picture."

An agronomy fact sheet issued at the University of Florida says: "SUNFLOWERS are grown for oil, meal, silage, birdfeed, human consumption, windbreaks and ornamentation. The oil is used in cooking and salad oils, for producing margarine and in paints. The meal that results from oil extraction contains 40 to 46 per cent protein and is used in livestock feed. Russian scientists have bred SUNFLOWERS that contain over 40 per cent oil in the seed. SUNFLOWERS are fed to birds either alone or mixed with other grain. For human consumption, SUNFLOWERS are normally roasted. Windbreaks of SUNFLOWER plants may be used to protect vegetable plants.

"In recent years, Russia has been the world's leading producer of SUNFLOWERS with plantings of several million acres. The United States has only a few hundred thousand acres, with North Dakota, Minnesota and California being the major producing states.

"The 1967 average yield of SUNFLOWER seed for oil in North Dakota was 1,100 pounds per acre. In variety trials at Gainesville, up to 2,500 pounds of seed per acre have been obtained from the better plots. The average yield has been around 1,500 pounds per acre. With good cultural practices, commercial yields in Florida should be from 1,000 to 1,500 pounds per acre. A recent discovery in the genetics of SUNFLOWERS is expected to lead to better yields.

"VARIETIES: The intended use of SUNFLOWERS will influence the variety that should be planted. Greystripe is the variety generally desired by the birdseed trade, however, black-seeded varieties are also used. Peredovik, NK H01 and Krasnodarets are varieties that have yielded well in Gainesville and are high in oil content. These are all black-seeded varieties. Since there are limited markets for SUNFLOWERS in Florida, information on varieties desired by the buyer should be obtained before planting a commercial crop of SUNFLOWERS. Seed are normally available from dealers that will later purchase the SUNFLOWERS."

## *Madia sativa* (Compositae) MADIA-OIL

Sturtevant says: "Western North and South America. This plant is cultivated in Chile, France, Germany and Italy for the sake of the limpid and sweet oil which is expressed from its seeds. This oil is used as a substitute for olive oil. The seeds yield about 41 per cent to analysis and from 26 to 28 per cent to the oil-press, according to Boussingault, whose experiment in 1840 gave 635 pounds of oil and 1,706 pounds of oil cake per acre. The plant is easily cultivated, requiring management similar to seed clover, but, owing to the glutinous nature of the stems and stalks, the seeds require to be threshed and sown as soon as the crop is cut, otherwise fermentation injures them."

## *Guizotia abyssinica* (Compositae) NIGER SEED

Purseglove: *Tropical Crops* says:
"A small genus of 5 species of herbs in Tropical Africa. The seeds yield a yellow, edible, semi-drying oil with little odour and a pleasant nutty taste. It is used for culinary purposes, as an illuminant and for soap. The seeds are fried and eaten in India and are used in chutneys and condiments.

"*G. abyssinica* is of African origin and occurs sporadically from Ethiopia to Malawi. NIGER seed is grown as a rain-fed crop in areas of moderate rainfall seldom exceeding 40 in. and will produce a reasonable crop on rather poor soil."

## *Carthamus tinctorius* (Compositae) SAFFLOWER

Purseglove: *Tropical Crops* says:
"About 30 species distributed in Asia, Africa and the Mediterranean region. The dried florets were the source of red dye, safflower carmin, in Egypt, the Middle East and India. The colour is fugitive and has tended to be displaced by aniline dyes. The seeds are edible, usually being roasted first.

"SAFFLOWER is only known in cultivation, with primary centres in Afghanistan and the Nile Valley and Ethiopia. It was introduced experimentally as an oil crop into the United States in 1925, where it has been grown on a commercial scale since 1950, particularly in California. Trials have been made in Australia and South Africa."

---

# Chapter 21
# PUMPKINS
# and
# GOURDS

Pumpkins, squash, gourds, melons — they are all the same thing to hungry people. The pulp of many of them is eaten as a vegetable all over the world, but the really important part of these fruits is the great quantity of seeds inside. These are rich in proteins and fats and are produced and eaten in great quantities by many people. Because they are hard-shelled seeds eaten by humans, they have a place in this book on nuts.

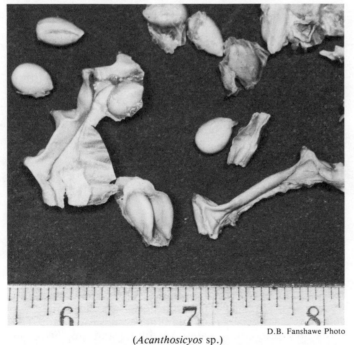

D.B. Fanshawe Photo

(*Acanthosicyos* sp.)

## *Acanthosicyos horrida* (Cucurbitaceae) NARAS

Sturtevant says: "Tropics of Africa. The fruit grows on a bush from four to five feet high, without leaves and with opposite thorns. It has a coriaceous rind, rough with prickles, is about 15-18 inches around and inside resembles a melon as to seed and pulp. When ripe it has a luscious sub-acid taste. The bushes grow on little knolls of sand. It is described, however, by Anderson as a creeper which produces a kind of prickly gourd about the size of a Swede turnip and of delicious flavor. It constitutes for several months of the year the chief food of the natives, and the seeds are dried and preserved for winter consumption."

Winn J. Tijmens, Botany Department, University of Stellenbosch, South Africa writes: "NARAS though few people know it, is an important source of food for the Topnaas Hottentots in the Southwest Africa desert near the Kuisel Valley. They are not cultivated (not yet but research may soon advise on commercial crops). The plants grow on these sand dunes and every family has its own area where they collect the squash-like fruits. Though every part is eaten, the seeds are most important for their high food value, and can be stored. Any surplus is sold to Capetown canneries as a substitute for almonds."

Regarding two species, *A. vulgaris* and *A. naudinianus*, Fanshawe writes from Zambia: "The Bushmen roast the seeds and pound them into flour."

Loyd O. Schaad writes from Botswana:

"*A. horrida* seed contains a butter-like substance which is greatly relished by the local inhabitants: seed parcels are sometimes sent to friends living away from the natural habitat (sandveld) of the plant. It is a densely bushy, spiny, leafless plant of the Namib sand dunes, up to 30 ft. in diameter. It flourishes only where subterranean water exists and to reach this, the root penetrates to over 45 ft. The plants produce globular spiny fruits, often as large as ostrich eggs and weighing up to 3 lbs. The pulp has a sourish-sweet taste, and, if eaten, produces a burning sensation of the mucous membranes.

"The seeds of *A. horrida* are also called 'butterpips' (pits). The seeds are rich in oil and after being boiled and dried, were sold locally (since 1877) for shipment to the Cape under this common name, for eating like nuts. As recently as 1915 still so sold in Cape Town. The kernel has the soft consistency of butter. Hottentots of the Namib extract the oil from the seeds by crude methods and use it as a food as well as for rubbing into the skin of the face, a practice that apparently long antedates the arrival of the European in the southern part of Africa."

Isaac Ho Sai-Yuen Photo

5 CM

WAX GOURD (*Benincasa hispida*)

## Benincasa hispida (Cucurbitaceae) WAX GOURD

This Asiatic gourd that gets 16 to 20 inches long and up to 12 inches in diameter, has been cultivated for its food value for a thousand years and is grown in many countries. One of its great values is that fruit keeps well if stored for a year without refrigeration.

The plant is a vine and because the fruits are heavy, it is often trained over buildings.

Burkill says: "The seeds contain a bland oil and are eaten fried by the Chinese."

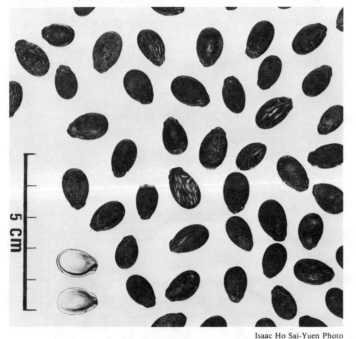

Isaac Ho Sai-Yuen Photo

BLACK MELON SEEDS (*Citrullus sp.*)

## Citrullus lanatus (Cucurbitaceae) WATERMELON

This is the most important of the three species. It is an African vine now cultivated all over the world. By selection the size has become enormous, up to 96 pounds or more. Not only is the sweet flesh enjoyed by millions, but the seeds are an important article of commerce.

Watt says: "The flattened and elliptic seeds yield a sweet, edible oil. In fact, the seeds of most of the members of the MELON, PUMPKIN, CUCUMBER, and GOURD family, contain oil, but the only kinds which are utilised to any considerable extent are those of the SWEET-MELON (*Cucumis Melo)* and the WATERMELON (*Citrullus lanatus*).

Howes says: "Although not nuts in the ordinary sense, WATERMELON seeds, with their oily kernels, are eaten out of hand after parching just like peanuts in many parts of the world. The practice of eating them like nuts is very common in southern China, especially in the province of Kwangtung, where the toasted seeds are a common article of food. They may be white, yellow, black, or reddish and with much variation in size. The kernels are also used in soups or stews and ground into meal or pounded into cakes. The oil in the kernel, which varies from 15 to 45 per cent may be extracted and used as a cooking oil. In Java the black seeds are first soaked in salt water and then roasted in a pan, when they are served as a delicacy. In west tropical Africa WATERMELONS are sometimes grown solely for the seeds. When ripe they are placed in heaps until the pulp has fermented. This renders the seeds much easier to extract."

Isaac Ho Sai-Yuen writes from Malaya: "The older generation of Chinese here are fond of eating dried WATERMELON seeds (both the black and red) as tidbits while watching a wayside opera or during their New Year."

## Colocynthis vulgaris (Cucurbitaceae) BITTER GOURD SIERRA LEONE GOURD

This is a cucumber-like vine from West Africa, often called Egusi. The boiled fruits are pickled or made into preserves. The seed kernels are also eaten. The variegated green and white orange-sized gourds are very ornamental and can be used for Halloween or Thanksgiving decorations.

Of the BITTER GOURD Sturtevant wrote: "This creeping plant grows abundantly in the Sahara, in Arabia, on the Coromandel coast and in some of the islands of the Aegean. The fruit as large as an orange, contains an extremely bitter pulp, from which the drug colocynth is obtained. Gypsies eat the kernel of the seed freed from the seedskin by a slight roasting. Fluckiger says the kernels are used as a food in the African desert, after being carefully deprived of their coatings. Stille says they are reported to be mild, oleaginous and nutritious. Captain Lyon speaks also of their use in northern Africa."

Dalziel says: "The seeds are known in West African markets as egusi, and their native uses are chiefly as a masticatory, and for medicine, food and oil. They are generally dried in the sun after extraction from the pulp, either by cutting up the latter when used as food, or after decomposition while left in heaps or buried for a few days. Analysis of seeds from Sierra Leone, Gold Coast and Nigeria showed that they are rich in fat — roughly 45%, and protein 34%. They are therefore of considerable food value, and the oil is easily refinable, and often preferred to other oils for cooking by Europeans. The oil is of the semi-drying type, a good substitute for COTTONSEED oil; that of certain varieties is fit for table use.

"Egusi seeds in Lagos are sold in at least two grades: (1) clean, white and fairly large; (2) smaller and rather dirty. As food they are put in soup, after roasting and grinding to pulp, or form an ingredient in sauce, or the oil may be used in cooking. Another food called igbalo is made from the seeds roasted, pounded, wrapped in a leaf and thus boiled; as sold in the market it is fried in the oil and red pepper added. The seeds can also be roasted as a substitute for coffee. The oil, extracted by boiling the mass of pounded seeds, or sometimes by either pressure or pounding after steaming the seeds, is used for cooking. The oil from the best seeds in Yoruba is used in cooking; it is probably suitable for use as a salad oil.

"The plant yields well on comparatively poor soils and requires only a small rainfall. In the deserts of South Tropical Africa it provides a food or a substitute for water for primitive tribes and for antelopes. The moisture of the pulp is made to exude by heating, and a sort of porridge is prepared from the kernels of the seeds."

Botanists now include this genus in *Citrullus*.

## Cucumis melo (Cucurbitaceae) SWEET MELON

*Cucumis* is a genus of about 25 kinds of MELONS, mostly African, plus the fruit we call CUCUMBER, but almost none of these has seeds that are eaten. In describing *C. melo*, Watt says:

"The flattened and elliptic seeds yield a sweet, edible oil. In fact, the seeds of most of the members of the MELON, PUMPKIN, CUCUMBER, and GOURD family, contain oil, but the only kinds which are utilised to any considerable extent are those of the SWEET-MELON (*C. melo*) and the WATERMELON (*C. lanatus*). From West Africa large quantities of MELON seeds are exported to France. China also does a considerable trade in them, but in India the fruit is chiefly eaten as such, and not allowed to ripen its seeds, and accordingly the supply of MELON oil is not extensive."

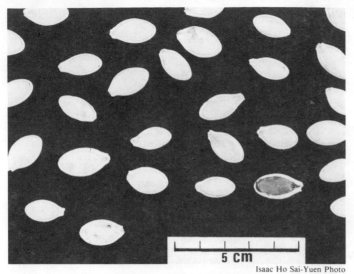

PUMPKIN (*Cucurbita maxima*)

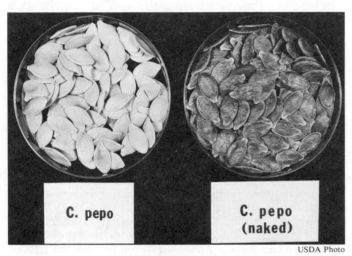

C. pepo

C. pepo (naked)

Lady Godiva PUMPKIN (*Cucurbita pepo*)

Lady Godiva PUMPKIN in the field

## *Cucurbita pepo*    (Cucurbitaceae)    SQUASH PUMPKIN GOURD

*Hortus Third* says of this genus: "Over 20 species of herbaceous plants, probably originally from the western hemisphere, . . . fruit an indehiscent, fleshy, corky berry, with hard rind, seeds many, horizontal."

The species *C. pepo* includes the PUMPKIN, SQUASH, GOURD and MARROW, and there are many varieties and hybrids of each.

Isaac Ho Sai-Yuen in Malaya writes: "The seeds of many of them are eaten by hungry people all over the world."

The U.S.D.A., Plant Science Research Division, in 1972 released the shell-less or naked-seeded PUMPKIN variety Lady Godiva. This variety produces seed yields large enough to make it feasible to grow the crop solely for the seeds, which have value as a snack food or as sources of protein and/or oil.

Lady Godiva was derived from a cross between PI 267663 and Beltsville Accession 102 which is a naked-seeded line received from the Agway Corporation in 1965. The former was one of five naked-seeded selections made by L. C. Curtis of the Connecticut Agricultural Experiment Station in the 1940's. It is a vining, naked-seeded, nearly round type pumpkin with slightly pale fruits. Accession 102 is also a vining, naked-seeded type with round green and yellow striped fruit. Both belong to the species *Cucurbita pepo*.

Like the parent lines, Lady Godiva is a vining type PUMPKIN producing 8 to 12 foot runners. The fruits are nearly round in shape and average 6.0 to 6.5 pounds. The external color of the mature fruits is a yellow orange and the internal flesh is a pale yellow color. The selections from which Lady Godiva were derived were made on the basis of high seed yielding ability, the attractiveness of the seed, and the freedom from splitting of the shell-less seeds in the mature fruit.

Commercialized PUMPKIN seeds as tidbits in plastic bag.

Lady Godiva seeds average about 9 x 16 mm in size and weigh about 200 mg each. The mature seeds are dark green. They average 35 to 40 per cent protein and 40 to 45 per cent oil. A comparison of the essential amino acid content of Lady Godiva seeds with the FAO reference protein is favorable except that they may be limiting in respect to total sulfur containing amino acids. Lady Godiva seeds have an excellent flavor eaten raw or roasted.

Regarding the BUFFALO GOURD (*C. foetidissima*), the book *Underexploited Tropical Plants* says:

"Demands for edible oil and protein in arid lands are increasing. Until recently wild gourds belonging to the SQUASH family, *Cucurbitaceae*, have been overlooked as a potential source of oil and protein for livestock and humans. Several of these are highly drought-tolerant, particularly the BUFFALO GOURD. On barren land the BUFFALO GOURD may match the performance of traditional protein and oil sources such as PEANUTS and SUNFLOWERS, which require more water. But little research has been conducted, and the BUFFALO GOURD is not yet commercially cultivated anywhere. Much research, particularly into the nutritional efficiency of the oil and protein, still remains to be done.

"The BUFFALO GOURD is a vigorous perennial. It grows wild on wastelands in the deserts of Mexico and the southwestern United States, and produces an abundant crop of fruit containing seed rich in oil and protein. Its large, fleshy, dahlia-like tubers grow as deep as 5 meters to obtain and store water. The plant is covered with a dull, wax coating. It produces yellow, hard-shelled, spherical fruit (to 8 cm. diameter) containing pulp and flat, white seeds 12 mm. long and 7 mm. wide. The fruit can be mechanically harvested and the flesh dries so completely in arid environments that the seed inside can be threshed out.

"Each fruit of the BUFFALO GOURD contains about 12 grams of seed and, on the basis of 60 fruits to the plant, 1 hectare of plants can produce 2.5 tons of seed. The seed contains 30-35 per cent protein and up to 34 per cent oil." These (estimated) yields compare favorably with other oil and protein-bearing crops such as soybeans and peanuts.

"The seeds can be crushed to obtain the edible polyunsaturated oil for food. The BUFFALO GOURD's enormous root can weigh as much as 30 kilograms (70 per cent moisture) after just two growing seasons. It is filled with starch.

"The plants are long lived; some are reportedly over 40 years old. The GOURD has been used by North American Indians for centuries."

Harold F. Winters, research scientist with the USDA at Beltsville, Md., wrote: "In Guatemala, I have eaten a confection of squash seeds resembling peanut brittle."

## *Hodgsonia macrocarpa* (Cucurbitaceae)

Howes says: "This plant is a member of the GOURD family and, like some of the WATERMELONS, has an oily seed which is eaten as an edible nut. The plant itself is a large vigorous climber found in Burma, Siam, and Malaysia. The gourd-like, though fibrous, fruit is about the size of a COCONUT and contains upwards of eight large flattish seeds. After baking the kernels are pleasant and wholesome, but when eaten raw are bitter and may contain deleterious substances. The oil content is from 50 to 60 per cent. In the Shan States where it is called 'mark-mun-mu', meaning literally 'lard seed', the nuts are crushed and cooked together with fish, meat, or vegetables. They are also crushed for oil used in cooking."

USDA Photo

NARANKA or DOLPHIN GOURD (*Lagenaria ciceraria*)

NARANKA GOURDS offered as jugs and vases

## *Lagenaria ciceraria*

(Cucurbitaceae)
BOTTLE GOURD
CALABASH CUCUMBER

There are six kinds of *Lagenaria* gourds, mostly in tropical Africa, commonly cultivated more for use in making utensils than for the food possibilities. Dalziel says:

"The seeds are commonly used as a masticatory, and some forms are cultivated for oil used in native cooking. The kernels of the seeds contain, according to variety, from 45-50% of a clear oil and 5% of protein."

Presumably, the word "masticatory" might be a synonym for chewing gum but Dalziel's further description indicates that the cud is swallowed and this becomes a nut in this book.

Photo from *Fifty Tropical Fruits of Nassau* by Kendal and Julia Morton
CHAYOTE (*Sechium edule*)

## *Sechium edule*   (Cucurbitaceae)   CHAYOTE

Sturtevant says: "This species is cultivated in tropical America, the West Indies and Madeira for its fruit, which is about 4 inches long, 3 inches in diameter, of a green color outside and white within. It is used as a vegetable. The seeds are very good boiled and fried in butter. In Mexico CHAYOTE was cultivated by the Aztecs."

Photo by J. S. Karmali, Nairobi
OYSTER NUT (*Telfairea pedata*)

Photo by J. S. Karmali, Nairobi
OYSTER NUT (*Telfairea pedata*)

## *Telfairea pedata*   (Cucurbitaceae)   OYSTER NUT
KWEME NUT

The OYSTER NUT grows on big vines all over Africa and in many other countries, smothering big trees with runners up to 100 feet if plenty of fertility and moisture are available. C. N. Hayter wrote in the *Rhodesian Agricultural Journal:*

"The OYSTER NUT is not a true nut, but belongs to the PUMPKIN family and the flat edible seeds or nuts are obtained from the large gourds. The female flowers produce large ribbed gourds of 12-20 inches long and 8-12 inches diameter. The gourds weigh 20-30 pounds and contain rows of nuts running longitudinally. They mature in 4-5 months. As the gourds ripen they become soft and fall off the plant and burst; the nuts (seeds) embedded in the pulp are then released and need to be washed free of pulp.

"The nuts are pale straw-colour, flat and nearly circular, about 1½ inches diameter, almost ½ inch thick, and very like the shape of an oyster, from which the name is taken. They average about 35-40 to the pound according to the size of the gourd, the larger ones always contain the largest nuts. Gourds give an average of 96 nuts.

"When the gourds are left to ripen naturally on the vines, this extra last 10 days of maturity has a very important effect on the nuts, as they have a much better flavour and higher viability.

"OYSTER NUTS are not as easy as ordinary nuts to crack open. The shell of each is covered by an outer fibrous layer which has to be cut through around the edge before prising the nut open. An easier method, however, is to rip the fibrous layer off, then holding the nut on edge, give a few sharp taps until the top and bottom shells crack, they then are easily separated and the kernel removed intact. The kernels are covered with a thin greenish membranous skin.

"In flavour, OYSTER NUT kernels are not unlike BRAZIL NUTS and are excellent to eat with a little salt. They may also be used in cooking, confectionery and in the manufacture of chocolate and sweets. A high quality cooking oil has been extracted from the nuts.

"OYSTER NUT plants are very gross feeders and, to become well established, need exceedingly fertile conditions, plus a fair supply of moisture, particularly when grown alongside supporting trees.

"No doubt exists regarding the value of the nuts for food purposes, and edible nuts of all kinds are required in

108

ever increasing quantities. Where growers have deep fertile soils, plentifully supplied with moisture, absence of sharp frosts and have strong supporting trees for the vines, OYSTER NUTS can be a very profitable side-line crop, for an extremely small amount of work and cost.''

J. B. Gillett of the East African Herbarium, Nairobi, writes:

"The seeds of *Telfairia pedata* are eaten here. They sometimes appear on the market. My wife and I tried eating them. They are quite nice but the trouble is to open them. The fibrous outer coat does not crack but simply bends and embeds itself in the edible substance if one uses a nutcracker. Thus they are so troublesome to open that we gave them up.''

### *Trichosanthes anguina*      (Cucurbitaceae)<br>CLUB GOURD<br>SERPENT CUCUMBER<br>SNAKE GOURD<br>VIPER'S GOURD

Sturtevant says: "The fruit of this India plant is a large, greenish-white, club-shaped gourd of the length of a man's arm and about four inches thick. The fruit is eaten sliced and dressed in the manner of French beans. The gourd is commonly cultivated about Bombay and is in very general demand for vegetable curries in Burma. In Central America, it is called SERPENT CUCUMBER or VIPER'S GOURD from the remarkable, snake-like appearance of its fruits, which are frequently 6 or more feet long, at first striped with different shades of green but ultimately a bright, orange color.

"The seeds of various cucurbits are eaten. There is, for instance, a hardy climbing perennial in the Markham Valley, New Guinea, which is probably a *Trichosanthes*.''

# Chapter 22
# WATER NUTS

Scattered over the globe are a large number of water plants that produce seeds that are edible. This applies to a considerable number of water lilies, so called, but also there are seaweeds like *Trapa* which is illustrated and described in this chapter. It is considered a noxious weed and therefore its seeds are denied admission to the United States. All you can do is look at a picture of the seeds supplied by a Malayan forester, Isaac Ho Sai-Yuen.

### *Enhalus*      (Hydrocharitaceae)      SEA FRUIT

A monotypic genus in the Indian and Pacific Oceans. *E. acoroides* is a marine plant found in the sea about and below water mark.

Brown: *Minor Products of Philippine Forests* says: "In some parts of the Malayan region the seeds of this plant are eaten either raw or cooked, but this use is not recorded from the Philippines. The fruits are about the size of a large walnut and contain eight or nine green seeds."

Burkill says: "In Sumatra the fruits of *E. koenigiia* are called SEA FRUIT. The seeds are slightly farinaceous and taste like chestnuts soaked in salt water. This fruit is round, hairy and generally much covered with mud.''

### *Euryale ferox*      (Nymphaceae)      FOX NUT<br>GORGON NUT

The word GORGON in Greek means terrible.

The *Botanical Magazine* says: "This curious plant is a native of the East Indies, and has been cultivated in China, according to the pretensions of the Chinese writers, more than a thousand years before the Christian era. The seeds which are involved in an insipid pulp, supposed to be of a cooling quality, are farinaceous, and considered a wholesome food.''

Bailey explains that the FOX NUTS are the spiny-covered edible seeds of a handsome floating water-plant of eastern India. It has long been cultivated in China and now to a considerable extent is common in the milder portions of the temperate United States.

Sturtevant says: "This PRICKLY WATER-LILY is frequently cultivated in India and China for its floury seeds.

The fruit is round, soft, pulpy and the size of a small orange; it contains from 8 to 15 round, black seeds as large as peas, which are eaten roasted."

Burkill says: "This water lily grows in still water in tropical Asia. The seeds are starchy, and are used both in India and China; as a light food for invalids, because they are believed to have tonic properties."

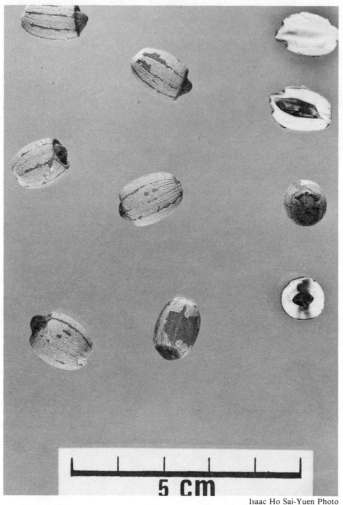

MALAYAN LOTUS seeds (*Nelumbo sp.*)

Isaac Ho Sai-Yuen Photo

INDIAN LOTUS (*Nelumbo nucifera*)

## *Nelumbo speciosa*      (Nelumbonaceae)
### WATER CINQUAPIN
### WATER-NUT
### RATTLE NUT

Willis says: "This water lily, growing now only in Asia and northeast Australia, is sometimes supposed to be the sacred LOTUS, no longer found in the Nile, but sacred in India, Tibet and China. It was introduced to Egypt about 500 B.C. The seeds of *N. nucifera* are used as food in Kashmir, etc."

Sturtevant says: "The LOTUS seems from time immemorial to have been, in native estimation, the type of the beautiful. It is held sacred throughout the East, and the deities of the various sects in that quarter of the world are almost invariably represented as either decorated with its flowers, seated or standing on a LOTUS throne or pedestal, or holding a sceptre framed from its flowers. It is fabled that the flowers obtained their red color by being dyed with the blood of Siva when Kama deva wounded him with the love-shaft arrow. Lakeshmi is called the lotus-born, from having ascended from the ocean on its flowers. The LOTUS is often referred to by the Hindu poets. The LOTUS floating in the water is the emblem of the world. It is also symbolic of the mountain Meru, the residence of the gods and the emblem of female beauty. Both the roots and seeds are esculent, sapid and wholesome and are used as food by the Egyptians. In China, some parts of India and in Ceylon, the black seeds of this plant, not unlike little acorns in shape, are served at table. Tennent found them of delicate flavor and not unlike the pine cones of the Apennines. In the southern provinces of China, large quantities are grown. The seeds and slices of its hairy root are served at banquets and the roots are pickled for winter use. In Japan, the stems are eaten. These stalks are not dissimilar in taste to our broad beet with a somewhat sharp after-taste. The seeds are also eaten like filberts."

Burkill says: "This water-lily, in a normal habitat, the rhizome lies deep in the mud under the water beyond the reach of frost. It grows in Asia in a natural way through the lowlands south of a line from the Caspian to Manchuria. It is interesting to note in passing that Ohga claims to have germinated seeds 120 years and possibly 200 to 400 years old, on filing the end of the seed-coat. If this is right, the plant may be very tenacious of its situations.

"It has many uses. In some countries its rhizomes are eaten all the year round; but it is grown less for food than for the beauty of its flowers.

"Today, the Chinese are the chief cultivators of it in Malaya. They eat the seeds when ripe. It is customary to prepare them by removing the intensely bitter embryo, and then boil or roast them; or they are eaten raw, when slightly unripe, as nuts. The Siamese use them freely.

"An analysis of the seed gives 62 per cent of starch and sugars, nearly 18 per cent of protein, 2 per cent of fat, and 12 per cent of moisture.

"The rhizomes may be seen on sale in the shops of towns. They are cooked for food or steamed for use in a salad; but it is said that in Indo-China, they may be eaten raw. They are pickled in salt, or in vinegar.

"The rhizome contains an abundance of starch. For eating it must be young, and then it tastes like artichokes."

Isaac S.Y. Ho, who made the accompanying photograph, wrote: "Malayan LOTUS seeds are eaten preserved in sugar during the Lunar (or Chinese) New Year in early February. Fruits all the year round in fishponds, and sometimes eaten raw in pods. The seeds are also dried and crushed to make paste-fillings inside bread by the Chinese. They are also offered to Deities in Temples in large quantities and are believed to bring immensely good luck. The Chinese call it LIN TZE."

Watt says: "The oblong nut-like seeds twice the size of peas, and when ripe so hard as to require a hammer to break them, are eaten by the natives either raw, roasted, or boiled."

Barrau says: "The Indian LOTUS, the seeds of which are edible, has been introduced into the Society Islands by the Chinese. This plant is today a common weed in some taro gardens, notably at Moorea. Its seeds may be known as a food, but their use is not widespread among Polynesians."

Sturtevant says of *N. luteum*: "North America and West Indies. The seeds are very agreeable to eat and are eagerly sought for by children and Indians."

Bailey says: "The small dark blue, nearly spherical seed of the AMERICAN LOTUS or great water lily, is about ½ inch in diameter, with smooth surface and a strong shell, within which is an edible kernel. *Nelumbo nucifera* is eaten in China as a nut."

### *Nuphar* (Nymphaceae)
#### YELLOW POND LILY SPATTER-DOCK

This comprises some 25 species in the north temperate zone. Sturtevant says of these:

"*N. advena*. Brown says the seeds are a staple article of diet among the Klamaths of southern Oregon. Newberry saw many hundred bushels collected for winter use among the Indians of the western coast and says the seeds taste like those of broom corn and are apparently very nutritious.

"*N. polysepalum*. This furnishes an important article of food, in its seeds, to the Indians."

Of this species Fernald & Kinsey wrote: "To some of the northwestern Indians the seeds are a very important food and they spend several weeks each year harvesting them. This species is so important to the Klamath Indians, that a detailed bulletin on their use and the preparation of the food 'Wokas' was prepared by Coville. Very briefly: the seeds are extracted after the pods have thoroughly dried and have been pounded to loosen the seeds; although the pods which have thoroughly ripened in the water and have begun to disintegrate contain more valuable seeds. The seeds are parched for ten minutes to loosen the kernel contained within, then pounded or lightly ground and winnowed to get rid of the hard, firm shell. The remaining white kernels, after the hard shells of the seeds have been removed, may be parched, when they swell considerably but do not crack like pop-corn. Thus prepared they are said to be 'a delicious food, particularly if slightly salted and eaten with cream.' The white kernels are also ground into flour for bread-making or the dried seeds with their shells on may be stored for winter use, to be parched and ground as needed.

"The large-flowered species of eastern America are so similar that it is highly probable our eastern species would furnish as valuable seeds."

### *Nymphaea lotus* (Nymphaceae)
#### EGYPTIAN WATER LILY LOTUS

This is believed to be the sacred LOTUS of ancient Egypt. It is a big water lily with either rose or white flowers, one species among 50 in the temperate and tropical zones. Willis says: "They grow in shallow water. The flowers float on the surface. The seeds float up on dehiscence of the fruit and float about."

Sturtevant says: "The small seeds are fried in heated sand and make a light, easily digestible food. The tubers are much sought after by the natives as an article of food. The capsules and seeds are either pickled or put into curries or ground and mixed with flour to make cakes."

Burkill says: "In India the seeds are eaten as a famine food, and sometimes in food in normal times by the poorest; they are eaten in the Philippine Islands. In India they are pounded and made into a kind of bread."

Describing another species in Malaya, *N. atellata*, Burkill says: "In India seeds are famine-foods."

Stuhlmann says: "The seeds are eaten in Africa."

*Nelumbo* (q.v.) which is also called LOTUS, arrived several thousand years after *Nymphaea*.

Isaac Ho Sai-Yuen Photo

TRAPA seeds. — The Chinese called them "Ling Kok," meaning "Spiritual Horn." *Trapa* are harvested and consumed during the mid-Autumn festival in September, to celebrate the overthrow of the Mongolians during the Yuan Dynasty in ancient China.

### *Trapa* (Trapaceae)

*Trapa* comprises some 30 species of herbs that grow in water in warm parts of Europe, Asia and Africa, and bear edible nuts in hard-shelled fruits which are important articles of food for millions of people. They are called by a wide variety of common names in different areas.

On all of them the fruit is a two-horned capsule much resembling the skull of an ox. Here are the chief kinds of *Trapa* and their local names:

111

*T. bicornuta* LING. This Chinese nut is about ¾'' high and wide. *T. natans* JESUIT NUT, WATER CALTROPS, WATER CHESTNUT. This is cultivated in southern Europe in lakes, ponds, or even tubs, and the seeds are ground into flour and made into bread. Sturtevant says of this species:

"The Thraceans, according to Pliny, baked bread from the flour of the seeds, and the seeds are thus used even now in some parts of southern Europe and, at Venice, are sold. Grant found *Trapa* nuts on the Victoria Nyanza in Africa, and the Waganda use the four-pronged nuts for food. It is enumerated by Thunberg among the edible plants of Japan. This water plant is extensively cultivated in China and furnishes, in its strangely-shaped fruits, a staple article of nutriment. Williams says its cultivation is in running water and the nuts are collected in autumn by people in punts or tubs, who look for the ripe ones as they pull themselves through the vines over the surface of the patch. The dried nuts are often ground into a sort of arrowroot flour. The taste of the fresh boiled nuts is like that of new cheese."

Hundley wrote this author from Burma:

"The fruits of a form of *T. natans* are made into rosaries and offered for sale in Italy. They will be on the market here in Rangoon, at the end of the rains, about September. Here they are boiled and eaten after removal of the skin."

Bailey says: "The seed of a water-plant of southern Europe, much sought after by the natives for their agreeable kernels which become inedible with the hardening of the shell. In form, these nuts are very irregular, measuring from 2 to 3 inches between the tips of the short stout horns, and about 1 inch in depth through the irregularly shaped head of the nut. These nuts are of a slatish brown color and their surface is quite smooth.

"*T. bispinosa*. SINGHARA-NUT. Asia and northern Africa. This plant has been grown in India from the most ancient times. In growing, the nuts mature under water and are gathered in November and December. In certain sections it is extensively cultivated, e.g. in Kashmir, the United and Central Provinces, etc. The kernel abounds in starch, and is eaten either raw or cooked, especially by the Hindus. It may be boiled whole, after soaking a night in water, roughly broken up and made into a sort of porridge, or ground to meal and into chapattis."

Sturtevant says: "This species grows abundantly in the lakes about Cashmere and at Wurler Lake and is said to yield annually ten million pounds of nuts. These are scooped up from the bottom of the lake in small nets and constitute almost the only food of at least 30,000 persons for five months of the year. When extracted from the shell, they are eaten raw, boiled, roasted, fried, or dressed in various ways after being reduced to flour. They are also eaten in Lahore."

Dalziel says: "The fruit is woody or crustaceous and horned by two lateral calyx lobes being enlarged and hardened; it sinks to the bottom when ripe.

"The Nigerian names mean "watergroundnut," and the fruit is eaten by pagans in the eastern districts of N. Nigeria, by whom it is cultivated in pools; also sometimes by the Fulani in Adamawa, etc. The plant is more abundant in the Nile and Zambesi regions."

## *Typhonodorum lindleyanum* (Araceae)

Williams says: "A giant aroid with a banana-like stem 4 to 6 feet high, and very large arrow-shaped leaves. It occurs as a pure stand in undeveloped freshwater swamps in Zanzibar and Pemba. The flower spathes bend over in fruit to form a large cluster of many brown, flattish seeds about 1 inch in diameter. The seeds are a common article of food, particularly during periods of food shortage. They are prepared for cooking by rubbing with wood ashes to remove certain toxic matter. After boiling the seeds for 15 to 20 minutes, the water, which has become darkly coloured, is poured off, and the seeds washed in fresh water and boiled again. This process is repeated twice more, after which they are soft and free from toxic matter. They are then finally prepared for eating by boiling in coconut juice."

## WATER LILY
## *Victoria regia* (Nymphaeceae) WATER MAIZE

Sturtevant says: "The Spaniards in Guyana collect the seeds and eat them roasted."

## *Zostera marina* (Zosteraceae) WATER NUT

*Underexploited Tropical Plants* says: "*Zostera marina* is a marine flowering plant that grows in shallow seawater. It is one of the few plants that grow and flower fully submerged in seawater. When ripe, the grain-bearing part breaks loose and floats to the surface where it drifts to the shore and can then be harvested. Although little is known about the use of *Zostera marina* as a grain crop, it yields well in warm, clear, sun-drenched water. It holds potential as a food crop that can be grown in tropical estuaries around the world.

"The only recorded case in which the sea has been used for grain production is that of the *Zostera marina* harvested by Seri Indians on the West Coast of Mexico. The Seri Indians prepared *Zostera marina* grain by threshing sun-dried plants with wooden clubs and loosening the fruit by rolling the seed heads between their palms. The product was winnowed (tossed in the air), then the grain was toasted, rewinnowed, and ground into flour. Cooked in water into a thick or thin gruel, the flour has a bland flavor. Traditionally it was combined with other food, usually sea turtle oil or honey."

# Chapter 23
# MANNA FROM HEAVEN
### (Miscellaneous Dicots)

Nuts are not confined to any special group of plants. They occur in all kinds of seed-bearing plants and hungry people have searched them out. Those in this chapter are just some leftover goodies on the platter. Some persons have experimented with seeds as food, which often proved dangerous and inadvisable, but hungry people are desperate.

In this chapter are perhaps a hundred kinds of nuts that belong to no special groups or plant families, but they are edible and millions of people eat them. Perhaps this chapter can serve as sort of a guide to the miscellaneous

INDIAN BUCKEYE (*Aesculus indicus*)

HORSE CHESTNUT (*Aesculus hippocastanum*)

## *Aesculus hippocastanum* (Hippocastanaceae)
### HORSE CHESTNUT

Bailey says flatly: "The inedible seeds are about equal in size to the largest of the European species, but less regular in form and having a somewhat stronger and more shining shell. They are in a one-to-three-celled prickly pod. The fruit of an ornamental tree familiar in the North Temperate Zone of both the Old World and the New."

This should put these "nuts" in the chapter on "Not Nuts" except that there are exceptions.

Balfour says: "The seeds in their ordinary condition are inedible but have been used as a substitute for coffee."

Regarding the Japanese species *A. turbinata*, Suzuki writes from Tokyo: "The starch produced from the seed has been eaten in a large quantity by the mountain-villagers."

Maheshwari of the National Botanic Garden in Lucknow, India writes of the Indian tree *A. indica*: "The fruits are eaten greedily in the Himalayas in times of scarcity by the hill tribes, after being steeped in water, and sometimes mixed with flour."

Sturtevant notes two other exceptions:

*A. parviflora* BUCKEYE. Southern states of America. The fruit, according to Browne, may be eaten boiled or roasted as a chestnut.

*A. californica* CALIFORNIA HORSE-CHESTNUT. A low-spreading tree of the Pacific Coast. The chestnuts are made into a gruel or soup by the western Indians. The Indians of California pulverize the nut, extract the bitterness by washing with water and form the residue into a cake to be used as food.

Kirk in his *Wild Edible Plants* says of this:

There are a number of ways of processing the fleshy nuts. One is as follows: the shiny brown nuts are first steamed in a firepit for several hours until they are the texture of boiled potatoes; they are then sliced thinly, placed in a basket and soaked in running water for 2 to 5 days, depending on the thickness of the slices, to remove the poison.

Another way is to steam them, remove the skin, mash them, and mix them with water to form a thin paste. This is then soaked from 1 to 10 hours in a sandfilter or running water.

The residue from either process is high in starch, quite nutritious, and not bad in flavor. It may be eaten cold or baked into bread or cakes.

## *Afraegle paniculata* (Rutaceae)

Dalziel says of this tree in Gold Coast and Nigeria:

"A small tree found only in villages, but said to occur wild, attaining 30-40 ft. The fruit is 3 in. or more in diameter, orange-like but with hard shell; on section it shows radiating carpels surrounded by a pulp which turns brown, and which is not edible. The seeds are large, and are enclosed in an abundant mucilage, clear at first, turning yellow-brown, which is gummy and adhesive, and is used as bird-lime and for cementing broken pottery. The seeds are said to be rich in fat, which is in some places extracted and used for food or in cooking. Small calabashes or snuff-boxes, etc., are made from the shell."

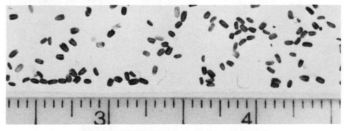

GIANT HYSSOP (*Agastache urticifolia*)

*(Balanites maughamii)*

## GIANT HYSSOP
*Agastache urticifolia* (Labiatae) HORSEMINT

Kirk in *Wild Edible Plants* says: "GIANT HYSSOP is a tall perennial herb. The nutlet-like seeds are dull brown. The seeds may be eaten raw or cooked."

The plant is found in moist, open soil mostly in coniferous forest areas throughout the West except for Arizona and New Mexico.

## *Agriophyllum gobicum* (Chenopodiaceae)

Sturtevant says: "Siberia. The seeds are used as food."

Isaac Ho Sai-Yuen Photo

ALOES WOOD (*Aquilaria malaccensis*)

## *Aquilaria malaccensis* (Thymelaceae) ALOES WOOD

This poorly defined genus of trees in southeast Asia, is important for its pathologically diseased, fragrant wood which is sought madly for trading, secretly and rather destructively. Healthy wood is scorned, diseased wood is precious.

The tree is important in this book only because Isaac S. Y. Ho of Malaysia writes: "These nuts are an essential ingredient for making hot curry in Malaysia."

## *Avicennia officinalis* (Verbenaceae) NEW ZEALAND MANGROVE

Sturtevant says: "Region of the Caspian. This plant transudes a gum which the natives of New Zealand esteem as a food. The kernels are bitter but edible."

*(Balanites pedicellaris)*

## *Balanites aegyptiaca* (Balanitaceae) SOAPBERRY TREE THORN TREE DESERT DATE

Some 25 *Balanites* trees have been described from Africa to Burma, characterized by fruits with rather thick, oil-containing flesh, and very thick, bony, 5-angled seeds that also contain oil.

Irvine says of *B. aegyptiaca*: "A most useful tree. A Bornu proverb runs: 'A BITO tree and a milk cow are just the same.'

"The fruit-pulp is edible, fibrous, oily, and gummy, with a bittersweet taste, and fruits are sometimes dried (DESERT DATES). They contain about 40 per cent of sugar, and have been suggested as a source of alcohol.

"The kernels contain over 40 per cent of oil which is edible. The kernels have distinct food value, and a kind of bread is sometimes made from them. In Bornu they are eaten in soup by the Shuwa Arabs, who also soak them for 4 days before sun-drying them, after which they can be stored for months."

Dalziel says of this tree: "The kernel yields over 40% of an oil highly prized both in the E. and W. Sudan; in some parts it is used as an edible oil. Barth mentions that in Baghirmi a sort of bread is made from them, and in E. Sudan they have been recorded as being given as a temporary food to slave gangs. The Shuwa Arabs east of Bornu use them in soup, and the fruit is often spread on roofs to dry."

Dale & Greenway say: "Savanna tree usually 15-20 ft. high, with a tangled mass of long thorny twigs. Fruit green at first, turning yellow as it ripens, broadly oblong-ellipsoid, containing a large, hard-pointed stone surrounded by yellow-brown sticky edible flesh.

"The dried fruit is sometimes called the DESERT DATE, and the unripe fruit Egyptian MYROBALAN. The kernel yields over 40 per cent of an oil, sometimes called Zachun Oil, believed to have been an ingredient in the spikenard mentioned in Scripture.

"*B. wilsoniana* (Syn. *B. maughamii*) MKONGA. Medium-sized tree. Lower stem deeply fluted, often with compound thorns in the concavities. Fruit unpleasantly scented, ovoid-ellipsoid, longitudinally 5-ribbed, yellow-green when ripe; seeds about 2 in. long and 1 in. diameter.

"The fruits are relished by elephants, who are mainly responsible for the distribution of the tree, the seeds passing through undigested."

ANNATTO (*Bixa orellana*)

(*Champereia malayana*)

### *Bixa orellana*      (Bixaceae)      LIPSTICK TREE      ANNATTO

The LIPSTICK TREE from tropical America is cultivated in Florida and elsewhere as an ornamental. It is a small tree with showy pink flowers followed by heartshaped scarlet fruits that turn brown.

Kennard & Winters wrote: "When fully mature, the fruits split open exposing the numerous seeds. Although it does not produce an edible fruit, the ANNATTO is widely grown for the orange-red pulp that covers the seeds. The ANNATTO dye, which is prepared by stirring the seeds in water, is used to color butter and cheese. It is also widely used in Latin America to color rice and other foods. In the Philippine Islands the seeds are ground and used as a condiment."

### *Bruguiera sp.*      (Rhizophoraceae)

This small group of big mangrove trees stretches along higher shores from Africa to the Pacific, much used for tannin and timber.

Barrau says: "At Yap and in the Palaus the embryo of the fruit of *B. sexangula* is eaten after grating, washing and cooking. It is utilized similarly in a number of islands of Melanesia and in the Celebes."

Burkill says of *B. cylindrica* that the young radicles from the seed are occasionally eaten, after boiling, as a vegetable or preserve. Of *B. parviflora* Burkill says: "Malays sometimes use the germinating embryo as a vegetable."

### *Cannabis sativa*      (Cannabaceae)      HEMP      MARIJUANA

*Hortus Third* says of this plant: "An important economic plant in many countries. The stems supply a strong, durable bast fibre (true HEMP); the fruit yields a drying oil (HEMP SEED OIL) and bird feed; and the dried flowering and fruiting tops of female plants produce drugs (MARIJUANA or CANNABIS, HASHISH or CHARAS, BHANG and GANJA). Methods of cultivation vary depending on the product desired. The species is usually grown for fibre in temperate regions and for drug production in warmer regions. In the United States it can be grown only under government permit."

### *Champereia malayana*      (Opiliaceae)

This is a genus of six species of shrubs in southeast Asia, belonging to the Opiliaceae, a family of root-parasitic plants.

Burkill reports that the fruits are eaten by the Sakai (aborigines).

Isaac Ho Sai-Yuen who made the accompanying picture, says the kernels of the seeds are boiled after the skin is discarded, in a pot of water with fish. When thus cooked they are eaten as a soup along with rice, and he adds: "Perhaps the seeds are too small for roasting."

(*Cordia subcordata*)

## Cordia subcordata (Ehretiaceae)

*Cordia* is a genus of 250 kinds of shrubs and trees in warm parts of the world, most of them bearing edible fruits.

Barrau says the nuts of this species are sometimes eaten, especially in the New Hebrides and elsewhere in Polynesia. The same tree grows in Kenya, usually along the seashore above the high water mark.

Of the SAPISTAN PLUM or ASSYRIAN PLUM (*C. myxa*) Irvine writes: "It was probably cultivated at one time in Sudan. The kernel and the sticky mucilaginous pulp are eaten, the latter also being a well-known bird-lime. In India the young fruits and the flowers are eaten as vegetables, the former also being pickled. This tree yields a gum in India."

Sturtevant says of this tree: "The tender, young fruit is eaten as a vegetable and is pickled in India. The ripe fruit is also eaten. The kernel tastes somewhat like a filbert and that of the cultivated tree is better."

Neal says of *C. myxa* in Hawaii: "Its half-inch, cherry-like fruit has edible mucilaginous pulp which surrounds a stone with one edible, filbert-like kernel." The same authority says that the GEIGER TREE (*C. sebestena*), common in south Florida, "has edible fruits about an inch long," but there is no reference to the seeds.

The North Queensland Naturalists' Club bulletin says of *C. dichotoma*: "Nut kernels edible."

## Crossostemma laurifolium (Passifloraceae)

This scrambling shrub or climber grows in the forests of West Africa from Guinea to Ghana. Its woody fruits contain smooth, black seeds ½ inch long, which Deakin says are edible.

## Cuervea kappleriana (Hippocrataceae) KAROSHIRI

The shrubs or lianas of this genus are found from Costa Rica to Peru, in the West Indies and elsewhere in northern South America.

Fanshawe wrote of this species in Guyana: "The fruit of this rather rare bush rope contain a number of more or less flattened, elliptical, red brown nuts with a pleasant flavour. The oil content of the nuts is low."

## Diplodiscus paniculatus (Tiliaceae) CALOBO

Brown says of this common Philippine tree: "*Diplodiscus* is a tree reaching a height of 20 meters and a diameter of 80 centimeters. The fruit is edible. The starchy seeds when boiled have a good flavor. When the fruits are mature they can frequently be gathered in very large quantities with little labor."

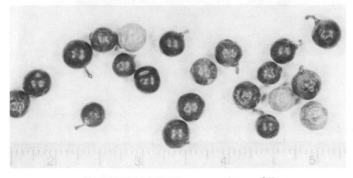

KARANDA NUT (*Elaeocarpus bancroftii*)

## Elaeocarpus bancroftii (Elaeocarpaceae) KARANDA NUT

This genus comprises 200 kinds of trees in the south Pacific, Australia and Indo-Malaysia. Brian Vicary who lives at Karanga, Queensland, recommends the KARANDA NUT. He says that it grows in the rain forest and is not at present cultivated. The nuts are 1 to 1½ inches long and are encased in a hard four-segmented shell that is easy to crack open. They "are delicious."

Maheshwari says the kernel of the KARANDA NUT is of good flavor.

Parham writes from Fiji on *E. chelonimorphus*. "The kernel of the fruit has been reported edible."

## Erisma japura (Vochysiaceae) JAPURA

*Erisma* is a genus of 20 trees in northern Brazil and Guyana.

This species grows in Rio Negro, Amazonas, and the kernels of the seeds are eaten by the people there.

Sturtevant writes: "The kernel of this red fruit is pleasant eating both raw and boiled. By a process of boiling and leaving in running water for several weeks, and then pounding in a mortar, it is made into a sort of butter, which is eaten with fish and game, being mixed in the gravy. People who can get over its vile smell, which is never lost, find it exceedingly savory."

KEULE (*Gomortega nitida*)

## Gomortega nitida (Gomortegaceae) KEULE

This genus contains only this one tree. Sturtevant says of it: "This is a large tree of Chile. The fruit is the size of a small peach; the edible part is yellow, not very juicy, but is of an excellent and most grateful taste."

Willis says: "Large tree, containing aromatic oil. Fruit drupaceous, with bony endocarp; seeds with much oily endosperm."

## Gomphia jabotapita (Ochnaceae) BUTTON TREE

Sturtevant says of it: "Tropical America. Piso says the carpels are stringent and are not only eaten raw, but that an oil is expressed from them, which is used in salads."

Of another species, Sturtevant says: "*G. parviflora* Brazil. The oil expressed from the fruit is used for salads."

116

## Gynandropsis pentaphylla (Cleomaceae)

Sturtevant says: "This plant is a well-known esculent in the Upper Nile and throughout equatorial Africa as far as the Congo. In India the seeds are used as a substitute for mustard and yield a good oil. In Jamaica, it is considered a wholesome plant but, from its being a little bitterish, requires repeated boilings to make it palatable."

USDA Photo

WITCH HAZEL (*Hamamelis virginiana*)

## Hamamelis virginiana (Hamamelidaceae)
### WITCH HAZEL

This in the United States is the commonest of five species, allied to one Asian, *H. japonica*. It is a coarse shrub in the Eastern States.
Sturtevant says: "The seeds are used as food, says Balfour. The kernels are oily and eatable, says Lindley. The seeds are about the size of a grain of barley and have a thick, bony coat."

## Hippocratea (Celastraceae)

These are twining shrubs in the tropics. Sturtevant says:
"*H. comosa*: Santo Domingo and West Indies. The seeds are oily and sweet.
"*H. grahamii*: East Indies. In India the seed is edible."

## Icacina senegalensis (Icacinaceae) FALSE YAM

This is an erect, woody herb or scant undershrub to 3 feet high, a common weed along roads in savannah forest from Senegal to the Sudan. Dalziel writes:
"The fruits are red when ripe, with a thin pulp and a single seed.
"In time of shortage of cereals some of the peoples of the Upper Shari region use a meal obtained from the seeds or more rarely the starch of the tuber. The fruits are dried in the sun and macerated in water; the seeds are then pounded and made into a paste with boiling water.
"The plant is troublesome. The enormous tuber, 12-18 in. long and 1 ft. or more in diameter with long penetrating roots, requires much labour to eradicate."

## Iris pseudacorus (Irideae) YELLOW IRIS

Sturtevant says: "In eastern Asia and Europe, the angular seeds of this plant when ripe, are said to form a good substitute for coffee, but must be well roasted before eating."

## Irvingia gabonensis (Ixonanthaceae)
### BREAD TREE
### WILD MANGO

*Irvingia* is a genus of ten trees in Africa, Indochina, Malaya and Borneo. Irvine says this species is a tree to 120

feet extending from Senegal to Zaire with a gray trunk, slightly buttressed.
Dalziel describes the importance of the seeds as food:
"The fruit is yellow when ripe and resembles a small mango; the pulp surrounding the fibrous-coated hard-shelled nut is said to be edible, though of a turpentine flavour, and in some cases bitter and acrid.
"The single seed is more important and ranks as an oil-seed. The fruits are collected as forest produce from the ground under the trees, and the nut is split open on the spot. The seeds, after removing the brown shiny coat, are dried in the sun or by fire; they split naturally and are sold in native markets. They are used in Nigeria, etc., in soup and as a seasoner for various native dishes. The kernels have a fairly pleasant taste with a slightly bitter after-taste. They yield from 54-67% of fatty matter, and their more important use is for the preparation of the paste known as Gaboon Chocolate, or Dika Bread, a staple article of food, obtained from the seeds of several species. This is obtained by grinding the kernels, heating in a pot (lined with banana leaves) to melt the fat, cooling to an irregular grey-brown mass, greasy to touch, and with a slightly bitter and astringent but not unpleasant taste and more or less aromatic odour, possibly disguised by the addition of pepper and other spices. The produce is often subjected to wood-smoke in the huts, and is made up in loaf-like cylindrical masses encased in a basket-like covering. The native use of this material is as a seasoner for fish, meat or plantain dishes, etc. In Gabon besides Dika Bread other preparations are made, viz. (1) a soft paste from the fresh kernels steeped in water for two or three weeks, then pressed by hand to yield a soft rather bitter paste which is kept wrapped in leaves and is used for cooking with fish, meat, etc.
"The crude dika paste yields by heating or boiling 70-80% of a pale yellow or nearly white solid fat — dika butter — which has a low iodine value and a high saponification value, and is comparable with cocoa-butter. Analysis of the native-prepared "dika chocolate" and of the kernels alone show differences which suggest that other articles, probably other seeds, enter into the composition of the former. Dika butter is imported into Europe in small quantity, and possibly serves as an adulterant of cocoa-butter or replaces it in the manufacture of the cheaper chocolates. When freed from its slight odour it can be regarded as a butter and cocoa-butter substitute suitable for European use in the preparation of margarine, etc.
"The residual kernel cake is rich in protein and might be used as a feeding-stuff similar to copra cake. It has the following percentage composition: protein, 31-16; fat, 10-0; carbohydrates, 38-82; crude fibre; 3-15; ash, 5-80; moisture, 11-07."

## Lallemantia iberica (Labiatae)

Sturtevant wrote: "Asia Minor and Syria. The seeds are very rich in fat and are used for food in the northwest districts of Persia."

### MENI OIL
## Lophira lanceolata (Ochnaceae) RED IRONWOOD

This tree is found from Sierra Leone to Uganda and Sudan.
Irvine writes: "A medium-sized savannah tree up to 40 feet: often stunted and gnarled as a result of bush fires. Seeds winged, wings often crimson and veined, up to 3 in. by nearly 1 in., surrounding a narrow beaked nut over 1 in. long.
"The tree is a beautiful sight when in full flower, and worthy of being grown for decorative purposes.

"The seeds, eaten by the Nzimas and in other parts of W. Africa, are said to taste like GROUNDNUTS. They contain 70-75 per cent of kernels which yield 40-50 per cent of creamy-yellow, semi-solid fat by expression, and this is known in W. Africa as MENI OIL. It is also extracted in Sudan, where it is much valued, even preferred to shea-oil as it has no odour. In Senegal and S. Leone it is used in cooking."

### *Mentzelia albicaulis* (Loaseae) PRAIRIE LILY

Sturtevant says: "The oily seeds are pounded and used by the Indians in California as an ingredient of their pinole mantica, a kind of cake."

### *Mesembryanthemum edule* (Aizoaceae) HOTTENTOT FIG

Of the 350 species of these ground plants in Africa, a few have fruits with edible pulp. Of one species in North Africa, *M. forskahlei*, Sturtevant writes: "The capsules are soaked and dried by the Bedouins, and the seeds separated for making bread, which, however, is not eaten by other Arabs."

HORSERADISH TREE (*Moringa oleifera*)

### *Moringa oleifera* (Moringaceae) HORSERADISH TREE BEN NUT

*Moringa*, the HORSERADISH TREE is a small, quick-grower that flowers in Florida every day in the year, and throughout the tropics produces food.

Sturtevant says: "India. The HORSERADISH TREE is cultivated for its fruit, which is eaten as a vegetable and preserved as a pickle, and for its leaves and flowers which are likewise eaten. According to Firminger, the unripe

seed-pods are used boiled in curries. It is also cultivated by the Burmese for its pods. In the West Indies, the oil expressed from the seeds is used in salads."

Irvine says: "The seeds contain up to 38 per cent of oil and a saponin. When fried they are said to taste like GROUNDNUTS. The oil, BEN OIL, suitable for food purposes, was formerly used for oiling clocks. It does not grow rancid, is an excellent salad oil. It has no scent and burns clearly without smoke. The oil consists of glycerides of oleic, palmitic, and stearic acids, together with another glyceride of very high melting-point."

(*Ochrosia elliptica*)

(*Ochrosia coccinea*)

### *Ochrosia* (Apocynaceae) PAKOIDAN

*Ochrosia* is a genus of 30 kinds of small trees scattered from Madagascar to Australia and from Hawaii to Polynesia. Brown writes of two kinds in the Philippines:

"The fruits are united at the base, 2.5 to 4 centimeters long and 1 to 1.5 centimeters in diameter. The outer part is fleshy and covers a stone containing food. This species is a tree 2 to 10 meters in height.

"*O. oppositifolia* is a fairly large tree. The fruit contains an edible seed."

Neal says of this species: "The FAO is a low to tall tree, native on shores from southern Polynesia west to the Mascarenes; flowers are small, white, crowded; leaves are more or less oval, blunt, to 12 by 15 inches; fruit is yellow, twinned, fibrous, ovoid, 2 to 3 inches long, the seed edible."

S. Gowers of the Department of Agriculture, New Hebrides, says the seeds of *O. oppositifolia* are eaten.

## *Ouratea jabotapita* (Ochnaceae)

*Ouratea* is a genus of 300 kinds of trees and shrubs in the tropics. Writing about this plant in Brazil, Hoehne said: "Some species produce an oily seed. This is one of them and in the Amazon region the oil is used for cooking. Another species *O. parviflora*, called BATIPUTA produces seeds which are used to produce 'Batiputa butter', an oil which is somewhat sweet and aromatic, solidifies at 17° C, and used to be used as a shortening."

Paul R. Wycherly Photo

DESERT WALNUT (*Owenia reticulata*)

Paul R. Wycherly Photo

EMU APPLE (*Owenia vernicosa*)

## *Owenia reticulata* (Meliaceae) DESERT WALNUT
## *O. vernicosa* EMU APPLE

These are small trees of tropical northwest Australia and extending into India. The fruits are green, 1 inch diameter, containing two edible cones.

Paul R. Wycherly, director of the Botanic Garden at Perth, writes: "The DESERT WALNUT is more widely distributed than the other. There are usually two seeds embedded in a mass of hard fibrous tissue. If one crushes

the fruit as harvested in a vice or tries to crack it with a hammer, so much force must be used that it is entirely broken up. The fragments of the seed so obtained are edible in the sense that they have a pleasing taste. I suspect that one would have to expend more energy in breaking it open than would be gained by eating. Nevertheless some people may find a morsel so difficult to win, more attractive for that reason. If the fruit as harvested are placed in sand, kept damp for months, even a year, there is no germination. In order to grow plants, we cut the fruit through with a hacksaw trying (not always successfully) to make the cut between the two seed, which can then be extracted. They will then germinate readily. We do not know how germination occurs in nature. We suspect that the fibrous material is eaten away by termites or some other insects. Fruit can pass through emus without any apparent effect."

Maheshwari writes of the EMU APPLE: "Fruit should be buried in the ground for several days before eating."

T. R. N. Lothian, director of the Botanic Garden at Adelaide writes of this fruit which he calls SOUR PLUM: "It was used by natives. So far as I am aware it has never been utilised by the white population of Australia."

## *Panda oleosa* (Pandaceae)

This is a tree to 60 feet in forests from Liberia to Gaboon and Zaire. It is the only species of this genus.

Willis says: "The fruit is a massive, stony endocarp, containing 3 one-seeded chambers, finally dehiscing by valves at germination."

Irvine says the 3 or 4 boat-shaped seeds fit special cells in the stone, and continues: "The seeds contain oil which is difficult to extract. The seeds are edible with a nutty flavour, and are eaten also by monkeys and certain game animals. The oil or crushed seeds makes a condiment or sauce in Cameroons and Gaboon."

Dalziel says: "The fruit is drupaceous, yellowish-green when ripe; the pulp is rich in tannin, rots quickly and is not edible. The seeds contain a white oily endosperm surrounding an embryo with two broad cotyledons. They have been recommended as oil-seeds, but the shell of the fruit, which is thick and rough, and the hard though spongy endocarp surrounding them would render extraction difficult. The oil or the crushed seeds are used in Cameroons and Gabon in food preparation as a condiment or sauce."

PANGI (*Pangium edule*)

## Pangium edule  (Flacourtiaceae)  PANGI

The *Pangium* is a big tree to 80 feet and 2 feet in diameter, found growing all over Malaysia and in the Philippines. Only one species is known. The rough brown fruits up to 6 inches or more long, contain several seeds embedded in a yellowish, sweet, aromatic edible pulp. While the pulp is used as food in some parts of the Philippines, this use is not general. There are reports that eating the pulp sometimes causes headache. Several authors who describe the properties and uses of *Pangium edule* in the Malay regions make no mention of the edibility of the pulp. The unripe fruit is said to be edible after very special preparation.

The seeds of *Pangium edule* are flattened and average about 5 centimeters long and 3 centimeters wide.

Burkill says: "The tree fruits at fifteen years, but lives to a great age. The seeds float for a long time in water, even in sea-water.

"The tree is poisonous enough for its name to be proverbial as an intoxicant; but the seeds are used as food, precautions being taken to prepare them in such a way as to remove the poison. The poison is hydrocyanic acid, which arises from the glucoside gynocardin, and pervades the plant.

"By boiling the seeds for an hour, the chemical interaction of the gynocardin and the accompanying enzyme gynocardase, by which the hydrocyanic acid is produced may be prevented; for the heat destroys the gynocardase.

"Ripe seeds contain less of the glucoside than unripe seeds. The theory is held that the function of the glucoside is to sterilize wounds in the active tissue of the plant, and, therefore, particularly in the vegetative parts; and as the seeds reach maturity the amount of glucoside decreases with the cessation of their active growth and their growing hardness. Immature fruits, such as needy men may take, are therefore more dangerous than the fully mature fruits.

"*Pangium* seeds are collected and sold sometimes in the markets.

"For use as food the seeds are crushed and boiled, then put into running water for a day, after which they are boiled again and eaten.

"Another method is to bury the boiled seeds with ashes and let fermentation set in, which happens very slowly, so that the whole preparation takes forty days; such a preparation is highly flavoured.

"A third preparation is carried through, starting as in the first process, and after the second boiling the dough is shaped into little lumps and left to ferment, which takes seven days only.

"A fourth preparation is to dig up the buried mass after fifteen days, boil, soak in running water, and allow it to ferment for four more days.

"The second, third, and fourth preparations are of a kind of kechap (see K. Heyne, Nutt. Plant. Ned. Ind. ed. of 1927 p. 1136).

"Oil of 'kepayang' is obtained in the following way: the ripe seeds are boiled for 2 to 3 hours; then their seed-coats are removed and any discoloured spots cut out; they are placed in running water for 24 hours, as is done when they are intended for food; then, instead of a second boiling, they are dried in the sun and subsequently pressed. The oil so obtained is a good cooking oil, and serves as a substitute for coconut oil; but it becomes rancid very soon. In cooking, should there be any glucoside mixed with the oil, the heat of the cooking-pot destroys it and the oil is innocuous."

Sturtevant says: "The nuts, when macerated in water, are rendered partially wholesome but are used only as a condiment."

Neal says: "A large to medium-sized, long-lived, deciduous tree of the Malay Archipelago has shiny, broad-ovate or heart-shaped leaves, 6 to 9 inches long, on stems 3 to 8 inches long, but larger and lobed on seedlings. The fruit is a brown, oblong, rather rough, thick-walled capsule, 6 to 12 by 3 to 5 inches, containing many somewhat flattened, oval, gray-white, hard seeds about 2 inches long. The tree is poisonous throughout, owing to the presence of prussic acid, which, however, can be removed by washing leaves and seeds and by cooking. Old leaves and ripe fruit, which are eaten by Malaysians, have less poison than young leaves and green fruit. Sometimes oil from the seeds is used for cooking. Leaves are used as wrappers to preserve meat."

## Papaver somniferum  (Papaveraceae) OPIUM POPPY

Sturtevant says: "Greece and the Orient. There are several varieties of which the two most prominent are called white and black from the color of their seeds. The OPIUM POPPY is a native of the Mediterranean region but is cultivated in India, Persia, Asiatic Turkey and occasionally, by way of experiment in the United States, for the purpose of procuring opium. It is grown in northern France and the south of Germany for its seeds. This poppy is supposed to have been cultivated by the ancient Greeks and is mentioned by Homer as a garden plant. Galen speaks of the seeds as good to season bread and says the white are better than the black. The Persians sprinkle the seeds of poppies over their rice, and the seeds are used in India as a food and a sweetmeat. The seeds are also eaten, says Masters, in Greece, Poland and elsewhere. In France, the seeds are made to yield by expression a bland oil, which is used as a substitute for olive oil. In Sikkim, Edgeworth remarks, the seeds afford oil as well as an agreeable food, remarkably refreshing during fatigue and abstinence."

## Paris polyphylla  (Trilliaceae)

Sturtevant says: "Himalayan region and China. The seeds are eaten by the Lepchas of the Himalayas. They are sweet but mawkish."

## Passiflora quadrangularis  (Passifloraceae) GRANADILLA

Sturtevant says: "Tropical America. The fruit is oval and of various sizes from a goose egg to a muskmelon; it is greenish-yellow, having a spongy rind about a finger in thickness, which becomes soft as the fruit ripens, contains a succulent pulp of a water color and sweet smell, is of a very agreeable, pleasant, sweet-acid taste and contains a multitude of black seeds, which are eaten with the pulp. Titford says it is delicious."

## Pittosporum ferruginium  (Pittosporaceae)

This tree, usually small but sometimes to 65 feet, ranges from Burma to Australia. It is ornamental and often used in gardens.

Ho Sai-Yuen writes from Malaysia: "The small, whitish seeds, the size of peeled GROUNDNUTS, can be eaten raw or can be boiled with fish as a soup dish."

Willis says there are 150 species of *Pittosporum* scattered from Africa to the Pacific and adds: "The seeds of some are sticky."

Greshoff in Kew Bulletin 1909, demonstrated that a number of species contain saponin.

## Poga oleosa (Anisaophylleaceae) INOI NUT AFRICAN BRAZIL NUT

This is a big forest tree, abundant in Nigeria and the Cameroons, not much exploited for timber because it is attacked by termites.

Dalziel says its use for plantation production of oilseed is limited, because the nature of the hard shell renders extraction of the kernel very difficult.

Dalziel continues: "The fruit is roughly spherical, 1½-2 in. in diameter, with a fleshy pericarp ¼ in. thick, which soon rots, and a very hard bony nut, tubercled or pitted and fenestrated on the surface, and containing two to four seeds. The seeds are white and oily on section. The clean kernel is equal to the BRAZIL NUT in flavour, but the seed-coat has a disagreeable taste. Kernels from Western Cameroons are described as sweet and pleasant to taste, like an almond, and yielding easily by cold pressure an oil of agreeable taste, which has on occasion been used locally as a substitute for olive oil for the table. In Nigeria the seeds are sold in markets, and are much appreciated by the people, while in Cameroons some tribes use the oil in cooking. In Gabon the kernels and the extracted oil are regarded as one of the best of native condiments. The residual meal was found to contain 41-5% of protein and 40-7% of carbohydrates."

## Raphiostylis beniniensis (Icacinaceae)

Of the 10 species in tropical Africa, Dalziel says of this one: "The seeds are said to be edible."

## Ravenala madagascariensis (Scitamineae) TRAVELERS' TREE

Food and water from Madagascar. Ellis: *Three Visits Madagascar* says: "The seed is edible. When a spear is struck into the thick firm end of the leaf-stalk, a stream of pure, clear water gushes out. There is a kind of natural cavity, or cistern, at the base of the stalk of each of the leaves, and the water collected on the broad and ribbed surface of the leaf, flows down a groove and is stored."

## Salvadora persica (Salvadoraceae) SALT BUSH

Willis says, of the 4 or 5 species in warm Africa and Asia, this one "has been thought by some (probably erroneously) to be the mustard of the Bible."

Dalziel says: "The seeds contain an oil, yielding about 45% of a fat of high melting point suitable if purified as to odour and taste, a possible substitute for vegetable butters in chocolate manufacture."

## Simmondsia chinensis (Simmondsiaceae) JOJOBA GOAT NUT DEER NUT

This rigid much-branched shrub to 5 feet, is the only species in the genus, native of California. Sturtevant says: "The ripe fruit is the size of a HAZELNUT and has a thin, smooth, three-valved husk, which, separating spontaneously, discloses a brown triangular kernel. This fruit, though edible, can hardly be termed palatable. Its taste is somewhat intermediate between filbert and acorn. It is employed by the Indians as an article of diet."

Kirk says: "The bitter nuts contain a nutritious oil and may be eaten raw, roasted, or parched. The bitter flavor is due to tannin. The nuts were once used as a substitute for coffee, prepared as follows: roast the seeds and grind the kernels together with the yolk of a hard-boiled egg; boil this pasty mass in water for several minutes; add sugar and cream or milk; flavor with vanilla for a savory drink. Of course, if you are a purist, you can drink it black!"

This shrub is closely related to boxwood. Willis says: "An unusual feature of *Simmondsia* is the storage and mobilization of waxes in the seed, instead of the more usual carbohydrates, proteins or fats."

## Spergularia rubra (Caryophyllaceae) SAND SPURREY

This European salt-loving, annual herb to 1 foot high, is naturalized in North America. In Finland and Scandinavia bread has sometimes been made of the seeds in time of scarcity.

## Theophrasta jussieui (Myrsineae)

Sturtevant says: "South America and Santo Domingo. The fruit is succulent, and bread is made from the seeds."

## Tilia (Tiliaceae) LINDEN BASSWOOD

Some 30 kinds of these ornamental shade trees of the Temperate Zone are cultivated in Europe and America and many cultivars are used in street planting.

The fruit is a nut containing three seeds.

Julia Rogers: *Trees* says: "Experiments in Germany have successfully extracted a table oil from the seed-balls. A nutritious paste resembling chocolate has been made from its nuts, which are delicious when fresh. In winter the buds, as well as the tiny nuts, stand between the lost trapper and starvation."

JOJOBA (*Simmondsia californica*)

AFRICAN BREADFRUIT (*Treculia africana*)

121

## Treculia africana (Urticaceae)
### AFRICAN BREADFRUIT

Fanshawe writes: "Seeds ground to a meal, cooked and added to soups in Malawi. Roasted seeds are palatable and contain an edible oil."

Dalziel says: "A large tree in forest and by streams, even in comparatively dry zones, and often seen near villages. The soil under the tree is moist throughout the dry season from condensation.

"The fruit attains 18 in. in diameter and 18-30 lbs. in weight; the seeds are numerous, brownish, ⅓ in. or less in length, buried in a spongy pulp. They are extracted after placing the fruit in water to macerate, and are an excellent food cooked and ground to a meal, which is generally used in soup. 'Almond milk' is a beverage made from the meal, used in the Portuguese African colonies. The seeds may also be boiled or roasted, peeled and eaten as a dessert nut quite palatable to European taste, or fried in oil. An edible oil is sometimes extracted from them. The fruits are eaten by antelopes and by the large forest snails.

"The tree is reputed to be poisonous to animals in S. Nigeria. Others refer the poisonous properties to the fruits, a belief widely held by the people, although they use the cooked seeds as food, but no poisonous properties have been found."

Sturtevant says: "A tropical African tree called Okwa. The nuts contain an edible embryo and are collected by the negroes and ground into meal."

Irvine says: "An unbuttressed medium to large tree up to 80 ft. high and 9 ft. girth; bole square with flutings up to 20 ft. Fruits (Feb.-Mar.) often abundant, on trunk and larger branches, weight, spherical, becoming yellow brown and soft, containing 8 cigarette tinfuls of small brown seeds; seeds nearly ½ in. long, ellipsoid.

"The small brown seeds are edible with a groundnut flavour. Vogel states that they are of the size of haricot beans, are ground, and used as meal, e.g. with maize. Aubreville mentions the tree's cultivation for this purpose. When food is scarce, the Ibos grind and cook them, re-cook, and mix with oil, and eat them in a mass. Boiled or roasted and skinned, or fried in oil, they are quite good as dessert nuts, though Ridley, on trying them, said that JAK seeds (Artocarpus) were more palatable. In Sudan the kernels are roasted and eaten whole or made into a paste for sauce."

Julia Morton Photo

LAND CALTROPS (Tribulus terrestris)

## Tribulus terrestris (Zygophylleae)
### LAND CALTROPS

Sturtevant reports: "The unexpanded capsules, reduced to powder and formed into cakes, served as food during a famine in Rajputana, India."

## Trichilia emetica (Meliaceae)

Some 300 species of Trichilia thrive from Mexico to tropical America, the West Indies and tropical Africa.

Dalziel says of this species in the Gold Coast and Nigeria: "The fruit is a brilliant red leathery stipitate capsule; the seeds have an orange-red or scarlet fleshy aril; the greasy reddish pulp is either used as food in some regions or chewed like KOLA.

"The seeds yield a variable amount of fat, up to 64%, the pulp also yielding up to 50%. It consists of about 55% olein and 45% palmitine. In Portuguese East Africa it was formerly exported to Marseilles, but now an oil and soap factory is established at Lourenco Marques. It is commonly used to make native soap, but in some parts it is also used as a cooking fat. The local method of obtaining the fat is to immerse in hot water and float off first the oil from the aril, after which the seeds are crushed and the solid fat expressed. It is yellowish, without much taste, and with an odour like cocoa-butter. The seeds of some samples from West Africa yield up to 44.7% of fat."

Fanshawe writes from Zambia: "The Valley Tonga cook and eat the seeds as a famine food. Seeds have to be husked before eating as the pericarp contains a poisonous principle."

Williamson says of T. roka: "A much-branched evergreen tree to 50 ft. tall with fruits globose, green, opening on the tree to show the black seeds largely covered with a scarlet aril. The fruits ripen in January to April. Common at Lake levels.

"Hot water is poured on the seeds; they are left to soak for a few hours and then rubbed between the hands. A sweet milky liquid is extracted from the arils which can be used as a drink or added to suitable side-dishes or mixed with bananas. The seeds yield a variable amount of fat up to 64 per cent. In Portuguese East Africa, it is used for soapmaking. It can also be used as cooking fat."

## Trichodesma zeylanicum (Boraginaceae)

Williamson says: "An annual much-branched herb in Malawi, with very rough leaves and small white or pale blue flowers. Common everywhere as a pioneer in abandoned cultivations at lower elevations. The seeds yield an oil which might be of commercial importance if the Africans could be induced to harvest the plants."

HINDI-PITTI (Ventilago madraspatana)

## Ventilago madraspatana (Rhamnaceae)
### HINDI-PITTI

Maheshwari says: "A climbing shrub, found in Maharashtra and S. India. The seeds are edible."

Watt says of V. calyculata: "A large climbing shrub, found throughout the hotter parts of India. An oil is obtained from the seeds, which resembles ghi in taste and is used in Chutia Nagpur for cooking purposes."

JUJUBE (*Zizyphus mauritiana*)

Julia Morton Photo

Sturtevant says: "East Indies and Malay, cultivated generally in the East Indies. More than 1200 years ago this plant was introduced into China by way of Persia and now yields an excellent dessert fruit for the Chinese, who recognize many varieties, differing in shape, color and size of the fruits. Those of one variety are called CHINESE DATE. In India, the fruit is more or less globose in the wild and common sorts and is ovoid or oblong in the cultivated and improved plant. The pulp is mealy, sweetish, with a pleasant taste, and, in South India, an oil is extracted from the kernel.

Regarding *Z. xylopyrus*, East Indies, Sturtevant says: "The fruits are not eaten by men but the kernels are."

*PART II. (Monocots)*

# Chapter 24

# The COCONUT and other Palms

Everybody recognizes the COCONUT as a nut. Its interior in commercial forms is called copra. Harvesting these nuts and reducing their contents to food is big business.

But the COCONUT is not alone. There are many relatives of this palm which have edible kernels and therefore are nuts, and if we were to define "kernel" as the core or heart of anything, scores of other palms make their way into the nuts book. In most of the latter group the edible part of the fruit is available only in the green, or immature, stage of the fruit's growth. At that point the edible part is a juice or juicy pulp which is extracted through holes in the shell, or by cracking, which of course ends the life of the seed. Later on that pulpy interior solidifies, in some instances becoming fibrous, in others becoming a sort of vegetable ivory, often so hard it is utilized in making buttons and billiard balls.

But all these edibles get into nuts book for the reader to get acquainted with.

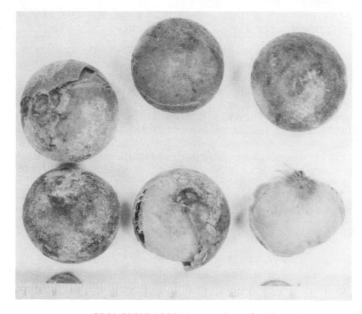

GRU-GRU PALM (*Acrocomia aculeata*)

MEXICAN GRU-GRU (*Acrocomia mexicana*)

## *Acrocomia aculeata*          GRU-GRU PALM

Williams says: "This palm is most abundant on dry hills in both Trinidad and Tobago. Height 20 to 30 feet, trunk erect about 1 foot in diameter, often swollen near the summit and armed with black spines. Leaves 12 to 14 feet with from 70 to 80 leaflets on either side of the main rib, which is covered with strong black spines. Flowers yellow and fragrant, the yellowish-brown round fruit, about the size of a billiard ball, borne in great abundance.

"GRU-GRU kernels yield a valuable oil. The sweet pulpy portion of the fruit as well as the kernel is edible."

Wadsworth says in Puerto Rico: "The fruits of certain palms are edible, particularly *Acrocomia media*, but it is virtually inaccessible and, in my judgment, not worth the effort."

Blossfeld writes from Brazil: "*A. totai* grows in the Chaco area and is important for oil extraction from the seeds in Bolivia and Paraguay, where it is used for oil lamps and in cooking.

"*A. sclerocarpa* most important locally, produces pulp which is about 50 per cent oil, used in soap manufacture. This oil, when obtained locally, is used in cooking because it is cheap. The nut can be eaten raw and it is often used to fatten hogs."

L. S. Lindo, forester at Belize, writes of *A. mexicana*, which he calls the SUPPA PALM: "In the northern plains and perhaps elsewhere; Mexico and Central America. A large palm with tall thick trunk densely armed with long slender dark spines; leaves very large, pinnate, with narrow segments, densely clustered at the top of the trunk, the dead leaves persisting below the living ones; segments of the leaves and midrib densely spiny; flower and fruit panicles large and heavy; pendent, spiny; fruit large, black, globose, smooth. This palm grows usually in open places and often in dry regions. The fruits are eaten by cattle, and the flesh is eaten sometimes by people. From the trunk there is obtained a sweet sap which after fermentation forms an agreeably flavoured palm wine."

F. C. Hoehne wrote of this genus: "Cattle appreciate very much the coconuts of *Acrocomia*, and the milk cows transmit to the milk the odor and yellowish color of the pulp which they ingest. They expel the seeds when they ruminate.

"From these same palm trees, which abound in southwest Brazil and as far as Mato Grosso, two good oils can be extracted: oil from the pulp for soap and oil from the almonds for nutrition.

"We have dozens of species which supply coconuts with mucilaginous pulp of a sweet and agreeable flavor, which many years ago children learned to make the most of. In the genus *Acrocomia*, which provides the 'Macaiuvas', 'Bacaiuvas' or 'Coco Catarro', there is a hard shell which adorns the fleshy part, but in others it is very thin and easily broken, so that you can enjoy them with no further effort by putting them into your mouth, which the young folk do everywhere in the interior, and also in the cities where these palms appear."

(*Actinorhytis calapparia*)

## *Actinorhytis calapparia*

This genus of small palms in Malaysia contains one or possibly two species. The young nut, says Rumpf, has a juicy kernel, pleasant in taste and fit to eat though tough when chewed.

Burkill says the ripe nut is medicinal, being chewed as BETEL by the Malays.

124

Fairchild Tropical Garden Photo

*(Aiphanes acanthophylla)*

## Aiphanes minima COYOR

This medium-sized palm from tropical America is often planted as an ornamental; the fruits are sometimes used for food. It bears long, sharp, black spines on the trunk, leaves, and stems of the inflorescences. The leaves are pinnate, 5 to 8 feet long, and are composed of closely spaced leaflets 8 to 15 inches long and 2 to 3 inches wide. The branched inflorescence, which is borne among the leaves, is 2 to 3 feet long. It bears many orange-red globose fruits each slightly less than 1 inch in diameter.

The thin, fleshy exterior of the fruit is edible and has a sweet, fruity flavor. Inside the hard shell of the single seed is a comparatively thick layer of white meat. In flavor and texture this meat resembles coconut meat, and it may be used in the same way. Propagation is by seeds.

## Allagoptera maritimum

This is a genus of ten kinds of palm trees in South America, formerly called *Diplothemium*. Sturtevant wrote:

"The fruit, an ovate or obovate drupe, is yellow and has a fibrous, acid-sweet flesh, which is eaten by the Indians."

J. K. Maheshwari Photo

*Arenga pinnata* in Calcutta Botanic Garden

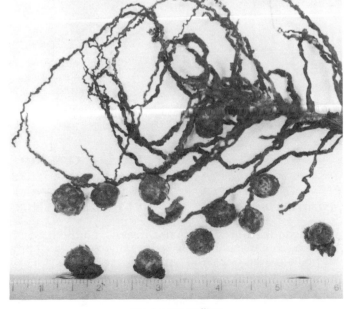

*(Aiphanes corallina)*

*(Arenga engleri)*

*(Arenga undularifolia)*

*(Astrocaryum aculeatum)*

## Arenga pinnata

KAONG
SUGAR PLUM

Brown: *Useful Plants of the Philippines* says:
"This rather large palm is characterized by its very long, ascending, pinnate leaves, which are up to 8.5 meters long with 100 or more pairs of linear leaflets which are whitish beneath, 1 to 1.5 meters long.

"*Arenga pinnata* has very numerous, crowded, green nuts, which turn yellow when mature. The fruits are about 5 centimeters in diameter and contain two or three seeds. Immature seeds are much eaten by the Filipinos, being usually boiled with sugar to form a kind of sweetmeat. In this form they are often sold in Manila markets. The buds make an excellent salad. The meat is white and crisped and has an agreeable, bland flavor."

*(Astrocaryum malybo)*

*(Astrocaryum tucumoides)*

*(Astrocaryum standleyanum)*

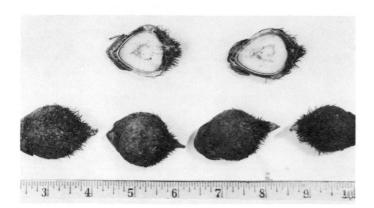

*(Astrocaryum mexicana)*

TUCAN NUTS, TUCUM NUTS,
AWARA NUTS, PANAMA NUTS,
GUERE-PALM NUTS,
MURU-MURU NUTS

## Astrocaryum

This confused genus of palm trees in northern South America, comprises about 30 species, many of which produce nuts rich in oil, though probably less satisfactory or of less value than the nuts of the African oil palm *Elaeis*. All the *Astrocaryum* trees are characterized by exceedingly spiny trunks, and the leaves and flower stalks are covered with long, sharp, black thorns.

126

The fruits of several species yield edible oil that finds commercial use in margarine and similar products.

*(Attalea speciosa)*

*(Attalea fagifolia)*

## *Attalea funifera*          COQUILLA NUT

*Attalea* comprises some 40 kinds of palm trees, mostly Brazilian, of which this species bears fruits 3 or 4 inches long, dark brown, with an extremely hard shell. This fruit is used as a substitute for ivory in the manufacture of buttons, doorknobs, and various other household items.

Blossfeld writes from Brazil: "*Attalea funifera* furnishes the famous plassava fiber largely exported for hard brooms and brushes. The fruit is too hard to be opened, still harder than BABASSU NUTS, and has been exported in old times to France and Germany for making buttons of the hard shell. How the seed manages to germinate through the tiny hole the shell has, is still a little wonder.

"*Attalea oleifera* is used in the way of BABASSU in Pernambuco: the nut is placed on the edge of an axe placed on a flat stone and fixed by two stones, one on each side, and then the man gives it an expert blow with a wooden club, which splits it in two, and two kernels can be extracted. Then the same operation is repeated twice with the halves, and the two remaining kernels are set free. In recent years, the shell is shipped to special factories and burnt to charcoal for certain metallurgic purposes. From the kernels, a very fine cooking oil is obtained, which has a ready market locally. I do not believe the kernels are eaten."

COHUNE NUT *(Attalea cohune)*

Regarding the COHUNE NUT (*A. cohune*), also called COHOON NUT, in Central America, Bailey says: "The oval or fusiform seeds measure from 2 to 2½ inches in length, by about 1½ inches in greatest diameter. Within the shell, which is fully 1/8 inch and very hard, is a single elliptical kernel. COHUNE NUT oil has long been used as an adulterant for coconut oil. At present there is practically an unlimited demand for all of these (palm) oils in the European margarine trade, where they are now preferred to oleo oil and neutral lard as a hardening ingredient."

Sturtevant says: "This tree bears a fruit, about the size of a large egg, growing in clusters resembling a bunch of grapes. The kernel tastes somewhat like that of the COCONUT but is far more oleaginous and the oil is superior."

L. S. Lindo, forester at Belize, wrote this author about the COHUNE PALM.

"The commonest palm of Central America, occurring extensively from sea level to an elevation of 540 meters, on all types of soil; Mexico, and probably as far south as Costa Rica. A tall, unarmed palm with very thick trunk,

127

usually with persisting leaf bases; leaves plumelike and graceful, sometimes as much as 10 metres long, with numerous narrow segments; flower and fruit panicles very large and heavy, pendent, 1 meter long or more, often containing 500-800 fruits, these 6 cm. long, shaped like young COCONUTS of corresponding size. This palm is of considerable importance locally. The leaves are much used for thatching, and the pole-like rachis of the leaf for forming the frame work of huts. Oil is obtained from the kernels, and the tender cabbages are eaten. During the World War large quantities of the nuts were exported to England for preparing charcoal used in gas masks. Attempts have been made to extract the oil, but these have failed heretofore, partly because of the difficulty of crushing the fruits, and also on account of the uncertainty of a continuous supply of them.''

Harold E. Moore, Jr. Photo

(Bactris gasipaes)

## Bactris gasipaes (Syn. Guilielma gasipaes)

PEACH PALM
PUPUNHA
PEJIBAYE

The PEACH PALM has been grown extensively for many years from Central America as far south as Ecuador. From September to March its fruit crop is important to millions. It is protected from animals on the tree by sharp spines below the clustered fruits, it keeps well on the tree as well as after harvesting, and it is used as food in many ways. The palm reaches 60 feet, often is allowed 4 or 5 stems from the base, and each tree bears up to 5 bunches of fruit, each weighing about 25 pounds.

(Bactris guineensis)

(Bactris majur)

In addition to the usefulness of the fruits as food, the seed kernels are eaten, which makes this a nut. Popenoe says: ''The flesh is dry, mealy, yet firm in texture, and pale orange to yellow in color. The single seed, from which the flesh separates very readily after the fruit has been boiled, is conical, somewhat angular in outline, about three-quarters of an inch long, black, with a thin but hard shell enclosing a white kernel resembling that of the coconut in character. The hard white kernel is eaten. It resembles the coconut in flavor and contains a high percentage of oil.''

Blossfeld writes: ''There are several varieties, and even a seedless form, that is, the seed of which has no shell or almost none. The fruit is two inches in diameter, first green, then turning yellow or in some varieties red, with a soft skin and a very small kernel which is starchy and oily. A good oil is extracted by boiling.''

Purseglove says: ''The oily kernels are also edible.''

Dr. Harold E. Moore of the Bailey Hortorium at Cornell University and the No. 1 authority on palms, writes: ''Guilielma has been considered a genus distinct from Bactris but most contemporary botanists fail to see any real basis for its separation. Thus I use Bactris gasipaes HBK (Guilielma gasipaes (HBK) L. H. Bailey). A more complete synonymy is to be found in my checklist of cultivated palms, Principes 7: 129, 1963.''

The book Unexploited Tropical Plants says: ''The chestnut-like fruit of this palm is probably the most nutritionally balanced of tropical foods. It contains carbohydrates, protein, oil, minerals, and vitamins. Suited to the wet tropics, the trees, once established, require little care and yield well.''

Howes says: ''In the lowlands of Colombia, Venezuela, and Ecuador this palm constitutes a staple foodstuff with many aboriginal tribes. As much as 50 kilos of fruit may be obtained from a single palm in a season. The fruits contain a single seed embedded in a dry mealy pulp. Both kernel and pulp are eaten. When boiled, which is best done in salted water for about three hours, the seeds are very palatable and strongly resemble chestnuts both in appearance and taste, hence the name 'palm chestnut', although much larger in size than an ordinary CHESTNUT. The kernel is rich in oil and tastes like COCONUT.''

F. C. Hoehne wrote:

''Among the fruit trees we must cite Bactris, the 'Popunha', which the inhabitants succeed in domesticating to the point of obtaining coconuts with the seed completely solidified, composed entirely of fibrous pulp. This and other plants of this family should be taken under the care of the agronomists and converted into a source of income. We believe that many of them could become as precious and as useful for the nourishment of men as the 'Tamareira' of Arabia and Africa. In Mato Grosso we saw, many times, how the dwellers of the back country who travel along the rivers know the fruits of many species of *Astrocaryum* and *Bactris* and know how to extract from them magnificent resources for their daily menus. Some have an acid flavor, others are sweet, so they use the one to make refreshing beverages and the other to eat.

"Regarding the industrialization of the oil of many seeds of the palm trees, we will say only that these great riches, largely still completely unknown, continue to be wasted. In the destruction and subsequent fires, thousands of palm trees perish in the northeast of Sao Paulo and in other parts of our country under the pretext that the lands are needed for grazing for fattening cattle, despite the fact that there are endless natural lands which so far have not been utilized by turning them into pastures."

## Borassodendron

This is a genus of one species of palm in the Malay peninsula.

P. F. Cockburn, forest research officer in Penyelidek, Sandakan, Malaya, wrote this author: "*Borassodendron* is a large jungle palm with sharp edges to the leaf stalks. It produces nuts similar in many respects to the COCOA-DE-MER, of Seychelles but much smaller. The young endosperm is eaten in much the same way I believe as COCONUT."

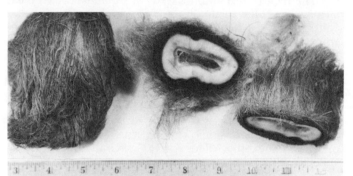

*(Borassus flabellifera)*

## Borassus flabellifer          PALMYRA PALM

This 80-foot tree from Asia and tropical Africa, is extensively cultivated in the drier parts of India and Ceylon. The fan-shaped leaves 8 to 10 feet wide, form a dense mass at the top of the tree and often for a long way down the trunk.

Williams & Freeman write: "It is one of the most useful palms of India. The wood is hard and durable; the leaves are used as thatch and as writing paper; fibre is obtained from the leaves, toddy from the inflorescence, and the fruit and young seedlings are used as food. Matting, bags, baskets, umbrellas, fans, etc., are also prepared from strips of the leaves."

Maheshwari writes: "When the fruits are tender, the seeds are of a soft, sweet gelatinous pulp with a little liquid in them. These are much relished in summer. The pulp gradually hardens into a bony kernel and develops a fibrous coat. The cotyledon, in germinating seeds, a cream-coloured substance of the consistency of cheese, is sweet and pleasant to taste. When seedlings are 2-3 months old, the tender shoots which are starchy, are edible and sometimes flour is made from them. It is reported that the young fleshy roots, about 4 months old, also contain starch and are eaten. In Ceylon, the soft, yellow, pulpy tissue, under the outer skin of ripe fruit, is squeezed out and the juice is dried in thick layers into an edible preparation called "punatoo". In Bengal this juice is consumed as such, or is made into sweets.

"About April to May, a certain number of the fruits are removed from the trees. The epicarp and the mesocarp are removed and rejected; the shell is split open and the seed is obtained. This constitutes the edible structure sold in Bengal under the name of 'talgaus'. The soft albuminous layer and the jelly-like fluid contained within it are eaten fresh, being regarded as cool and refreshing. They are sometimes cut into small pieces and flavoured with sugar and rose-water. In this condition they are viewed as a delicacy. In India it is very rarely the case that either the fresh seed or the above preparation from it is eaten by Europeans.

"In July and August, when the fruits are ripe they are removed from the tree. The mesocarp or succulent and fibrous layer, after being passed through a preparatory process, is eaten as an article of food. The yellow pulp surrounding the seeds (nuts) of the ripe fruit is sweet, heavy and indigestible. It is extracted by rubbing the seeds over a wooden scratcher and with the addition of a little lime, it settles into a jelly, which is ready mode of taking the pulp. It is also made into cakes with flour and other ingredients. The fibrous tissue which ramifies through the succulent mesocarp is attached to the endocarp or shell of the nut. The succulent pulp scraped away from this tissue has a peculiar odour and is sweetish; it is either eaten raw, or is mashed and strained with a little flour and sugar, completely mixed up to form a mess and is then made into small flat cakes and is fried in ghee or mustard oil. The cakes are known as 'patali' or 'petha'. In order to make the first kind of cake ('patali') the scraped pulp is mixed with lime and coconut, spread evenly on a plate in which it is allowed to stand for an hour, after which it is found in a solid state, owing to the effect of the lime on the pulp. In order to make 'pitha', the pulp is mixed with rice or wheat flour and then fried in oil. In Bengal 'tal' pulp is not preserved, does not form an important article of food, and there is no trade in it. In short, the 'tal' occupies a very unimportant place among the Bengal fruits.

"In Ceylon, the pulp is known as 'Punatu'. The pulp of the fruit is preserved for use in the following manner. The ripe fruits are put into baskets containing water, and are then squeezed by the hand till the pulp forms a jelly. Layers of this jelly are spread on palmyra-leaf mats to dry on stages. Layer after layer is deposited to the number about fifteen. These are left in the sun about a fortnight or three weeks, only covered at night and protected from the dew and rain. The best sort is called 'Punatu'. 'Punatu' is sold by the mat at 3 to 5 sh. each and is the chief food of the islands of Ceylon and of the poorer classes of the Peninsula, for several months of the year."

Dr. Alfred Heasty, a medical missionary who lives on a hill in the Sudan, writes of the *Borassus* palms that grow around him:

"The *Doleib* palm tree is hollow on the inside. It grows about 30 feet tall or taller. It has a lot of deep roots. The trunk is very straight and too big around to climb. There are male and female trees.

"The female trees produce once a year. Each tree will produce from 50 to 100 nuts or more. The nuts have one, two or three seeds. Very rarely there will be four seeds. When the nut ripens it falls with a thud on the ground sounding like "tuck" (with a long u). The Shilluck name for the nut is Tuk (again with a long u).

"The nuts will fall from January through June. Through the years this has made a food through the famine (dry) season.

"The nut itself is so hard, you have to beat it with a club to soften the fibers and fruit or pulp before you can eat it. The meat part of the nut is fibrous like a mango. There is not as much meat as a mango. The fibers are much larger and stronger. Most people tasting it for the first time do not like it, but it tastes good to a fellow raised on the Doleib nuts.

"I've never seen the seed used for anything. In the dry season cracks open up in the clay soil, the seeds fall down in and a new tree is born. It takes years for a tree to grow. Some of the trees in Doleib Hill were there when the first missionaries came in the early 1900's.

"Now-a-days the people use the palm fronds for ropes, or anklet or bracelet decorations during a dance. This of course kills the tree, so there are very few new trees. It is against their traditional religion to destroy any tree. Now it is even against the law to kill any tree."

George L. Avery of South Miami, technical advisor to this author, writes of Dr. Heasty's palm tree: "I looked into the floras of northeastern Africa for *Borassus deleb* (this is the correct spelling) in Beccari's original publication on this palm in *Webbia*, is in Italian, concerning the range, it says: "*B. deleb* seems to be restricted to the river basin of the upper Nile."

"I now strongly suspect that the tree Dr. Heasty is writing about is this *B. deleb*. He is located in the very area where this species is native. Furthermore, he gives us a picture of the palm on his stationery, which does not display the swollen trunk typical of *B. aethiopum*."

*(Calamus maneu)*

*(Calamus tumidus)*

## *Calamus spp.* RATTANS

Purseglove: *Tropical Crops* describes these well:

"RATTANS are climbing palms of the Orient belonging to several genera, of which the largest is *Calamus* with 250-300 spp., extending from West Africa to Taiwan, Australasia and Fiji, but with the greatest number in the Dipterocarp rain forests of the Malayan archipelago. They have long, woody, flexible, solid stems which may reach nearly 200 m. (680 feet). They scramble by means of modified leaf-tips or leaf-sheath whips; both are barbed with vicious recurved spines which hook onto the trees over which they clamber. When the support gives way, the stems loop between the trees or coil on the forest floor, and the crown subsides until the hooks catch on again to continue scrambling. The hooked whips tear at the unwary traveller in the Malesian forests and only pachyderms may be immune from their assault.

"RATTANS vary in thickness from 0.3-3 cm. Some spp. produce a number of stems from a single clump. *Calumus* fruit have imbricate scales and a thin layer of pulp surrounding a stoneless seed; some have edible fruits.

"The canes are usually obtained from wild plants in the Malesian forests, the RATTANS being pulled from the trees, cut into suitable lengths, cleaned and coiled. This is done mainly by the local people; they sell them to the traders, who are often Chinese."

Malayan forester Isaac Ho Sai-Yuen writes from Kuala Lumpur:

"The fruit (pulp) and the seeds of *Calamus* are edible at a ripe stage. I have eaten both. The edibility of the seeds is confirmed by a plant collector who is an aborigine and whose knowledge of jungle lore is fantastic. Sometimes as a substitute for *Areca* (BETEL NUT) the aboriginees chew these seeds. From the forest I was able to collect the ripe fruits of *Calamus tumidus* and have photographed them for you."

Regarding *C. rotang* in the East Indies, Sturtevant says: "When ripe this fruit is roundish, as large as a HAZELNUT and is covered with small, shining scales, laid like shingles, one upon the other. The natives generally suck out the subacid pulp which surrounds the kernels by way of quenching their thirst. Sometimes the fruit is pickled with salt and eaten at tea-time."

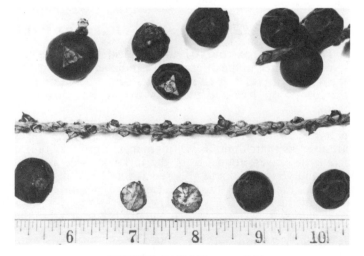

FISHTAIL PALM *(Caryota mitis)*

FISHTAIL PALM *(Caryota sp.)*

## *Caryota mitis*       FISHTAIL PALM

This Asiatic palm with up to 40 clustered stems, rising 25 to 40 feet, each stem up to 4 inches in diameter, is much planted in South Florida as an ornamental.

Burkill says: "The fruits, like those of *C. aequatorialis*, have edible seeds inside a poisonous fruit wall. Monkeys may be seen eating them, no doubt discarding as much as possible of the wall. The people of Cochin-China use these fruits as a masticatory, along with BETEL, for which purpose they are specially prepared by macerating for 4-6 days in water, and beating to free the coat."

Dr. Harold E. Moore, Jr., author of *Natural History of Palms*, writes this author: "I would not recommend anyone eating the fruit of *Caryota*. Dransfield in *Principes* 18:93 — 1974 wrote: 'As in all Caryotoidea, the mesacarp contains many irritant oxylate crystals. How does the hornbill survive the crystals where even to the human hand the mesacarp is wildly irritating?' In similar fashion the fruits or *Arenga* are extremely irritant, just to handle, as are those of many species of *Chamaedorea*."

COCONUT *(Cocos nucifera)*

## *Cocos nucifera*       COCONUT

The COCONUT is by far the most important nut in the world commercially. It is prized first of all for the meat and drink within the hull with their riches of food and fat. The nut is valued too for the charcoal derived from the shells, for the coir fibre that comes from the husk to make brushes, cloth, rope and a thousand other products, and last but not least, for the lumber derived from the trunk to build homes; and for the leaves that thatch the roof. The thousand necessities of life derived from it supply hundreds of millions of people throughout the tropics.

The tree's enormous annual crop grows bigger and bigger as the years wear on, continuing its production often for 60 years or more, mostly from uncultivated soil, not needing man's fertilizer or industry to maintain its production level. It is by all standards the biggest money crop in the world and its continuance does more to feed people than any government agency so far devised by man.

Aside from money value of the crop, the nut is produced on one of the most ornamental of palm trees, highly prized for its aesthetic value on the landscape. Florida's development as a land of palm trees grew out of the shipwreck of the bark Providencia, laden with coconuts from the south seas, on the beach near Lake Worth on January 9, 1878, and these within ten years had produced 350,000 trees.

Wm. F. Whitman Photo
MALAYAN DWARF COCONUT *(Cocos sp.)*

Because of tree losses by a disease called "lethal yellowing" in Florida, the common coconut is being widely replaced by a so-called Malayan dwarf form, which really is not a dwarf. But it is disease-resistant.

Typical of experiences in many lands is a note from Harry Blossfeld in Brazil. He writes: "Four or five varieties of coconut are eaten here. One of these is *C. coronata*, here called LICURI which in the Brazilian state of Bahia is a native palm that sustains thousands of people and most of their hogs, goats and even chickens. Hogs break the shell easily, goats crush them partially and on ruminating, expel the hard shells and learn to spit them out, while they eat the nut. Chickens are fed on the fruits crushed by hand by the people. And many people live for months on at least a partial diet of LICURI nuts.

"*C. oleracea*, the native name GUARIROBA. This grows in Goias and southern Minas Gerais and has big clusters of fruits, the pulp of which is sweet and eaten by cattle and children, and after drying and cleaning the kernel, this is sold on the local markets for direct eating as a nut, and where plentiful, the kernels are pressed and an oil is obtained, which is used for cooking."

Bailey says of the COCONUT:

"From the nuts, which are borne incased in very thick fibrous husks, is obtained the world's greatest food-supply. The flesh is wholesome either green or ripe, and either raw or cooked. The milk affords a very refreshing drink and the dried flesh, called 'copra' is exported in enormous quantities. Coconut oil is one of the chief articles of export from the tropics. It is used in the manufacture of transparent and 'marine' soaps. It is also largely used in pharmacy as a substitute for lard because of its less tendency to rancidity."

William F. Whitman of Bal Harbour, has written this study of the Malayan dwarf COCONUT for the Rare Fruit Council International, Inc.:

"The rapid spread of the 'Lethal Yellowing' coconut disease has resulted in a worldwide search of tropical countries for resistant coconut varieties. One tolerant strain is the 'Malayan Dwarf' which is being used to replace coconuts killed by the above disease in Jamaica, South Florida and other coconut growing areas. This dwarf palm comes in three color variations, the green, the yellow and the red. In South Florida the red usually is referred to as the golden and is considered the most ornamental of the three types.

"The Malayan Dwarf, under favorable conditions, bears when about four or five years old with only two or three feet of bare trunk exposed. The nuts are small but the crop can be heavy. These tend to remain on the tree and don't fall to the ground when ripe as the nuts produced by the tall varieties do.

"The Malayan Dwarf differs from the typical tall coconut of commerce in a number of ways. Among these is its ability to come into bearing much sooner, with full production in the ninth or tenth year when the trees are first commencing to bloom. Their ultimate height and life expectancy are a third less to half that obtained by the common tall forms."

USDA photo

*(Copernicia cereifera)*

## Copernicia prunifera

### WAX PALM
### CARNA-UBA

This comprises some 30 species in the West Indies and tropical America. The leaves of this species are coated both sides with wax which is removed by shaking and is used in making gramophone records, candles, etc. The ovoid fruits are 1 inch long or more.

Of the tree in India Maheshwari writes: "Immature seed kernels eaten. Ripe seed kernels grated or pounded for eating raw."

USDA Subtropical Research Sta. Photo

This tremendous burst of seeds in the tip-top of Corypha umbraculifera comes after 40 years of growing. When the seeds ripen, the palm dies.

USDA Subtropical Horticultural Research Photo

A handful of Corypha seeds.

## *Corypha umbraculifera*     TALIPOT PALM

*Corypha* is a genus of 8 species of palms in Indo-malaysia, this species in Ceylon reaching nearly 100 feet. When about 40 years old all the *Corypha* palms suddenly flower magnificently in the tip-top of the trunk, set seed, then die. Like the CENTURY PLANT, they die for their young. All the *Corypha* palms have enormous fan leaves, often 10 feet wide and that much or more long, something to be under when it rains.

Burkill says of one species: "In flowering, a big pyramid of flowers is thrown up. The young kernels can be turned into a sweetmeat by boiling in syrup. As they ripen they become poisonous, and at ripeness are hard enough to serve for the manufacture of buttons."

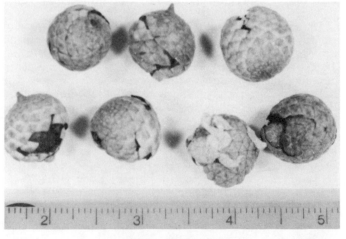

*(Daemonorhops affn. longipes)*

## *Daemonorhops Sp.*

This is a genus of a hundred kinds of palms in Malaysia, most of them climbers. They supply rattans about as good as those from *Calamus*.

Burkill says: "The fruits of some contain a little edible flesh."

132

AFRICAN OIL PALM *(Elaeis guineensis)*. Young fruits.

Francis G. Hallé Photo

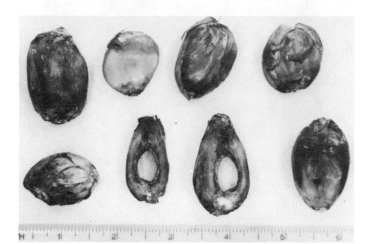

AFRICAN OIL PALM SEEDS *(Elaeis guineensis)*

## *Elaeis guineensis*      AFRICAN OIL PALM

This palm, originating in Africa but now cultivated throughout the world tropics, is by far the most important source of edible oil.

Bailey says: "The small irregularly formed seeds measure from 1 to 1½ inches in length by about ¾ inch in greatest thickness. They are very hard, have a thick ivory-like flesh and a small cavity in the center. The nuts are encased in a fibrous covering which contains the oil. According to the Kew Bulletin 'Three varieties of nut trees are distinguished, having orange, red, and black nuts respectively, the first having the finest oil but small kernels, the others less oil but large nuts.'

"MANKETTI NUTS, mentioned in the Daily Consular and Trade Reports, October 23, 1912, comprised a trial shipment of 22,500 pounds, recently made to Europe from German southwest Africa, with a view to testing their commercial value. The nuts were gathered from wild trees in the neighborhood of Tsumed. According to this report, the natives and bushmen eat the fruit without any ill effects. Efforts to find reference to the name 'manketti' in botanical works have thus far met with failure. It is suspected, however, that the article had reference to the palm nut, *Elaeis guineensis*."

Sturtevant writes: "The bright yellow drupe with shiny, purple-black point, though nauseous to the taste, is eaten in Africa. *Mawezi*, or palm oil, of the consistency of honey, is rudely extracted from this palm and despite its flavor, is universally used in cooking. Palm chop, a dish prepared at Angola from the fresh nut, is pronounced most excellent by Montiero. Lunan says the roasted nuts taste very much like the outside fat of roasted mutton, and that the negroes are fond of the oil which sometimes makes an ingredient in their foods. Hartt says this palm is the *dendes* of Brazil, the *caiauhe* of the Amazons, and that the oil is much used for culinary purposes."

Mors & Rizzini explain the construction of the nut: "The fruit, or nut, is fairly large (about 4 cm. in diameter) and hard. The stone-hard endocarp, which contains the seed, is enveloped by a fibrous, orange-colored pulp. The fruit yields two different oils. The fruit pulp supplies a deep yellow oil used by the native population and known as *zaeite de dende*. The oil, which has a sweet odor and a peculiar but not disagreeable taste, has manifold household uses.

"The second product of this fruit, the palm kernel oil, comes from the seed. It is whitish in color and practically odorless and tasteless; it is not extensively used for industrial purposes. Enormous quantities of this oil are used throughout the world, in the manufacture of soap and margarine. In Africa the natives prepare the oil from the pulp for their own use, but the kernels are cleaned and dried and subsequently exported for the manufacture of kernel oil. These palm kernels became one of the most exportable products and it was upon them that Lever Brothers of Port Sunlight, Liverpool, England based their worldwide soap empire at the turn of the century. According to analyses of the Brazilian Oil Institute, the fruit pulp contains 47 to 63 per cent, the kernel 42 to 46 per cent oil."

Dalziel reports on difficulties of oil extraction: "Efforts are made to adapt some simple and cheap but efficient apparatus for local family use, some form of cooker-or hand-press, easily worked and cleaned, involving steam or boiling to loosen and sterilise. With an efficient cooker-press the thin-shelled and mantled fruits are the more valuable, and the yield of oil may be increased 100% over the native method, and 50% for the thick-shelled types. As different types of fruit predominate east and west of the Niger, the development of thin-shell plantations may depend upon the adoption by the people of the cooker-press or other improved process. Otherwise the thick shelled are the more valuable, because by native methods the proportion of oil recovered is more, and because the yield per palm and the amount of kernels are both greater."

Schaad writes from Angola: "The palm nuts *(dende)* are the inside kernel or seed left over after the fleshy fibrous covering is removed for the palm oil. The palm nuts, aside from their commercial value, are used by the local natives as a relished common nut. The hard shell is cracked by the children with stones, with our own children participating in these feasts. As a food they are eaten raw, roasted or cooked. At times they are seasoned with cinnamon or sugar for added taste."

The Nigerian Institute for Oil Palm Research near Benin City, Nigeria, explains its objectives:

"This Institute deals principally with *Elaeis*. The components of the oil palm seed are —
  (1) *fleshy mesocarp* from which palm oil is extracted
  (2) *nut* (consisting of shell and kernel) not eaten as such, but crushed to give palm kernel oil and palm kernel cake."

Wilson Popenoe, famed plant explorer, who was largely responsible for the establishment of enormous oil palm plantations in Tropical America, wrote this author: "The fleshy pericarp is used, but also the oil from the seed kernels. There are now more than 50,000 acres of African oil palms in Tropical America. This crop was introduced commercially to the American Tropics, through the experimental plantings we made at Lancetilla Experiment Station in Honduras in the late 1920's."

The AMERICAN OIL PALM (*Elaeis oleifera*) formerly known as *Cordozo oleifera*, is now identified as allied to the AFRICAN OIL PALM. It grows in Central America and northeastern South America. The stems are procumbent with an erect apex. The leaves are 10 feet or more long and the fruits about 1 inch diameter. They supply oil like the African tree.

Hoehne wrote of Brazil: "More than three centuries ago there was introduced into Bahia the 'DENDEZEIRO' *(E. guineensis)* which, cultivated in regular quantity, produces the 'Azeita de Dende' (DENDE OIL) which finds so many uses in the Bahiana cooking. But in the state of Amazonas, and as far as Costa Rica, grows *melanococca*, which provides the same material."

Harold E. Moore, Jr. Photo

STILT ROOT PALM *(Eugeissona utile)*

Isaac Ho Sai-Yuen Photo

*(Eugeissona tristis)*

## *Eugeissona utile*  STILT-ROOT PALM

This is a genus of short-stemmed or tufted palms in Malaysia and Borneo.

Isaac Ho Sai-Yuen, forester at Kuala Lumpur, writes: "The fruits (pulp) and the seeds of *Eugeissona* are edible at a ripe stage. I have eaten both, and the edibility of the seeds is confirmed by a plant-collector who is an aborigine."

Burkill writes of *E. tristis*: "The fruit when young is edible.

COROJO *(Gastrococos crispa)*

## *Gastrococos crispa*  COROJO

This native of Cuba has showy yellow flowers, rich green fronds and no known insect or disease problems. The edible seeds are hard-shelled and difficult to germinate. The stem of this unusual palm "grows in reverse," downward, for several years while larger and larger leaves are produced; this is apparently a means of protection against fires in its native habitat. Suddenly, the direction of the shoot is reversed and the stem elongates upward quite rapidly producing the unusual bulged and tapered trunk.

DOUM PALM *(Hyphaene ventricosa)*

Fruits of the DOUM PALM *(Hyphaene ventricosa)*

134

## Hyphaene ventricosa

### GINGERBREAD PALM
### DOUM NUT

*Hyphaene* is a genus of 30 kinds of palm trees in Arabia, tropical Africa and Madagascar. The trunk is frequently branched, a rare occurrence in palms.

Tourists at Victoria Falls get a souvenir slip that reads:

### HYPHAENE VENTRICOSA PALM
#### Native Name: Mulala
#### Popular Name: Vegetable Ivory Palm

This beautiful Palm Tree grows principally on the islands and banks of the Zambesi River, in the vicinity of the Victoria Falls. The Palm attains a height of 60 feet or more.

The fruit is the shape and size of a small orange. It is covered on the outside by a thin shiny brown skin. Beneath this is a thicker layer of a fibrous nature which forms a popular diet for elephants, monkeys and baboons. This portion of the fruit is also edible to humans. A third very hard fibrous layer encases the kernel, which is inedible, extremely hard, and is extensively used in the manufacture of curios. Until the advent of plastics, Vegetable Ivory was used for the manufacture of studs, buttons, etc.

Nuts, Cut and Polished, with Card — 1/9 each — SOPER'S CURIOS, VICTORIA FALLS.

Palm Society Photo

Fruits of the GINGERBREAD PALM *(Hyphaene thebaica)*

Palm Society Photo

VEGETABLE IVORY PALM *(Hyphaene thebaica)*. This palm is unique because it is one of the few palms having branches. Sexes are on different trees. Female trees bear bunches of irregularly-shaped, yellow-brown edible fruits that do taste like gingerbread. Egypt.

G. L. Guy wrote from Zambia: "*H. ventricosa* fruits can be eaten when young — like coconuts."

Bailey writes of DOUM NUTS: "The seeds of a slow-growing African palm. It appears that there are at least two quite different types of nuts appearing under this name, both of which have been considerably employed as substitutes for the more expensive IVORY-NUTS *(Phytelephas Seemannii)* of South America. Nuts of one of these types are of a light yellowish outer color, irregularly jug-shaped, approximately 2 inches thick by 2½ inches long, and covered with a smooth-surfaced fibrous husk 1/8 inch thick. Nuts of the other type are somewhat larger, less regular in form and of a buff-color, but having much the same sort of outer husk and inner characters. The thick wall of pure white, hard flesh within the woody shell of each is used in the making of buttons, but reports from American and German manufacturers are that buttons of this material are much inclined to warp and shrivel."

Purseglove writes of *H. thebaica*: "The palm is fire-resistant, and may form dense stands in hot dry valleys. It is distributed by nomadic tribes, as well as by the elephants and baboons which eat the fruits. The seeds are among the commonest objects found in tombs in ancient Egypt, where the palm was cultivated and was considered sacred. Fruit a dry indehiscent drupe, unilocular by abortion, brown, smooth, ovoid, about 7.5 x 5 cm, ripening in 8-12 months; mesocarp smelling and tasting of gingerbread; endocarp dark brown, hard, about 4 mm. thick; seed ovoid, 4 x 3 cm; endosperm white, very hard, with hollow centre.

"The mesocarp is edible and diuretic; it may be made into syrup or may be ground to a meal, which is made into cakes and sweetmeats. Forms with sweet or bitter pulp are known. The seeds are used as vegetable ivory. The unripe kernel is edible. The endocarp is used for small containers, such as snuff-boxes."

Irvine says of *H. thebaica*: "The cabbage is edible, as also is the thin, dry, but sweet rind of the fruit. This rind is sometimes pounded into a meal and used as food or made into cakes and sweetmeats, e.g. with ground-nuts. The unripe kernels, too, are edible, and in N. Nigeria the nuts are pounded to provide a food which is sold instead of millet in districts farther south. The portion of the seedling just below the ground can also be eaten."

Dalziel says: "The hard nut is used as a ball, or strung together to form a weapon."

135

## Jessenia polycarpa                                SEJE

*Underexploited Tropical Plants* says: "*Jessenia* is a palm that produces oil closely resembling olive oil. It grows abundantly in some lowland areas of the Amazon region of Venezuela and Colombia. Its extraordinarily large and heavy fruit clusters are comparable to those of the AFRICAN OIL PALM. It is much used in its homeland.

"The purple fruit, 3 cm. long, has a thin, oily, edible pulp enclosing a fibrous husk that surrounds a horny seed. The pulp constitutes almost 40 per cent (dry weight basis) of the whole fruit; it is approximately 50 per cent oil. Adult palms average two fruit clusters per year or 30 kg. of fruit, from which 22 kg. of oil (24 liters) can be extracted.

"The yellow oil from the pulp is sold in markets in Colombia. It is equally satisfactory for food, soap, or cosmetics. The seeds are eaten mainly by the poor."

PALMA DE CONQUITOS *(Jubaea chilensis)*

David Noel Photo

*(Jubaea spectabilis)*

### HONEY PALM
### COQUITO NUT
## Jubaea chilensis                     LITTLE COKERNUT

*Hortus Third* says: "A solitary, massive, unarmed, monoecious palm of coastal central Chile. Much grown worldwide in Mediterranean-type climate, including southern California. Does not thrive in Florida. In Chile the massive trunks have long been felled as a source of sap yielding commercial palm honey, and few wild stands remain."

Bailey says: "Small globular nuts, 1 inch or less in diameter, having a smooth-surfaced, rather thick and very

hard shell, within which is a flesh and open center, much like that of the COCONUT."

Sturtevant says: "The nuts are used by the Chilean confectioners in the preparation of sweetmeats and have a pleasant nutty taste."

Howes says: "The fruits hang in bunches and each contains a hard-shelled nut about 1½ inches in diameter with a pleasant edible kernel, not unlike COCONUT in taste. These nuts are known as 'cognito' to the Chileans and are to be seen in the markets and shops of the larger towns. They were perhaps used more in the past than at the present time and were employed in the preparation of various delicacies. From time to time they have been imported into Britain as edible nuts and frequently sold under the name of 'pigmy coconuts'. The palm itself is of interest in that it is the most southerly representative of the palm family in South America."

## Livistona

This is a genus of 30 kinds of tall palms in southeast Asia from Malaya to the Philippines. Uphof says of *L. cochinchinensis*: "Ripe fruits are eaten by natives of N. Annam and Tonkin.

"*L. jenkinsiana.* Tall palm. N. E. India. Leaves used for thatch and hats. Likewise *L. speciosa* Kurz in Chittagong; *L. chinensis* Mart. in Philippine Islands; *L. australis* Mart. in Australia.

"*L. sariba*, Philippine Islands: The endosperm is eaten in Indo-China after maceration in vinegar or in salt solution."

Wolfe Photo

SEYCHELLES PALM NUT *(Lodoicea maldavici)*

136

Commercializing BIG NUTS in a BIG WAY (five languages). This Malayan circular advertises a cough medicine made from the pulpy interior of the COCO-DE-MER when fruit is a year old. The circular calls it "African Sea Coconut" but it does not grow in Africa, it is not a COCONUT, and it does not grow in the sea. The circular says the medicine cures coughs instantly. What a nut that is!

## *Lodoicea maldavici*          COCO-DE-MER

This palm is famous for many things: first, because for thousands of years its natural habitat was shrouded in mystery; because it grows only on two islands of twelve in the Seychelles, rocky spots in the Indian Ocean between India and Madagascar; because the mature trees there are 100 feet high and probably 800 years old. The tree produces the largest fruit in the plant world, usually weighing 20 to 40 pounds but occasionally twice that much; and for other reasons detailed in Menninger: *Fantastic Trees*.

Seychelles palms do not bear till they are one hundred years old or more. No one knows how old the biggest palms on Praslin are, or what age they finally reach.

Some persons make the mistake of calling this the double coconut, but it is not a coconut. It grows on a fan-leaf palm with sexes on different trees; the coconut grows on a feather-leaf palm with both sexes on the same tree. The outer husk of the Seychelles nut is smooth, brown, and less than 1 inch thick, and it splits off; the thick greenish-yellow shell beneath is not double but lobed. The fruit is usually two-lobed, sometimes three-lobed, and very rarely six-lobed.

When the fruit is ten to twelve months old it has reached its maximum size and at this stage it is frequently eaten. Its jelly-like interior is much appreciated throughout the Seychelles.

Whether the big fruit is a nut hinges on whether the contents are eaten by people, although 40 pounds of nut meat in one mass sounds a bit overwhelming.

Guy Lionnet, Minister of Agriculture writes: "The COCO-DE-MER kernel is only edible when the nut is about a year old. The kernel is then jelly-like, and translucent, with a sweetish taste, and is considered a dessert delicacy. This jelly must be eaten still fresh as it does not keep. It can however be kept for several days if refrigerated.

"COCO-DE-MER cannot be said to be plentiful since only some 2,000 nuts are produced annually, out of which about 200 are eaten green. The rest is utilized in the curios industry."

This answers the question, and the Seychelles palm fruit is a nut when it is a year old, but it ceases to be a nut when it is ripe six years later.

## *Manicaria saccifera*          MONKEY CAP PALM

This is one of four kinds of these tall palms in Central and South America. Uphof says: "The seeds are the source of oil, 'Ubusou', similar to coconut oil. Locally used for food and feed for animals."

Harold E. Moore, Jr. Photo
*(Mauritia pinifera)* On Ecuador market.

## Mauritia flexuosa

ITA PALM<br>TREE OF LIFE<br>BURITI NUT

Bailey says: "The wine-colored seed, with flattened ends, of a lofty tropical American palm. This seed is covered with very regular, close-fitting scales, underneath which is a tough shell, encasing a single ivory-like, globular, and farinaceous kernel about 1 inch in diameter. Much used as a food by the natives."

This tree grows only in flooded savannahs or marshlands, in northern South America. The fruit is 2 inches diameter, 1¾ inches long.

Dr. Harold E. Moore, Jr. writes of this palm: "The fruit is used in making ice creams and a refreshing drink."

## Maximiliana regia

CUCURITE PALM<br>INAJA PALM

Harry Blossfeld writes from Brazil:

"The kernels are really eaten on the lower Amazon. The pulp too is relished by people and cattle. The kernels have a rather thin shell, so are easily obtained by cracking. But these nuts will not enter the commerce in any quantity, they are consumed locally.

"When the natives eat the kernels, they use the shells as fuel to feed the fires in drying rubber along the lower Amazon. These fruits grow in a large cluster to 10 feet long, several bushels of nuts weighing up to 300 pounds. Individual nuts are the size of an apple."

Harold E. Moore, Jr. Photo

SAGO PALM *(Metroxylon sp.)*

## Metroxylon

SAGO PALM

These are two kinds of palm trees in Malaya that supply large quantities of sago, a starch, flour, to many hungry people. If properly prepared it can be stored. The tree is cut down to get the starch.

The fruits are only incidental. Burkill quotes Low as saying the fruit can be eaten and it was the custom to preserve it in Malacca.

Burkill explains the tree's growth: "Palms of fair height which throw up stems in succession from the underground parts, each stem in turn flowering, fruiting, and dying, after a life of about 15 years."

Harold E. Moore, Jr. Photo

*(Neoveitchia storckii)*

## Neoveitchia storckii

VULEITO

This genus of palms with only one species, grows in the Fiji Islands. J. H. Parham, author of *Plants of Fiji*, wrote this author: "The fruits of this palm have been reported as edible."

P. F. Cockburn Photo

NYPA PALM *(Nipa fruticans)*

*(Nipa fruticans)*

ingly very similar to those of olive oil. Although the kernel also contains oil (1 to 7%), this oil is not exploited.''

BABASSU PALM *(Orbignya barbosiana)*

## *Nipa fruticans*    NIPA PALM

NIPA is a palm with short prostrate, branched trunk, on the ends of which arise pinnate leaves, 20 feet and more in length. It grows in tidal mud, from the mouths of the Ganges to Australia, and is also in Ceylon.

The palm supplies roofing, thatching, baskets, matting, cigarette wrappers, fuel, alcohol, sugar, toddy and other products.

Brown: *Useful Plants of the Philippines* says:

"The immature seeds are used for food, their taste and consistency being similar to those of the flesh of immature COCONUTS. They are sometimes made into a kind of sweetmeat. The mature seeds are too hard to be eaten.''

NIPA fruits which are flat, about 12 centimeters long by 10 centimeters broad, are crowded in a very large, globose, fruiting head, which is up to 30 cm. in diameter and borne on an erect stalk.

Of the tree in India Maheshwari writes: "Immature seed kernels eaten. Ripe seed kernels grated or pounded for eating raw.''

In *Nipa fruticans* seeds is a jelly which is eaten by the marsh dwellers of New Guinea.

## *Oenocarpus*    PATAUA

This is a genus of 16 kinds of palm trees in South America, many of them very large, and several of them yield edible oil. Mors & Rizzini: *Useful Plants of Brazil*, wrote:

"*O. distichus* is distinguished by the fan-like stand of its leaves. Its fruits are violet outside and green inside. The oil, which is generally obtained by boiling with water, constitutes 8 to 10 per cent of the nutritive tissue. This oil is much appreciated all over the Amazon region for edible purposes. Its physical properties are surpris-

*(Orbignya barbosiana)* fruits

## *Orbignya barbosiana*    BABASSU PALM

*Orbignya* is a rather confused genus of some 25 species in Central and South America. Regarding this BABASSU in Brazil, Harry Blossfeld wrote this author:

"BABACU. This is a native of Maranhao, Bahia and northern Minas Gerais south to Matto Grosso, almost half of the interior of Brazil. The nut contains several kernels but the shell is so hard, that up to the present, no machines proved satisfactory to break the shell and set free the kernels. After a few days or weeks, the machines wear out, or crush the nut in a way that the kernels cannot be separated from the hulls.

"It seems that only a few years ago, a Brazilian inventor received a patent for a crushing machine, operating on *Aleurites moluccana* and BABACU successfully, without crushing the kernels. This will set free an immense economical wealth. BABACU nuts are obtained — about three to four times the quantity stated in official statistics, the remainder is consumed on the spot. It is obtained by splitting it by hand. The nut is put on a cleft of two suitable stones and a skilled worker manages to split it open with one violent blow of a heavy hatchet. The operation must be repeated four or five times, to set free all the almonds of a hull. Another method is used in Maranhao: The man keeps an axe between his feet, blade upwards, and puts the nut on the blade and then blows a tremendous hit on top of the nut with a kidgel of very hard wood. The kidgel wears out after a few weeks, but can be replaced, without cost, which is essential for the people who could not afford to buy a hammer. They keep the axe as their biggest treasure for a lifetime. The man may obtain five pounds of clean kernels in a day's work. The kernels are rarely eaten raw, but pigs are reared on the broken chips that are not bought by the oil factories, because the oil extracted from chips is quickly rancid. There is, however, a rather important oil industry on BABACU, because it is one of the best for soap production."

*Underexploited Tropical Plants* says:

"The BABASSU produces an abundance of fruit containing up to 72 per cent oil. BABASSU kernels taste, smell, and look like COCONUT meat, but they contain more oil. The palm grows wild throughout more than 35 million acres of the Amazon basin. Various levels of yield are reported for individual trees; a BABASSU palm may produce a ton of nuts a year, representing 90 kg of kernels.

"BABASSU is a tall (as high as 20 m), majestic, fan-shaped palm with large, elegant, curved leaves that grow to 9 m long. Its bunches of oblong or conical fruit often reach up to 1 m in length. The bunches weigh from 14 to 90 kg and contain 200-600 fruits; 1-4 bunches per year are produced from the time the tree is 8-10 years old. The fruit (8-15 cm long and 5-9 cm thick) resembles a small COCONUT, weighs 150-200 grams, and contains 3-8 kernels. The kernels contain 60-70 per cent oil and constitute 10 per cent of the fruit's weight. The kernel is surrounded by a pulp that is 10 per cent starch, enclosed by a hard, woody shell nearly 12 mm thick."

IVORY NUT *(Phytelephas macrocarpa)*

## *Phytelephas macrocarpa*
### IVORY-NUT NEGRO'S-HEAD

Bailey says: "The rounded, somewhat wedge-shaped seeds, or nuts of a low-growing reclining Central American palm, which in size and form greatly resemble very large chestnuts. Each nut is covered with a smooth, thin but strong shell of a light yellowish color, mottled with brown. The flesh is solid, pure white or creamy white, and capable of taking a very high polish. When cut or turned, they are used as a substitute for ivory in

the manufacture of buttons, toys, and various kinds of ornamental work.

"These seeds are borne in large compound chambers compactly joined together into heads a foot or more in diameter and covered with a sharp thorny surface, of a gray color. Each chamber contains from four to nine of the nuts, each of which is encased within its own shell.

"The manufacturing of useful articles from IVORY-NUTS for the household is a very important industry in Germany, Hamburg being one of the chief centers."

Burkill says: "The palms begin to fruit when 6 years old and produce 4 to 9 fruits per annum over 50 to 100 years. Each fruit weighs about 25 pounds. When young they are eaten. Towards ripeness they harden."

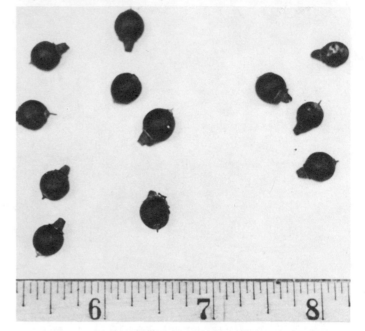

*(Pritchardia thurstonii)*

*(Pritchardia beccariana)*

## *Pritchardia*

Of the 36 kinds of these palms, 31 are natives of Hawaii. Neal: *In Gardens of Hawaii* says:

"Most are fine-looking trees, with ringed trunks, each bearing a rounded cluster of large, rigid, ordinarily broadly wedge-shaped and shallowly cut leaves. The short-stemmed fruit is a drupe, ranging in color from green to yellow, red, or black. It is smooth, with a fleshy or fibrous layer covering a thin woody shell,

140

which, in turn, covers a nutlike seed. Hawaiians eat the unripe seeds, which taste somewhat like COCONUT. As the seeds are also eaten by rats, wild pigs, and insects, the palms do not have much chance of survival.''

Sturtevant writes of *Pritchardia filifera*: "This species is found in rocky canyons near San Felipe, Cal., attaining a height of 50 feet. The fruit is small, black and pulpy and is used as food by the Indians.''

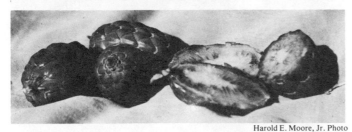

Harold E. Moore, Jr. Photo

RAFFIA *(Raphia farinifera)*

## *Raphia farinifera*      RAFFIA

This species of fibre-producing swamp-loving palms is chiefly in Africa and Madagascar, but a few of the 40 species are in South America. They grow close to the ground, but produce enormous leaves up to 65 feet long. These are the biggest leaves in the plant world. The fruit contains a single nut. Dalziel says:

"The single nut has a sculptured surface and between it and the scaly husk is a yellow oily pulp eaten as food or as a rather bitter flavourer. It varies in amount and importance in different species of *Raphia*, in some fairly sweet and edible, in others bitter. By treating with boiling water a yellow fat, 'Raphia butter,' is got, of good taste when fresh. In various parts of West Africa an oil, 'piassava oil,' is extracted from the pulp, used in lighting, as a lubricant, pomade, or even for cooking. The fruit of *R. Sese* in the Congo is said to yield most oil.

"In N. Nigeria the Fulani use the fruit, eating the boiled kernel, which also contains a little oil; in the Benue region the kernels are sold as food to the people. In Gabon the kernels of some species are edible, roasted in ashes.''

The fruit is top-shaped, about 2½ inches long and Burkill says the fruit of *R. vinifera* is bitter but sometimes eaten in Africa, and that there is a little oil in it which is sometimes extracted.

## *Rhyticocos amara*      OVERTOP PALM

Uphof says of this tall West Indian palm tree: "The orange colored fruits were used to prepare a fermented drink.''

K. L. Brown Photo

CABBAGE PALM *(Sabal palmetto)*

## *Sabal palmetto*      CABBAGE PALM

Fewer than 20 kinds of dwarf to mostly stout unarmed trees, the *Sabal* palms grow from Bermuda and the

southeastern United States to the West Indies and South America. The CABBAGE PALM is common in Florida. Sturtevant says of it:

"The drupes are said to afford nourishing food to the Indians and hunters but are not palatable to whites until they become accustomed to them. In *Plaine Description of Barmudas*, (1613) it is said: 'There is a tree called a PALMITO tree, which hath a very sweet berry, upon which the hogs doe most feede; but our men, finding the sweetnesse of them, did willingly share with the hogs for them, they being very pleasant and wholesome, which made them carelesse almost of any bread with their meate'.''

Isaac Ho Sai-Yuen Photo

SALAK *(Salacca conferta)*

## *Salacca edulis*      SALAK

This genus comprises 10 species in Malaya. Wm. F. Whitman wrote for the Rare Fruit Council International:

"The SALAK is indigenous to the Asiatic tropics where it is extensively grown. The fruit of this small, spiny, pinnate-leaved palm is held in high esteem and considered one of the finest of all palm fruits for eating out of hand. The rich yellow-white meat is slightly crisp with a delicate delicious blend of acidity and sugars.''

Sturtevant says: "The fruit is about the size of a walnut and is covered with scales like those of a lizard; below the scales are two or three sweet, yellow kernels, which the Malays eat.''

Purseglove wrote: "The seeds are globose-ovoid or ellipsoid-triangular with a globose back, dull dark brown or brownish black, hard, and 2-3 cm. long.''

Burkill wrote of *S. macrostachya*: "The acid seeds are used in curries.''

Harold E. Moore, Jr. Photo

*Scheelea sp.* in Peru

## Scheelea magdalenica                     MAMARRON

A Dugand wrote this author: "This species and *S. macrocarpa* which grow in my part of northern Colombia, are edible nuts, but the kernels are so extremely hard that they practically are not eatable as one eats a cashew nut."

Of the 40 species of this palm in tropical America, a score are listed by Uphof as a source of oil from the nuts.

## Serenoa repens                          SAW PALMETTO

The stems are mostly prostrate, forming great clusters in the wild, rarely erect. Uphof says: "South Carolina to Florida and Louisiana. The seeds were an important food to the aborigines."

*(Syagrus romanzoffianum)* PALMA PINDO, CHIRIVA

## Syagrus sp.

This is a genus of 50 kinds of palm trees in South America. F. C. Hoehne in his *Flora of Brazil* wrote:

"Actually, the genus *Cocos* is subdivided into many others, of which *Arecastrum* and *Syagrus* provide fruit with a fibrous pulp rich in mucilaginous sweetness which children enjoy greatly. We wish to mention, at this point, with special emphasis on this characteristic, the *Syagrus flexuosa* which appears in the areas near Tatui, Tiete, etc., lifting its thin trunk to a maximum height of three meters and producing bunches with a few coconuts the size of a little egg, which are yellowish and have the seed covered with a thick layer of fibrous pulp, rich in saccharin oil with a pleasing taste. Also delicious are the coconuts of *Syagrus edulis* which appear in Espirito Santo as far as the Northeast of Brazil. Of the more than 50 species today making up this genus, probably more than 20 could be classified as nutritive because of their pulpy cover, while others have coconuts with a hard skin."

Uphof says *S. cocoides* produces seeds which are the source of a kernel oil called PURURIMA oil.

He says of *S. coronata*, the OURICURU PALM: "The pulp of the fruits is consumed by the natives, also used as food for domestic animals. Seeds are source of kernel oil, non-drying. Exported to U.S.A. and Europe. Used for manufacture of margarine."

*(Syagrus capiyata)*

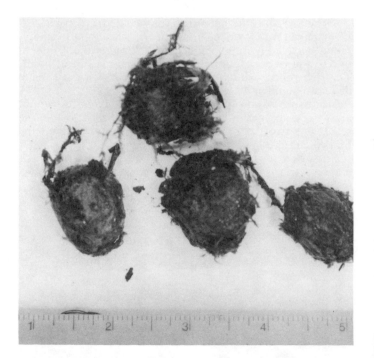

*(Syagrus coronata)*

*(Veitchia merrillii)*

142

## Veitchia joannis

Sturtevant says that of the fruits of this palm, the kernel has a slightly astringent taste but is eaten readily by the natives of Viti, Fiji Islands, especially the youngsters.

*Veitchia merrillii*, often called ADONIDIA, is a pretty tree much cultivated in South Florida as an ornamental. Brown: *Useful Plants of the Philippines* says:

"This species is known only from the Philippines. The bright-crimson fruits, contrasting with the whitish fruit stalks and sheaths, are very ornamental. The fruits are said sometimes to be used as a substitute for the BETEL NUT, in chewing."

## Washingtonia filifera

Sturtevant says: "This palm is found in rocky canyons near San Felipe, California, attaining a height of 50 feet. The fruit is small, black, pulpy and is used as food by the Indians."

Uphof says: "The fruits are eaten dry or fresh, or ground into meal."

CANON PALM *(Washingtonia filifera)*

# Chapter 25
# PANDANUS
## Often the Undergrowth in Palm Forests

The 650 different kinds of *Pandanus* or SCREW PINE in the Old World tropics, are much used by the natives, the leaves for all kinds of woven things, the nuts for food. They are allied to the palms and are added to them in this book. Although native of the old world, *Pandanus* is much planted in tropical areas of the new world too.

Confusion in the wild. Lots of *Pandanus utilis* nuts for hungry people. A 2-foot cluster of MONGO fruits in New Guinea weighs up to 60 pounds.

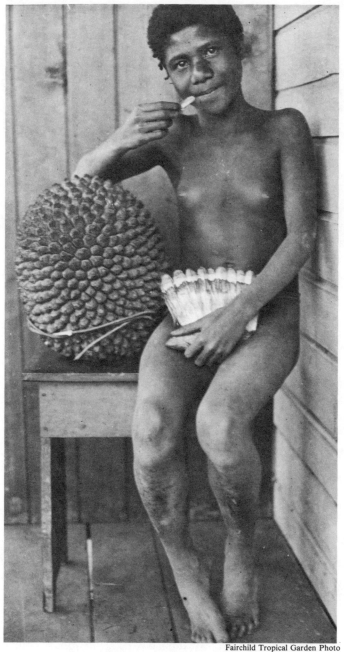

Native girl has found some PANDANUS nuts to eat.

## *Pandanus* (Pandanaceae) SCREW PINE

The 650 or more different kinds of *Pandanus* abounding on seashores and often at higher elevations all over the tropical world, provide millions of people with food, shelter, fibres, clothing, sails, paper, pouches, floral decorations, remedies, fish lures, and magic or ceremonial items. No tree could possibly serve more different purposes. But the species are ill-defined and confused.

The fruit is a spherical, buoyant mass of closely fitting, plug-like seeds, superficially resembling a pineapple or a fir cone. In size this mass may measure in diameter 1 inch to 18 inches or more.

The biggest fruits in New Guinea, called MONGO by the natives were described in the Fairchild Tropical Garden Bulletin of December 1954, thus:

> For the enormous fruit, two feet long by 18 inches in diameter, weighing from 40 to 60 pounds, Papuans have only one use: to eat them. White people would extract the oil from them, and use it for food, medicine, lubrication, paint, fuel, etc. But our Papuans are not interested in that.
>
> To New Guineaites the nut is a food and no more. It may be eaten either fresh or smoke-cured. The fresh kernel can

be eaten raw or cooked. The same applies to the smoked nut, which has the advantage that it can be kept for a year or more.

The process of smoking is simple and is the same for all the *Pandanus* fruits. Firstly, the fruit is cut in halves and all the woody pith of the center is carefully cut out, and the fibrous envelope of the outside is thrown away.

PANDANUS fruits pulled from the cluster.

If the village is not too far, the cleaned nuts are carried home and kept under the roof, where there is plenty of smoke and not too much heat from the fire.

In the far-away *Pandanus* forest, miles from the village, there are houses built for that special purpose, where every day and every night for weeks, firewood is burnt under the *Pandanus* fruits until the nuts are perfectly smoke-cured.

John S. Womersley, for 29 years a forestry executive at Lae, New Guinea, wrote this author: "*Pandanus* use as a nut is restricted to two or three species of which *P. julianetti* is the most common. These are the KARUKA nuts. Other species of *Pandanus* produce MARITA which is a red fruit, usually long-conical in shape. Each syncarp is surrounded by red fleshy pericarp which is boiled into a sort of soup."

*P. julianetti* is the species more fully described in the Fairchild Tropical Garden Bulletin of October, 1961 which reads:

> A New Guinea species, *Pandanus julianettii*, is among the largest of the species, growing in great colonies a hundred feet in height. Its leaves are over 15 feet long and fruits weigh 40 to 60 pounds each. Not only is the pulp of the fruits eaten, but the large seeds are cracked for their oily kernels."

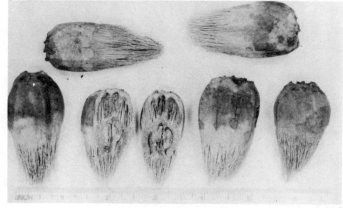

*(Pandanus odoratissimus)*

Bishop Museum Bulletin

Papuan house with attic, where PANDANUS fruits are smoked.

Sturtevant writes: "*P. leram*. In the Nicobar Islands the immense fruit cones consist of several single, wedge-shaped fruits, which, when raw, are uneatable, but, boiled in water and subjected to pressure, they give out a sort of mealy mass. This is also occasionally used with the fleshy interior of the ripe fruit and forms the daily bread of the islanders. The flavor of the mass thus prepared strongly resembles that of apple marmalade and is by no means unpalatable to Europeans.

"*P. pedunculatus*. Australia and New Holland. Fraser says this plant is called BREADFRUIT and is eagerly eaten by the natives. The stones, though very hard, contain a pleasant kernel."

Barrau in Bishop Museum Bulletin #223, says:

"In most Pacific atolls, *Pandanus* is, or has been, a staple food plant. Its importance in the traditional economy of low, coral islands is such that the inhabitants of certain atolls have been described as 'Pandanus peoples.'"

Bishop Museum Bulletin #219 says: "It is known that the oily kernels of various *Pandanus* species found in the New Guinea highlands are extensively eaten. *Pandanus* plays a part comparable to that of the COCONUT in coastal districts. The most common are *P. julianettii* and *P. brosimos*. The kernels are often preserved by drying and smoking. As the fruits are stored in house attics, they undergo continuous smoking. Such a house was seen at Kerau in the Papuan highlands, at almost 10,000 feet altitude."

# Chapter 26
# GRAINS and GRASSES

Grains and grasses get into this book because they are hard seeds and their kernels are eaten by humans — in a big way. Of course botanists balk at the thought of regarding wheat as a nut, but after all, what structural difference is there between a grain of wheat and a pecan, except that the wheat's covering is not as hard or tough as is the shell of the pecan?

This chapter makes no pretense of being exhaustive or complete; it merely points the way in the study of human food sources. Grains are one of the most important of all human foods, and are grown by mankind in every part of the world as No. 1 in his family's food needs.

### *Achyranthes bidentata* (Amarantaceae)

Sturtevant says: "Tropical Asia. The seeds were used as food during a famine in Rajputana, India. Bread made from the seeds was very good. This was considered the best of all substitutes for the usual cereals."

USDA Photo

PIGWEED *(Amaranthus cruentus)*

145

## Amaranthus cruentus
### (Amaranthaceae)
### Prince's Feather
### Red Amaranth

Sturtevant says: "North America and naturalized in the Orient. This plant is extensively cultivated in India for its seed which is ground into flour. It is very productive. Roxburgh says it will bear half a pound of floury, nutritious seed on a square yard of ground."

Willis says that of the 60 species in the tropics and temperate zones, this and *A. caudatus* produce "edible grains which are used as cereals in tropical Asia."

## Arundinaria          (Gramineae)          Cane

Sturtevant says: "This is the species which forms cane brakes in Virginia, Kentucky and southward. Flint says: 'It produces an abundant crop of seed with heads very like those of broom corn. The seeds are farinaceous and are said to be not much inferior to wheat, for which the Indians and occasionally the first settlers substituted it.'"

OATS *(Avena sativa)*
USDA Photo

## Avena fatua          (Gramineae)          Wild Oat

Sturtevant says: "Europe, the Orient and Asia. This is the common Wild Oat of California. It may have been introduced by the Spaniards but it is now spread over the whole country many miles from the coast. The grain is gathered by the Indians of California and is used as a bread corn. In 1852 Professor Buckman sowed a plat of ground with seeds collected in 1851 and in 1856 had for the produce poor, but true, samples of what are known as the potato and Tartarean oat. In 1860, the produce was good white Tartarean and potato oats.

"*A. sativa*. The native land of the common Oat is Abyssinia. Unger says the Celts and the Germans, as far as can be ascertained, cultivated this oat 2,000 years ago, and it seems to have been distributed from Europe into the temperate and cold regions of the whole world.

"This grain is not mentioned in Scripture and hence would seem to be unknown to Egypt or Syria. The plant is noticed by Virgil with the implication that its culture was known. Pliny mentions the plant. It is, hence, quite probable that the Romans knew the Oat principally as a forage crop. Pliny says that the Germans used oatmeal porridge as food. This cereal was sown on the Elizabeth Islands, Massachusetts, in 1602; it was growing at Lynn, Mass., in 1629-33. It was cultivated in Virginia previous to 1648. The Egyptian, or winter oat, was known in the South in 1800. In 1880, 36 named kinds were grown in the state of Kansas. The Oat grows in Norway and Sweden as far north as 64° to 65° but is scarcely known in the south of France, Spain or Italy, and in tropical countries its culture is not attempted."

BAMBOO *(Bambusa arundinaceae)*
USDA Photo

## Bambusa          (Gramineae)          Bamboo

Bamboo comprises 100 kinds of big, clump-forming grasses.

Sturtevant says: "In India, the *Bambusa* flowers so frequently that in Mysore and Orissa the seeds are mixed with honey and eaten like rice. The farina of the seeds is eaten in China. In the Himalayas the seeds of a variety in Sikkim are boiled and made into cakes or into beer.

"*B. arundinaceae*. East Indies. The seeds of this and other species of *Bambusa* have often saved the lives of thousands in times of scarcity in India, as in Orissa in 1812, in Kanara in 1864 and in 1866 in Malda. The plant bears whitish seed, like Rice, and these seeds are eaten by the poorer classes."

See also *Phyllostachys aurea*.

## Beckmannia erucaeformis          (Gramineae)

Sturtevant records that this grass grows in Europe, temperate Asia and North America. According to Engelmann, the seeds are collected for food by the Utah Indians.

HEMP *(Cannabis sativa)*
USDA Photo

## Cannabis sativa          (Urticaceae)          Hemp

Sturtevant says: "Hemp is spontaneous in the north of India and in Siberia. It has also been found wild in the Caucasus and in the north of China.

"HEMPSEED was served fried for dessert by the ancients. In Russia, Poland and neighboring countries, the peasants are extremely fond of parched HEMPSEED and it is eaten even by the nobility. The oil expressed from the seed is much used as food during the time of the fasts in the Volga region."

## Carum (Umbelliferae) CARAWAY

Sturtevant says: "Europe, Orient and northern Asia. CARAWAY is now cultivated largely for its seed in England, particularly in Essex, in Iceland where it is apparently wild, in Morocco and elsewhere. The seeds are exported from Finland, Russia, Germany, Prussia, North Holland and Morocco. The seeds are used in confectionery and distillation. In England the seed is used by cottagers to mix with their bread."

USDA Photo

LAMBSQUARTER *(Chenopodium album)*

PETTY RICE
## Chenopodium quinoa (Chenopodiaceae) QUINUA

*Chenopodium* comprises close to 150 kinds of herbs (a few shrubs and trees), in dry areas all over the world, many of them eaten like spinach. This species is South American. Sturtevant says of it:

"This plant, indigenous to the Pacific slopes of the Andes, constituted the most important article of food of the inhabitants of New Granada, Peru and Chile at the time of the discovery of America, and at the present day is still extensively cultivated on account of its seeds, which are used extensively by the poorer inhabitants. There are several varieties, of which the white is cultivated in Europe as a spinach plant, rather than for its seeds. However prepared, the seed, says Thompson, is unpalatable to strangers. Gibbon, who saw the plant in Bolivia, says that when boiled like rice and eaten with milk, the seeds are very savory."

Regarding *C. album*, called LAMB'S QUARTERS, Sturtevant says:

"In the United States, it is used as a spinach. The young tender plants are collected by the Navajoes, the Pueblo Indians of New Mexico, all the tribes of Arizona, the Diggers of California and the Utahs, and boiled as a spinach or are eaten raw. The seeds are gathered by many tribes, ground into a flour and made into a bread or mush."

## Dendrocalamus strictus MALE BAMBOO

Irvine: *Woody plants of Ghana* says: "A green-stemmed BAMBOO up to 80-100 ft. high, forming dense clumps and sending out whip-like branches from the ground upwards; stems solid 5-in. girth at 3 ft. from ground.

"Gamble states that the seed is used in India as food grain, in times of famine, and while wheat sold at 12 seers for the rupee, BAMBOO seed sold at from 40 to 50 seers. The seeds are powdered and eaten by aboriginal peoples of C. India."

## Eleusine aegyptiaca (Gramineae) ELEUSINE
CROW'S FOOT GRASS

Sturtevant says: "Cosmopolitan tropics and subtropics. This grass grows most abundantly on waste ground, also on the flat roofs of the Arab houses in Unganyembe. The natives gather the ears, dry them in the sun, beat out the grain on the rocks, grind and make a stir-about of it. Its grain is used in southern India.

"*E. coracana*. South America, East Indies and Egypt. This grass is cultivated on a large scale in many tropical countries. It is the most productive of all the Indian cereals, and is the staple grain of the Mysore country. On the Coromandel coast, it is a useful and most valuable grain, which is eaten and prized by the natives. The grain is either made into cakes, or is eaten as a porridge; it is pleasant to the taste. Grant found this grass cultivated everywhere along his route through central Africa. Its flour, if soaked for a night in water, makes a very fair unleavened bread."

Burkill says: "*E. coracana*, a cultigen of greater vigour and a more generous yield. It is cultivated throughout tropical Africa, in India and in backward parts of Malaysia."

USDA Photo

BUCKWHEAT *(Fagopyrum cymosum)*

## Fagopyrum cymosum (Polygonaceae) BUCKWHEAT

Sturtevant says: "*F. esculentum*. Europe and northern Asia. BUCKWHEAT seems to have been unknown to the Greeks and Romans. It grows wild in Nepal, China and Siberia and is supposed to have been brought to Europe at the beginning of the sixteenth century. It must have secured early admittance to America, for samples of American growth were sent to Holland as early as 1626. It is at present cultivated in the United States as a field crop, as also in northern Europe, in China, Japan and elsewhere.

"Notch-seeded BUCKWHEAT is a native of the mountainous districts of China and Nepal, where it is cultivated for its seeds."

## Glyceria fluitans (Gramineae) MANNA GRASS

Sturtevant says: "Northern temperate regions. The seeds of this grass are collected on the continent and sold as MANNA seeds for making puddings and gruel. According to Von Heer, it is cultivated in Poland."

USDA Photo

COTTON *(Gossypium hirsutum)*
(Chemically delinted)

USDA Photo

COTTONSEED — before cleaning (right, after cleaning to remove fuzz (lower right), and after treatment to keep it disease-free after planting (other three piles).

## Gossypium herbaceum (Malvaceae) COTTON

This Old World species of COTTON is one of perhaps 20 kinds, of which four are producers of the fibre COTTON and have edible seeds. Sturtevant says of this kind: "During the War of the Rebellion, COTTON seed came into some use as a substitute for coffee, the seed having been parched and ground. The oil expressed from the seed makes a fine salad oil and is also used for cooking and as a butter substitute."

The seeds of these plants are covered with long hairs forming the material known as COTTON. Usually cultivated in the United States is *G. hirsutum*. SEA ISLAND COTTON of this country is *G. barbadense*; the cotton separates more easily from the seed. In the Old World *G. arboreum* is used along with *G. herbaceum*. Willis says:

"From the seeds of all the species, cottonseed oil is obtained by crushing and the oil cake left behind is largely used for feeding cattle."

## Guizotia abysinica (Compositae) RAMTIL

Sturtevant writes of this cereal: "Native of Abyssinia, where it is cultivated, as well as in India, for the sake of its seeds, which yield an oil to pressure, bland like that of SESAME. The oil is sweet and is used as a condiment. It is much used for dressing food in Mysore."

Watt says: "Extensively cultivated as an oil-seed in various parts of India. The oil is much used for culinary purposes and as a substitute for ghi by the poorer classes in the regions where it is cultivated. In Madras the seeds are sometimes fried with oil or ghi and eaten."

USDA Photo

BARLEY *(Hordeum vulgare)*

## Hordeum deficiens (Gramineae) BARLEY

Sturtevant says: "This is the common BARLEY of cultivation and occurs in numerous varieties. Meyer found it growing wild between Lenkoran and Baku; Koch in the southeast of the Caucasus; Kotschy in South Persia. It is mentioned as among the things that were destroyed by the plagues of Egypt. The flour of BARLEY was the food of the Jewish soldiers."

### Hyptis spicigara (Labiatae)

This genus comprises 400 kinds of herbs and shrubs, mostly tropical American.

Sturtevant says: "This plant of tropical Africa is cultivated by the natives of Gani as a grain. It is eaten roasted by them. They also extract an oil from the seeds, both black and white, of this strongly smelling plant. Schweinfurth says the tiny seeds are brazed to a jelly and are used by the natives of central Africa as an adjunct to their stews and gravies."

### Melocanna bambusoides (Gramineae)

Sturtevant says: "East Indies. The fruit is very large, fleshy like an apple and contains a seed which is said to be very pleasant eating."

### Panicum miliaceum (Gramineae) MILLET

This tropical species was known to the Romans in the time of Julius Caesar.

Sturtevant states: "It thrives excellently in Gaul and is the best protection against famine. In France, this MILLET is cultivated at present for forage; in Germany for the grain and also for fodder; in England it is unknown. It is cultivated largely in southern and western Asia, in northeastern Africa and to some extent in Italy and in Spain. It appears little known as an agricultural crop in America.

"*P. pilosum*. This South American grain is cultivated in India as a bread corn.

"*P. sanguinale*. This grain grows in abundance in Poland where it is sometimes cultivated for its seed and is in cultivation in waste ground in America, naturalized from Europe. In Europe, the small-hulled fruit furnishes a wholesome and palatable nourishment called MANNA GRIT. This is the common CRAB GRASS of America."

USDA Photo

RICE — A new, high-yielding variety from India gives forth an abundance.

Commercialized BROWN RICE roasted tidbits in plastic bag.

USDA Photo

RICE *(Oryza sativa)*

### Oryza sativa (Gramineae) RICE

This grain, which supplies food for a greater number of human beings than are fed on the produce of any other known plant, is supposed to be of Asiatic origin. RICE had been introduced into China 3000 years before Christ.

Sturtevant says: "RICE was introduced into Virginia by Sir William Berkeley in 1647. It was first brought into Charleston, South Carolina, by a Dutch brig from Madagascar in 1694.

"The varieties of RICE are almost endless. The most general divisions are into upland rice, valley rice, summer rice and spring rice. The finest RICE in the world is that raised in North and South Carolina. RICE in the husk is called paddy."

149

Seeds in the hull and cleaned seeds of a hardy BAMBOO, *Phyllostachys aurea*, grown near Victoria, British Columbia, Canada.

## *Phyllostachys aurea*     FISHPOLE BAMBOO

This comprises some 30 kinds of tall, evergreen BAMBOO from eastern Asia, frequently cultivated as ornamentals. HORTUS THIRD describes a dozen of these. This species is often planted in the United States.

## *Paspalum ciliatum*     (Gramineae)

This is a perennial, a lauded cereal grass of Brazil.
Dalziel says: "*P. exile* is a food grass in west Africa.
"*P. scrobiculatum* var. *Commersonii* — BASTARD or DITCH MILLET. A wild grass with edible grain, not cultivated in West Africa, but often collected in scarcity and ground on stones like MILLET.
"In Sierra Leone it is common in rice fields, and is harvested with hill rice and mixed with it for food; the best crop is said to be from dry land rather than swamp."

## *Pennisetum typhoides*     (Gramineae) BULLRUSH MILLET

Williams says: "An annual, erect grass of tropical Asia and Africa, up to 9 feet high, with slender, pointed stems and a dark brown or black, cylindrical inflorescence resembling the bullrush, tapered at both ends, 7 inches or more long. It is cultivated in the Protectorate, particularly on the drier coral rag areas of Pemba, for its small seeds, which are a well-known cereal food, the clean grain being eaten in the same way as rice, or pounded and made into paste or bread."
Williamson says: "This grain is stored on a stand usually inside the house, under which a fire is kindled from time to time. It is kept here for about two months, then the heads are pounded and the freed grain stored in very large baskets which hold 200-300 lbs. of grain.
"If the grain is still on the heads, a bundle of these is taken, broken across and put into the mortar. The contents are then pounded slowly as the heads are very likely to spring out. The grain is sifted off from the debris. The grain is given two poundings as with maize. The first, is a short one after which the bran is shaken off. A little water is added and the grain well pounded until it sticks together in a mass. Now it is turned into a flat sifting basket, broken up by hand and as it dries the bran is shaken off. The grain is now washed well and then pounded, to form a fine flour. The latter is spread on a mat to dry in the sun."
Sturtevant says: "Barth, in *Travels in Northern Africa*, says at Agades the slaves were busy collecting and pounding the seeds of the *P. dasystachyum* the KARENGIA, which constitutes a great part of their food. Livingstone says the seeds are collected regularly by the slaves over a large portion of central Africa and are used as food.
"*P. typhoideum* — SPIKED MILLET is extensively cultivated about Bombay and forms a very important article of food to the natives. In Africa Livingstone found it cultivated in great quantities as food."

## *Poa abyssinica*     (Gramineae)     TEFF

Sturtevant says: "A mountain plant of Abyssinia, cultivated everywhere there, at a height of from 2,500 to 8,000 feet where gentle heat and rain favor its development. Its seeds furnish the favorite bread of the Abyssinians in the form of thin, highly leavened and spongy cakes. Four varieties of this grain are cultivated. Parkyns writes that TEFF is considered by the Abyssinians wholesome and digestible, but so far from being satisfied of this, he is doubtful of its containing much nutritive property and as for its taste, he says 'fancy yourself chewing a piece of sour sponge and you will have a good idea of what is considered the best bread in Abyssinia.' "

RYE *(Secale cereale)*

## *Secale cereale*     (Gramineae)     RYE

Sturtevant says: "RYE, according to Karl Koch, is found wild in the mountains of the Crimea. DeCandolle thinks he discovered RYE in a wild state in Australia, and a species seems to have existed in the Bronze Age of Europe. Kotzebur found it growing wild near Fort Ross, North America, where it is gathered by the Indians.
"RYE is now found in Norway, at 67° north, but its cultivation is usually given as extending between 50° and 60° north in Europe and Asia and in America between 40° and 50° north. It is less variable than other cultivated plants and there are but few varieties."

## *Setaria*     (Gramineae)     ITALIAN MILLET

Sturtevant says: "This MILLET forms a valued crop in southern Europe as also in some parts of central Europe. In India this MILLET is considered by the natives as one of the most delicious of cultivated grains and is held in high estimation by the Brahmans."
In north Australia the Naturalists' Club bulletin says of *S. italica*: "Native of China and Japan. Seeds pounded to flour for bread-making. Supposed to have been the chief flour grain of pre-historic people."

SUDAN GRASS *(Sorghum sudanense)*

HARD RED WINTER WHEAT *(Triticum aestivum)*

*Sorghum vulgare* (Gramineae) **BROOM CORN KAFFIR CORN**

Sturtevant says: "This is supposed to be a native of Africa, and has been cultivated in China from a remote period. Doolittle says the Chinese make a coarse kind of bread from the flour of the seeds, eaten principally by the poorer classes. The best kind of Chinese whiskey, often called Chinese wine, is distilled from the seeds. This Chinese form was imported into France from the north of China about 1851 and in 1854 distributed in the United States."

*Sporobolus* (Graminae)

This genus comprises 150 kinds of grasses growing in the warmer parts of the earth.

The North Queensland Naturalists' Club bulletin describes these two species in Australia of which the grain is edible:

"*S. caroli.* YAK-KAPARI. Seeds pounded to flour for bread-making.

"*S. actinocladus.* KA-TOO-RA. Seeds pounded to flour for bread-making."

DURUM WHEAT *(Triticum durum)*

*Triticum aestivum* (Graminae) **WHEAT**

This is the world's most important grain, particularly in the Temperate zones. WHEAT is native of the plains about the Caspian.

It was introduced into China about 3000 B.C. Standing crops of bearded WHEAT are figured in Egypt about 2440 B.C. In Europe WHEAT was cultivated before the period of written history.

The varieties of WHEAT are almost endless, and their characteristics vary widely under the influence of cultivation and climate. There are 180 distinct sorts in the museum of Cornell University.

*Tropaeolum majus* (Geraniaceae) **INDIAN CRESS TALL NASTURTIUM**

Sturtevant says: "This Peruvian plant is grown more for ornament than for food, but the seeds gathered while young and green, are used for pickling and as an excellent substitute for capers."

CLUB WHEAT *(Triticum compactum)*

| | | **BULRUSH** |
|---|---|---|
| *Typha latifolia* | **(Typhaceae)** | **CAT TAIL** |

Sturtevant quotes Long as saying: "The seeds are esculent, roasted."

CORN *(Zea mays)*

USDA Photo

Commercialized CORN nuts *(Zea)* in plastic bag.

| | | **CORN** |
|---|---|---|
| | | **INDIAN CORN** |
| *Zea mays* | **(Graminae)** | **MAIZE** |

This comprises two or three species of robust annual grasses native to tropical America, some often 15 feet high. The fruit has fed millions for thousands of years. Recently the 5% oil in the seed has come into demand because of its unsaturated form. Up to 30 rows of seeds are produced on an almost woody cob, the grains white, yellow, red or black. It is one of the world's most important food plants for both man and beast.

| | | **INDIAN RICE** |
|---|---|---|
| *Zizania aquatica* | **(Gramineae)** | **WILD RICE** |

Sturtevant says: "North America and eastern Asia. WILD RICE is found on the swampy borders of streams and in shallow water, common in the United States, especially northwestward. Gould has found it nine feet tall at the foot of Lake Champlain and in places on the Hudson and Delaware Rivers, where the tide ebbs and flows, over twelve feet high. The seeds have furnished food from early times to the Indians and the plant has been considered worthy of cultivation. In 1791 seeds from Canada were sent to England and attempts were made at its culture. Father Hennepin, in 1680, in his voyage on the upper Mississippi, ate the grain and pronounced it better and more wholesome than rice. In 1784 Jonathan Carver speaks of wild rice as being the most valuable of all the spontaneous productions of the Northwest. Jefferys 1760 says the people of Louisiana gather the seeds and make them into a bread. Flint says, but for this grain the Canadian traders and hunters could hardly exist. Pinkerton says, 'this plant seems to be designed by nature to become the bread corn of the north.' Almost every observer who has mentioned it has used terms of praise. Gould says the plant seems especially adapted for the soiling of cattle and that its use increases the yield and the richness of milk. In Louisiana, its use is recommended for hay, and in Savannah, Georgia, says Elliott, under the name of wild oats, it is used almost exclusively during the summer as green fodder for cows and horses. The one objection to its culture seems to come from the seed dropping so readily when ripe. The northern Indians, of the lakes and rivers between the Mississippi and Lake Superior, gather the seed by pushing the canoe amongst the stems and shaking the heads over the boat. An acre of wild rice is supposed to be equal to an acre of wheat in the nutriment afforded. The seeds are black, smooth, narrow, cylindrical, about half an inch long, white and farinaceous when cooked and are very palatable.

"This is the kaw-sun of China and is found in the lakes of Anam, Manchuria, China and Japan. From Dr. Hance, we know that the solid base of the stem forms a very choice vegetable largely used in China, where it is cultivated."

# Chapter 27

# THE PINE FAMILY
# (PINYONS)
## (Pinaceae)

# and Their Relatives

## Robt. L. Egolf

There are about 80 different pines in the world, distributed in the northern hemisphere, being most numerous in the cooler latitudes. They are evergreen, needle-leaved trees, bearing their seeds in cones, and cousins to the familiar spruces, firs, and hemlocks. Among the more familiar pines in this country are the eastern WHITE PINE (*Pinus strobus*), the LONGLEAF or YELLOW PINE of the Gulf States (*P. palustris*), the common SCRUB PINE (*P. virginiana*), and in the western states the PONDEROSA or WESTERN YELLOW PINE (*P. ponderosa*), and the LODGEPOLE PINE (*P. contorta*). The pines belong to the Gymnosperms, literally bearers of naked seeds. Pines, and all other Gymnosperms, do not have true flowers. Their reproductive structures are called strobilii (singular; strobilus). In the pines male and female strobilii occur separately on the same tree, the male in short, catkin-like clusters at the base of the new season's growth, the female singly or in pairs farther out along the branchlets. The male strobilii are shed very quickly after releasing their pollen; the female persist, developing into the characteristic cones which ordinarily ripen in the second year on the tree. At maturity the cones open to shed the seeds that are carried exposed or naked on the woody cone scales.

Pine nuts play a small role in the total economy of pine products. Lumber, pulp, resins and other products extracted from the sap and wood, and even fuel are all more important. Pines may not cone heavily until they are seventy-five years old. Lack of heavy demand, together with slow growth and low per acre yield, make it economically unrewarding to cultivate pine nuts in orchards, although planted stands for timber and pulp are common enough. Most pine nuts are too small or too sparsely borne to be worth gathering, and many have a resinous or turpentiny flavor. Men cannot compete with small animals and birds in gathering nuts shed from cones in the tops of large trees. For this reason where the gathering of pine nuts is a commercial enterprise the cones are often gathered green and allowed to dry and open on the ground. The ideal nut-bearing pine should be of scrubby growth, with large cones and nuts, and bear early.

Pine nuts are used in many ways. Mostly they are eaten whole, either from the tree or after being roasted. To eat a pine nut pop it into your mouth, crack the shell with your teeth, extract the kernel, and spit out the hull. With practice the whole operation is rapid, done in one quick motion. Pine nuts are also made into a flour for cakes, pressed into candies, used to garnish pastries, and the residue from commercial packing operations in Europe yields an oil for soap from broken kernels, the cones are used as fuel, and even the left over shells are used in the tanning of leather, and yield a dye used to color fish nets.

Bailey says: "The seeds of a considerable number of both foreign and American pines have rich, edible kernels which form an important article of food in many sections where the species are indigenous.

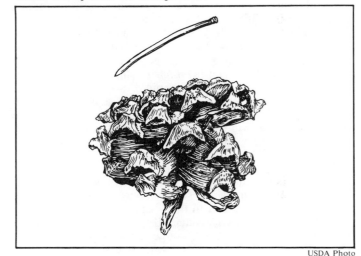

USDA Photo

*(Pinus monophylla)*

"Of commonest appearance in our American markets are the seeds of the STONE PINE (*P. pinea*) of southern Europe, which are sold under the names of PIGNOLIA, or PINE-NUTS and to an increasing extent under the Mexican name PINION, which originally was applied only to the seeds of certain American pines of the Southwest. As marketed, these nuts usually appear without the shells, in which condition they greatly resemble puffed rice.

"Although some 12 or 15 species of American pines yield edible nuts, their product is seldom seen in any but the western markets, as it is largely consumed locally by the Indians of the Southwest and the Mexicans. These nuts are known as PINONS, PINE-NUTS, and INDIAN-NUTS.

"While none of the seeds of the American group are large, they vary greatly in size, form and color. In flavor of kernel they are much alike. Usually they are irregular in form, longer than thick, sometimes slender but generally of about the same diameter each way. They range from 1/8 to 7/8 inch in length. In color they run from a light yellow, on one side at the basal end, to a brownish black at the opposite end, with a coffee-brown probably predominating."

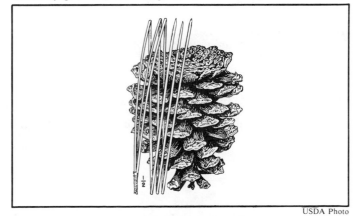

USDA Photo

LONG LEAF PINE *(Pinus palustris)*

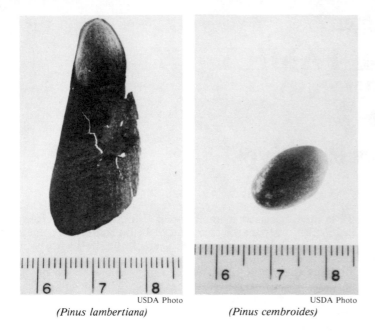

USDA Photo
(Pinus lambertiana)

USDA Photo
(Pinus cembroides)

## Pinus cembroides

### MEXICAN NUT PINE
### PINYON

This is occasionally a broad-headed tree to 40 feet in favorable locations, but often less, and sometimes stunted and shrub-like. It needs a hot, dry climate in summer, cold but still relatively dry in winter. The semi-arid highlands of southwestern United States in California, Arizona, and New Mexico, extending down through Mexico in the central highlands at least as far as Puebla. Variety *edulis* is widely distributed in Arizona, New Mexico, Utah, and Colorado, while varieties *monophylla* and *quadrifolia* extend into Nevada and California.

The cones of these nut pines are small and red-brown in color, 1 to 2½ inches long, with a small number of cone scales, opening widely at maturity to reveal the edible seeds. These are ½ to ¾ inches long, covered by a hard, red-brown shell with some yellow mottling.

On the basis of an average annual yield of five tons of nuts per square mile of good PINYON timber, the potential harvest of pine nuts in the southwestern United States has been estimated at a half million tons a year. Barely more than one percent of this is actually picked. The nuts from natural stands of PINYONS are gathered and sold in local markets where they grow, and some are shipped to larger cities in the east where PIGNOLIA NUTS, from the European STONE PINE, are known and relished.

There are three other pines of the PINYON group of common occurrence in North America, occupying continuous or overlapping ranges.

Williams Photo
PINYONS *(Pinus edulis)*

These are often considered to be distinct species, but sometimes as naturally occurring varieties of *P. cembroides*. The four intergrade in such a way as to make their exact terminology uncertain. The three other PINYONS, besides *P. cembroides*, are the TWO-LEAVED or NEVADA NUT PINE, (var. *edulis*,) the SINGLE-LEAVED or NEVADA NUT PINE, (var. *monophylla*,) and Parry's or FOUR-LEAVED NUT PINE, (var. *quadrifolia*). Of the four the most important as a bearer of edible nuts is the var. *edulis*. The varieties may be distinguished from *P. cembroides* by their stiffer, shorter needles, and from each other by the number of needles in each leaf bundle, as implied by the common name. The nuts of all four are mostly indistinguishable although those of the variety *edulis* are said to be of better quality than the rest.

Four other PINYONS have recently been described from Mexico. These are rare and occur very locally. Although described as species they may also eventually be reduced to the status of natural varieties. These four are *P. culminicola*, *P. maximartinezii*, *P. pinceana*, and *P. nelsonii*.

Pine nuts from *P. cembroides* and its near relatives have been an important staple of diet for the Indian tribes where they grow for thousands of years, and were described by the Spanish explorer Cabeza de Vaca (whose name translates into English as "Head of a Cow") as early as 1535. The Hopis, Navajos, and other tribes eat the kernels whole, make a flour of them for baking into cakes, and also pound them into a paste to be used like butter.

From the period before the Second World War the U.S. Forest Service has encouraged the development of a pine nut industry among existing stands of timber in the southwest. Although there is some commercial interest in the gathering of pine nuts, making an agricultural crop of them is a formidable task. Tree growth is exceedingly slow, little more than 2 to 6 inches a year. Bearing trees are generally 25 years old, and may not be in heavy production for another 50 years after that. PINYONS cone heavily once in 3 or 4 years, and in different localities each year. It is difficult to sustain commercial interest in an undependable crop. Unless the trees can be made to yield timber or some other useful product their cultivation is uneconomic. Harvest time in PINYON country, in September and October, takes on something of a festive atmosphere. Whole families make outings in the woods to gather the nuts, in which undertaking they compete with a countless horde of birds, squirrels, and other small animals, all equally enjoying the bounty nature has provided.

## Pinus koraiensis

### KOREAN NUT PINE
### CEDAR PINE

This is a very hardy pine, through eastern Asia in a broad belt along the Sea of Japan in Russia, Manchuria, China, and Korea, becoming rather scattered in South Korea. Also found in the mountain forests of central Honshu in Japan. The common names are rather anomalous as the main distribution of *P. koraiensis* is north of Korea.

This is a tree to 100-150 feet, pyramidal in outline when young, spreading in age with stout ascending branches.

The cones of *P. koraiensis* are 3 to 6 inches long and about 3 inches across, with leathery cone scales. The nuts are about 5/8 inches long, wingless, often persistent in the cone.

154

DIGGER PINE *(Pinus sabiniana)*
JEFFREY PINE *(Pinus jeffreyi)*

USDA Photo

## *Pinus sabiniana* — DIGGER PINE

The DIGGER PINE is a medium sized tree 50 to 75 feet tall, usually forking near the ground into two or more irregular trunks, with a very sparse, thinly clothed crown. It has wiry needle leaves 7 to 13 inches long, of a distinctive pale gray-green color, in bundles of three. The leaf bundles are in sparse tufts at the ends of the branches.

The tree grows on the eastern slopes and foothills of the Sierra Nevada and coast ranges in California, in the most arid locations. It prefers hot and dry summers, a little cooler in winter but still dry, occurring at about 500 feet in the north, but ascending to 2,000 to 5,000 feet in the southern part of its range in Santa Barbara County.

The large cones 6 to 10 inches long and 6 inches across, remain on the tree as long as seven years after shedding the seeds. The nuts are about ¾ inch long with a short wing.

This pine is named DIGGER after the Indians who settled, to live on the nuts, where it grew most abundantly. It is common in the Spanish Mission country, down the trail of the Camino Real. There was no tribe of Digger Indians in California. Rather the name is a contemptuous one, bestowed indiscriminately on all the California tribes by the early settlers.

A pine nearly related to *P. sabiniana* is the BIG CONE PINE, *P. coulteri*. It grows in much the same range, although generally at higher elevations, often in company with PONDEROSA PINE. Cones of the BIG CONE PINE are the largest of any pine. They are 10 to 20 inches long and 6 inches across, often weighing 5 lbs. when still green. The cone scales are armed with remarkably large, recurved spines resembling the talons of a falcon or hawk. The edible nuts of the BIG CONE PINE are not quite so large as those of the DIGGER PINE, but have a slightly longer wing.

## *Pinus pinea* — STONE PINE / PARASOL PINE

This is a very picturesque tree in age, with an irregular spreading, flat-topped crown, from 40 to 100 feet tall depending upon location. It is widely distributed along the northern littoral of the Mediterranean Sea, from Lebanon in the east to Spain and Portugal. The STONE PINE has been planted in these parts for centuries. It is hot dry summers and cool wet winters that suit it best.

The cones are egg-shaped, 4 to 6 inches long and 4 inches across, maturing in the third year. The nuts are about ¾ inch long with a hard shell. They are called PIGNOLIAS in England, PIGNONS in France, PINONES in Spain and Italy, the same as the wooden marionette of the children's tale, Pinnochio.

Of all the nut-bearing pines, this one provides the largest crop commercially. The nuts are harvested from the groves of Italy and Spain where the trees grow in nearly pure stands. The cones are gathered while still green by pickers armed with long hooked poles. After being piled in the sun to ripen the nuts are extracted by hand or mechanical threshing. The very best unbroken kernels are packed for sale and export. Broken kernels yield an oil. There is one cultivated form, 'Fragilis', called the TARENTINA PINE, with very thin shelled nuts.

The species name of this pine, *pinea*, is classical Latin for pine nut. Pliny mentions them preserved in honey. The shells have been found in Pompeii and even in the refuse heaps of Roman camps in Britain. In the Bible pine nuts are spoken of in the fourteenth chapter of the book of the prophet Hosea. In a beautiful poetic exhortation beginning "O Israel, Return unto the Lord" occurs this passage, remarkable for its references to plants,

I will be as the dew unto Israel.
He shall grow as the lily, and cast forth his roots
as Lebanon. (CEDAR of LEBANON, *Cedrus libani*)
His branches shall spread, and his beauty shall be
as the olive tree, and his smell as Lebanon.
They that dwell under his shadow shall return;
The scent thereof shall be as the vine of Lebanon.
Ephraim shall say, 'What have I to do any more
with idols?'
I have heard him, and observed him:
I am like a green fir tree.
From me is thy fruit found.

This green fir tree almost certainly is the STONE PINE. Although biblical references to conifers are often frustratingly vague, the STONE PINE alone would be referred to as bearing a fruit.

## *Pinus lambertiana* — SUGAR PINE / BIG PINE

This is the largest of all the pines. It grows to well over 200 feet with a clear trunk from the ground of a hundred feet or more. The crown is distinguished by the unequal length of the lateral branches, giving it a rugged, irregular appearance. It has stiff needle leaves in bundles of five, more or less evenly distributed along the branches.

It is a tree of the high mountain ranges of the Pacific coast, occurring as low as 2,000 feet in the Cascades of Oregon but ascending toward the south until it is scarcely found below 8,000 feet in the San Pedro Martirs of Baja California. It grows in the company of other large conifers in the magnificent forests of these regions. It enjoys cool dry summers at high altitudes and cold winters with heavy snowfall.

The nuts are about a half inch long with a wing a little more than an inch long. They are not much eaten by virtue of being so inaccessible, not only the nut from the ground but also the tree from civilization. The cones of the SUGAR PINE may reach 24 inches in length and a breadth of 4 or 5 inches when open.

The SUGAR PINE derives its common name from the very sweet but laxative resinous exudations that collect on the bark and injured portions of the tree.

The WESTERN WHITE PINE, also called SILVER PINE and IDAHO PINE, (*P. monticola*), is similar to the SUGAR PINE in its vegetative parts, but quite different in appearance. It is smaller, although still upwards of 200 feet tall, and has a very narrow, conical crown, densely clothed in needles. SUGAR PINE and WESTERN WHITE PINE sometimes grow together, but the range of the latter is of greater extent, generally at lower elevations. Like the SUGAR PINE its nuts are small and of greater importance to birds and squirrels than men.

TOP: Left to Right — *Pinus albicaulis, P. edulis, P. flexilis*
BOTTOM: *P. peuce, P. siberica*

### Pinus albicaulis
### WHITEBARK PINE · ALPINE PINE

This is a pine of the timberlines, occurring between 3,000 and 12,000 feet on high mountain peaks, from western Canada south along the Cascades, the Sierra Nevada, and the Rockies into upper Mexico. It is an upright bushy tree to 50 feet often contorted through exposure, at highest elevations a low matted shrub. Stout, rigid needles 1 to 2½ inches long, in bundles of five.

The cones are 2 or 3 inches long, smooth outside. The scales do not open at maturity, and the nuts escape only through decay of the cone, or by birds or small animals tearing the cones apart to get the nuts. The seeds are about a half inch long and sweet.

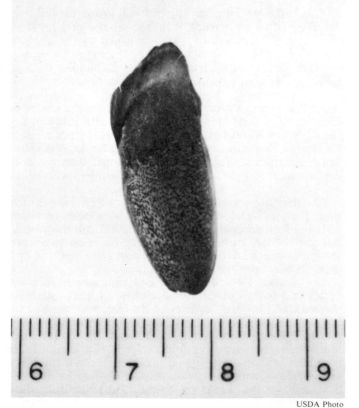

*(Pinus torreyana)*

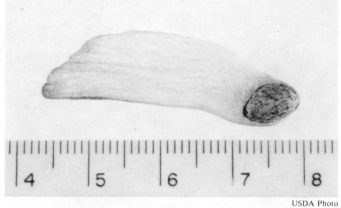

*(Pinus ponderosa* var. *ponderosa)*

### Pinus ponderosa
### PONDEROSA PINE · BULL PINE

This is a large tree, occasionally more than 200 feet tall with a trunk diameter of 8 feet, but probably averaging 125 feet or a little more and 3 or 4 feet through the trunk. The crown is narrow for the size of the tree and confined to the upper half of the trunk. Needle leaves 4 to 11 inches long, are in bundles of three in dense tufts at the ends of the branches.

The PONDEROSA PINE is found in most of the western part of North America, from British Columbia in the north to Lower California and into northern Mexico, from the Pacific coast eastward to Nebraska, Colorado and Texas.

It is very adaptable. It will grow in wet or dry regions, on good soil and poor, and withstand wide variations in temperature. In the southern part of its range it tends to be found at higher elevations above 4,000 feet.

Although pine nuts from the PONDEROSA PINE are edible they are not much eaten being quite small, only a quarter inch long, and difficult to gather from such a large tree. The cones are about 5 inches long by 2 inches broad, mature in a single season, and set heavily only every 3 or 4 years.

Another closely related pine with edible nuts, sometimes considered a variety of *P. ponderosa*, is the JEFFREY PINE (*P. jeffreyi*), found in the Sierra Nevadas from Oregon to Lower California. It differs from the PONDEROSA PINE in having longer, heavier cones and larger seeds. A broken twig of PONDEROSA PINE smells distinctly of turpentine, while the odor of JEFFREY PINE is nearer to pineapple.

### Pinus torreyana
### SOLEDAD PINE · TORREY PINE

This is a small tree of 20 feet in the wild, often leaning and of asymmetrical growth from constant exposure to the sea wind. When grown in more protected locations the SOLEDAD PINE may become large and luxuriant, very unlike its ordinary appearance. The needle leaves 8 to 13 inches long, are in bundles of five, in dense tufts at the ends of the branches.

This tree is confined to a very small area on the California coast near the mouth of the Soledad River at Del Mar in San Diego County, and on the eastern extremity of Santa Rosa Island in the Santa Barbara Channel. The California coast where this pine grows has a Mediterranean climate with hot dry summers and cool wet winters.

The edible seeds of *P. torreyana* are about an inch long, the kernel half as big, covered by a heavy seed coat and nearly encircled by a short membranous wing. They are borne in a heavy cone weighing nearly a pound, 4 to 5½ inches long and nearly as broad across the base, with heavy cone scales, maturing in the third year on the tree.

This is an extremely local tree, all of the specimens in the natural range probably not numbering more than a few hundred. It is undoubtedly a remnant from an earlier geological period when the islands off the Santa Barbara Channel were part of the mainland and the climate was more congenial for this tree's growth.

*(Pinus gerardiana)* Left: seeds complete; right, seed coat removed.

## Pinus gerardiana
### CHILGOZA PINE
### NOOSA PINE

This is a conifer of compact appearance with short lateral branches, reaching 50 to 80 feet in height, often dividing near the ground into several large ascending branches. The bark is thin, shedding in small plates rather like a SYCAMORE. The dark green, slender needle leaves 2 to 4 inches long, are in bundles of three.

This tree grows in the northwestern Himalayan Mountains between Kashmir, Tibet, and northern Afghanistan, on dry stony ground at elevations 6,000 and 12,000 feet. At the higher altitudes where these pines grow nearly all of the annual precipitation falls as snow.

The cones of *P. gerardiana* are 6 to 8 inches long and about 4 inches across the base. The heavy cone scales become strongly reflexed at maturity. The edible seeds are cylindrical, an inch or slightly less long, with a vestigial wing.

CHILGOZA nuts are greatly appreciated in that part of the world where they grow. They are gathered and sold in native markets, and large numbers are imported into India. The value of the nuts is such that standing trees are almost never cut for timber. Attempts have been made to grow the CHILGOZA PINE in England and America without much success. In spite of its Himalayan origin the tree is winter tender at lower altitudes and does not thrive.

A very similar pine in northwestern China is the LACE-BARK PINE, *P. bungeana*, also with distinctive peeling bark. It is a more tractable tree in cultivation than *P. gerardiana*, and hardy in the United States as far north as Massachusetts. The seeds of the LACE-BARK PINE are eaten in China, but they are quite small and borne in smaller cones, and so are not as important an article of food as the nuts of *P. gerardiana*.

In India, according to Watt, "the chief product of *P. gerardiana* is the almond-like seed, contained in the cones. The cones ripen in October, are plucked before they open, and heated to make the scales expand. The seed is then easily taken out. They are largely eaten by the Natives, and are stored for winter use. According to Brandis they form a staple food of the inhabitants of Kunawar, by whom they are often eaten ground and mixed with flour. Amongst these people the proverb is current, 'one tree, a man's life in winter.' They are also exported to the plains, from the

hills of the Panjab, and large quantities are imported annually into India from Afghanistan by the Khyber and Bolan passes.

"No statistics are available of the probable annual production, but a full-sized cone yields more than 100 seeds, and each tree produces from 15 to 25 cones. The seed is considerably eaten as a dessert fruit by Europeans, in the same way as PISTACHIO nuts. It is somewhat oily and difficult of digestion, but has a very delicate terebinthinous flavour."

BUNYA-BUNYA PINE *(Araucaria bidwillii)*

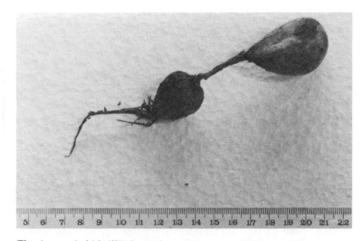

The *Araucaria bidwillii* photo shows a fact not widely known; the tree nut of the BUNYA germinates and the root penetrates the ground. On the end of this another nut grows, which may exist without root or stalk for a year, till rains come. Both the true nut and the "earth nut" are edible; the latter quite coconut-like in flavor.

## Araucaria bidwilli
### (Coniferae)
### BUNYA-BUNYA PINE

Several of the huge *Araucaria* trees produce edible nuts, sometimes in great abundance and they are relished by the natives of the countries where they grow.

Maiden wrote of this Australian tree: "The cones shed their seeds, which are two to two-and-a-half inches long by three-quarters of an inch broad; they are sweet before being perfectly ripe, and after that, resemble roasted chestnuts in taste. They are plentiful once in three years, and when the ripening season arrives, which is generally in the month of January, the aborigines assemble in large numbers from a great distance around, and feast upon them. Each tribe has its own particular set of trees, and of these each family has a certain number allotted, which are handed down from generation to generation with great exactness. The BUNYA is remarkable as being the only hereditary property which any of the aborigines are known to possess, and it is therefore protected by law. The food seems to have a fattening effect on the aborigines, and they eat large quantities of it after roasting it at the fire. Contrary to their usual habits, they sometimes store up the BUNYA nuts, hiding them in a water-hole for a month or two. Here they germinate and become offensive to a white man's palate, but they are considered by the blacks to have acquired an improved flavour."

157

Womersley writes from New Guinea that seeds of *A. bidwilli* and of the NORFOLK ISLAND PINE *(A. excelsa)* are nibbled by children there, but "are not really eaten by people."

*(Araucaria araucana)*

The situation is different in Chile where the famous MONKEY PUZZLE TREE *(A. araucana)* grows. Long ago a writer in the English *Popular Gardening* magazine, was poking back into history and started off by saying that Captain Vancouver, on his way home from settling a little trouble between the Spaniards and the English at Nooka Sound, put into Valparaiso for water and food. And here I quote:

> Brought into the presence of the Viceroy of Chile, he was astounded to find himself being addressed in a broad Irish brogue by that gentleman! He was, in fact, an Irishman naturalized as a Spaniard who, having risen high in royal favour, had been made Viceroy there. With true Irish hospitality a viceregal banquet was arrayed for the visitors.
>
> At this point, you must be introduced to the Discovery's surgeon, Archibald Menzies. Doubtless an able doctor, he was certainly a not inconsiderable botanist, even constructing a small greenhouse on deck to enable him to bring home new plants.
>
> Imagine his interest at dinner in peculiar and delicious nuts quite unlike anything he had seen before. He surreptitiously purloined a few and sowed them on board ship, so that when he returned he had four young nut trees to hand over to Kew. These were the first of the MONKEY PUZZLES in Britain.

The MONKEY PUZZLE is an evergreen 50 to 200 feet high, native to the mountains of southern Chile and northern Patagonia. Burkill says: "The sharp, thick, scale-like leaves of the MONKEY PUZZLE closely cover all its branches, giving rise to the legend that having climbed it the monkey cannot descend. It may easily be distinguished from the BUNYA by its leaves being thickly overlapping, which in the BUNYA are arranged in two rows. It is very beautiful and symmetrical."

Sturtevant says of this tree: "The seeds are eaten by the Indians, either fresh, boiled or roasted, and from them is distilled a spirituous liquor. Eighteen good-sized trees will yield enough for a man's sustenance all the year round. The seeds are sold as an article of food in the streets of Rio de Janeiro."

The BRAZILIAN PINE or CANDELABRA TREE *(A brasiliana)* is an evergreen tree to 100 feet or more, with branches in whorls. Specimens are very handsome and branched to the base, but old trees shed the lower branches, leaving a cluster of leafy branches at the summit.

Blossfeld writes from Sao Paulo: "*A. brasiliana* seeds are edible, and they are good, though a heavy diet, very nutritious and eaten since thousands of years by the native Indian tribes of southern Brazil, who actively disseminated the tree by wanderings. Apparently man never planted it purposely, but dropped seed here and there and it grew. Thus we find patches of this tree in the mountains of Minas Gerais. But this is a conifer seed, enclosed in a true, huge cone. The seed must be boiled several hours, then the shell peels off with some difficulty. But you can bite on it if you know the exact spot where to bite, and then it bursts and the nut suddenly comes out. But if it should be rotten, you are late to realize it and are likely to change the system to peeling. The flavour of the kernel is mealy and somewhat sweet, resembling a little the taste of sweet potatoes."

F. C. Hoehne wrote: "In our country the Araucaria family has three indigenous species. Only one the PINHAO is widely known as a food for men and animals. A highly nutritive flour can be made from it.

"*A. angustifolia*, survives in Panama, Sao Paulo, and in Minas Gerais. However, it is being unpatriotically and impiously destroyed to get lumber widely used in reinforced concrete construction, ceilings and light-weight furniture. Few people know the true value of this forest tree as the produce of PINHOES which are of the greatest use in nutrition."

The historic sights at Cressbrook, Queensland, are presided over to this day by a tree. A bulletin by the Australian Council of National Trusts says:

"The frontage at Cressbrook is still dominated by a towering BUNYA PINE *(Araucaria bidwilli)* which has almost as much historic significance as the homestead itself. Though climate, rainfall, soil, etc., have always restricted this tree uniquely to the Bunya Bunya mountains and foothills, it grows there densely and was the source of the most prolific and nutritious nut known to the aborigines. Every third year its crop of nuts is prodigally profuse and its season was the signal for an assembly of natives from thousands of square miles — from the west inland as far as the Balonne River, north to the valley of the Dawson, and south as far as the Tweed River in New South Wales. With a curious coincidental correspondence with the four-yearly Olympiads of ancient Greece, the jealous inviolability of tribal boundaries was waived, and the great assembly was the occasion for a feast that went on for weeks, with contests of skill and valour, in song, coroboree, spear and boomerang throwing and actual duels; and a triennial 'parliament' among the elders.

"In 1841 and 1844 the resolutions of this aboriginal Senate were simple and grim; to ambush and slaughter every white man with their flocks and herds, until the tribal lands were again free from them. The forests, which were felled and burned in steadily increasing clearings, could then grow again to shelter their kangaroos and other game, which were disappearing even more quickly as the forest thinned. This led to the guerilla war — the Black War — which flared or smouldered. They failed to realize the vast numbers of white men behind the few they saw, or the conclusive fire power of the gun against their own easily expendable spears and throwing sticks. The great BUNYA PINE at Cressbrook is a solitary momento of their fate."

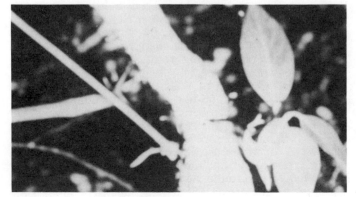

*(Gnetum montanum)* Female cones.

158

*(Gnetum gnemon)*

## Gnetum gnemon        (Gnetaceae)

This genus comprises 30 species in Indomalaysia, Fiji, northern South America and west tropical Africa. Burkill says:

"The Gnetaceae are found in the tropics. One third of them are trees and the rest woody climbers often of very great size. Probably the seeds of most species can be eaten, if care is taken to remove the irritating spicules of the seed-coat; *G. edule*, as its name suggests, is one of those used. *G. gnemon* is made into a delicacy in Java and elsewhere. Smaller fruits than these may only be worth picking for food in times of scarcity.

"*G. brunonianum*. A shrub in forests of southern Jahore and Malaya. Foxworthy records that its fruits are sweet and are eaten.

"*G. gnemon*. A tree of 60 feet, found wild in eastern Malaysia; cultivated here and there in the Malay Peninsula, sometimes abundantly, as in parts of Trengganu. It is a tree of such islands in Malaysia as have distinctly alternating seasons and is clearly not at home in the moister parts of the Peninsula.

"The fruits are eaten, and it is for them that it is grown in the Peninsula. They are of the size of an acorn, and when ripe are yellow or red. They are eaten raw, in which state they are hard and difficult to chew. They never appear in quantities in the markets, as they do, for instance, in Java, where they are abundantly sold either fresh or prepared by boiling, or better still by removing the outer coat, roasting in an iron pan, husking, moulding into cakes by beating and subsequently drying. The cakes need frying before eating."

Sturtevant says of this species: "The seeds are eaten in Amboina, roasted, boiled or fried."

Burkill's description of other species continues:

"*G. latifolium*, grows sparingly in the Malay Peninsula. In Celebes and the Philippine Islands the seeds are eaten cooked. The inner hairy seed coat must be removed as the hairs are irritant. They may be preserved in syrup: for the purpose they are boiled entire until soft; then the husk is carefully removed, and they are boiled again in syrup. They may also be eaten fried.

"*G. tenuifolium*. A slender twiner found throughout the Malay Peninsula and into southern Siam. It is a very important food of the jungle tribes, who eat the seeds and root. It is usual to boil the fruit for food, and throw away the skins."

Watt says of *G. scandens* (Syn. *G. edule*): "A lofty dioecious climbing shrub, in the Tropical Himalayas from Sikkim eastwards, to Assam, Singapore, and the Andaman Islands; also in the hills of the Deccan from the Konkan to the Nilghiris.

"The shrub, which flowers in March and April, yields an edible fruit in September and October. It is rather larger than the largest olive, and, when ripe, is smooth and orange-coloured. The outer succulent coat or pulp is commonly eaten by the natives, and the seeds, when roasted, are also employed as an article of food."

Brown: *Useful Plants of the Philippines* says:

"*Gnetum* fruit contains a single large starchy seed which is eaten either boiled or roasted, while the young leaves and tender tips are frequently used as a vegetable. The kernel of *Gnetum gnemon* contains 30 per cent moisture; 1.7 per cent ash; 10.88 per cent protein; 1.59 per cent fat, 50.4 per cent starch; 4.54 per cent other carbohydrates; 0.89 per cent crude fiber, and gives 2,774 calories per kilo. This analysis shows that the kernels are a nutritious food. This species is commonly cultivated in some of the towns of Batangas and Rizal for its edible leaves and fruits.

"According to Heyne the young leaves, flowers, and fruits are favorites for stews. He says that in Java the ripe fruits are roasted and pounded while hot into thin, round cakes which are cooked in boiling oil, when they puff up into a porous, crisp cake."

Shen Photo

*(Torreya grandis)*

## Torreya nucifera (Taxaceae)   JAPANESE TORREYA KAYA

The JAPANESE TORREYA is an evergreen tree, eventually reaching 80 feet but often much less, with a compact pyramidal crown much resembling a yew.

It grows in the forests of Southern and Central Honshu in the islands of Japan. It is hardy in the British Isles and to Zone 5 in the United States.

The foliage is flattened, yew-like, needle leaves ending in a spiny point, carried in two ranks along the twigs. Each needle is about an inch long and an eighth to a quarter inch broad, dark glossy green on the upper surface, curved and rather rigid. The leaves release a very pungent odor when broken or crushed.

STINKING CEDAR *(Torreya taxifolia)*

*Torreya*, in common with other conifers, has no true flowers. The structures corresponding to flowers are called strobilii, the male and female occurring separately on the same or different trees. In *Torreya* both are found on the current year's growth, the female at the base of the branchlet and the male further along toward the tip.

The nuts are in pairs near the base of the previous year's growth, the nuts requiring two seasons to ripen. They are ovoid, about an inch long, and green tinged with purple in color. There is a fleshy outer coat or aril, a woody shell, and an inner kernel irregularly folded into the shell, like a nutmeg.

Howes says: "The tree bears nuts 1-1½ inches long, not unlike acorns in appearance, which are edible and eaten as dessert nuts in the Orient. They have an agreeable although slightly resinous taste. The name KAYA is applied to the nut in Japan. There an oil used in cooking is extracted from it. The nuts are regarded by some as being mildly laxative and anthelmintic. They have been exported from Shanghai and Canton in the past.

CALIFORNIA NUTMEG *(Torreya californica)*

"The nuts of an allied species in China (*T. grandis*) are also eaten as edible nuts and used medicinally."

The genus *Torreya* is notable for its peculiar distribution. Two species occur in China, one in Japan and the two in this country, *T. californica* and *T. taxifolia*, in very restricted, widely separated ranges. Nearly the entire range of the STINKING CEDAR, and certainly that part of it where the tree can be said to be at all common, is encompassed by the boundaries of a rather small state park on the banks of the Apalachicola River in Florida.

### *Juniperus sp.*      (Cupressaceae)      JUNIPER

JUNIPER comprises some 70 kinds of needle-leaved trees and shrubs, mostly small, throughout the Temperate Zone and even into the Arctic. Many kinds and hybrids are planted as ornamentals. The "berries" of JUNIPERS growing throughout the western United States, really the seeds, are sweet and mealy and slightly resinous. These include the ALLIGATOR JUNIPER (*J. pachyphlaea*), the CALIFORNIA JUNIPER (*J. occidentalis*), and the UTAH JUNIPER (*J. osteosperma*). All of these have been eaten by Indians either raw or ground and prepared as cakes. They have been food for untold thousands of humans for hundreds of years.

ROASTED KAYA NUTS *(Torreya nucifera)*

# Chapter 28
# THE CYCADS
## *(Cycadaceae)*
### The Nuts That Dinosaurs Ate

## Robert G. Egolf

A hundred million years ago, during that incredibly remote era called the Mesozoic, dinosaurs ruled the earth. Some dinosaurs were carnivores, feeding on the flesh of their fellows, but most were inoffensive herbivores, foraging on the plants that grew in the lakes and streams and along the shores of that time. This vegetation bore a strange and somber aspect. There were no flowers, no grasses to carpet the earth, no towering pines or rugged oaks. Instead there were giant horsetails, ferns of every size and description, and strange fern-like trees. Dominant among these plants on land were the CYCADS and their near relatives, the BENNETTITALES. The BENNETTITALES are now extinct, gone with the dinosaurs, but the CYCADS remain, still much as they were, although greatly reduced in numbers. Less than a hundred different kinds survive, remnants of a mighty horde, now living fossils on the earth.

SAGO PALM *(Cycas circinalis)*. This female flower has opened out from the tree's crown, extending its "petals" in between the mature green leaves so that the flower now covers a spread 2 feet across. Seeds sit in nests along the edges of the "petals."

Would you like to eat the CYCAD nuts that dinosaurs might once have browsed upon? You can, possibly, but you may not want to. You won't find them in any store. They aren't very tasty. Even where they grow, in the tropics and the subtropical regions of the earth, they are mostly regarded as something to eat when there isn't anything else. Worst of all, without preparation the CYCADS are poisonous, root, stem, leaf, and nut.

CYCAD nuts are rather large, many of them an inch across. They are fat and rounded, full of starch, and mostly covered by a brilliant orange or reddish outer coat. They look as if they are meant to be good to eat. The poisonous substance in Cycads is soluble in water. It can be leached from the nuts or from the starchy center of the trunk by water, rendering them fit to eat. It is impossible

now to tell what primitive genius first discovered that such tempting nuts could be made free of their poison. Perhaps some tribesman, wits sharpened by hunger, found that CYCAD nuts shed into a jungle pool, partially decomposed by water, could be eaten whereas those fresh from the plant could not. Where the nuts are eaten they may be treated whole, with repeated changes of water, and then beaten to a flour for cooking, or the raw nuts may be beaten and the pulp washed in water and strained through a cloth. This is much like the making of sago starch, long a staple of food in the western Pacific, from the trunks of several Palms and also a CYCAD, the SAGO PALM *(Cycas revoluta)* in its range from Japan to Australia. It may be that the processes are related and that one discovery led to the other. However it happened, in nearly every tropical country where CYCADS grow men sooner or later found they could use the nuts for food. They are not an important staple because nowhere do CYCADS grow in dense profusion, but in times of famine, when there is little else to eat, they are as welcome as the finest delicacy.

In northern Australia stockmen and farmers kill the CYCAD, *Macrozamia moorei*, wherever they can find it. Under a government program holes are cut in the trunks, arsenic inserted, and soon the leaves droop and the plants die. In times of drought, where the CYCADS are undisturbed, cattle driven by hunger forage on the leaves, and develop a peculiar paralysis of the hindquarters called "rickets" by the local stockmen. Unless found and destroyed by the herders the afflicted animals die, not of the poison, but of slow starvation, being unable to feed.

Where CYCADS grow they are usually called palms, and the resemblance is indeed striking. Typically the CYCAD has a stout, unbranched trunk topped by a palm-like crown of large, glossy-green leaves. Most of the "palm fronds" used in churches on Palm Sunday are actually CYCAD leaves from the SAGO PALM *(Cycas revoluta)*, which will stay green and fresh longer than any real palm frond. Although CYCADS look like palms they are not at all related. Compared to CYCADS the palms are Johnnies-come-lately on the earth. If we are to find relatives of the CYCADS it is to the conifers we must look, and to such plants as the equally ancient *Ginkgo*. Botanists call these plants Gymnosperms. In technical terms they bear their seeds, not enclosed in a fleshy pulp like an apple, but entirely naked, attached to the woody scales of a cone. Like pine trees, CYCADS bear their seeds in cones, but what cones! The cones of the CYCADS are larger than any other in the world. The female cone of *Macrozamia denisonii*, a CYCAD of the Tambourine Mountains in Australia, may be two feet long and weigh 80 pounds, while that of *Encephalartos caffer*, from South Africa, has been weighed at 92 pounds. These are exceptional, but cone weights of 30 and 40 pounds are not at all unusual.

One of the most engaging things about the CYCADS is their incredible toughness. Perhaps we should expect this of these ancient sojourners, from the very fact of their survival. In his classic book on the Cycads Professor Charles J. Chamberlain tells of the leaves of an Australian CYCAD, *Bowenia spectabilis*, lying on a hotel veranda in the blazing tropical sun of Queensland for three days, with

161

never a sign of wilting. Another CYCAD, *Encephalartos altensteinii* of African origin, bombed out of a Hanoverian greenhouse in Germany in 1944 was dug up, thrown into a cellar for two years devoid of leaves or roots, then replanted to stand lifeless for another ten years, and at last produced one leaf, then another, and finally a whole crown more than fifteen years after its apparent destruction. CYCADS are long-lived as well. Although one cannot count rings in their trunk, each leaf as it falls leaves behind a scar, visible on the trunk throughout the life of the plant. These scars, or persistent leaf bases, can be counted, and because the leaves appear slowly and with predictable regularity the age of the plant can be calculated from the number of leaves it has borne. By this way of estimation many CYCADS less than ten feet in height would appear to be more than a thousand years old.

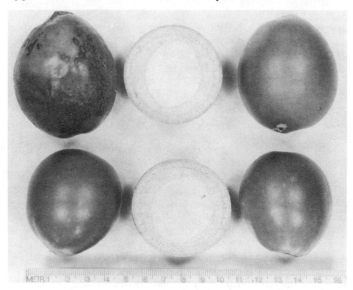

SAGO PALM *(Cycas circinalis)*

## *Cycas circinalis*  (Cycadaceae)

About 20 species of these fernlike plants are found native from Madagascar and the coasts of Africa to the islands of the Pacific. Burkill feels that the African species *C. thouarsii* is identical with this one which grows in Ceylon and India, and with *C. rumphii* which extends into the Pacific. Northwards in China where the tropics have been left, appears the distinct *C. revoluta*. Apparently all these, as well as other species of CYCAS, produce edible nuts which must be treated to remove poisons.

JAPANESE FERN PALM *(Cycas revoluta)*

Regarding *C. revoluta* in China, Burkill says: "The seeds are said to be eaten by the Annamese of southern Annam, though rarely, as the preparation is tedious. On analysis they are found to be rich in food as they contain 14 per cent of crude protein and 68 per cent of soluble non-nitrogenous substances."

Then Burkill reverts to *C. circinalis* and continues: "The large seeds are the most important product which the plant yields. They are poisonous in a fresh state, but a kind of flour is prepared from them for food. The seeds of *C. thouarsii* are so used in the Comoro Islands. Those of *C. circinalis* serve similarly in Ceylon, being made into cakes and considered to possess some vague medicinal value. The seeds in India are used in times of scarcity, and at all times by the hill tribes of India. The Andamahese eat them."

Both Wray and Schebesta state that the Sakai of upper Perak eat the seeds.

"Seeds are eaten, also, in the northern Philippine Islands, and in the southern Islands and Guam. Safford, writing of the islanders of Guam, states 'in the times of famine following hurricanes, they resort to the woods for the nuts of *C. circinalis*, the poisonous properties of which they remove by pounding, soaking, and repeatedly changing the water, after which the macerated starchy substance is ground and baked' or it may be sun-dried and stored for later use. If used for any length of time this food sets up intestinal trouble."

Hasskarl stated that in the Dutch Indies the seeds might be cooked, then soaked for two days and pounded to get out the juice, before consumption. Ochse calls the preparation a complicated treatment.

"Bacon found 31 per cent, of starch in the ripe seeds."

AUSTRALIAN NUT PALM *(Cycas media)*

*C. media* is a small tree of India and tropical Australia. Maheshwari says the 1½-inch seeds are used to make flour after special treatment.

*C. revoluta*, commonly called SAGO PALM, is native of China, Japan and the East Indies.

Burkill says *C. circinalis* and *C. rumphii* appear to be identical. Of *C. rumphii* Brown says:

"In times of famine the ripe seeds of this plant are prepared as food in some of the isolated parts of the Philippines, such as the Batanes Islands. In Guam, according to Safford, *Cycas* seeds are a staple article of food in times when better foods are scarce. As the untreated seeds are poisonous, it is necessary first to eliminate the poisonous principle. In order to do this, the ripe seeds are crushed and the resulting product is soaked in water which must be changed several times. The product is then dried, and the flourlike substance cooked in the form of small cakes or as porridge. Bacon found the starch content of mature seeds to be 31.2 per cent."

162

CHESTNUT DIOON *(Dioon edule)*

## *Dioon edule* (Cycadaceae)

The name, in Greek, means two eggs, because each scale covers two ovules, and the seeds are in pairs.

This is a Mexican plant of which Bailey says: "*D. edule* has a rigid frond which is more easily kept free from scale insects than *Cycas revoluta*, the commonest species of the family in cultivation. A specimen at Kew had a trunk 3-4 ft. high and 8-10 in. thick, the crown spreading 8-10 ft. and containing 50 fronds, each 4-5 ft. long and 6-9 in. wide. The seeds, which are about the size of SPANISH CHESTNUTS are eaten by the Mexicans."

Martinez: *Useful Plants in Mexican Flora* says: "The flowers are produced in scaly cones; the male ones measure about 25 centimeters and have woolly scales, and in the lower part of these are found pollen sacks from which abundant pollen issues. The female cones measure about 50 centimeters and also are scaly and woolly. The scales protect seeds the size of a PECAN. These seeds are foul in odor but are customarily used as food."

AFRICAN CYCAD *(Encephalartos sp.)*

BREAD TREE *(Encephalartos altensteinii)*

*(Encephalartos paucidentatus)*

## *Encephalartos hildebrandtii* (Zamiaceae)

This appears to be the chief species among the 30 kinds of these CYCADS that grow in tropical and South Africa. In the *East African Medical Journal* of Dec. 1968 appears this introduction to a 6-page study of "The Toxic Properties of *Encephalartos hildebrandtii*" by G. M. Mugera and P. Nderito:

"*Encephalartos* species is a palm-like plant which bears large pineapple-like cones. When the cones mature they fall off and expose the seeds. The seed consists of a hard nut-like kernel covered by a thick fleshy red layer known as the husk. The stems and seeds of the plants provide a source of edible starch. *Encephalartos* is found in South Africa, Central Africa, East Africa, Southwest Sudan and the West African states from Chad to Ghana.

In East Africa, the preparation of *Encephalartos hildebrandtii* is similar in most parts of East Africa. In Kilifi and Lamu districts of Kenya, a small tribe known as Wasanya use this plant's flour. They collect the ripe seeds and remove the husks which are then normally dried in the sun for one or two days before being ground to a fine flour. This flour, which is red, is used immediately for making porridge ('ugali' and 'chapatii'). It is said that 'ugali' and 'chapatii' prepared from this flour is very tasty and keeps well for a long time. The husks are used any time that they are available, by the Wasanya.

"The hard nut-oke kernel which remains after removal of the husks consists of an outer hard shell and a firm, whitish starchy endosperm containing the embryo. The preparation of the starch from these seeds is laborious and the Wasanya do not use it immediately. It is normally kept outside the house and prepared when there is a shortage of food, especially during the dry season when the people are not busy with garden work. It is prepared by breaking off the outer hard shell of the nut leaving the starchy kernel. The kernel is cut into small pieces which are then dried in the sun. The pieces are then ground into a white coarse flour. This flour is placed in a drum full of water and the water changed daily for eight days. After this, the coarse flour is dried and ground to a fine powder which is used for preparation of 'ugali', 'chapatii' and porridge. The dry flour keeps very well and can be stored indefinitely. 'Ugali' and 'chapatii' is a common food for most tribes in Kenya and is prepared usually from wheat or maize flour. The Wasanya are unique in using the starchy kernel flour of the CYCAD for preparation of this type of meal.

"All the Wasanya know that the starchy kernel and its flour, before it is detoxified with water, is very poisonous. It is believed that all the toxic factors dissolve in water and that cattle, goats, sheep and dogs die if they drink the water from the washings. According to the Wasanya, animals get 'drunk' after drinking the washings and then die. If the animals eat the starchy kernels whilst being dried, they become sick with bloody diarrhoea and die within a few days.

"In man, if adults eat the starchy kernels or eat starch which has been inadequately prepared, they show symptoms of gastrointestinal irritation (vomiting, anorexia and diarrhoea), apathy and headache, (Mugera et al. 1967). If children eat similar food, they die usually showing jaundice within two to six days."

*(Macrozamia spiralis)*

### *Macrozamia riedlii*     (Zamiaceae) QUEENSLAND NUT

This genus comprises 14 big CYCADS in tropical Australia. Of this species Dr. John S. Beard, when he was director of the King's Park Botanic Garden at Perth, wrote this author:

"Female plants bear large cones shaped like pineapples containing bright red fruits. The outer rind is believed to be poisonous but the kernel can be eaten if roasted."

P. R. Wycherly, a later director of the same garden, wrote this author: "This CYCAD is at present producing new cones and until new fruits ripen I cannot get suitable photographs for you. Uncooked and unleached these are indigestible and poisonous. They are prepared and eaten by the aborigines, but even so I think they should be classed as poverty fare."

Burkill wrote: "The largest species reaches 60 feet in height; all look like palms, and several are in cultivation in botanic gardens, because of their great interest.

*(Lepidozamia hopei)*

"The leaves are poisonous; cattle, as a result of eating them become paralysed in the hind quarters; and seeds sometimes kill sheep. On this account attempts have been made to destroy the plant in its home.

"The nut is poisonous also; but as the poison is volatile it is removed by roasting, and the nut can then be eaten. There is 56 per cent of starch on dry weight in the nuts of one species and 22 per cent of albuminoids."

Regarding *M. hopei*, commonly called ARUMBA, which grows at Cairns, Maheshwari wrote: "Nuts used for flour after treatment."

COONTIE *(Zamia floridiana)*

### COONTIE COMPTIE *Zamia floridiana* (Zamiaceae) SEMINOLE BREAD

This genus includes some 40 species in the West Indies and other tropical American areas, including Florida where this species and one other, *Z. pumila*, are found growing in central and on the east coast in south Florida, usually in moist areas.

Sturtevant says of *Z. integrifolia*: "West Indies and Florida. SAGO CYCAD. This CYCAD furnishes the Seminole Indians with their white meal. An arrowroot has been prepared from it at St. Augustine. It is now cultivated to a limited extent."

Bailey, however, says that the Florida plants sometimes called *Z. integrifolia*, are all *Z. pumila* or *Z. floridiana*.

Sturtevant describes another species with edible seeds:

"*Z. chigua*. New Granada. The seeds are boiled and reduced to a mash which is served with milk and sugar. Bread is also made from them."

Some 40 kinds of *Zamia* have been described. The genus is much confused and the above common names are applied to several different species.

164

# Chapter 29

# THE GINKGO

## A Pre-Historic Tree that Survives

The Ginkgo, often called MAIDENHAIR TREE, is one of the prehistoric trees that still survives. It is native of ancient China, but it also grew in this country a few million years ago.

MAIDENHAIR TREE *(Ginkgo biloba)*

### *Ginkgo biloba* (Ginkgoaceae) MAIDENHAIR TREE

Bailey describes this familiar tree much used along avenues in the northeastern United States:

"The oval, creamy white seeds of the GINKGO or MAIDENHAIR TREE from China and Japan, have smooth and thin, but stout shells, within which are single green kernels of rather sweetish flavor. When roasted, the kernels are highly prized by the Chinese.

"The fruit of the GINKGO considerably resembles that of the native persimmon in color, size and character, but differs from it in that the GINKGO flesh is of a disagreeable odor."

The GINKGO is never eaten by Americans because in ripening the hull of the nut stinks to high heaven, but in China when the hulls fall off, the Chinese pick them up, paint them bright red and use them strung in festoons as decorations at weddings. Then they crack the nuts and eat the contents which have no odor. No American gets that far.

The GINKGO is called MAIDENHAIR TREE, because of the resemblance of its two-lobed leaves to the fanlike leaflets of some maidenhair ferns.

The petrified GINKGO forest near Ellenberg, Wash., on the north bank of the Columbia River shows that these trees were growing there 15,000,000 years ago, before the Rocky Mountains were born. This area then was a rain forest; it was destroyed when the earth opened and belched molten lava to blanket the land where the forest had stood. The trees were green and wet; no oxygen was present to permit them to burn, so they turned to stone.

The ripe nuts are green or yellowish, oval, about an inch across. They are borne singly on long stems from the clusters of leaves. They have a thin, very foul outer flesh, a thin stony shell, and a large inner kernel. They have no commercial value as an agricultural crop although the nuts from chance trees are gathered and sold in China and Japan. They are grown nowhere strictly for the nuts. Because of the litter and smell, female trees are rare in ornamental plantings.

# Chapter 30
# NOT NUTS

Many fruits, tubers and other things in the plant world are called "nuts" but they are not eaten by anybody. This chapter is devoted to some of these mis-called "nuts", many of which are commonly cultivated.

Most conspicuous "not nut" is the BETEL NUT in India. It is the fruit of an *Areca* palm and is chewed by millions, but when they get tired chewing, they spit out the cud. It occupies the same place in the lives of those other-world peoples as chewing gum does in the lives of Americans. When we get tired chewing, we spit it out.

Julia Morton Photo

LOVE NUT or ROSARY PEA *(Abrus pracecatorius)*

### LOVE NUT
## *Abrus precatorius* (Leguminosae) ROSARY PEA

This old world scandent shrub produces quantities of small, bright red, black-tipped seeds used in necklaces. Don says the seeds are the hardest and most indigestible of all the pea tribe. Williamson says: "The seeds if eaten whole are harmless but if crushed or macerated are extremely poisonous."

## *Afrolicania* (Elaeospermaceae) PO-YOAK

Dalziel says: "Fruits from Sierra Leone are ellipsoid-ovoid, 1¼-1½ in. long, ¾-1½ in. across, the shell crustaceous and comparatively thin, densely warty when young, dark brown and slightly rough when mature. The seed or nut is single, up to 1¼ in. long, with two thick fleshy concave cotyledons enclosing a rather large cavity. The kernels yield by extraction 52.44% of a yellow oil, drying fairly rapidly to a varnish-like mass. The oil from PO-YOAK nuts is described as pale yellow, strongly drying, with a high iodine value. It was recommended as a substitute for linseed oil in the manufacture of paints and varnishes."

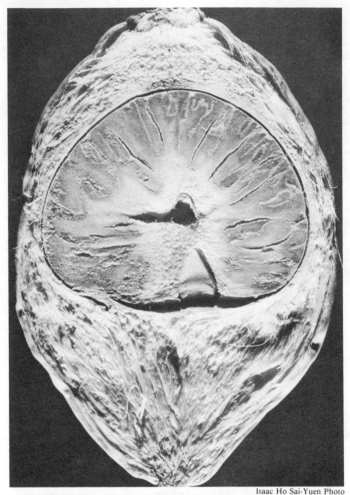

Isaac Ho Sai-Yuen Photo

*(Areca catechu).* Cross section of kernel of BETEL NUT.

Isaac Ho Sai-Yuen Photo

BETEL NUT *(Areca catechu)*

## *Areca catechu* (Palmae) BETEL NUT

The tree that produces the BETEL NUT is a single-trunked palm, tall and very slender. It is usually 30 or 40 feet but occasionally 100 feet. The trunk of a mature specimen may be no more than 4 or 5 inches in diameter at the base. On this feather-leaved palm, the leaves are 4 to 6 feet long, with closely spaced leaflets 18 inches long and a little more than an inch broad.

BETEL NUT palms are widely diffused among the tropical islands of the southwestern Pacific and adjacent shores. The palm has been spread to the climatic limits of its culture by the trade in BETEL NUTS for hundreds of years, becoming naturalized in favorable localities so that the original home is now a matter of conjecture.

The nuts are 2 or 3 inches long, encased in an orange or scarlet fibrous covering. The kernels inside are about ¾ inch long and reddish-yellow.

BETEL NUTS are an important article of commerce in those parts of the world where they are chewed, but their use is mostly confined to the peoples of the underdeveloped nations from India eastwards across southeast Asia and the islands of the southwestern Pacific Ocean. It is difficult to assign a dollar value to a trade so largely unregulated or done by barter.

Besides the nuts of *A. catechu*, the nuts of other species are often substituted, including *A. concinna, A. nagensis, A. glandiformis, A. valiso, A. ipot, A. macrocalyx, A. pumila,* and *A. triandra.*

P. Maheshwari Photo

BETEL NUT cluster *(Areca catechu)*

Burkill points out that betel chewing is the most complex of any of the luxuries, or vices, of its kind. Not only is the palm nut required, but also the leaf of the BETEL PEPPER (*Piper betle*), a little finely ground lime and such other spices and condiments as are occasionally added to the quid. The nuts are themselves picked and prepared for use in a variety of ways. Nuts picked when still green are considered better and bring a higher price, but do not last as well as fully ripened ones in damp climates. The nuts may be boiled after picking, or they may be left to dry in the sun either split open or whole. Each method of preparation produces its own distinct product. When the nut is to be chewed a slice is taken, sprinkled with the lime, and wrapped in the leaf of the pepper. A pinch of tobacco may be added, or a little cutch, gambier, clove or cardamon. BETEL NUT is offered among friends or at meals much as cigarettes are in western countries. The habit is most definitely an acquired taste. The primary sensation to the person unaccustomed to it is a choking or slight constriction of the throat, brought on by the natural astringency of the materials. There is no narcotic or addictive principle involved. Habitual betel chewers have rosy red saliva and blackened teeth. It is said that betel chewing causes early decay of the teeth, but in backward nations where the daily ritual of the toothbrush is not established, bad dentition is all too common under any circumstance.

Purseglove says: "The hard dried endosperm of ripe and unripe seeds, miscalled 'nuts', is chewed as a narcotic by some 400 million people from Zanzibar to India and the central Pacific, thus outrivalling chewing gum as a masticatory in popularity on a world basis. It may be chewed alone, but the usual practice is to wrap small slices or pieces of the nut in a leaf of betel-pepper, to which a dab of slaked lime has been added. The quid is placed in the check and chewed slowly. It causes continuous salivation and the saliva is turned bright red, hence 'the bloody gouts' that spatter roads and pavements in countries where betel is chewed. The quid is not swallowed, but is eventually spat out.

"The habit of chewing the betel quid has spread more slowly than smoking tobacco, possibly because several materials are used in its preparation; nevertheless, it has taken an extremely firm hold on the peoples who use it. 'It is prevalent among all classes of people, of all communities and religions, rich and poor, men and women, and young and old'. It is chewed after meals and on all auspicious occasions; 'none of their feasts and greetings being polite without it'; it has a prominent place in local religious observances and mythology. In the early Indian writings it is said 'to expel wind, to remove phlegm, to kill germs and to subdue bad odour, to beautify the mouth, to remove impurities, and to induce love'. It is believed to make the teeth strong and prevent their decay, but blackens them and eventually grinds them down. The mouth and lips are stained red. (It is obvious that many people in India like to paint the inside of their faces, much as the American Indians used to decorate the outside.) Burkill (1966) says that 'beginners do not find chewing pleasant, but acquire the taste; at first they feel dizzy, and the throat burns and feels constricted. Excessive chewing is said to be harmful. Corner recalls that 'the late Professor J. B. S. Haldane, on being asked what betel-chewing was like, rolled his eyes to heaven and continued chewing'."

BONDUC or NICKER NUT *(Caesalpinia crista)*

### Caesalpinia crista (Leguminosae) BONDUC NICKER NUT

This woody Indian climber is sometimes cultivated. The hard, brown, round seeds about ¾ inch diameter, are used as marbles by children in warm countries.

### Calodendrum capense (Rutaceae) CAPE CHESTNUT WILD CHESTNUT

Bailey says: "The shining black irregularly rounded and some wedge-shaped, seed of a subtropical tree of southern Africa, of about ¾ inch in length. These seeds have a stout but thin shell and a single farinaceous kernel, which resembles somewhat the texture of a chestnut. Cultivated mainly as an ornamental."

*Indigenous Trees of Southern Africa* by von Breitenbach says: "The seed yields about 25 per cent of a lemon-yellow, rather bitter oil, which is not edible but can be used for soap-making and, for the latter purpose, it equals cotton-seed oil."

*Trees of Southern Africa*, Palmer and N. Pittman says:
"These (seeds) are not generally popular with mammals or birds, but Samango monkeys strip off the black outer skin to eat the nut within, and the Pigeons *(Columba arquatrix)* eat the seeds whole. The kernel yields a lemon-yellow, rather bitter, fixed oil which is not considered edible but which can be used for soap making."

### Coelococus amicarum (Palmae) IVORY NUT

Brown says: "The IVORY-NUT palm is a native of the Caroline Islands. The globose fruits, up to 10 centimeters in diameter, are covered with closely overlapping, hard, shiny, brownish scales. The large seeds are very hard, ivorylike in texture and appearance and are commercially utilized for making buttons."

### Cyperus esculentus (Cyperaceae) CHUFA NUT EARTH ALMOND BUSH NUT

Bailey says: "The small edible tubers of a sedge plant which, to a considerable extent, are grown in warm climates as a food for swine. Native to southern Europe."

### Elaeocarpus ganitrus (Elaeocarpaceae) OLIVE NUT

This tree is found in India, Java and Australia. Howes says: "The seeds are often strung as beads, and have been used as rosaries, the heads of hatpins, and other ornamental articles."

### Euadenia eminens (Capparidaceae)

Irvine says this is a strongly scented, soft-wooded shrub to 6 feet in the forest undergrowth of Sierra Leone and Ghana, and adds: "This is a decorative plant worth introducing into cultivation."

The *Botanical Magazine* says this species has "a singularly handsome inflorescence which resembles a candelabrum, the yellow petals looking like pairs of gas jets on each branch."

However, it is not a "nut" in this book. The pulp of the fruit, according to Dalziel, is eaten and is a powerful aphrodisiac. The seeds which have a peppery taste, are chewed. This classes the seeds with other chewing gums. Chevalier says the plant is poisonous.

CHALMOOGRA NUTS *(Hydnocarpus kurzii)*

Cross-section of CHALMOOGRA NUTS *(Hydnocarpus kurzii)*

## Hydnocarpus sp. (Flacourtiaceae)
### CHALMOOGRA NUTS

The nuts of the 40 kinds of *Hydnocarpus* trees in Indomalaysia, have been treasured for centuries by the people of that part of the world, because of the oil derived from them and used in the treatment of leprosy. The genus was once called *Tartogenos.'* Burkill says: "The fruits of *Hydnocarpus* are like cannonballs. They are produced on the trunk, and ripen under the canopy of foliage, where, as the trees occur in rain-forest, there is considerable moisture. These big, hard fruits fall to the ground where they are broken open by animals.

"*H. kurzii* is a tree of the forests of Burma and Siam, the chief source of chaulmoogric acid and the reason for wishing to cultivate it is to obtain pure supplies of good seed. Bears are very fond of the flesh of the fruit, and wild pigs eat the seeds. It is considered inadvisable to eat the pork of pigs when they have been feeding on the seeds, as it produces nausea and vomiting. Further, fish that have fed on the seeds must not be eaten."

"Cases of human poisoning with oils from *Hydnocarpus* have been recorded.

"*H. anthelmintica*, is a tree of Indo-China and Siam with a girth of over 15 feet at 6 feet from the ground. Its seeds are brought to market in Bangkok where they are used as a vermifuge, and the oil, locally, as a remedy for leprosy and skin complaints. The tree is very ornamental when in good soil."

Julia Morton Photo

PHYSIC NUT *(Jatropha curcas)*

### PHYSIC NUT
### BARBADOS-NUT
## Jatropha curcas (Euphorbiaceae) PURGING NUT

Bailey says: "Small, oblong, rounded seeds of about ¾ inch long, 1/16 inch wide, by 3/8 inch thick, of a slatish color, and having a thin strong shell, of a shrubby, tropical American tree. From the kernel, which is white and solid, there is obtained a strong purgative oil (curcas oil) which is also used for illuminating purposes. To some extent, this tree is known as a hedge plant in Florida. The kernel of the fruit, when it ripens, is tasty but eating it is dangerous."

Harry Blossfeld writes from Brazil: "*Pachystroma acanthophylla* is a synonym for *Jatropha acanthophylla*, a big shrub of the dry desert of northeastern Brazil, known as FAVELEIRA locally and this has a fruit like a nut, indeed. But it is as poisonous as *Jatropha curcas*, the PHYSIC NUT

and the leaves of the tree are caustic in contact with the skin.

"The same happens with *Jatropha urens*, which I do not know, but which is said to furnish an oil, extracted by cooking the seeds, and which may be used for culinary purposes. The seeds, after roasting, are said to be edible, but I heard also they are dangerous to eat. It may be the poisonous substance in the oily seed gets destroyed by heat, after a certain time of exposure only, thus simple roasting may not be sufficient."

Steinmetz Photo

Col. Wm. R. Grove, holder of the Congressional Medal of Honor, established Florida's largest LYCHEE NUT orchard at Laurel, Fla.

### LITCHI NUT
### CHINESE HAZEL
## Litchi chinensis (Sapindaceae) DAWA NUT

Bailey says of this Chinese fruit, of which the aril but not the kernel, is edible: "A brown-colored, warty appearing fruit resembling a strawberry, with an outer thin, papery shell, within which is a central smooth hard-shelled seed, surrounded by a brownish pulp of a delicious, subacid flavor. The fruit of a low-growing, tender tree native to China."

## Ophiocaryon paradoxum (Sabiaceae) SNAKE NUT

Bailey says: "A large, roundish fruit, about the size of a black walnut, the product of a large tree of British Guiana. This nut takes its name of SNAKE-NUT from the peculiar form of the embryo of the seed, which is curled up spirally. The Indians, thinking there must be some virtue in form, use these nuts as an antidote for snake-bites, although so far as known to science they do not possess any medicinal properties."

## Pterocarya fraxini (Juglandaceae)
### WINGED WALNUT
### CAUCASIAN WALNUT

Bailey says: "Small, angular, winged seeds, having hard shells, of a tree native to western Asia. Of no economic importance."

Tang from Hong Kong writes that the nut is not edible.

### Pycnocoma macrophylla (Euphorbiaceae) BOMAH-NUT

Bailey says: "The seed of an African shrub used in tanning, and which yields a fixed oil."

### Pyrularia pubera (Santalaceae) BUFFALO NUT OIL NUT MOUNTAIN COGNUT

This comprises four species of woody plants of southeastern United States, the Himalayas and Chile. Small says this species is a shrub to 3 meters tall, with a drupe 2.4 cm. long, and continues: "A curious shrub, inconspicuous in flower, but obvious in fruit by the dangling drupes, which are, at first light-green and later yellowish. An oil resembling olive oil, but ill-scented and poisonous, has been pressed from the drupes."

### Sapium sabiferum (Euphorbiaceae) TALLOW NUT

Bailey says: "The whitish colored fruits, about 1/8 inch in diameter of a Chinese tree. The nuts consist of relatively large, brown seeds, having hard shells with a thick coating of a fatty substance, which is used in various ways as a substitute for animal tallow."

### Staphylea trifolia (Staphyleaceae) BLADDER NUT

This shrub common in eastern United States, bears fruits ¾ " x 1½ " with a reddish, papery shell. The fruit has 3 cells, each containing 2 or 3 hard, shiny seeds. They are not edible. They are noticed because they hang on all winter.

Ed Hallicy Photo

*(Strychnos spinosa)*

### Strychnos potatorum (Loganiaceae) CLEARING NUT INDIAN GUM NUT

Bailey says: "The seed of an oriental tree, which is largely employed by the natives because of its power of causing

impurities in water to settle to the bottom. Receptacles in which water is to be placed are vigorously rubbed with one of the nuts; later the water is poured in and the impurities quickly unite together at the bottom, leaving the water perfectly clear."

Bailey says of *S. spinosa*, a tropical African tree cultivated in South Florida, that the pulp of the 3-inch, hard-shelled fruits is edible and the seeds abundant, but Maheshwari writes from India that the seeds are "considered unwholesome." Chevalier mentions symptoms of violent vomiting after eating two or three fruits 'along with the seeds'."

Williamson says of this fruit: "The seeds are poisonous. The flesh is also said to be poisonous if not fully ripe."

Julia Morton Photo

PORTIA NUT *(Thespesia populnea)*

### Thespesia populnea (Malvaceae) PORTIA NUT

This *Hibiscus* relative, common in Florida though native to the old world, has inedible fruits. Bailey says: "The small obovoid brown seeds, have a netted veined surface, yellowish brown pubescence on inner edges, especially at apex, and a thin but stout shell. PORTIA-NUTS yield an oil used as an illuminant."

Julia Morton Photo

LUCKY NUT *(Thevetia peruviana)*

### *Thevetia peruviana* (Apocynaceae) LUCKY NUT

Williams: *Useful and Ornamental Trees of Zanzibar and Pemba* says: "A small tree, native of the West Indies and Central America, with poisonous, milky juice. The fruit are yellow when ripe, containing a single, somewhat triangular, seed, ¾ by 1¼ inches, lined around the margin and down the centre. The seeds, LUCKY NUTS, are carried by natives of the West Indies in their purses, worn as watch charms, or given to represent good luck; they are also put into the hands of babies at birth for the same purpose. In India they are known as a cattle poison. The tree being evergreen and of very rapid growth, is useful where a screen or light shade is required quickly. In Zanzibar it is used for ornamental hedges."

---

# BIBLIOGRAPHY

Allen, Paul H: *The Rain Forests of Golfo Dulce.* Univ. of Florida Press, Gainesville, 1956.

Anderson, R. H.: *Trees of New South Wales,* Thomas Henry Tennant, Gov't Printer, Sydney, 1947.

Bailey, L. H.: *Standard Cyclopedia of Horticulture,* MacMillan, New York, 1935. *Hortus III,* MacMillan, New York, Sept. 1977.

Barrau, J.: *The Sago Palm and other Food Plants of the Marsh Dwellers in the South Pacific Islands.* Econ. Bot., 13,151-62. (1959)

Black, J. M.: *Flora of South Australia,* 2d ed., Government Printer, Adelaide, 1948. (Supplement, 1962.)

Brandis, Dietrich: *Forest Flora of Northwest and Central India.* Wm. H. Allen & Co., London, 1874.

Brooks, Reid M., and Olmo, H. P.: *Register of New Fruit and Nut Varieties, 1920-50.* Univ. of Calif. Press, 1952.

Burkill, I. H.: *A Dictionary of the Economic Products of the Malay Peninsula.* Government Printer, Singapore, 1935.

Bush, Carroll D.: *Nut Grower's Handbook.* Orange Judd Pub. Co. Inc., 1941. Rev. edit. 1953.

Corner, E. J. H.: *The Life of Plants.* Weidenfeld and Nicolson, London, 1964. *"Wayside Trees of Malaya,"* Govt. Printer, Singapore — 1958.

Corsa, William Pinckney: *Nut Culture in the United States,* Wash. Govt. Print. Off. 1896.

Dale, Ivan R. and Greenway, P. J.: *Kenya Trees and Shrubs,* published by authority of the Government of the Colony and Protectorate of Kenya, 1961.

Dalziel, J. M.: *Useful Plants of West Tropical Africa.* Crown Agents for the Colonies, London, 1948.

Ewart, A. J.: *Handbook of Forest Trees for Victorian Foresters.*

Fanshawe, D. B.: *The Dum Palm — Hyphaene thebaica* (Del.) Mart. East Afr. agric. for J., 32, 108-16. Also *Forest Products of British Guiana,* Georgetown, 1950.

Fernald, M. L. and Kinsey, A. C.: *Edible Wild Plants of Eastern North America,* Idlewild Press, Cornwall, N.Y. 1943.

Francis, W. D.: *Australian Rain Forest Trees.* Forestry and Timber Bureau, Canberra, 1951.

Fuller, Andrew Samuel: *The Nut Culturist.* Orange Judd Co., 1896. Sept. 1906.

Furtado, C. X.: *The Genus Calamus in the Malay Peninsula.* Gardens' Bull., Singapore,15, 32-265.

Gardner, C. A.: *Trees of Western Australia.* Publication by W. A. Dept. of Agriculture.

Hall, Norman; Johnson, R. D. and Chippendale, G. M.: *Forest Trees of Australia.* Australian Govt. Pub. Serv. Canberra, 1957-Sept. 1975.

Howes, Frank Norman: *Nuts: Their Production and Everyday Uses.* London, Faber and Faber, 1948.

Irvine, F. R.: *Woody Plants of Ghana,* Oxford University Press, New York, 1961.

*Handbook of North American Nut Trees* — The Nut Growers Assoc. (Jaynes — 1969)

Kennard, William C., and Winters, Harold F.: *Some Fruits and Nuts for the Tropics.* Federal Experiment Station in Puerto Rico, Mayaguez, P.R. Misc. Publication No. 801 Agri. Research Service U.S. Dept. of Agric.

Laing, Robert Malcolm and Blackwell, Ellen W.: *Plants of New Zealand.* 7th Edit. Whitcombe & Tombs, Ltd., Christchurch, N.Z. 1964.

Maiden, J. H.: *Forest Flora of New South Wales, Useful Native Plants of Australia,* 1889.

MacMillan, H. F.: *Tropical Planting and Gardening.* MacMillan, London, 5th ed. 1948.

Maril, Lee.: *Crack & Crunch, nuts in fact and fancy.* New York, Coward-McCann, 1945.

Morris, Robert Tuttle: *Nut Growing.* The MacMillan Co., 1921, rev. ed. 1931.

Mors, Walter B. and Rizzini, Carlos T.: *Useful Plants of Brazil,* Holden Day, Inc., San Francisco, 1966.

Morton, Julia F.: *Wild Plants for Survival in South Florida.* Hurricane House Publishers, Inc., Coconut Grove, Fla. 1962.

Oakman, H.: *Trees of Australia.* International Pub. Serv. 1970.

Ochse, J. J. et al: *Tropical and Subtropical Agriculture.* MacMillan, 1961.

Palmer, Eve, and Pitman, Norah: *Trees of South Africa.* A. A. Balkema, Cape Town, 1961.

Parry, John R.: *Nuts for Profit.* N.J.S. Chew, Printer, 1897.

Purseglove, J. W.: *Tropical Crops.* (2-vols.) John Wiley & Sons, 1972.

Reed, Clarence A. and Davidson, John: *The Improved Nut Trees of North America and how to grow them.* Devin-Adair, 1954.

The Royal Horticultural Society: *Dictionary of Gardening.* Clarendon Press, 1974.

Smith, Gilbert L.: *Practical Nut Growing.* Benton & Smith Nut Tree Nursery, 1949.

Standley, Paul C.: *Flora of Costa Rica,* Field Museum of Natural History, Chicago 1919.

Sturtevant, E. Lewis: *Sturtevant's Notes on Edible Plants* (Hedrick Ed.) New York Ag. Sta., Geneva. 1919. Sept. 1972 — Dover.

Watt, George: *A Dictionary of the Economic Products of India,* Periodical Experts. 1889, 2nd Sept. 1972.

Weschcke, Carl: *Growing Nuts in the North.* Webb Pub. Co. 1953 (1954).

Williamson: *Useful Plants of Nyasaland.*

Willis, J. C.: *Dictionary of the Flowering Plants and Ferns.* Cambridge University Press, 6th ed., revised, 1955.

Woodroof, J. G.: *Tree Nuts — Production, Processing, Products.* Vols. 1 and 2. Avi Pub. Co. 1967.

171

# INDEX

175